White Stones and .

(a story of conflict between the British and the Boers)

by

Ronnie Hammond

Published by R Hammond 2012
Copyright R Hammond 2012 © All Rights Reserved
ISBN 978-1-4716-1334-0

INTRODUCTION AND ACKNOWLEDGEMENTS

This work is not a scholarly chronicle of the history of South Africa or of the Boer War, but simply a search into the past to find, and if possible to understand the passions and the imperatives which drove the two principal white races in South Africa to a state of mortal enmity and bloody conflict.

I am the South African product of a Boer mother and an English speaking Cape Colonial father – my grandparents fought on opposing sides during the Boer War with all the hatred and venom that they had inherited from over a century of confrontation and conflict. Because of this I have always been driven by an insatiable need to understand where I personally stood in all this. This rapacious quest was constantly fuelled by discussions with anyone and everyone who would be patient enough to put up with me – my parents, grandparents, relatives, friends, teachers, schools, university - books, historical references, libraries, whatever and whenever!.

In this book I have tried to describe my journey through some 350 years of South African history. It is an attempt at a personal narrative of the events which were set in motion with the arrival of the first white settlers at the Cape and which culminated in bitter and bloody conflict between the British and the Boers at very end of the 19th century. The sentiments and the feelings are mine but not being an accredited historian I needed to seek help from the professional scholars and writers for detailed descriptions of battles and personalities. In this regard I am profoundly indebted to all the following authors without whose help I would never have completed my story – **Thomas Pakenham, Rayne Kruger, Michael Barthrop, John J. Stephens, Ian Castle, Oliver Ransford, Peter Trew, Alister Sparks and Steven Debroey.**

Finally, on a more personal basis, I wish to express my gratitude and thanks to my many friends who encouraged and helped me in producing this work. In particular I wish to name my friends **Tom Pate and Jeremy Cross** who patiently ploughed through my drafts and highlighted the many spelling and grammatical errors that my p.c. keyboard insisting on producing. Jeremy particularly, spent many, many hours restructuring grammatical presentations, correcting errors and offering advice and critiscism of immeasurable value. And then there is Graeme Black whose help with the production of drawings and illustrations was also invaluable and, almost as a PS. my very "recently acquired" friend **Douglas Brown** whose account of his personal interest in the 13th Battalion of The Imperial Yeomanry led me to re-write, expand and enliven a large section of my narrative.

Ronnie Hammond
Guthrie, Scotland

WHITE STONES and LITTLE CROSSES

CONTENTS

ILLUSTRATIONS and DIAGRAMS
(CATALOGUE OF SKETCHES, PICTURES and MAPS

White Stones and Little Crosses
(a story of conflict between the British and the Boers)

by

Ronnie Hammond

THE DEDICATION

I stood on the summit of Spioenkop and looked across towards Twin Peaks in the distance, then over to Aloe Knoll and Conical Hill, and finally, at my feet, the "acre of massacre", and I was stricken with a profound melancholy. Ghostly echoes of that terrible day, 105 years ago, drummed through my head as I tried to imagine those sixteen endless and bloody hours of point-blank rifle-, artillery-, and crossfire. For it was here that 75 dead and 150 bleeding Boers mingled with 350 dead and 1,200 mangled British soldiers as payment of a truly ghastly price for one of the most pointless and badly managed military engagements of all times....

There had to be some explanation, some sort of justification for the gruesome price that was paid that day for the honour of lying beneath those blanched stones and little crosses on that barren hill in that remote and far-flung corner of the earth.

In silence I gazed on those awful white-washed boulders that trace the main trenches of mindless slaughter and resolved to try and find some reason for it all – to discover why it happened – where it started and how it all ended.

PROLOGUE

It was inevitable that the soldiers who plodded painfully in the black night up the steep south-west spur of a remote hill, in an even remoter corner of the world, were destined, in a few hours time to blunder into mortal combat with the burghers encamped at the foot of the north-western slopes of that same hill. For the ensuing sixteen dreadful hours, they would bash it out, blow by blow like two punch-drunk pugilists, until the hill was littered with hundreds of corpses and bleeding wounded.

The soldiers, as well as the burghers, may have had some notion of why they were there and of what they were doing. The troops, men mainly from Lancashire, were told that they had been chosen to travel some seven thousand miles to South Africa on the behalf of their beloved Queen to 'whip the Boers' and 'give that nasty 'Kroojer' a bloody nose' for being so cruel and unkind to Her Gracious Majesty's loyal subjects in Johannesburg. The Officers, were informed that they were *fighting to protect our legitimate interests in South Africa and to protect our kith and kin from oppression by the tyrannous government of President Kruger'*

The burghers on the other side of the hill were gathered together to *'save their country from the rapacious designs of the predatory, empire-building English'*. For some of the less informed back-veld farmers the concept may have seemed a bit vague, but the stark visions of their families pillaged and their farms destroyed by their hereditary enemies were too alarmingly real.

What had also become obvious to both sides on the summit of that hill on that day was that the war, which had started just over three months ago, on the 11th October, 1899, and was predicted to be 'over by Christmas', would, in fact, turn into something very different. In reality, by the end of the year the over-confident British Army had already met with some horrible and entirely unexpected reverses, suffering more than 675 serious casualties during the opening days of the war alone. In Ladysmith, General White, with 14,000 of his crack troops was under siege by the Boers. At Nicholson's Nek, just a few miles north of Ladysmith, more than 900 soldiers had surrendered to the Boers and severe casualties had been inflicted on the British at the battles of Belmont, Modder River, Magersfontein, and Stormberg. At Colenso, the elite of the British Army was destroyed by a handful of untrained farmers from the Transvaal and Free State, and in addition, by this time the border town of Mafeking as well as the diamond-rich city of Kimberley were both securely under siege by the Boers.

Was this encounter on this day and on this hill going to be the key to a final glorious British vindication, and for the Boers, their arrival at the 'bitter-end'? Alas, how far off the mark they were. In reality, it was merely an insignificant incident in a long-standing conflict between two peoples - a conflict that started more than a hundred years before and which would continue for a further implacable and bitter hundred years, until the initial causes for this inherent hatred and distrust had long disappeared in the mists of passing time....

It could be argued validly that the seeds of discontent between those engaged on the hill that day were sewn, nay, not a hundred years prior to the Battle of Spioenkop, but 300 years before that. It was during the years from 1600 to 1800, that the pulsating British commercial and imperial endeavours were already in conflict with those of the Dutch and their French allies. In addition, by that time all the major European states were honed for armed conflict in an imperative to protect their commercial and political interest at home and abroad at any cost in human life or limb.

Soldiers and burghers – from where did they come? What were they doing here and why were they desperately struggling to inflict mortal damage upon each other? In the early half of the seventeenth century, a loose collection of Netherlands states succeeded in rebelling against the ruling authority of an ailing and waning Spain. They soon emerged on the international scene as the lively and enterprising Dutch Republic which, not being primarily concerned with territorial gains, either at home or abroad, would rapidly develop into Europe's foremost overseas trading nation. It was inevitable, therefore, that, sooner or later, English, French and Dutch involvements overseas would be destined to become inextricably intertwined. In the end the Dutch gradually ceded their territorial interests both in North America and elsewhere to the more rapacious and possessive French and English, and it may have been at this time that that the first seeds of discontent between the Dutch and the English were sown. It may also have been from here that these first seeds developed into the ultimate discord and enmity that would eventually manifest itself on the summit of Spioenkop in January 1900, and for half a century beyond that.

Out of the ensuing conflict of territorial interests between the leading European overseas trading nations there soon arose a culture of military power and conquest, which evolved to the point where a small elite of colonising states would eventually dominate the entire world. With this a cult of war was inevitably engendered, bringing with it a tradition of superiority based on a pre-ordained order of status, rank and obedience. From the highest rank to the meanest, no act would be perpetrated without the sanction of an order to which instant and unquestioning obedience was attributed. Every soldier whatever his rank, was paid to defend the honour and the safety of his country even to the extent of unwaveringly sacrificing his life in the process of its purpose.

It was in this way, that the English soldier (to become the 'British soldier' after the Act of Union in 1707) evolved into the paramount fighting unit in Europe and throughout the world, going into battle with the universally accepted and well tested European martial attitudes of the time. It was widely held that the most effective engagement tactic was that of preliminary heavy bombardment (the 'softening up') followed by close-order marching advance with the troops pausing periodically to deliver mass volley fire. These formatives were the easiest to teach the men and allowed the officers to maintain maximum control and mass obedience to orders. Sometimes open-order formations were permitted as well as the use of cover, but both were subordinated to the need to maintain formation and impetus. There was no provision at all for any soldier, irrespective of rank, to act on his own account or initiative outside the strict parameters of the 'order from the top'

9

On the other hand, the armed burghers who confronted the British military machine in 1899, had developed along completely different martial concepts, and could in no way even be described as an 'army' or a 'military force' in the strictest sense of the concept. The principal Boer combat unit, the 'commando' evolved, painstakingly over the preceding 250 years from the needs of handfuls of frontiersmen spontaneously gathering together from time to time to make punitive raids on marauding natives, or to take up mass defensive stands against belligerent tribes who resisted the slow but irrevocable erosion of their land and their cattle.

The Boers fought essentially as a civil militia unit made up from the obligation of every male capable of bearing arms to turn up, equipped at his own expense, whenever the occasion demanded. They fought in every-day farming clothes with no bright uniforms, insignias, colours or badges of rank to distinguish themselves from one another or from the natural colours of the veld that nurtured them. For them there was no honour in death in battle and their fighting was done best from long range with the rifle. They especially spurned hand-to-hand combat at all costs and had no qualms to mounting on their ponies and riding away from battle to 'live to fight another day'. .

The commandos varied in number according to the size of the population of any particular area. Every commando was led by a 'Commandant' elected by the burghers under his command. He was assisted by one, two or sometimes three similarly elected 'veldt-kornets' (junior 'officers') and 'corporals', individuals elected to represent the informal groups of burghers camping together in campaign laagers. Neither commandants not veldt-kornets, nor anyone else, including the President of the Republic, possessed any legal powers to discipline the burghers under their command, nor force them to do anything against their will. Orders could be issued, but the men were not obliged to obey them, and if an individual disagreed with any command, he would be quite at liberty to ignore it. Nor could he be prevented from leaving the battle area whenever he chose to do so – with farms and families back home to attend to it was quite understandable that periodic absences from the front were necessary and inevitable.

In general, most command decisions were made at a 'krijgsraad' (council of war) at which everyone could attend and have a right to speak. Individuals also had a right to refuse or endorse the decisions of the council, but once they did give it their support they were morally bound to follow its actions. It was quite understandable therefore, that because of this general absence of formalised discipline and obedience and this lack of total commitment to the state and its leaders, the British, often to their own very dear cost, tended to disregard the Boers as an inefficient, ill-disciplined and cowardly combat entity.

And so it came about that the predators who ravished the 'jungle' of the African veld and koppies at that time, were animals of a very different kind – the imperious lion stalking and killing for sustenance, and the scraggy hyena slinking and killing for survival. It was on the plains and hills of Natal in 1899 that these two beasts would eventually come face-to-face in mortal combat...

PART ONE

CONFRONTATION

1
THE BEGINNING

The story of the Anglo-Boer War, fought from October 1899 to May 1902 in the southernmost part of the African continent, is the story of a bitter conflict between the burghers of the Transvaal and the Orange Free State Republics on the one hand, and the forces of Great Britain on the other hand. Britain's colonial administrations in the Cape Province and Natal, together with her imperial allies from all parts of the world, joined in the conflict against the Boers.

First though, it is interesting to look at some of the events which contributed to the origins and reasons for the bitter acrimony that existed between these two adversaries, and to trace the long and tortuous road, which eventually brought them together to the final point of bloodletting in October 1899. The war it self, is covered in detail in Parts 2 and 3 and Part 4 examines the aftermath of the conflict.

Originally, the southern tip of Africa was not part of the British Empire. In fact, 150 years separated the advent of European settlement at the Cape in 1652 and the eventual, almost inevitable, arrival of the British in 1805. It has been suggested that the British occupation was unintentional, almost accidental, created by threats to British survival from Napoleon's France. It would be more accurate, however, to suggest that the occupation came about as a deliberate result of fundamentally complex and complicated economic and political factors. These origins had been in the frame for a very long time with their beginnings buried in England's imperative need to trade with the world at large, and, in order to do so successfully, her need to exclude all her rivals from those areas where her own economic and commercial interests lay.

In his book 'Fuelling the Empire' John J. Stephen writes, at page xiii, paragraph 1, *'Empires are not inherently evil, they merely had a bad press. They are the creations of highly organised societies of people that, from a particular confluence of circumstances and opportunities, act collectively to <u>impose their influence over vast regions of the planet and the people who inhabit them.</u> Being of human creation they display in their histories all the good and evil of which humans are capable'* (my underlines)

By the time Britain had completed her final occupation of the Cape in 1805 the need for the addition of yet another bit of the globe's surface had become decisive. Yet if the British Empire was not built on a deliberate and co-ordinated plan to establish a world empire for its own sake, where then did this imperative lie? As far back as the early 1500's the Spanish and the Portuguese were actively involved in stripping Central and South America of gold and other treasures in an orgy of empire-building forays which, in stark reality, were no more than bullion raids on a grand scale. The English, for their part, were quite content to lie in wait for the treasure-laden Spanish galleons plying their way back to Europe, and to take it all away from them, amassing in the process priceless booty on an already 'packed and sealed' basis.

Elizabethan England soon learnt that the benefits of these raids could be transformed into very profitable commodities, which in turn could be pumped back into ready-made markets abroad. In pursuance of these activities there soon followed a period of very rapid and aggressive expansion of colonial settlements in Central and North America as well as in India and the Far East.

At the same time, none of the European states had ever seriously considered colonising the African continent in spite of their centuries old fascination with it. Their only involvement in Africa consisted of the lucrative coastal trade in slaves, an enterprise which required no more effort than to call into port, take on an already prepared cargo of miserable and manacled human beings, and set off to sea again. Apart from the slave trade, the further exploration of the African coast in a southerly direction was aimed principally at the discovery, and then the maintenance of a sea-route to the east where the true European trading interests lay. To achieve this, the need to establish victualling stations for vessels on their long and hazardous travels to and from the east, was paramount. It was this imperative that goaded the East Indian Companies of the English, Dutch and French, during the seventeenth century, to consider the creation of victualling stations along the trading routes to India, the East Indies and the Far East

In the end it was the Dutch alone who took any positive initiative in this regard, and so it happened that on April 6ᵗʰ 1652. Jan van Riebeeck, on behalf of the V.O.C. (*Vereenigde Oost-Indische Compagnie or Dutch East India Company*), stepped ashore in Table Bay where he built the first permanent structure in the southern sub-continent of Africa, a wooden fort. He then established a vegetable garden, a hospital and facilities to enable ships to take on fresh water, meat and other supplies. In spite of the fact that all these early initiatives came from the Dutch, the servicing facility at the Cape was at no time intended to be exclusively for the benefit of Dutch shipping. It became evident that right from the start both British and French merchantmen, plying their way along the East Indies trade route, regularly and routinely put in at the Cape for servicing.

It was also from the outset that the Dutch authorities made their intentions vis a vis the establishment at the Cape very clear by issuing succinct instructions to Van Riebeeck that no one was to harm any of the native inhabitants of the Cape, nor to take away anything that belonged to them without appropriate recompense. His instructions were simply to build a fort to protect the Company's investments, to develop a vegetable garden, to establish stock pastures, and especially to foster and maintain good relations with the local inhabitants with a view to the peaceful procurement of cattle and other items to provide him with fresh water, meat, fruit and vegetables for calling ships.

Another significant instruction that the V.O.C made to Van Riebeeck was to avoid being embroiled in any contest of 'empire building'. '...*if any other nations wished to establish themselves in the southern tip of Africa you must live in peace with them. You must only establish the perimeters of the Company's possessions in the Cape clearly on a map of the area you need to occupy in order to fulfil the duties imposed upon you by the Company'*

As far as the Cape being a halfway station to the Indies was concerned, it clearly served its purpose well, especially as the settlement grew more efficient in its ability to provide food and services for passing vessels. It soon became obvious that the lucrative trade with the east would have been virtually impossible without this essential facility; a happy situation that was set to continue and grow and probably would have done so unfettered if it were not for the advent of Napoleon Bonaparte at the end of the eighteenth century.

Van Riebeeck's tiny refurbishing station at the Cape settled down to serious business and soon an average of 6,000 persons passing by the Cape on their way to and from the far east were being catered for and tended to. Relationships with the local Khoikhoi inhabitants were precarious. For the incoming Europeans the Khoi were quite bizarre beings and often described in many different ways. For example, one John Maxwell, an Englishman who was passing by wrote of them as *'easily distinguished from the negroes and from the white Europeans insofar as their hair was woolly and curly, with flat noses and thick lips and with a skin as white as ours.... For they smear their whole body with ranking kidney fat and other oily substances to protect their pale brown skins from the scorching sun and so creating such a stink that they are disagreeably discernable from quite a long way off downwind'*

The Khoikhoi (Hottentots) that Van Riebeeck encountered around Table Bay, as well as the San (Bushmen) and other tribes he met later on, were mainly cattle herders with large herds, which they moved from one area to another, continuously in search of grazing and water. They lived off the spoils of hunting, fishing and their cattle stock, as well as from wild plants, herbs and honey, and were therefore able to exercise quite an independent self-servicing livelihood. It soon became clear to the incomers that the Khoikhoi, although owners of many thousands of head of cattle, were exceedingly reluctant to dispense with even one beast if it were not direly necessary to do so.

Van Riebeeck and his fellow settlers, rude and rough as the bulk of them were, made a profound impact on the primitive Khoikhoi and San. The Dutch did indeed bring with them a particularly intellectual background and psychology that would become critical in the eventual shaping of the mind of the *'Afrikaner Volk'* in this alien environment. The world they had just left behind was one astir with new energies and new ideas. Europe had just recently burst its way out of the somnolent middle ages and was in the throes of a revolutionary transformation, with changes in a man's environment and an expansion of his intellectual horizons such a people had never seen before. Gutenburg had just invented the printing press opening the way to popular education, and it was also an age of brilliant artists and philosophers, of the birth of science and the rise of capitalism with new wealth flowing in to the merchants and a new self-confidence to the individual.

Holland was in forefront of all these events. Fired by Calvinist republicanism and led by their very own beloved Prince William of Orange, the Dutch had emerged from eighty years of bitter struggle to win their political and religious independence from the tyrannous domination of Hapsburg Spain. Now it was surging forward as the world's leading trading nation whose ships would bring goods from all parts of the world for transhipment up the Rhine and into the heartland of Europe. It was the Golden Age of Dutch civilisation – its society was the most literate in Europe – its cities were full of arts, literature and philosophy – it was home to Rembrandt and Frans Hals – to Vermeer, Jan Steen, Descartes, Spinoza and a multitude of others. As Jan van Riebeeck readied himself to sail for the Cape in the spring of 1652, Amsterdam was without any doubt the greatest commercial centre in the world, and the V.O.C. the world's biggest commercial enterprise.

Exactly how sophisticated the men who sailed with Van Riebeeck were is of course a matter of conjecture. Certainly they were not, by a long chance, 'intellectuals' except perhaps for van Riebeeck himself who was a medical doctor and whose parents were people of substance (his grandfather was the mayor of Culemburg and the centre of the social and political life of the community). The rest of his men came from the so-called 'grauw' (rubble) of Dutch society, a mixture of day labourers, vagrants and unemployed, many of whom had drifted into the big cities from the nearby lowlands of Germany.

It was matter of singular importance in the shaping of the Afrikaner mind, that the Cape was initially settled, not by the Dutch government, but by the V.O.C., a commercial company whose impelling motivation was profit and not patriotism. It had no interest in establishing a colony in South Africa, only in operating a well-defined service utility. The outpost was to consist merely of a fort and a garden, and the Company was not interested in developing the place or exploiting its resources. The Cape was simply a base that was to have a minimum involvement with the locality and its inhabitants. The V.O.C.'s instructions to Van Riebeeck were explicit – he was to keep his distance from the indigenous inhabitants – only to trade with them by exchanging trinkets for cattle in order to provide meat for passing ships. In no way was he to conquer them, nor seek to colonise them or to employ them.

The fundamental fact that the Cape was settled by a commercial company and not by a state, a nation or a government, was of singular importance in the shaping of the future of the country and its inhabitants. Although the V.O.C. had powers to make laws and to conduct military operations, its impelling motivation was profit and not possession, and it had absolutely no interest nor intention of establishing a colony in South Africa. This primary occupation with costs and commercial viability meant that van Riebeeck was under intense pressure from Amsterdam to show profit, which would mainly be achieved by reducing overheads and increasing output. This led to a constant search for profitability through higher output by reduced personnel, and he was strongly encouraged to cut back the number of Company employees and at the same time to increase output.

Thus it was inevitable that sooner than later, Company employees would be 'laid off'. In fact, it would barely take four years after the arrival at the Cape for the first batch of 'free burghers' to be cut off from the payroll and to be settled on 28-acre allotments along the Liesbeeck River, in what are today Cape Town's most affluent suburbs. This group of nine burghers was encouraged to grow produce in its own right and to sell it back at fixed prices, to the Company. Soon more and more workers were released from the payroll to set up their own 28-acre farms to till, plant and produce for the benefit of the Company's remit to service the ever increasing volume of sea-traffic calling in at the Cape 'half-way house' for refurbishing and replenishing.

This arrangement suited everyone except the Khoi who saw with the release of every 'free burgher', the disappearance of yet another chunk of traditional Khoi grazing land. Van Riebeeck was surprised when the Khoi, taking exception to this state of affairs, took to arms in order to reclaim what they considered to be their own land, thereby giving birth to South Africa's very first war of resistance. When the brief conflict was over and the Khoi soundly beaten the disputed land was claimed for the Company by right of conquest, thereby creating a precedence to a tradition that, for the white South African, all the wide open land around him was available for the taking by simple occupation.

This action heralded a very long process of land acquisition, which combined with slavery and cheap labour, would eventually create a tradition of resentment and antagonism against authority, and eventually give birth to a belief of 'white supremacy'. It was here as well that the seeds were sewn of the Boer concept of the 'chosen people', which would lead in the final analysis to the conflict that would find its ultimate expression in the bitter blood letting of the Boer War some 200 years later.

These initial 'free burghers' were the first white South Africans, cast loose in a vast continent without proper government or civil administration, who would begin to move inland beyond the reach of the V.O.C. and its irritatingly restrictive regulations. The 'free burghers' progressively gobbled up the land to which they now believed to be freely entitled, and the V.O.C. had neither the ability nor the disposition to incur the expense of attempting to pursue them, nor of policing them except in a most token manner. As their numbers grew, there took place at the southern tip of the African continent one of the most remarkable settlements in the history of colonisation – a small and scattered community of white men drifting away beyond the effective reach of any law or administrative arm and losing themselves in the vastness of Africa for a century and a half. They lived on their own, out of touch with the world at large, without roads, railways, newspapers, telegraph, radio or even a postal service. Their only contact with the outside world was through the occasional itinerant trader or hunter-explorer who might bring some snippets of months-old news from Cape Town.

In his book 'The Mind of South Africa' (p.40,para.4) Allister Sarks neatly summed up the peculiar psyche of these early Cape frontiersmen in the following words: '*Always it was the most intransigent and disputatious spirits who trekked the furthest – driving deeper and deeper into isolation as they went. It sank into their souls, feeding their pride and intensifying their obduracy with each man becoming a king unto himself, unwilling to tolerate any challenge to his authority or questioning of his judgement. They became a schismatic people who never acquired the habit of settling disputes through negotiation or compromise, turning, instead, their backs on any disagreement, pulling up stakes and trekking off to new pastures where their authority would once again be unchallenged.*'

Within the first two or three years of Van Riebeeck's installation at the Cape relationships with the local Khoi clans became more and more strained. It was a fact that the Khoi possessed vast herds of cattle but they were very reluctant to part with them – even those which had been exchanged in fair barter for copper, beads, tobacco and alcohol. It was quite common for cattle exchanged in such a manner, to be 'reclaimed' by the Khoi in the dark of the night, and made away together with all the other bits and bobs which had been received in fair exchange. Naturally, the settlers were furious and also very frustrated because van Riebeeck consistently failed to get permission from his bosses in Amsterdam to smoke out and confront the offending Khoi and to punish them accordingly.

During this time, the servicing activities at the Cape were rapidly growing, and to meet the increasing demand for fresh produce, more and more Company employees were encouraged to farm for themselves. Van Riebeeck was also anxious to increase the output of servicing requirements, so from the start he prevailed upon the Governors of the Company to allow the importation of slaves to perform the more arduous and non-productive chores such as lumbering and quarrying. The Company, already deeply involved in slave labour in the East Indies, wasted little time in agreeing to Van Riebeeck's request, and from 1652, the very year of his arrival in the Cape, the first trickle started arriving, and by 1658 over 500 men, women and children were already in labour with the Company and its employees at the Cape. It was in that year that the first school in South Africa was established, exclusively for slave children, for at that time there were still no white children of school age.

During these early years of the settlement at the Cape, the absence of more than a few white women resulted in men marrying, or taking on as slaves indigenous women, thus creating mixed race families, who would eventually be known as "Cape Coloureds". These 'coloured babies' were the forerunner of a subsequent development in the Colony, which would leave a lasting impact on South Africa, even to this very day.

As the settlement at the Cape expanded, more and more people arrived there, mainly from Holland but also from France, Germany, Flanders and even Sweden and elsewhere, and soon their numbers warranted the creation of a 'Burgher Raad' (Burgher Council) to deal with parochial matters concerning the free burghers at the Cape. On June 22nd 1658 the first Burgher Council was constituted and consisted of two burghers selected by the Company from a short-list of four candidates which had been proposed by the free burghers themselves. To take care of official matters a 'Politieke Raad' (Political Council) was created consisting initially of the'Opperkoopman' (Chief Procurer) or Commander, (Jan van Riebeeck himself), a 'Deputy Procurer' and a 'Sergeant of the Garrison'. Whenever an official fleet, to or from the East Indies, was in dock at Cape Town, the senior official of the visiting fleet would join the Political Council as its Chairman, to constitute 'De Brede Raad' (the Broad Council).

So, gradually there developed outside the confines of the Company's compound a co-ordinated and self-functioning settlement composed of free land-owning burghers with their Khoi servants, and slaves from Malay, providing produce for itself and for the

Company's victualling requirements for passing maritime traffic. Other skills and occupations soon blossomed, and very soon, enterprises such as brick- and wagon-making, tailoring, plough and tool making and so on, emerged. Buildings were erected and a huge communal barn, De Groote Schuur, was built. Van Riebeeck himself acquired a tract of land for his own private use, and in February 1659 he pressed his first own wine on his farm called Bosheuvel, which is where the present-date suburb of Wynberg is situated. At the same time another free burgher set up the first water-mill which gave birth to a successful bread baking and confectionary business which was soon to be followed by beer brewing and other domestic businesses.

In the beginning, the Company exercised a tight control over the disposal of the products farmed by the free burghers, restricting them to providing for the Company's needs first, at prices fixed by the Company. It did not take the burghers long to realise that they could procure far better deals by by-passing the Company and trading directly with calling vessels. When Van Riebeeck tried to stop this clandestine trading, the burghers were not tardy in presenting him with a strong worded petition containing a long list of complaints. Their grievances were mostly about being barred from trading freely at profitable prices for their products, but instead being forced to sell to the Company at ridiculously low prices. Complaints also included trivia such as the Company's omission to provide the free wood and the cattle grant promised as part of the deal with them on their release from the Company's employ.

Could it be that the seeds of the later Boers' strong resentment to interference in their independence and the evolution and formation of their particularly positive and instinctive reaction to restricting government from above, be traced to this very early incident in the history of their development? For a handful of very vulnerable people who only months before had been humbly paid servants of an international commercial trading company, their reaction was very strong and extremely provocative. The menacing tone of the petition left no doubts as to their attitude in respect of the Company and its control. In it the burghers categorically stated that that if they were to be harassed any longer they would be obliged to stop working the land as they had *'no intention of becoming your (the Company's) slaves because instead of being helped by you we are in fact being oppressed'*

Although Van Riebeeck responded to the petition point by point and intimated his willingness to propose a relaxation of the rules to the Council, he was well aware that he had a big problem on his hands, and that the burghers would become more and more difficult to control. It was also at this time that the burghers became increasingly aware of another threat, this time from the Khoi clans living around Table Bay. They were being harassed by the Khoi, who were making off with their cattle, sheep, goats and chickens and spoiling their fields and cutting their nets. There were even instances of murder, with herders killed while protecting their herds and flocks. Active and open opposition from the Khoi increased when they began to realise that the settlers had come to stay and were not going to leave as their predecessors from visiting vessels invariably did. Traditionally, the Khoi was basically a nomadic people who did not actually 'possess' any of the land over which they moved, nor did they build houses or permanent settlements on specific sites. Instead, they roamed from one grazing area to another and followed their herds, to-and-fro across the vast expanses in and around the Cape. However, they came to look on the settlers as usurpers who claimed possession of 'their' land by tilling and building upon it, and by so doing depriving the Khoi of their traditional grazing grounds.

For their part the burghers laid claim to this land by right of occupation and possession, and in order to maintain and exercise this prerogative, they set about creating the very first South African 'commando', in their words to 'protect our lives and our property at the Cape'. Soon the gun proved deadlier than the poison-tipped arrow, and the Khoi and the San were gradually pushed further and further away from the settlement at the Cape. It was now that another tradition was born – that of the aphorism that 'might was right', a convention that would nurture and grow with the centuries to develop into another fundamental aspect of the white South African psyche.

2
THE FIRST YEARS

After ten years of service as Commander at the Cape, Van Riebeeck and his family finally set off for Batavia on the 7th May 1662, his successor, Zacharias Wagenaar having been sworn in the previous day as the new Commander. Conditions in the Cape continued to be unstable during the management of Wagenaar as well as that of his two successors, Isdbrandt Goske and Johann Brox who was in control from March 1676 until the arrival of Simon van der Stel in October 1679. The V.O.C. urged Van der Stel to get the situation at the Cape under proper control as quickly as possible, so his immediate imperatives included the urgent need to win over the confidence of the dissatisfied and estranged burghers and to improve the agricultural production system in order to bring it into a viable investment mode as soon as possible.

Van der Stel put about his tasks with alacrity and enthusiasm, and within the first few weeks in office he set out on an inland expedition to investigate the possibilities of profitably exploiting the areas in the vicinity of Table Bay and to the north. He soon claimed possession of some very fertile and well watered nearby valleys, and immediately set about installing some twenty free-burghers on as much ground as they could cultivate in return for a portion of one-tenth of their grain output for the Company's granary. They received as many slaves as they needed to meet the requirements imposed upon them by the Company. A town was established and named Stellenbosch, after the Governor. A preacher cum teacher and a medical orderly were appointed to manage the affairs of the infant community.

At the beginning of Van der Stel's administration there were 87 free-burghers at the Cape, with 55 spouses, 117 Dutch and 'mixed blood' children, and 37 white Company 'servants'. The Governor was convinced that he could not succeed with this number, and continually put pressure on the Council of the V.O.C. to send as many more settlers to the Cape as possible. The process was a slow one as Amsterdam favoured a system of 'natural progression' rather than artificially enlarging the settlement with immigrants. However, Van der Stel was not to be discouraged, and assiduously continued with his programme of expansion.

There soon emerged a policy of building and construction, the laying out of proper roads and avenues, the requisition of suitable arable and grazing lands further a field, and to the establishment of recognisable towns at Table Bay and at Stellenbosch. In order to finance these projects Van der Stel introduced local levies and taxes including the payment of ten gulden per annum for grazing rights for 100 sheep or 20 head of cattle. To maintain the church and cemetery, a universal levy of six gulden per annum per adult male, was also imposed on them.

Education too was not neglected either. Schools and nurseries were established for all the children regardless of whether they were 'free born or slaves'. They were instructed in basic reading, writing and elements of protestant religion. In order to prepare them for defence and for protection of their 'lives and goods against wild beasts and marauders', every able lad between the ages of 9 and 13 years had to assemble 'every

Saturday and every afternoon in the square for small arms instruction and drill'. A 'home-guard' scheme (De Burgherwacht), was also introduced, involving all eligible male burghers capable of handling a firearm or any other appropriate defence weapon. Other developments were encouraged such as the construction of a hospital for 500 patients, of an abattoir, of additional vegetable gardens and other civilian amenities aimed at benefiting the Company's continued commitment to the servicing of ships calling at the Cape to replenish their supplies

In 1687 a group of German soldiers returning to Europe from Company duty in Java requested, and received, permission to land at the Cape and to settle there. Van der Stel was delighted with this fresh intake and invested them in a fertile valley just north of Stellenbosch, which he named Drakenstein. This small German enclave gradually grew bigger, as more and more, German immigrants trickled in during the course of the next two decades.

Coupled with the growth of the population and activities in the tiny settlement, came the need for better judicial and fiscal management of the affairs of the settlers and the settlement itself. On the 31st August 1682 a 'Commission for Minor Matters' was set up to handle cases involving deals and disputes of less than 300 gulden, and that same day four free-burgers were appointed as 'Heemraden (administration officers). Three years later a 'Landdrost' (magistrate) was added to establish the Judiciary College of Landdrost and Heemraden. The Landdrost was also appointed to the 'Political Council' and had powers to requisition transport, slaves and draught oxen for use in the construction and maintenance of public works, tax collection and so on. He was also appointed commander-in-chief of the police force, and gradually as the 'colony' grew larger and larger the responsibilities and powers of the Landdrost increased, but always, however remaining subordinate to the Political Council whose authority covered every person in the colony, even those settled in the remotest regions.

Simon van der Stel contributed more to the positive and rapid expansion of the colony at the Cape than any of his predecessors, including Van Riebeeck. Apart from the dramatic innovations outlined above, his one single action that was to have a profound and lasting impact on the Afrikaners in Africa was his involvement in the settlement of the French Huguenots in the regions around Stellenbosch, Paarl and Olifantshoek, later to be renamed Franschoek ('French Corner')

The Huguenots came to the Cape in response to Van der Stel's repeated requests to the Council of Seventeen for the permanent establishment of more settlers in his growing colony. At that time there were many fugitives seeking refuge from the French religious persecution policies, who were living in Holland, Germany, Flanders and even England. The Council considered it a good thing to offer them a new life of freedom in the colonies, and to this end the Company provided free transportation for the Huguenots and granted them land and provisions to establish a new life for them and their families. When the first group of 200 Huguenots landed at the Cape in 1688, they were set up with adequate grants and fertile farming land along the Berg River in the Stellenbosch area, and encouraged to mix freely with the neighbouring Dutch settlers already there.

The Huguenots were an industrious and hard-working lot. Many were qualified artisans and others were skilled agriculturists, especially in wine farming, and soon their influence and example began to make its mark on the progress and development of the colony as they progressively integrated themselves into the local community, more often than not outshining and out-stripping their Dutch and German counterparts. By and large the Huguenots belonged to a higher social class than the bulk of the Dutch and German immigrants and were undoubtedly more qualified and skilled in general farming, trading and industrial skills

It is important at this stage to assess the influence of another group of white settlers at the Cape at this time, namely the Germans. Much has been said and written about the significant contributions made by the Dutch and Huguenot settlers, while the impact of those immigrants who came from Germany, has generally been glossed over or simply ignored, regardless of the fact that there had been a steady inflow of Germans practically from the very first landing of Van Riebeeck in 1652. Although figures vary from one historian to another it is now generally accepted that by 1795 the white population was made up of 36.8% of settlers of Dutch origin, 35% of German origin, 14.6% oh Huguenots, and the remaining 13 odd percent from various other European countries. Perhaps the reason for this neglect stems from the very nature of the German integration into the local Cape scene. From the beginning they arrived in small groups of ones, twos and threes in a steady trickle over the decades following the establishment of the V.O.C. at the Cape, and that there was never an 'en bloc' arrival at any time as was the case with the Huguenots. In spite of this it is well known that as early as 1656 there were already 28 Germans employed in the Company's garrison in Cape Town and in the following year, their percentage was increased by an additional intake of a further 22 Germans. It is also interesting to note that in 1656 three out of the first nine Company employees to be released from the payroll and given grants of land and equipment to farm on their own account were Germans.

Although many German immigrants remained in and around Cape Town, a large number of them also moved away during the Trekboer era. They settled and established farms in the Caledon, Ceres and Swellendam areas and others trekking further afield and as far away as the eastern frontier regions, and eventually settled down in remote areas such as Graaff-Reneit in the Small Karoo, and Uitenhage near present-day Port Elizabeth.

On the 11th February 1699 Simon van der Stel's son, Willem Adriaan, at the age of 34, took over the management of the Company. Unlike his father, Willem Adriaan did very little, either for the advancement of the Company's interests or for the benefits of the settlers. He was very energetic, however, in ruthlessly enriching himself at the expense of the Company, the burghers and even the hapless Khoi. Willem Adriaan gathered about himself a sycophantic coterie of acolytes who enthusiastically shared his own ambition of self-enrichment at the expense of everyone and everything else. He cast himself wholeheartedly into his role of Governor by acquiring vast acreages of land to expand his own interests in agricultural and especially pastoral activities. He granted generous privileges to himself and his hangers-on, mostly without the knowledge of his masters in Amsterdam, and to the detriment of the Company and the free-burghers at the Cape. His frequent forages into the hinterland gained him vast herds of cattle and sheep, mostly at the expense of the defenceless Khoi. On his massive newly-gained lands he ruthlessly made use of Company slaves and Company equipment and supplies, to launch into big scale cattle, grain, fruit, vegetable and wine farming enterprises, the fruits of which were sold directly to passing fleets at artificially inflated prices. All this was achieved simply by by-passing the Company and the burghers. At the same time, Ordinances were passed which prohibited the burghers from dealing directly with passing vessels. Instead, they were obliged to dispose of their produce through the Company alone at ridiculously lowly fixed prices.

This effectively excluded the burghers from any possible outlets for their products, and forced them to look at other means of earning even a minimum subsistence living. Understandably, they did not take very kindly to this state of affairs, and it was at this stage that the trek into the hinterland began. It started with a trickle and soon developed, over the following years, into a regular flow of very independent and very irate free burghers. Packing up their earthly possessions, they moved eastward and over the mountains with their families, their servants and their cattle stock, pushing any Khoi who happened to be standing in their way further and further back into the hostile regions beyond the distant mountains in the northeast

Those who chose to remain at the Cape, and there were many, were also determined not to take things lying down. Amongst the leading antagonists were some very wealthy and successful free burghers who had attained success through hard work and application during the Simon van der Stel era. The principal complainants against the activities of the Governor and his cronies were Henning Hussing, Jacobus Van der Heijden and Adam Tas, a burgher of great import who would later himself become Governor. Adam Tas was also the intellectual amongst the burghers in uproar, and acting as their scribe, penned a Protocol of Complaints against the Governor and his administration, which was submitted to the Council of Seventeen for its urgent and serious consideration. Amongst the many complaints levelled against the Governor the most significant were:

- The free burghers at the Cape believed that the 'unjust and rapacious' attitude of the Governor was reducing the burghers to a status of 'slaves'

- The Governor's totally unwarranted acquisition of thousands of hectares of land for his own use at the expense and detriment of the burghers was illegal and unnecessary. In fact, any one of his many estates was large enough to provide as much as it would take fifty average sized burgher farms to produce in a year.

- The Governor had seconded sixty employees of the Company to work solely for him, and apart from his own 200 personal slaves, he had at least 100 of the best of the Company slaves also working on his lands. In order to account for their physical absence from Company duties they had been recorded as 'deceased' in the official Company records.

- The Governor's 18,000 sheep and 1,000 head of cattle were reared and pastured on his fifteen 'ranches' situated throughout the colony. The returns from these holdings were sufficient to provide for the total needs of the Company and its servants, the garrison, the hospital and for all the ships that would call in for revictualling during the course of an entire year. In addition, all this together with all the fruit, vegetables, grain and wine was available to the consumers before a single beast or bushel was allowed to be sold by the burghers, even at the ridiculously low prices imposed by the Company officials.

- The Governor granted unfair advantages and opportunities to his kith and kin at the expense of the interest of the burghers. In this way his brother, Hans de Jonker, 'who never did a fair days work in his life' was enriched beyond his dreams, and the predikant, Rev. Petrus Kalden, was favoured 'to pay more attention to his own land holdings than to his pulpit or to his flock'

In response to this Protocol Willem Adriaan tried to bring a case against the so-called 'rebels' by faking a petition containing the signatures of 240 well wishing burghers, and tried to meet out 'just and adequate punishment' for the 'ringleaders', whom he banished from the Cape and rapidly sent away on the very first out-going vessel available. He soon regretted this course of action, because on board the ship carrying the five 'trouble-makers', was a highly placed Dutch official returning to Rotterdam after a spell of duty in Batavia. On hearing, at first hand, the grievances of the Cape burghers, he made appropriate representations to the Council of Seventeen to force an in-depth investigation into the alleged state of affairs at the Cape. As a result the Governor, Willem Adriaan van der Stel, his second-in-command, Samuel Elsevier, the predikant, Rev. Petrus Kalden, and the Landdrost, Johannes Starrenberg were all stripped of office and ordered back to the Netherlands. When this news was made public, a universal jubilation in the Cape broke out. One young buck, the 17-year old Hendrik Bribant, was heard to rejoice, claiming that - '*I am an "Afrikaner" and even if they throw me in jail or put me to death, I shall not waver'*. It was here for the first time ever, but surely not the last, that these words '*I am an Afrikaner'*, were spoken in public – a description that would eventually become universal in South Africa and remain so this very day....

The Council of Seventeen strove for a rapid return to normality in the Cape, and particularly encouraged the burghers to continue production and at the same time forbidding the Governor or any other senior Company official to undertake any private commercial activity whatsoever, especially in respect of provisions for fleets calling in at the Cape. Regrettably, by now, the massive over-production by Willem Adriaan and his friends had stuffed the granaries with excess stock, which required to be disposed of, and which consequently left little demand for any burgher production. As a result increasing numbers of private producers turned to pastoral farming and started moving further inland in search of fresh grazing and water for their beasts.

The era of the 'trekboer' had begun....!

24

Unlike the grand exodus of the Great Trek, which, was to take place a century later, the movement away from the Cape in the early eighteenth century was a slow, erratic and disorganised affair. To maintain its viability the Company's requirements became increasingly burdensome for the free burgher, and many became totally disenchanted and disgruntled with their lot. Although they were supposedly 'free' burghers, their activities were, seriously curtailed by restrictions, taxes and levies imposed upon them. With this pitiless mismanagement and suppression of Willem Adriaan's regime, for many the very last straw had landed on the camel's back. No longer able to eke out any form of viable existence from agricultural activity, the burghers set about acquiring large stocks of cattle and sheep, more often than not illegally from the unfortunate Khoi, and moving inland in search of fresh grazing. Between 1700 and 1760, the total number of cattle owned by free burghers grew from 8,000 to 20,000 and sheep from 54,000 to 131,000. To counteract the effect of this privately owned stock on its own profits, the Company imposed heavy duties on cattle, sheep and goats, causing even more hardship for the suffering burghers and encouraging them to move even further away from the Company's sphere of influence and authority, and in so doing becoming lost to the Cape forever.

Those first streaks of intolerance and independence displayed against Jan van Riebeeck in the early 1650's, by now developed into full force. By 1710, the white colonist's quest for independence and urge for freedom had moulded him into a proud, intolerant, and fiercely independent individual who would brook no threat or imposition on his self-ordained style of living. After the 'benefits' of being served by slaves and Khoi servants from the beginning, he held a profound resentment against working for any other white person or for hard tasks of any kind, which, being traditionally the duty of slaves or servants had become beneath the white man's dignity to perform. It was this continual search for fresh land, which drove the trekboer further and further inland and which led him into a near nomadic way of life wherein his individual rights and authority extended as far as his border with his neighbour's land. It was a boundary which he continually strived to push as far away from him and his family as possible, so that by 1735, some of these trekboers had reached limits as far as 250 miles from Cape Town and were still moving further and further into the hinterland.

Although the exodus of these first families of burghers who moved away from the Cape and the disciplines of the Company and its administration constituted a fundamental influence on the evolution and development of the tiny settlement, it is important to note that it was by no means the end of the beginning. In fact, for as many of those who moved away, as large a number lingered close to Cape Town, to the Company and to the vital communication lines with the outside world. They settled in the lush valleys of the Western Cape where they grew wheat and made wine and established a 'rural society' with gracious gabled houses and carriages, living on fine estates, serviced by plenty of indentured labourers from among the Khoi people and the slaves from Malaya. This lifestyle of leisure and grace and open hospitality acquired by those burghers who settled in and around the Cape, set them quite apart from their rough-hewn brothers who had trekked off into the distant eastern frontier area. It was this separation, which would eventually become a permanent dichotomy of the Afrikaans psyche.

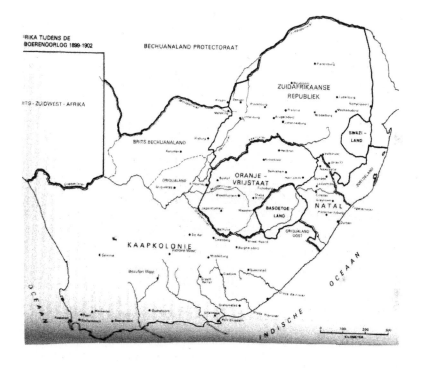

RIKA TIJDENS DE
BOERENOORLOG 1899-1902

BECHUANALAND PROTECTORAAT

ZUIDAFRIKAANSE
REPUBLIEK

ITS - ZUIDWEST - AFRIKA

SWAZI -
LAND

BRITS BECHUANALAND

ORIQUALAND

ORANJE -
VRIJSTAAT

NATAL

BASOETOE -
LAND

ORIQUALAND
OOST

KAAPKOLONIE

INDISCHE OCEAAN

OCEAAN

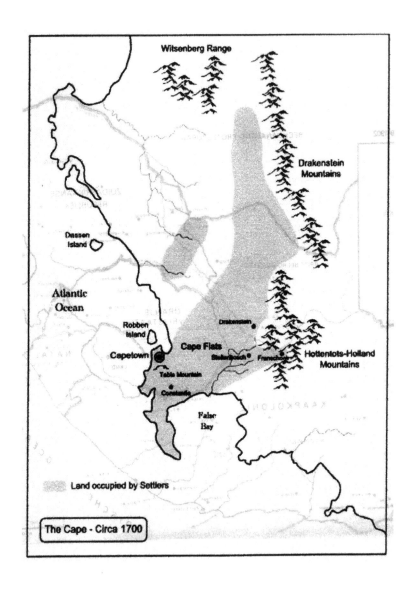

Witsenberg Range

Drakenstein Mountains

Dassen Island

Atlantic Ocean

Robben Island

Drakenstein

Cape Flats

Capetown

Stellenbosch

Franschhoek

Hottentots-Holland Mountains

Table Mountain

Constantia

False Bay

Land occupied by Settlers

The Cape - Circa 1700

From now on the term *'Boer'* will be used many times so it would be the appropriate moment to identify the various non-indigenous groups of 'white' people in the Cape in that epoch. In the Dutch language the term *'boer'* simply means *'a farmer'* and *'te boer'* is *'to farm'*. The same word, when spelt with a capital 'B' (as in *'Boer'*) became to be identified with those Dutch-speaking *'white'* inhabitants of the later Boer republics regardless of whether they were farmers or not. Those Dutch-speaking people who remained at the Cape, were only called *'boere'* if they were farmers and actually engaged in farming. As a group they became identified as *'Afrikaners'* and never as *'Boers'* – the term *'Afrikaner'* served to express their 'Africa-ness' and the permanent adoption of Africa as their home, and their acknowledgment that they no longer considered themselves as *Europeans*. So broadly speaking those *'white'* people who remained in the Cape became known as *'Afrikaners'*, whilst those *'whites'* who moved away, initially to the Eastern Cape frontier and subsequently into the southern African hinterland were called *'Boers'*.

During the latter half of the nineteenth century, Afrikaners came to appreciate that the language they were speaking was no longer *'proper' Dutch*. It had in fact developed into a separate language from a Cape-Dutch patois, which had itself been the linguistic result of the melting pot of cultures and languages at the Cape. The language came to be known as *'Afrikaans'* by its speakers who included many of those who were not accepted as *'Afrikaners'* Later the terms *'Boer'* and *'Afrikaner'* became interchangeable. This interchange only developed late in the life of the Transvaal Republic, and gained growing acceptance after the South African War when the Boers wished to identify themselves with the aspirations of the Afrikaners at the Cape. Before that, they never thought or referred to themselves as Afrikaners, or to the language they spoke as anything but Dutch.

The Boers of the later republics and the Afrikaners at the Cape were related by blood and thus easily identified with each other. In fact, the Boers merely represented those Dutch-speaking people, mostly white, but including some of mixed descent, who had moved further away from the Cape through the *'trekboer'* phenomena and later the Great Trek. Nevertheless, the Dutch at the Cape and the Boers were, in the end, sufficiently separated by time and historical experience to allow a significant cultural gap to develop between them, and furthermore, during the time of the Boer Republics, relations with the Cape Dutch were not always cordial, nor did their interests always coincide. Keeping all above in mind and for the sake of clarity, from now on reference to the people who remained at the Cape will be referred to as the *'Afrikaners'* and those that moved away to the eastern Cape borders and eventually trekked north to Natal, the Free State and Transvaal as the *'Boers'*

The so-called 'Cape Melting Pot' out of which emerged, among others, the 'trekboers', the 'Eastern Frontier Boers', the 'Boers' in general, and finally the 'Afrikaners' was an interesting and intricate amalgamation of European, Asian and African peoples living and evolving together in the small area around Table Bay from 1652 onwards. Grants of farms to the free burghers of the V.O.C. encouraged the immigration of white European women to the colony but for many decades, white males would substantially outnumber white females in the settlement. It was inevitable, therefore, that many unions were forged between white males and indigenous African and imported Asian female slaves, thereby engendering a progeny of mixed race and colour.

The V.O.C. had the whole of continental Europe from which to draw its servants, and so it did, and gradually the settlement at the Cape grew on an *ad hoc* basis. After 1750 the company decided to encourage organised settlement in the Cape, and succeeded in drawing substantially more German speakers than Dutch. Yet the German language never flourished at the Cape, mainly because the settlers included more males than females, and these men eventually married Dutch women as well as some free black women. Their children were brought-up in the Dutch idiom, speaking and thinking High Dutch. Notwithstanding the diversity of their backgrounds, the European population at the Cape rapidly became more culturally uniform, speaking Dutch and practising the religion of the Dutch Reformed Church.

To this European mix must also be added the influence of the Khoikhoi and the slaves imported from various parts of Africa and the Far East, especially Malaya, who enriched the local culture not only with the admixture of their own cultures, but also with their rich and spicy cuisines. Added to the French love of wine and good food, a unique and flavourful Cape Malay cuisine of great variety and sophistication developed.

A substantial amount of inter-marriage and crossbreeding between all these groups took place, and some of the offspring were accepted into so-called 'white society', while others, especially those of the Muslim faith, remained outside the enclave of privilege. This resulted in the gradual development of a free, but subservient, Dutch-speaking 'Cape Coloured' community, evolved from Malay, free blacks and Khoikhoi, and 'mixed-race' people living side by side with the European community at the Cape. When the British finally emancipated all the slaves between 1838 and 1840, their numbers greatly increased.

The fact remains however that within a few decades the European community had become the dominant group, all others having been relegated to a position of legal, political and social inferiority. This was not only the situation in fact but its existence came to accepted as 'God ordained', and thus any question as to its correctness was regarded as sacrilege. Raising the perception of inequality to the status of divine revelation put it beyond rational debate for more than three centuries, at least as far as the dominant Europeans were concerned.

The reasons for this development were quite straightforward – European domination had been part-and-parcel of the V.O.C. policy since it wielded, after all, both the necessary economic, as well as the military power to dictate the terms of settlement at the Cape. The resultant situation and its concomitant racial attitudes came about specifically because the V.O.C. servants and free burghers could hold or gain political power in the official hierarchy of the colony, while the others could not. The fact that the Company recruited its servants and free immigrants in Europe, and brought in very few Asian or Eurasian employees and settlers to the Cape, created a precedent of political, economic and social elitism which was almost exclusively European.

By importing slaves, none of whom were European, intensified the correlation between legal status and race, and by regarding the Khoikhoi, initially as aliens and later as subjects who were not free burghers, effectively precluded them from political and economic advancement in colonial society. It is also significant that the same attitudes towards race found at the Cape, were not unique amongst settlers from Europe. These same attitudes existed in other parts of the world where Europeans settled. The colonies in North- and South America, for example, also developed ideas about race similar to those at the Cape and their colonisation policies closely followed the pattern of the V.O.C. at the Cape. In other colonies too, their policies resulted in European ownership of land and political and economic privilege, contrasted with black servility and powerlessness. It is fair, therefore, to assert that the racial attitudes of the South African whites, and more particularly of the Afrikaners, owes and traces its origins directly to policies of European imperialism during the seventeenth and the eighteenth centuries.

3
EXPANSION

A lot has been said and written about the disgruntled and distressed burghers, who as a result of the contrived and grossly unfair competition from the V.O.C., as well as the heartless treatment of Willem Adriaan van der Stel and his cronies, switched from crop-to stock-farming. As we have seen this change eventually drove them further and further inland in an endless pursuit of fresh grazing and an adequate water supply. However, contrary to the belief that a mass movement into the hinterland suddenly erupted, the numbers of individuals who initially trekked inland was, in fact, a very insignificant one, and for a long while went almost unnoticed in Cape Town and Stellenbosch, where the vast majority of the burghers settled. Even in the V.O.C, it self there were not many people who were aware of any change in the situation.

Life 'on the trek' into the parched and hostile hinterland beyond the mountains was an exceedingly hard one, and the struggle for survival, let alone for success, was not to be considered lightly. In fact, in the very beginning many stock-farmers continued to live in Stellenbosch and to establish inland 'stock posts', seeking out grazing lands where the herds would be cared for by some member of the family aided by a few slaves or Khoi servants. These herders ('vee boere') would live in their ox-wagons or in rudely constructed reed and clay 'bothies' which were easy to construct, and whenever the time came to move further on, just as easy to demolish.

Soon however, as the flocks moved further and further away, a farmer here, and then another there, would pack up and load an ox-wagon or two, and with their families, their servants and all their worldly possessions, follow their herds further and further away from the Cape and from the outside world itself. This slow trickle continued throughout the ensuing decades until the 'Great Trek' itself in 1834-1835, and comprised individuals rather than groups of people, and never amounted to anything beyond a slow and erratic displacement of peoples from one part of the colony to another. It was estimated that at the height of the 'trekboer' movement, there was never more than about 10% of the burgher population who actually set off and severed, to all intents and purposes, their relationship with the Cape and its administration. For the trekboer the land ahead was endless, and there for the taking of as much of it as they could handle. They had no scruples when it came to moving any Khoi or San who happened to be in their way, but simply drove them off with their superior weapons.

In 1714 the V.O.C. introduced, purely for revenue purposes, a grazing fee, through the introduction of a 'grazing licence', which for the cost of 1 Rijksdalder per month allowed a person to graze his herds on any land available for any length of time he wished. The cost of the licence was later doubled, but even at that, it was a ridiculously small price to pay for the free use of any land, regardless of size. This land was available for whatever purpose desired, and it was relatively easy for many burghers to come into 'ownership' of vast quantities of ranching land, which, they believed they legitimately owned as long as they held a valid grazing licence.

By 1730 many of these stock farmers had established themselves as far away as 200 miles from Stellenbosch, which they still considered to be their 'home' or 'church-town' and to which they would return once or twice a year for the 'Nachtmael' (Communion), to meet old friends and families and to replenish stores and supplies. Farmers visited Cape Town, itself, for purposes of marriage, baptism and payment of grazing licences only, and very often periods of years would go by before they went there.

In time an additional tradition of regular contact with the Cape developed though the advent of the 'smouse', itinerant traders who travelled far into the hinterland bringing stores, supplies and news from the Cape and the outside world, and even grazing licences to the trekboers wherever they may be found. In return, the 'smous' would take back with him to Cape Town, news of the trekboers and their families as well as their grazing licence payments.

Life on the trek was not an easy one. These pioneers lived in isolation, ignorance and poverty – a journey to Cape Town could well entail an absence of two to three months, and their children would more often than not only visit the Cape once in their lifetime, and that would be to get 'properly' married by a real 'predikant' (Dutch Reformed Church minister). For the children there was no question of organised schooling, and their standard of living was extremely basic, and life in general exacting and telling. Nevertheless, once the movement started, it grew into a steady trickle of farmers, moving further and further away from the Cape, and deeper and deeper into the northeast hinterland, with 'the bible in one hand and the gun in the other'

There has been much debate about the motivation and reasons for this development but it seems reasonably certain that it was not significantly motivated by business principles. Although the trekboers needed certain vital supplies from civilisation such as guns and gunpowder, they rapidly became self-sufficient. Indeed, at the time of the Great Trek in 1835, a man's clothes, from his shoes and trousers to his shirt and hat were mostly D.I.Y. from game and cattle hide. He used the tail tallow from his scrub sheep for candles and soap making – he shot game for his meal, and used the skin to make blankets, clothing and leather strips for binding and for furniture, even beds.

There was by now, very little that the authorities in Europe, be they Dutch (or subsequently British) could do to contain the size of the colony. The free-burghers simply moved off into new territory yet never truly severing their ties, tenuous as they were, with the Cape. The authorities at the Cape had no option but to recognise and accept the de facto growth of the land area of the colony. This they did by the establishment of administrative centres further and further away from the government hub at the Cape and in an attempt to exert some control over the moving frontiers, Drostdye (magistracies) were set-up at Swellendam in 1743, at Graaf-Reinet in 1785 and at Uitenhage in 1803. These wandering farmers were, after all, Cape colonial subjects, and to a greater or lesser extent, the authorities at the Cape were obliged to accept and accord responsibility for them and their actions.

Landrosten (magistrates) and Heemraden (councillors), were appointed by the Company to represent the Cape administration on the frontier, at least to ensure some sort of system of justice in the ever-expanding colony. Local burghers were also nominated as 'Veldtkornetten', officers endowed with some policing and judicial authority, and with specific powers to call up commandos and keep records of all able-bodied male citizens who were liable for military service. All actions against indigenous people in which groups of Boers participated as organised commandos were considered to be 'military operations'.

During their outward movement the trekboers were initially opposed by the Khoikhoi and the San, but they managed to push them out of the way and then gradually move them further and further inland until they were eventually rendered totally ineffective. The gradual arrival of the trekboers in those areas historically occupied by the San and the Khoi, and later in the eastern frontier region, by the Xhosa tribes who were moving in from the north, caused a serious upheaval in the traditional ways of life of these indigenous peoples. Back at the Cape, many of the weaker Khoi communities were decimated by recurring epidemics of small pox, introduced from the East Indies, and to which the Khoi had no natural resistance. Those who managed to survive the ravages of smallpox succumbed to the evils of tobacco and alcohol, introduced by the white settlers, which soon reduced them to a miserable existence of poverty and need, forcing them to enter in menial service with their white 'masters'. The more resilient Khoi tribes, who refused to subject themselves to white dominion, moved away into the hinterland and continued to pursue their traditional lifestyle to the best of their ability in the circumstances. Yet, all this endeavour would come to nothing in the end, for as the land-hungry Boers trekked even deeper inland, they remorselessly drove the Khoi further and further away until they were eventually forced to bide at last in the remotest and most inhospitable recesses of the hostile interior.

The fate of the San was even worse than that of the Khoi. The Boers considered the San to be a dreadful menace, who in their endeavour to protect their own historic hunting grounds, stole Boer cattle and set fire to Boer crops. For this, the Boers branded them as vermin, and they set about systematically eradicating the San by hunting them down and shooting them dead as if they were game or marauding beasts. Eventually the Boers came face-to-face with the first black nation, the Nguni speaking Xhosa, who proved to be an infinitely more serious obstacle than the indigenous Khoi and San, particularly as the Xhosa shared with the Boers an insatiable appetite for more land. Thus, it was clear that a future conflict between them would be inevitable.

By the end of the eighteenth century, the situation in the Cape had developed into an uncontrollable monster that neither the V.O.C. nor the government in the Netherlands had anticipated nor desired. By then, the Trekboers had reached and had settled in the furthest eastern regions as far away as present day Port Elizabeth. The South African historian, F. J. van Jaarsveld described the typical Boer as a *'swerwer met wa en osse – oral tuis – beweeglik, rusteloos en sy oe gerig op die verre horizon. Sy geweer en perd en vee was deel van hom'* ('He was a wanderer with a wagon and oxen – at home anywhere – forever on the move – restless and with his eyes fixed on the distant horizon. His gun, his horse and his cattle were part of him').

Wherever the trekboers encountered the Xhosas, their wanderings were blocked and their outward movement halted. The pioneers, or 'frontier Boers' as they were by now called, would then settle with their families and their stocks on a more or less permanent basis, and would come into regular conflict with those Xhosa tribes who sought and fought for the same vast tracts of land as the Boers.

An informal head-count in 1773 revealed that the total white population of the Cape Colony consisted of 2,165 Company employees and 8,554 colonials, including women and children. About one-half of the colonists lived in and around Cape Town, which meant that the remaining 5,000 inhabitants occupied an area twelve times larger than Belgium.

The situation in Cape Town itself was not a very satisfactory one either. Unrest and complaints against the V.O.C. were coming in fast and furious. One such was a petition, signed in 1779 by three to four hundred burghers, against the Company and its officials. Rather than handing it to the Governor, van Plettenberg, it was addressed directly to the Council of Seventeen (the V.O.C.'s Executive) with a request that it be presented directly to the Chief Executive of the States General of the United Netherlands for immediate consideration. The petition contained direct and damning accusations, with concrete evidence of dishonesty, fraud and mismanagement perpetrated by named senior members of the Company administration in the Cape, but not the Governor himself who's only fault was his omission to take punitive action against his subordinates for their misdemeanours. It also made demands for increased civil and political rights and for increased burgher representation on the Political and Judicial Councils in the Cape.

It took the authorities in Amsterdam five years to complete their enquiry into the state of affairs in the Cape, and to make a ruling on the contents of the petition. In 1784, a reply was finally published finding the accused not guilty of the charges brought against them, but relieving them, nevertheless, of their duties in the Cape and recalling them to Amsterdam, including Governor Van Plettenberg. By now the financial state of the Company in Cape Town had fallen into such disarray through dishonesty and mismanagement, that all efforts to sort out and rectify matters were in vain, and its demise was inevitable and only a matter of time.

The crisis at the Cape was not relieved in any way by the unrest in the border areas where the frontier Boers had begun to pit their strength against the Company's local administrators. In Graaff Reinet, two hundred armed burghers accosted the Landdrost from Cape Town, and relieved him of his duties and ordered him back home. Following the Graaff Reinet affair came Swellendam's turn, where the Landdrost, Faure, was 'kicked out of his office 'by sixty armed burghers under the command of 'National Commandant-General Petrus Jacobus Delport' and other leaders of the self appointed 'National Convention'

In Holland, the bell was also tolling the death knell of the V.O.C. After France invaded the Netherlands in 1795, Prince William of Orange was forced to flee to England and while he was there, he invited Britain to occupy the Cape in order to deny the French safe access to the Dutch colonies in the Far East. In the wings, the British were waiting for the inevitable stage call that would at last bring them to Southern Africa, and where they would remain for the next 150 years.

By the end of the eighteenth century therefore, we see the emergence of dominant white groups in the southern tip of the African continent, some living in and around Cape Town in comparatively prosperous and settled conditions and surrounded and served by slaves, 'coloured' and Khoi servants. Further inland, we find the same white dominance, not acquired through peaceful and gracious evolution but rather through the rough and tumble of outback encounter and conflict. These hinterland Boers had missed out on a century of enlightenment and social reform, and were culturally sterile, totally de-urbanised, living in rude isolation, and cut off from civilisation. They had become intensely individualistic, suspicious and resentful of interference from anyone or anything beyond the limited of their own property. For the Boers in in this situation the local inhabitants were either servants or enemies, and treated accordingly.

Finally, in the north, the San were practically wiped-out, and being replaced by land-hungry and hostile Xhosa tribes who were heading rapidly into head-on collision with the frontier Boers. The potato which the British were about to inherit in the southern tip of the African continent would turn out to be a very hot one indeed....!

4
THE ARRIVAL OF THE BRITISH

Recently Christian Tyler published a revue in the Financial Times magazine on a book written by Roger Osborne entitled "Civilisation: a new History of the Western World" In summing up Osborne's book Tyler wrote the following: *'In outline, Osborne's case is that the west developed a sense of exclusive superiority that permitted it to bully others. The fantasy was peddled by a social elite that exploited the lower classes and enjoyed killing barbarians. So the conquistadors massacred the uncomprehending Aztecs and Incas; European traders threw Africans into slavery; American pioneers wiped out native peoples and empire builders grabbed half the world. A superior wisdom blessed the cruelties of the French Revolution and the appalling conditions of the Victorian factory worker. Coercion was reinforced by a cult of warfare and by the emergence of the notion of state demanding the loyalty of its citizens in return for protection'*

It is uncanny just how accurately this assessment related to the British government's dealings with South Africa and its inhabitants during the nineteenth century, for with possession of the Cape in 1805, came the responsibility for some 80,000 people spread over some 90,000 square miles. In the area around Cape Town there lived approximately 50,000 burghers who were the most prosperous members of the colony. They were mainly of Dutch, German and French origin and all spoke a Dutch dialect, which was later to develop into the cultural language of Afrikaans. A slave population accounted for another 35,000 souls, thus bringing the total number of people living in and around Cape Town in settled conditions to about 85,000.

By the time of the French Revolution in 1794, England was, already well established as the leading world colonising nation, the dominant maritime power and the most important state on the European stage. This status was however, soon, to be challenged. With the advent of the Napoleonic wars, Britain found herself threatened by the continental trade blockade imposed against her by Napoleon. It was during this period that France invaded, and then occupied, the Netherlands, William, Prince of Orange, fleeing to England where his government-in-exile requested the British to protect the V.O.C. interests in the Dutch East Indies. By now, British influence had largely supplanted that of the Dutch in the East Indies, and the Cape sea route had become an infinitely more important trading lifeline for Britain than for any other European power. They were, therefore, rightly concerned that their sea-lines to the east could be severed, should access to the Cape ever be denied them. The British received authorisation from the exiled Prince of Orange to send an expedition to take possession of the Cape with an understanding that it would be returned to the Dutch when a general peace was eventually attained.

At the end of August 1795, Sir James Craig was handed a letter from the Prince of Orange requiring the Commissioner-General of the Cape to surrender the government of the colony, and on the 16th September 1795, following a brief skirmish, Slysken, the local Governor, formally handed the administration of the Cape over to the British.

At this time, the British had absolutely no territorial designs on the Cape – their sole intention was to secure the trading route to the Indies for British shipping. Neither colonial acquisition for its own sake, nor colonisation was even remotely within their contemplation at that time, and Craig quite correctly saw his administration as a temporary one, and he made as few changes to the existing system as possible. The current legal system was retained intact while Roman-Dutch law remained the common law of the colony. Local rules and regulations were left undisturbed, and local administrative and community affairs remained in the hands of the burgher councillors of Cape Town.

Craig, nevertheless, did make one change, which would signify, more than anything else, what was destined to become a root problem, then and later on, between the British and the burghers of the colony. He required 'humane treatment' for all the peoples of the colony and immediately after his arrival in the Cape he outlawed all judicial torture and other more bizarre methods of execution that had hitherto been carried out in public. By that time 'humane treatment' of black slaves, for example, was totally anathema to the locals. The Cape Court of Justice protested strongly in a letter to Craig, which he promptly rejected. Yet, although the frontier Boers remained somewhat restive and despite an inconsequential rebellion led by one Marthinus Prinsloo, the British occupation and administration of the Cape continued without any serious challenge for eight years, until 1803.

In 1802 the Treaty of Amiens was signed, bringing a temporary peace in Europe. The United Netherlands was renamed the Batavian Republic, and the Cape was handed back to the Dutch. The British withdrawal from the Cape, was followed by the appointment of Governor J.W. Janssens and Commissioner-General J.A. de Mist as principal administrators of the colony, and so matters remained until 1806 when a British force once again landed at the Cape, this time to take over and stay put. With the resumption of hostilities in 1803, the British had once again become wary of Napoleon's intensions with regard to the facilities of the Batavian Republic, and as a consequence it became inevitable that they would wish to protect their interest in the Cape, where they returned in January 1806.

During the period between the British departure in 1803 and their return in 1806 the Batavian Republic did little to bring about any consequential policy changes in the Cape. During the short while that they were in control, however, they did succeed in effecting a few very sound administrative functional and procedural changes. Unhappily, they also managed seriously to alienate Cape opinion and support. It was not that the Batavians failed to manage affairs at the Cape properly, nor that they considered looked upon as intruders. The real problem stemmed from the same source as that which had arisen between the British during their brief stay in the Cape, namely the 'burgher ideology'. The burghers judged the Batavians guilty of supreme blasphemy in their tolerance of creeds and beliefs other than those of the established Dutch Reformed Church as well as their willingness to secularise marriage and education and in their attitudes of liberal humanitarianism. These were devilish innovations of a kind which the colonists had long learned to view with extreme suspicion.

The importance of the Batavian interlude is the light that it sheds on the cultural chasm that had developed between the Cape burghers and their European roots. Many later historians, especially Afrikaners, tend to stress the difference in philosophy between the Boers and the British, but the truth is that the Boers would have suffered exactly the same frustrations with any administration from any other Western power. Indeed, had they enjoyed longer tenure at the Cape the idealistic Batavians, filled with milk of human kindness, would probably have offended the sensibilities of the Cape colonists much more and much sooner than the more pragmatic British did.

The basic problem was that the perceptions and value systems of the western world had moved on since the time of Van Riebeeck and that during those long years of isolation, the Western European Enlightenment had passed them by. The burghers entertained cardinal misconceptions of the principles of the Enlightenment. Some historians still emphasise the links of the Kaapse Patriooten (Cape Patriots) Movement with the liberal continental Hollanders, and suggest that they had assimilated the liberal doctrines of their European mentors. Recent scholars are justifiably more sceptical, giving evidence that the Patriooten differed fundamentally in their views from the new European liberalism. For example, they displayed no interest at all in those modern European concepts of the universal rights of man nor in popular sovereignty or even on independence. Indeed, with some substantial individual exceptions, the history of the Afrikaners right up to the end of the twentieth century displays a total blind spot for the universality of the concepts of rights and justice, and a particularly special disdain for popular sovereignty. The appreciation of this philosophical chasm that had developed between the colonists and their own cultural heritage is fundamental to the understanding of later events in the Transvaal and the Free State, and indeed in twentieth century South Africa as a whole.

When in January 1806, the British force of 6,706 troops landed on Bloubergstrand in Table Bay, Governer Janssens sent out a small force to oppose them, but it was quickly defeated. The Napoleonic Wars were to last for another nine years but this time the British had arrived to stay for an indefinite period. Their aim, like the first time round, was unchanged; the trade route to the Indies around the Cape of Good Hope had to be protected at all costs, and the fact that there was a sizeable and territorially over-expanding colony allotted to the Cape was an unfortunate nuisance that would be dealt with on an *ad hoc* basis. This time, however, there was a significant difference in the occupational intent of the British as compared to that of the Batavians. The Batavians had come to 'inaugurate a social revolution' whereas the British had come specifically to 'occupy a fortress'. At the end of the Napoleonic Wars in 1815 there was a general pacification among the countries of Europe and Britain returned to the Netherlands all its frontier colonies that they taken in possession with the exception of Guinea and the Cape. A treaty transferred the Cape Colony to Britain in return for payment of £6million, which was in fact the equivalent of the Netherlands' financial commitments owed to other European powers during the war.

Du Pre Alexander, Earl of Caledon was appointed first British Governor of the Cape, and in terms of his instructions, he ruled autocratically, by proclamation, and was responsible only to the Secretary for War and the Colonies in London. For the next thirty years, consecutive British governors viewed the Cape primarily as a military outpost with the result that the first governors were all military men. In September 1811, Sir John Cradock succeeded Caledon, and in April 1814, Cradock was followed by Lord Charles Somerset. All these initial governors set about making the British presence as permanent and as economically viable as possible.

Traditionally, the single most important principle of British colonial policy was that the colony should not be a liability to the mother country. The whole purpose of obtaining colonies was to gain advantages and not burdens and to transform colonial investments into economic sources for raw materials and lucrative markets for exports. The case of the Cape however, was quite different. The benefits expected from it were two-fold – in the long term it expected the Cape to protect the very lucrative trade route to the Indies, and in the short term to secure the island of St. Helena where Napoleon was held prisoner. It was not seen as a 'promising' investment, and consequently running costs were to be pared to a minimum in order to ensure the expected benefits of occupation at the lowest possible cost. It was in realising this expectation that Britain was to find its greatest challenge, and in the end, its greatest failure.

The biggest dilemma for the British was that for military and naval purposes alone, they only needed the Cape peninsula and False Bay, but with these two strategic landmarks also came a hugely extensive colony, sparsely populated by a few unruly Dutch farmers, by formidable black nations pressing on its borders, and demoralised Khoikhoi and San scattered about. It was only in the Cape that there was any form of the amenities of civilisation or settled forms of administration, or law and order.

The succession of British governors at the Cape resolutely shouldered the burden, and carried on trying to make the best of matters. Sadly, there never was a consistent British policy at the Cape, and in the circumstances it could hardly have been expected. Yet in the broadest possible sense, there was absolute consistency in the *aims* of the policy, whatever its details and method of management by successive governors and administrations might be. And that, in essence, was what they all strove to achieve, namely the protection of the sea route around the Cape at the minimum of cost to the Exchequer, and in so doing their expectations were expanded to achieve the following at least:

-ensure that the settled population of the colony would be peaceful and loyal subjects of the Crown

-establish and maintain an effective agricultural community that would not only sustain the colony itself, but would also be able to generate sufficient surplus to sustain a resident British garrison, victual ships and export produce

- promote a just and equitable administration of the law according to the precepts of generally accepted civilised norms of justice within the colony

- stabilise the colony's borders along defensible frontiers

- establish and ensure lasting peace with peoples neighbouring the colony's frontiers

Although it was largely successful in achieving the first three policy aims, the British administration in the Cape only managed to do so against bitter opposition from the Dutch inhabitants, especially those on the eastern frontier. The last two aims were, alas, never to be. Due to many various circumstances, the British presence in South Africa would become increasingly expensive, and would finally end in a bloody and bitter head-on confrontation with the descendants of the peoples inhabiting the colony at the time of the British arrival in 1806.

In their endeavour to enhance the social conditions of the Khoikhoi and other indigenous inhabitants, the British administration encouraged the arrival of missionaries, but this too was soon to become another bane for the Boers. The work of Christian missionaries among the indigenous population in many respects exercised a more than substantial influence on the turn of events. Shortly after the arrival of the British in 1795, the first Christian Protestant missionaries also arrived. The declared aim of the London Missionary Society was to '*send the Glorious Gospel of the Blessed God to the Heathen*'.

The missionary invasion started in the Cape with the arrival of the first missionaries from the L.M.S. in 1799 led by Dr. Theodorus van der Kemp. The missionary zeal, in quick succession, brought the Anglican Church Missionary Society, The Basel Society (Swiss Calvinists), the Paris Society and the American Missionary Society to the shores of southern Africa. It was inevitable that the Boers and the missionaries would eventually find themselves on a collision course, the Boer 'weltanschaung' diverging so much from that of the rest of the civilised world, and especially from that of dedicated missionaries, that they would be predictably and totally incompatible.

Soon after the establishment of the L.M.S. at Bethelsdorp, east of Cape Town, Khoi servants were encouraged to bring charges of maltreatment against their white employers, and soon a steady stream of complaints were made against the Boers. Dr. van der Kemp and Sir James Read, his chief assistant, were both characters of epic proportion, totally dedicated to the Mission and to the protection of its Khoikhoi neophytes, and following the arrival of the British, their efforts to stop the labour-hungry Boers from indenturing and exploiting their charges were intensified.

The proliferation of trivial charges was bound to cause serious disruptions in the day-to-day management of affairs in the Cape, and it came as no surprise that the local British Officer, Colonel Collins (who had previously been Commissioner of the Eastern District) displayed very little sympathy for the missionaries and their protestations. Collins ordered an investigation into the activities of the mission station at Bethelsdorp, and as a result, opined that, in reality, it was of little if any benefit, either to the community or to the Khoi. He recommended its closure, a course of action that would have benefited the Boers because it would have released those Khoi inhabitants at the mission station for free labour for the farmers. In response, James Read vigorously took up the cause of a number of coloured servants who had claimed to have suffered maltreatment by their employers and soon a stream of complaints became a flood which eventually found its way to the highest quarters in London.

It may be interesting to look at the state of the law in the Cape Colony at this time. When the British arrived, they had deliberately retained the Roman-Dutch legal system as the common law at the Cape. Roman-Dutch had been the common law of the Netherlands until the Napoleonic Wars and it had been in force at the Cape since the arrival of Van Riebeeck in 1652. It was not only possible but even feasible for the British to leave the legal system unchanged because, despite some differences of detail, it and English common law were both based on Roman Law and were therefore entirely compatible in their precepts and attitudes to justice and fairness. Both systems were accusative in procedure as opposed to the less compatible inquisitorial systems of France and other continental countries.

However, the normally high principles of justice by Roman-Dutch law were in practice, severely compromised at the Cape, and even more so in the eastern frontier regions. People of colour received harsher sentences than the Europeans did for the same offence, and the evidence of white people was always accepted over that of the Khoikhoi witness, or witnesses from any other indigenous person for that matter. In many areas, no criminal or civil complaints by coloured people against their masters were even entertained.

In the wake of the missionaries' complaints, which were investigated in London, the governor of the Cape, Lord Caledon, was urged to test this flood of allegations in a proper court of law. As a result he was allowed in 1810 to institute circuit courts with a quorum of Justices of the Supreme Court with powers to review the decisions of the Landdrosten , and to try the more serious cases itself. The first Circuit Court of 1811 went about its business without incident – the frontier Boers were not against the exercise of the judicial function at all. The problem, in fact, did not lie in the law itself but in the concept of equality before the law. The second circuit, in 1812, was to become infamous amongst the Boers who dubbed it the 'Black Circuit' (De Zwarte Omgang). As Lord Caledon had intended, the Circuit Court was to be the opportune and appropriate forum to sort the wheat from the chaff as far as complaints against the Boers were concerned. Read and Van der Kemp had encouraged their flock to place every possible complaint they could think of before the court, and in the final count, the tally came to over 100 murders allegedly having been committed, with some individual Boers standing trial on some eight or nine counts.

Because of the profusion of complaints, many of them blatantly flawed, the judges were inclined to attach little if any weight to purely Khoikhoi evidence, most of which was openly fabricated, and so a vast majority of the cases were dismissed outright. Nevertheless, there were some convictions and this infuriated the Boers to the extent that it became a black day in their history and was eventually to lead to one of the most serious causes for the collapse of future relations between them and the British.

The Boers' main complaint was that those whom they regarded as their inferiors, had been allowed to accuse them in the first place. They deemed it an extreme injustice that they had to face trial in a court of law on the complaint of a party who was not white. Thus, implicit in their attitude was that such lowly beings as the Khoikhoi and blacks had no right to be heard in a court, and certainly not to complain against their 'betters.

Then a second incident was to occur in 1815, which would become yet another festering sore in the wound of Boer relations with the British administration. Complaints of maltreatment were brought against one Freek Bezuidenhout, a prominent renegade amongst the so-called 'wetloozen' (outlaw) farmers in the wild country over the hills in the far-off Graaff-Reinet area. Johannes Auret, Veldkornett in charge of that district, was sent with some troops to issue the summons for Bezuidenhout to appear in court. Bezuidenhout was in an ugly mood, and started firing on Aurett and his party, and during the ensuing shoot-out, was killed. His brother, Hans Jan Bezuiudenhout, swore revenge, and persuaded some of his friends to join him in armed defiance of the authorities. The Landdrost, Jacob Cuyler, responded by acting severely against the rebels, and beat them into surrender. In the skirmishes that followed, Hans Jan and one Khoikhoi soldier were killed. After the trial in the Circuit Court, five of the ringleaders were sentenced to death, and were brought to a place called Slachtersnek for the hanging. When the first of the five was hanged, the rope broke and the execution was suspended for two hours whilst a new rope was sought. Because of this, the mood of the disenchanted onlookers became uglier by the minute. The hanging resumed, and in due course, the five men duly met their fate.

The so-called 'Slachtersnek Rebellion', a misnomer for it did not take place at Slachtersnek, nor could it be called a rebellion, engendered an inglorious episode of lawlessness into the Afrikaans mythology as further proof of the unrelenting persecution of the Boers by the evil British!

Perhaps it was at this time that the British administration at the Cape, as well as in London, began to realise that the frontier Boers would never come round to accepting the British conception of justice and fair play for all. In 1814, Lord Charles Somerset, the new Governor at the Cape, received instructions from the Colonial Secretary in London, to encourage the Dutch in South Africa to realise that they lived in a British colony, with British institutions and a British way of life, and that they needed to accept the ways and the language of Britain. As a result, Somerset sought to replace Dutch by English in all spheres of public life. In due course English became the sole language of the Cape legislature, although all laws and regulations were published in the Dutch language as well. In 1822, a proclamation was issued declaring that, during an initial trial period of five years, English would be the exclusive language of the courts. This would not preclude the accused or a witness from using Dutch or whatever other language was preferred, but it would entail making use of an interpreter. In the schools, special incentives were given to teachers who employed the medium of English and it was clear that Dutch education suffered in the process, especially in the country areas where English was hardly ever spoken by anyone. The result was that school attendance became a particular ordeal for the bulk of the children, who had great difficulty in communicating with their teachers.

In the Dutch Reformed Church, there was also a dire shortage of adequately qualified ministers, and Somerset managed to secure the services of a team of Scottish clergymen to fill the pulpits in South Africa. This in fact, turned out to be one of the rare actions of his that did not engender any ensuing hard feelings on behalf of the local whites, because the Scots had all learnt to speak Dutch even before they had left for South

Africa, and they eventually integrated into Afrikaner society quite seamlessly. In time, their descendants would become leading members of Afrikaner society.

Although the Anglicization policy did not in the end make much of an impact, especially on the eastern frontier Boers, they still perceived it as a malicious part of a whole process of relentless British imposition, and would later be cited as evidence of their self-perception of victims of ruthless British persecution.

At this time incidents of violence increased all along the colony's eastern frontier as the Boers pressed further and further into the face of the advancing Xhosa tribes from the north. In December 1811, Andries Stockenstrom, a local Landdrost, was murdered by some black inhabitants of the region. The newly appointed Eastern Commissioner, Col. John Graham, ruthlessly exacted revenge. At the head of a mixed force of Boers, regulars and the newly formed Khoikhoi Cape Regiment, he cleared the area, then known as the Zuurveld, of its indigenous inhabitants, destroyed all their crops, burnt their kraals and took away all their cattle. London was not pleased. - to them the Governor's job was to protect the sea-route and not conduct wars and expand the colony, and Somerset received specific instructions to settle disputes more diplomatically and less belligerently. By now, it had become abundantly obvious that peace and stability would never be realised along the colony's eastern borders. For as long as the land-hungry Boers were pressing ferociously against the equally land-hungry and fiercely resisting Xhosa tribes from the north, these two counter-pressures would inevitably result in constant cross-border clashes.

Somerset decided to annexe the recently cleared-out Zuurveld and rename it the District of Albany. This new district extended up to the line of the Fish River, and Somerset envisaged filling the new area with more stable immigrants directly from Britain. At first, the Colonial Office was slow to react but soon, during the first half of 1820, some four thousand settlers eventually arrived from Britain. Most of the males amongst them were either farmers or tradesmen, but included a sprinkling of soldiers, teachers and clergymen. The settlement was a huge success, although not for the intended purpose of establishing peace on the border, nor for containing the growth of the colony. Clashes with the Xhosa were to continue for a further fifty years, long after the bulk of the Boers had set off on their great trek to the north between 1835 and 1838. In fact, territory further to the east, would be added to the Cape in a piecemeal fashion until it finally met up with the Natal border in the far north.

The settlers quickly acclimatised to their new surroundings and developed a toughness of character that was common to the inhabitants of all the turbulent frontiers areas throughout the world. The Albany settlement was seen by the British administration as a serious attempt to stem the outward movement of the frontier Boers, but it was doubtful whether they succeeded in this aim. In many instances the settlers joined the Boers in their quest for land and labour, and in their need for protection against the encroaching Xhosa tribes. Indeed, many of their offspring married Boer sons and daughters, and some of them even set off with the Boers on their eventual great trek out of the colony. In the end, however, the British attempt at the Anglicization of the Cape Colony came to be seen as one of the major factors in the continued process of alienating the Boers from the British and their administration in the Cape.

It would be tempting to make quick and easy judgements about who was right and who was wrong, but in the final analysis blame and merit must be laid at both doors. The frontier Boers had wilfully and systematically estranged themselves, firstly from the Company, then from the Batavian Republic, and finally from the British. They purposely and wilfully ignored official policies discouraging territorial expansion, of humane treatment of indigenous peoples who stood in their way, and of the economic exigencies of the Cape authorities. They expected, nay *demanded,* just and fair legal treatment for themselves from the administrative system, yet they denied the same to their servants, slaves and any other beings they considered their 'inferiors.' The very way of life which they chose to adopt, turned them into intolerant, quick tempered and intensely rapacious isolationists, seeking in the end more land and more labour at the expense of everyone and everything else. Yet, they were exceedingly brave and enterprising in opening up the hinterland in the face of hostile and fierce resistance from invading Xhosa tribes from the north.

On the other hand, treatment of the Boers by the British administration in the Cape was deplorable. Regardless of their contribution of 150 years of civilising stability and progress as an independent and European colonial entity, they were treated by the British in a most condescending and patronising manner, as if they were uncivilised 'natives' of some obscure outpost of their mighty Empire. Britain made no effort either to understand nor to appreciate and accommodate the 150 years of evolved lifestyle, needs and aspirations of a sizeable chunk of their subjects. Lord Charles Somerset's deliberate policy of Anglicisation only served to antagonise them. The imposition of restrictive laws on the usage of the Dutch language in all spheres of life, including the schools and the legislature, was insulting, insensitive and downright humiliating to the non-British inhabitants of the Cape Colony. This resentment was also shared by a vast percentage of the coloured population who had no English at all, and whose *lingua franca* was the evolving Dutch derivative that was later to develop into the Afrikaans language.

This, then, was the animal which by 1830, was poised to sever, unequivocally, 180 years of association with the Dutch, Batavian and British administrations in the Cape and head north into a new wilderness, a new identity and a new destiny.

The British impact on the Afrikaners was enormous. Having entirely missed the eighteenth century, the nineteenth burst in on them with a bang. They had lived as free men with almost no administrative restraints, so they would have felt entangled, and subsequently strangled by the arrival of the rule of law, and the pervasive orderliness of a major imperial power. The intrusion at first irked them, and then gradually irritated them, and finally angered them, and by so doing fuelled a spirit of nationalism, which eventually turned a loosely knit community of undisciplined individualists into a cohesive national entity, which would baffle the world with its obduracy. And therein lay the seeds of deeply engrained antipathy, mistrust and eventually outright antagonism against the British. For the Afrikaners the arrival of the British on the scene at the beginning of the nineteenth century resulted in the disruption of a relatively stable, albeit somewhat primitive way of life.

Their impact on the indigenous inhabitants of the southern tip of Africa was equally as profound. The Africans, having encountered one kind of expansionist white intruder, who had engaged them aggressively but with limited powers of destruction, were now to come against another who spoke softly and deceitfully of Christian values and humanitarian ideals, but who at the same time, introduced the concepts of total war and territorial expansion and conquest. By the time the Bantu tribes encountered the Trekboers on the eastern frontier, the latter, whether they would admit it or not, had developed a lifestyle not much different from that of the Bantu. It was only with the arrival of the British that both Boer and Bantu would fall victim to the destabilising impact of the modern world on their traditional institutions and way of life. Herein lay another reason for Boer antipathy towards the British. It was they who had to bear the notoriety of being the instrument of black subjugation, when in fact, it was the British who first broke the power of the black tribes in southern Africa by crushing them in war, annexing their territories and eroding their institutions with Christianisation, education and finally industrialisation and urbanisation. The frontier Boers deeply resented this intrusion on their own chosen lifestyle. They deeply resented the paternalistic liberalism, which was the hallmark of Victorian imperialists. As the Empire spread around the world, Britain instituted herself as the self-appointed guardian to millions of the earth's inhabitants, taking on an air of smug superiority and a belief that what they were doing was for the inestimable good of the less fortunate souls they were dominating. Thus the spirit of imperialism and democracy, of exploitation and Christian charity, were all reconciled in the notion of the 'White Man's Burden'.

In 1839, Thomas Carlyle wrote: *'surely of all the 'Rights of Man' (this) right of the ignorant man to be guided by the wiser, to be gently, or even forcibly, held in the true course by him, is the most indisputable'*. The frontier Boers saw themselves as those who, in the eyes of the imperialists, were described as *'less fortunate souls'*, and as Thomas Carlyle's *'the ignorant man to be guided'*. For this they resisted the British intrusion with a seething resentment for did not they in their own right consider themselves as being 'superior' to the less fortunate black tribes around them, and tantamount to the modern day 'chosen people' of Old Testament tradition.

So it was that the Boers finally came to believe that, not only did the British want to possess their land and their homes, but their very souls as well. For them to retain their traditional ways of life, which they had built over the past 180 years the only answer was to pack up their ox-wagons and leave the colony, lock, stock and barrel, and move as far away from the British as possible.

5
EXODUS and PURSUIT

The Great Trek

Over a period of two years, between 1834 and 1836, over 4,000 Voortrekkers ('forerunner trekkers') set off from the Cape Colony in a dramatic last-bid attempt to put as many miles between them and the British. It is significant to note that this momentous event did not take place in one single movement at any one appointed time, but was made up of small individual parties of people gathering under appointed leaders, and setting off, perhaps picking up one or two more groups here and there on their way. In their tented ox-wagons they took with them all their earthly belongings, a few slaves and as many servants and labourers as were willing to accompany them into the unknown wilderness. They also carried with them a deep-rooted resentment against the 'verdomde Engelse' (damned English), who within the short space of thirty years had succeeded in impinging on their long-established mores and customs, and in taking away their farms, their land and possessions, and above all their pride and their dignity.

It was here that the principal cause of the mistrust and enmity between these two peoples will be found. It was a deep lying antipathy which would, over the next 130 years, survive relentless pursuit, conflict, invasion, annexation, colonisation, two major wars, a painfully humiliating peace, a slow and agonising healing process, and eventually with the creation of the Republic of South Africa in 1965, the final and irrevocable break with the British, the Empire and the Crown.

The groups did not set off with a dramatic 'exeunt' with the leader prancing about on his lively pony - gun in hand – a shot fired in the air – a shout of 'yippeeee' and a dozen or more wagons rolling away into the distant vastness.... On the contrary, usually a few families only, in some particular area would set off quietly, often with great grief and sober dignity, and as they progressed they would be joined, here and there, by the odd wagon or two as additional individual families decided to accompany them in their flight for freedom. It is also worth noting that the trekkers did not all come from the eastern border region either. Many families from the central region of the colony and even as close to Cape Town as Caledon and Ceres, joined them in their escape to the north (*)

The trek was certainly not an idyllic romp with campfire capers and banjo sing-a-longs, but a hard and arduous undertaking fraught with danger and risk as the wagons trundled northwards, week in week-out, month in-month-out, until time itself seemed to disappear beyond those endless flat and distant horizons.

(*) *One such was the family of Lourens Badenhorst, the author's mother's great-grandfather who set off from the Swellendam area and later joined the Andries Pretorius group in Natal just before the battle of Blood River.*

From the very start evidence of Boer 'contentiousness' was revealed as groups quarrelled and split into factions arguing about which leader to follow and which direction to take. Eventually they settled for two main, divergent routes, one heading north and finally ending up in the Transvaal, and the other curving around to the east across the Drakensberg and into Natal. Both groups soon ran head-on into collision with the two principal black military powers of the day, the Ndebele on the highveld, and the Zulus in Natal. On the highveld Mzilikazi's Ndebele fell upon the northbound trekkers, led by the tall and peppery Hendrik Potgieter, at Vegkop in the northern Free State in October 1836. At the end of the day the Ndebele drove off thousands of Boer cattle, but the trekkers survived and in due course they mounted a punishing reprisal attack, and succeeded in driving Mzilikazi and his Ndebeli right out of the country. Potgieter now proceeded to set up two Voortrekker communities, one around the the modern day town of Winburg in the Free State, and the other on the banks of the Mooi River in the western Transvaal. This latter party would flourish and eventually evolve into the dominant Boer stronghold in South Africa.

The Mooi River settlement differed from those in Natal, in so far as it covered no specific territory, but much more flexibly, exercised its authority over whatever land it proceeded to possess. This 'policy' caused a lot of friction amongst the Boers, and soon the irascible Potgieter predictably fell out with his fellows and moved his party off to the eastern Transvaal to settle in the region of present-day Ohrigstadt. By now it was well known that his intense Anglophobia constantly motivated his urgent imperative to move anywhere north of the ill-fated 25th parallel that had been defined by the 'Cape of Good Hope Punishment Act, 1836'. It was here, in the eastern Transvaal, that some trekkers from Natal joined the Potgieter group following the British annexation of Natal.

Alas, wherever one found Potgieter, one also found dissent and it was not long before he fell out with the newcomers from Natal who strongly resented his overbearing bullying and autocratic style of leadership. The outcome was that Potgieter once again moved off, this time to an area in the Zoutpansberg in the far northern Transvaal and close to the Limpopo River, and further away than ever from the hated British!

Potgieter's original encounter with a major black tribe in Africa was soon to be replicated in Natal. As the eastward bound trekkers crossed over the Drakensberg and into Natal, Piet Retief, the oldest and most venerable of all the Trek leaders, decided to seek a negotiated land deal with the Zulus. By then, Shaka, the founder of the Zulu empire had already been assassinated by his half-brother Dingane, who had then declared himself the new paramount chief of the Zulus. Dingane was a man of unstable temperament, sadly lacking Shaka's intelligence and leadership qualities, and was paranoid about losing his power at the hands of his enemies in the same way as he himself had wrenched it from Shaka.

During his reign Shaka had met some early white traders, mostly British, who had long since settled at Port Natal, and whom he had treated with friendly curiosity and without any animosity whatsoever. On the other hand, Dingane was very nervous about these people, and feared them as a threat, and later, when informed of the in-coming Boers, he

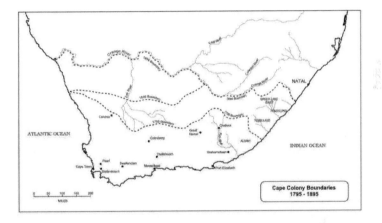

Cape Colony Boundaries
1795 - 1895

48

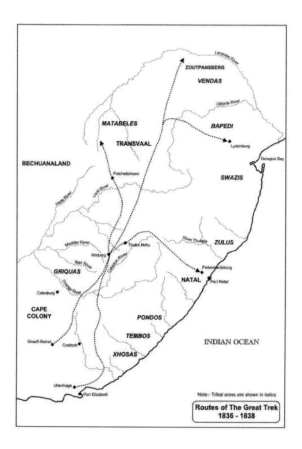

Routes of The Great Trek
1836 - 1838

became convinced that he and his people were in grave danger of destruction. In this he was right excepting that it was not to be Boers that would eradicate his nation but the British themselves He purported to agree to Retief's land request, and placed his mark on a treaty granting a generous portion of land to the Boers, but it was a deceitful trick. After inviting Retief and his party to a celebration, he ordered his warriors to slaughter the whites, and he then despatched his impis to the main Boer encampment, where they attacked the unsuspecting trekker families, killing 281 white men, women and children and some 200 coloured servants. The Boers later named the place where this occurred, 'Weenen' or 'the place of weeping'

It was then that the 'Vow of the Covenant' was sworn. The surviving Voortrekkers in Natal, reinforced by newcomers from the Cape Colony, mustered a powerful commando against the Zulus. Led by Andries Pretorius, it trekked into the heart of Zululand and formed a laager beside the Ncome River. There the Boers swore a vow imploring the Lord God to be with them and deliver them from the enemy, promising to build a church there and observe in perpetuity that date as a day of sacred deliverance And the Lord did indeed deliver the enemy into their hands. On the morning of the 16th December 1838, the Zulu army of perhaps 10,000 warriors, attacked the Boer laager containing 530 Boer marks-men, only to be shot down in such vast swathes that the adjacent river ran red with the blood of the slain and the wounded. In the end the Boers raised a commando, and rode out in pursuit of the fleeing warriors and proceeded to cut them to pieces. More than 3,000 Zulus fell that day at what would become known as the 'Battle of Blood River'.

After the battle, the victorious commando found Retief's body with Dingane's treaty still intact in a coat pocket. With it they proceeded to lay legitimate claim to the land, and settled there to found the Republic of Natalia and established the seat of administration at Pietermaritzburg, some 50 miles inland from the seaport at Durban.

In summarising the complex ethnic situation in Southern Africa at the time of the 'great dispersal', the historian, Allister Sparks writes, in his fascinating book entitled 'The Mind of South Africa', '*By the second decade of the nineteenth century the ethnic stage was set for the enactment of an epic drama. Four groups of people as different from one another as any on God's earth were cast together in a closed setting on the eastern frontier of South Africa. There were the world's most isolated whites, locked in their seventeenth century time capsule, convinced of the God given rights over the un-elected pagans around them, and offended by the doctrine of black rights that was being foisted on them. There were the world's most advanced whites, bringing with them the spirit of a new age but sewing confusion as they did so with their ambiguous blend of racial superiority and philanthropy, of exploitation and humanism. There were the black tribes, proud and secure in their own immemorial culture but bewildered by the strangers now blocking their path and the turmoil that was beginning to build up in their rear. And there were the Khoikhoi and the slaves, stripped of land and cultural heritage and merging together into a new racially defined category of servile workers.*

The Trekkers entered upon a land that was largely abandoned by its original occupants who had fled the ravages of the "Difaquane" – the domino effect of tribal displacements initiated by Shaka Zulu's aggressive empire expansion activities – and as they headed into their new territory they also headed into a maelstrom of unrest. Originally, when the Xhosa tribes on the coastal strip had stood in the way of the white expansion that had been going on for a century or so, the Trekkers simply changed direction and headed north, inland and around the Xhosas just as before.

Now, as already mentioned, in the north, standing in their way, they were soon to encounter the two military powers that had arrived there earlier, and were putting all the smaller ones to flight – the Ndebele on the highveld and the Zulus on the Natal coastal plain. Although the Voortrekkers eventually overcame both, they first had to pay a heavy price in blood and suffering, but they endured their disasters and hardened their resolve, forging themselves as they went along into a people of formidable resolve and resilience, which soon, within the next fifty years, the British were to discover to their bitter surprise and cost.

Slowly the Boers took over the land, confining the indigenous peoples to an arc of shrunken territory that curved around the central plateau, forcing thousands into servitude. The Boers' pioneering opened up the interior of South Africa but it did not develop it. Unlike the pioneers who opened up the Australian interior or the American West, the Voortrekkers were not fortune seekers in search of new opportunities neither were they driven by the impulses of the industrial age to conquer the wilderness and wring new wealth from it. In fact they were fugitives from that age, and not the bearers of its ethics, and were in essence simply seeking to escape the nineteenth century and rediscover the arcadian simplicity of the seventeenth, as they had known it before the arrival of the British.

Thus, they entered the interior and languished there with their imaginations lying fallow and their minds inert once again and for the next two generations their children and grandchildren continued to receive the education of the farm, the veld and the Boer home carrying their non-literary and non-industrial attitudes and habits of mind right through to the end of the nineteenth century (de Kiewiet "A History of South Africa – Social and Economic" (London 1941)

The Boer republics acquired a curious kind of 'equalitarianism – within – the – family' attitude. Since whites alone owned all the land, and the blacks they had conquered did all the manual labour, no white person had to work for another white, and all were equal in the racial aristocracy. All were fierce individualists with their own individual estates, so no one dared interfere with another's affairs or order him about. And, since it was basically government from which they had escaped in the Cape Colony they saw to it that government was kept to a minimum in their republics. Taxation was frowned upon and the collection of it nearly impossible. This meant that such government as they did have was weak and inefficient for want of revenue. Nothing could be done except by general consent of the equal and opinionated individualists who made up the nation which was highly democratic but which totally excluded all people of colour. Ironically, in the very first independent African republics the Africans themselves were the aliens!

For the blacks it was the start of their subjugation. Until then they had confronted the whites as equals, albeit mostly as enemies, each in his own territory and secure in his own culture. Now the whites took their land away from them and forced them into servitude. The relationship was no longer one of equals but of master and servant in a situation where the servant worked under compulsion and the constant threat of violence. With the eventual defeat of the Ndebele and the Zulus, black power in the north was broken, and now there were only the stubborn Xhosas on the eastern frontier who remained unconquered. Between 1778 and 1878, they waged nine frontier wars against the whites, and although they were frequently defeated, they were never subdued. In the end, they broke themselves by self-imposed destruction based on witchcraft and tribal mythology and the disastrous vision of a maiden. A young girl told her uncle, a powerful 'witch doctor' in the tribe, that she had a vision of an ancestral tribal chief ordering her to prophesy the destruction of the white invaders. For this to come about, the Xhosas had to slaughter all their cattle and burn all their grain, and on the given day the sun would rise in the east, reach its zenith at noon and return to set in east from whence it had come. At this sign, the graves of the dead would open and return all the great warriors of the past, the empty kraals and pits would be filled, once again with fat cattle and grain, and all around wagon loads of guns and ammunition would appear. Then a great wind would arise and drive the enemy into the sea. It all ended in a terrible disaster as thousands of Xhosas died of starvation and of deprivation. and many thousands more were left to struggle across the border into 'white man's land' and perpetual servitude.

In the meanwhile, the pursuit of the Boers went on. Like the flight of the Israelites out of Egypt in Old Testament days, the Great Trek was a concerted effort to escape from the British, a positive act to move outside the Empire's sphere of influence and authority. And, like the Pharaoh of that time, the British refused to let them go, but hounded them relentlessly, seeking to bring them back into imperial dominion.

And so it was that Sir George Napier, the new British governor at the Cape, rather absurdly maintained by proclamation, that the defected Boers would continue to remain British subjects regardless of the fact that they had quit the colony and openly denied its sovereignty over them. By so proclaiming, Napier was effectively imposing restrictive jurisdiction on a self-declared independent people who no longer wished to have anything more to do with the British and their Empire. In order to 'legitimise and legalise' Napier's absurdity, the British Prime Minister, Lord Melbourne pushed through parliament the 'Cape of Good Hope Punishment Act of 1836' unilaterally declaring British jurisdiction in all of Southern Africa south of the 25th parallel. This Act, therefore, summarily outlawed the Voortrekkers and subjugated all the black peoples of Southern Africa who occupied all the territories between Cape Agulhas, the southernmost tip of the African continent to a line, from the Atlantic to the Indian oceans, some fifty miles north of present-day Pretoria.

The British had neither the means nor the intention of controlling such a vast tract of land, over three-quarters of which did not even belong to them, and it was obvious that the claimed jurisdiction was nothing more than a legal fiction and a vindictive ploy to alienate the Boers even more. Nevertheless, it did provide a convenient vehicle for Napier, and his successors, to use to consider the possible annexation of the newly formed Boer Republics of Natal, the Free State, the Transvaal, plus Zululand and a host of other minor African nations. It was Napier himself, who summed up the whole situation by stating that '*annexation must be seen as the only practical solution to the British design'.* He summarised the British point of view quite neatly when he wrote – '*The British Nation will never consent either to allow the emigrants to perish from want or the sword, or to permit them to attack and slaughter the natives of the countries they have invaded'*

It is an interesting thought that although Napier and the British appeared to be so concerned over the actions of the emigrants, there was no evidence of any thought or concern over the well-being and sovereignty of the many indigenous realms and peoples that were existent within the area of Melbourne's Act of 1836.

In Natal, everything now seemed to be perfect for the Boers. They had succeeded in ridding themselves of the British, and in eliminating of the main threat to their future by conquering the Zulus at Blood River. Finally, they succeeded in the establishment of their own long dreamed-of republic in an idyllically beautiful and fertile land. However, it soon transpired that even now they could not free themselves from the ever spreading tentacles of the, apparently, insatiable British empirical quest. Ever since 1824, a small British trading settlement had existed under Zulu sufferance at Port Natal. The settlers had made periodic requests to the Cape for the annexation of their small settlement by the Crown, but to no avail. Eventually, after the discovery of coal in Natal and the growing awareness of the strategic importance of a port at Durban, the British authorities began to reconsider their attitude. Searching around for a feasible 'causus belli' they contrived reports of Boer ill-treatment of natives in Natal, as well as a spurious threat of invasion by the Zulus in the north. Both reasons were purely fabricated excuses, but were sufficient to justify the occupation of Durban in May 1842, when two companies of the 27th (Inniskilling) Regiment marched in and raised the British standard.

The Boers had no intention of submitting themselves once again, to British rule, and their leader, Pretorius, sought negotiations with Capt. T. C. Smith, the commander of the British garrison at Durban. It was a foregone conclusions that the negotiations would fail, and in consequence Pretorius led a commando against Smith, who outnumbered 3 to 1, fell back to his laager, and sent Dick King on an epic 458 mile ride south in search of reinforcements. When support eventually came, there were skirmishes against Pretorius and his commando, and eventually the Boers, dismayed by the re-appearance of the power of Britain in their back yard, upped sticks and moved away over the Drakensberg and back into the Transvaal. Britain finally annexed Natal as a Crown Colony in 1843.

The Boers were distressed – it appeared that no matter where and how far they went they could not escape the imperial reach. Those of them who had established the Orange Free State, north of the Orange River, also soon found the British on their doorstep. Again, the excuse of friction between the Boers and the Griquas was given to justify this action. The Griquas were a collection of mixed race settlers in the extreme western area of the Orange Free State, who regarded themselves, as British subjects and who were recognised as such.

In April 1845, fighting broke out between the Griquas and the Boers, and the 7th Dragoon Guards under Lt. Col. Richardson were despatched from the Cape to restore order. Encountering a 400-strong commando at Zwartkoppies, Richardson dislodged the Boers from their positions and all fighting ceased. A British Resident, Major Warden, with the assistance of a detachment of Cape Mounted Rifles, was appointed to maintain order. After that, apart from a successful skirmish against some disaffected Boers at the Vet River in 1846, the country remained quiet for a year or so.

On the 3rd of February, 1848, Sir Harry Smith, British Governor at the Cape, made the decision to annexe the Free State as the "Orange River Sovereignty". The Boers reacted rapidly, and Pretorius, with 200 burghers from the Transvaal, joined 800 Free State burghers, and after forcing Warden out of Bloemfontein, proceeded southwards to take up a position at Boomplaats to ambush the British advance that was sure to follow. Capt. Smith, recently arrived from Natal, took up the challenge and marched north across the Orange River on the 26th August 1848 with 600 men. Pretorius concealed his burghers along a ridge of low hills forming a horseshoe around the road up which Smith had to advance. Behind the ridge were a stream and a range of higher hills, on which Pretorius placed a party of burghers and a field gun to make Smith believe that this was his main position and to which his forward lines would retire if necessary. On the 29th of August, Smith approached. He sent the CMR (Cape Mounted Rifles) forward to scout the hillocks on the right of the road and came under fire from the Boer left. At the same time, the Boer centre opened fire and Smith withdrew the CMR to his left and sent forward the 45th and the Rifle Brigade to outflank the Boer left. It was now that the Boer right rode out from cover to attack Smith's wagons but they were driven back by gun-fire from the artillery and rifle-fire from the CMR. Meanwhile, the infantry on the right was advancing so rapidly that the Boers opposing them were unable to regain their horses and were forced to run back towards their centre under fire from the artillery, which had come into action quickly on the captured position. The Boers now fell back to make a stand before the stream but Smith's infantry continued to press forward covered by the guns, and only one hour after the first shots had been fired, the Boers were in full retreat. They did make some attempt at a rear-guard action but they were so hard-pressed that they finally dispersed.

Despite their mobility, marksmanship and sound choice of terrain, they had been unable to resist Smith's co-ordination of guns and infantry and the speed of his attack. Consequently, the apparent ease with which small British Regular forces had up untill now overcome superior numbers of armed Boers on three separate occasions, bequeathed a legacy among the British, of contempt for the fighting quality of the Boers.

After the collapse of Boer opposition in Natal in 1843, and especially at Boomplaats in the Free State in 1848, Britain finally found herself securely established in the driving seat in Southern Africa. In 1848, Sir Harry Smith, the British Governor at the Cape, formally annexed the territory north of the Orange River, as the Orange River Sovereignty .and there, for the time being, matters appeared to rest. Paradoxically, however, it was at this stage that an anti-colonial mood gripped the British government. There had been growing concern over the rapid and substantial drainage on resources caused by the costs of operations in South Africa against the Boers in the Transvaal and the Free State, as well as against the Xhosas, who were at that time constantly threatening the eastern frontiers of the Cape Colony. As a result, Sir Harry Smith was recalled to London in 1852, and in the same year, the independence of the Transvaal was recognised and guaranteed by the British Government at the Sand River Convention. Two years later, at the Bloemfontein Convention in 1854, Britain also granted independence to the Orange River Sovereignty and named it the Orange Free State.

The Boers, at last, had crossed their Jordan and could now settle down in peace in their very own Canaan where all their problems would finally come to rest...

CONQUEST and ACQUISITION

After the independence settlements of 1852 and 1854, the Anglo-Boer strife in Southern Africa appeared to have finally ended. But this proved to be a false dawn, and it was not long before perfidious Albany once again reared her head. In the early years of the 1870's she resumed, once again, an increasingly aggressive thrust into the whole of the African sub-continent. In the course of the following two decades Basutoland, Griqualand West, Matabeleland, Mashonaland, the two South African Republics, the Transkei and Bechuanaland were all conquered, and the Zulu and BaPedi kingdoms utterly defeated and their lands brought under imperial control.

What brought about this sudden and imperative urge for conquest and acquisition?

Prior to 1870 there were two kinds of explanation – the overt one for the universal record, for the public, the voters and all others, and the covert one for the official secrets files and of inner-ring of government cabinet ministers and policy jugglers. The liberal justification was the philanthropic drive to unify the "barbaric" and "uncultivated" areas under the benevolence of British control, fuelled by the belief that integration was a rational step towards civilization and progress, and motivated by humanitarian concern for the protection of the alleged maltreatment of the Africans in the Boer republics.

Modern historians now stress another reason, namely that the new thrust inland was part of a wider scramble for empire, particularly in Africa, amongst European powers. Anxious to prevent their continental rivals from gaining access to the trade of the interior, the British surged forward for direct control of as much territory as they could wrench from the weaker and less prosperous indigenous inhabitants in vast areas of the world..

In this respect, South Africa was particularly important because of the British need to protect the naval base at Cape Town in order to secure the lucrative sea routes to India and the east. Of even greater significance was the discovery in 1867 of diamonds on the Vaal-Harts River junction, followed by the diamond rush to the Kimberley diamond fields, and the massive growth of the mining industry that ensued. It was an undeniable fact that the discovery of valuable mineral deposits, and the need to secure the labour supplies needed to mine them, made the South African interior a highly desirable region for the British to control directly. It was also apparent that none of the existing African nations, including the Cape had neither the will nor the capability to deal with the demands of the mining industry, particularly in its need for a suitable transport infrastructure, and for adequate labour. Furthermore, the Colonial Office had received complaints that the Transvaal government was inhibiting the free flow of labour to the diamond fields as well as to the farms and plantations of the Cape and Natal, through the introduction of pass laws enacted in 1874 and 1879. Direct control over the Transvaal would therefore, enable a variety of entrepreneurs, traders and investors to secure and regulate a controlled and critically vital supply of cheap and abundant African labour.

Between 1874 and 1879, Lord Carnarvon, the British Colonial Secretary, was persuaded by Theophilus Shepstone, the Natal Secretary for Native Affairs, to push for a union of the South African colonies and the two republics under British sovereignty. The reason for Shepstone's anxiety to press for annexation of the Boer Republics was clear - the discovery of diamonds and gold deposits in various parts of the Transvaal had resulted in the diversion of vital migrant labour supplies from the thriving sugar plantations of Natal, to the more lucrative mining areas of the Transvaal. The dilemma was even more serious for British commercial interests at home and in the Cape Colony. Migrant labour streams traditionally heading for the diamond fields at Kimberley, travelled from Zululand, Swaziland, Mozambique and Sekhukhuneland, through the Transvaal where they were regularly waylaid, and diverted to meet the labour requirements of the Republic instead.

Carnarvon's avowed justifications for British participation in affairs in South Africa were purported to be about the security of naval bases, and the philanthropic intent to protect the indigenous populations against the ravages of the Boers. However, there is no evidence to suggest that he did not sincerely believe that it was essential for British interests in Southern Africa to secure and ensure an adequate supply of African labour for the mines and the plantations. Any opposition to this aim from the Boers, or even the Africans themselves, needed to be eliminated, preferably through negotiation, but if necessary, by force. Steadfast in his commitment, Carnarvon stated in an address to parliament that his intentions behind confederation were *"to replace the existing categories of weak, poor and un-progressive states by a single, strong and efficient one. It would possess the credit and security necessary to develop the country and to bring to an end the political and economic dependence of the Africans and incorporate them as the working class of the economically and geographically expanding new dominion, which would be a source of strength for the Empire"*

It is against this background that the events of the 1870s and the 1880s developed. Soon after the discovery of the diamond fields the British, true to their intent, moved rapidly to pre-empt attempts by the Boer republics to divide the region between them, although, geographically speaking, they both had legitimate territorial claims to the area, especially the Orange Free State. Britain immediately backed both of the inhabitant tribes, the Thlaping and the Griquas, and their respective claims to the area, simply by annexing them, naming the area "Griqualand West" and then squeezing out the more militant and less cooperative   Thlaping inhabitants. In 1880, Griqualand West was handed over to the Cape Colony, while British expansion in the region continued with the annexation of Bechuanaland in 1884/5, ostensibly to resist Transvaal occupation of part of the area, but in reality, to secure vital sources of timber and labour supplies for Kimberley.

In the eastern regions of the Transvaal, the situation was equally confused. The most assertive inhabitants of that area were the BaPedi, a Bantu tribe that had moved in from the north under the supremacy of a very wily and astute paramount chief named Sekhukune. The BaPedi were an industrious and prosperous people, securely ensconced in the mountainous regions of the Eastern Transvaal, subsisting principally in cattle farming. Further east were the Swazis who, although not as powerful as the BaPedi, were nevertheless in constant conflict with them especially in respect of grazing lands. It was inevitable that the neighbouring Transvaal Boers would become involved with both the BaPedi as well as the Swazis. With the opening up of the diamond fields in the west and the start of small scale gold mining in the Lydenburg area of the Eastern Transvaal, there came the urgent need for Native labour, and the Boers lost no time at all in creating a lucrative traffic of workers from both Sekhukuneland and Swaziland.

Fanning traditional tribal enmities between the BaPedi and the Swazis, the Boers enticed the latter to create diversions on the Pedi border areas, while they summarily staked claims to large areas of land under aegis of Sekhukune. When the BaPedi resisted Boer attempts to claim rents and taxes from the inhabitants of these illegally acquired areas, and in return charged the Boer labour recruitment officers a fee for all workers indentured in the areas under dispute, the Boers joined with the Swazis in joint military action against Sekhukune. All their efforts were thwarted by the BaPedi who repelled them in a series of highly successful skirmishes, inflicting resounding defeats on them. As a result the Swazis, having now lost complete confidence in the Boer commandos, appealed to Britain for protection, which was eventually accorded. The Transvaal administration fell into disarray as the wasteful and unnecessary campaign against the BaPedi left their Treasury in total ruin, and the creditability of the Transvaal president, Schalk Burger in tatters.

It was at this stage that Britain became convinced of the need to include both the BaPedi and the Swazis into its confederation plans, and Shepstone was encouraged to set about immediately in laying impossible and crushing indemnity demands on the BaPedi, who being unable to meet them, were, in 1879, crushed in a major British attack. The BaPedi had stood in the way of colonial land and labour policies, and now had to pay the costs!

The unrest in the northeast regions of South Africa regrettably did not end with the defeat of the BaPedi and Swaziland. There were stirrings in Zululand, which were causing alarm for Shepstone, for the Cape administration and for the Colonial Secretary in London. The Natal settlers had long resented their inability to extract labour from Zululand, forcing their sugar planters to employ costly indentured workers imported from India. There was also the fear of the growing presence of refugees fleeing the Zulu authority and seeking unauthorised shelter in Natal. These wandering and workless refugees not only gave the white settlers concern for their security and safety but constituted a real threat of reprisal from Zululand itself.

Previously, the Natal colony had entered into an uneasy alliance with Cetshewayo, the Zulu king, and supported him in his claims against the Boers for some disputed territories. Following the defeat of the Boers in Sekhukuneland and the settlement of the BaPedi and Swaziland issues, Shepstone found him confident enough to lay claim over some disputed territory between the Transvaal and Zululand. The land in question was vital for the sugar economy in Natal because it constituted an important corridor for migrant labour from the north.

Cetshewayo opposed Shepstone's claims and in reply demanded the return of all the Zulus who had sought refuge in Natal. Thwarted by Cetshewayo's refusal and fearing for Zulu reprisals against the refugees in Natal, Shepstone appealed to Frere, the British High Commissioner in South Africa, and as a result, a British Resident Official was sent to Zululand. This official was empowered with the authority to demand the return of cattle stolen from Natal, and to order Cetshewayo to disarm and disband the powerful Zulu army. Cetshewayo resented this unwarranted intrusion in the affairs of his independent and paramount authority, and rejected Frere's demands outright. Seeing Zululand as a serious threat to the security of Natal and a major barrier to confederation of the southern African states, Frere sent in a strong British force under Lord Chelmsford, to bring Cetshewayo to heel. After a disastrous defeat at Isandhlandwana, followed by massive casualties at Rorkes Drift, Chelmsford went on to rout the Zulus at Ulundi, imposing direct control upon them and finally incorporating Zululand into Natal in 1897.

Since the 1840's, the British had slowly penetrated the eastern seaboard of South Africa, north of Port Elizabeth, and claimed sovereignty over vast areas bordering the Cape Colony, including the Transkei and Pondoland. Then they drove the Boers out of Natal, proceeded to defeat the Tswana, the BaPedi and the Zulus, and finally establish 'protectorates' over Swaziland and Basutoland. Yet, by the end of 1880, whilst effectively exerting control over a vast number of African states, they were still unable to achieve their ultimate goal of a universal Southern African Confederation. The major resistance to their ambitions were the Boers in the Transvaal, and it was imperative for this block to be removed at any cost, even if it meant going to war to do so.

The last three decades of the nineteenth century were manifested by an aggressive policy of imperial intervention, motivated by the need to secure labour for the mines and plantations and to reap maximum benefits from the rapidly evolving economic and financial potential of the African sub-continent. In the process, the individual freedom and independence of most of the indigenous peoples were lost, and in the end, only the two Boer republics remained. It would take two major wars and massive devastation for a final settlement in South Africa eventually to be achieved.

The Annexation of the Transvaal
In order to exploit the situation to the maximum, it was obvious that something drastic and urgent was needed to straighten out the tangle of British colonies, Boer republics, and the many African kingdoms scattered throughout southern Africa. Moreover, it needed to be done clinically, cleanly and, of course, totally subject to British control. As a result, Lord Carnavon began plotting and planning his policy of confederation, aimed at bringing together all the separate lands, republics and kingdoms under British control. It was almost pre-destined that exactly at this very precise moment, events dramatically veered in a direction that would play precisely into the hands of the authorities in London, Cape Town and Durban, who were actively engineering the road to confederation.

The unsuccessful and wasteful campaign that the Transvaal had undertaken against Sekhukune and his BaPedi kingdom had created utter financial and political disaster for the Transvaal government. Schalk Burger, the president, was obliged to impose a crippling war tax of £5 per head on every burgher in the Transvaal, which the majority, of course, refused to pay! The national debt reached the staggering amount of £215,000 whilst the Treasury, at the same time, could only count the sum of 12/6d in liquid assets! The South African Republic, surrounded by potential hostile black neighbours and dangerously exposed and bankrupt to boot, desperately needed help, and this played neatly into British hands who, taking advantage of the Transvaal's dilemma, proposed assistance by appointing Sir Theophilus Shepstone as Special Commissioner to the South African Republic with a mandate to annex the country as soon as possible.

Shepstone had the half-hearted support of President Burger and most of his ministers, as well as that of the mercantile bankers and the large English population around Pretoria. He raised the Union Flag over the capital on the 27th April 1877 with hardly any opposition from the local inhabitants. President Burgher was granted a State pension and was ordered to leave the Transvaal immediately. Encouraged by this apparent acquiescence, Shepstone then made a number of promises for the future of the Transvaal, promises which neither he, Britain nor Lanyon, the Resident British Commissioner, had any intention of keeping. Lanyon, in particular, was disdainful and almost entirely dismissive of the aspirations of the Boers.

When Shepstone's promises failed to materialise, the Boers, particularly in the country areas, became increasingly unhappy and angry over the British rule. Also, it was becoming quite clear by now that the annexation of the Transvaal was by no means as popular among the burghers as Shepstone and Carnavon first believed. Resentment against British occupation and administration began to crystallize around Paul Kruger, who, before annexation, became Vice-President in opposition to President Burger's liberal policies. Kruger led two protest delegations to Britain, and on the second visit, he armed himself with a petition opposing annexation, signed by over 6,000 of the 8,000 suffrage-eligible burghers in the Transvaal. Although the British government undertook to consider the possibility of local autonomy for the Transvaal for sometime in the future, they made it clear that the restoration of complete independence was not on the agenda and would not be considered. Kruger returned to South Africa, rebuffed, humiliated and revengeful, and Boer indignation was increased by the British administration's overt sympathy towards the interests of the Africans, as well as its insensitivity towards Boer mores and customs. Resentment was further fuelled by the appointment of Col. Owen Lanyon in Shepstone's place as Administrator of the Transvaal. Lanyon was an overbearing, arrogant, and very deliberate sort of person, whose dark complexion did nothing to endear him to highly prejudiced Boer minds about his racial origin.

By now, the situation had become very tenuous; the British were, on the one hand, totally unconcerned about the aspirations of the Boers, whilst on the other hand the Boers were in no mood for compromise. On the contrary, far from being grateful to the British for crushing the power of the Zulus and BaPedi, the Transvaal maintained that the removal of these threats now meant that the British military occupation of their country was no longer justifiable. Mass protest meetings against British occupation and British denial of legitimate Boer rights were held, and to avert rebellion Sir Bartle Frere, the High Commissioner for South Africa, urged the home government to grant some sort of self-government to the Transvaal. However, Frere, who was out of favour for precipitating the Zulu war, was recalled and his responsibilities for the Transvaal were handed over to Sir Garnet Wolseley, who lost no time in reminding the Boers that *"the Vaal River would flow backwards through the Drakensberg sooner than the British would be withdrawn from the Transvaal"*

By the end of 1879, the Boer nationalists were becoming more and more militant and Wolseley started deploying his 3,600 troops all over the Transvaal, with a mobile column centred at Pretoria – a force that he considered to be, "amply sufficient to destroy any armed opposition the Boers could muster." The Boers, led by Kruger and Piet Joubert, still believed that their aims could be achieved peacefully, especially since in March 1880, Gladstone and the Liberals, who when in opposition had repeatedly denounced annexation, had replaced the Conservative government which had been in power in Britain since 1874. Now, confident that independence would soon be granted, the hotheads and agitators in the Transvaal quietened down. Wolseley however, believing that it was his show of military force that had served to cow the Boers into submission, asked for, and was granted permission to hand over his duties in the Transvaal to Maj. Gen. Sir George Pomeroy-Colley. Colley, encouraged by the apparent calm, and assured by the obtuse Lanyon that the Boers could not and would not fight and pressed by the new government in Westminster to make economies in South Africa, reduced the number of outlying garrisons as well as the strength of his total force in the Transvaal.

Meanwhile, in London, Gladstone's cabinet was divided over the Transvaal – there were those that believed that only the continued British rule would protect and bolster British interests. Others believed that the Boer demands be met and yet a third group strongly urged the maintenance of British prestige in southern Africa and throughout the world. Gladstone himself was very pre-occupied with the more serious and closer-to-home Irish problem, and for him retention of office and the unity of his cabinet were far more important than the grumblings of a handful of disaffected farmers thousands of miles away on the other side of the world. However, ultimately, Gladstone reassured by over complacent reports from officials in South Africa decided to inform Kruger that, *"the Queen cannot be advised to relinquish her sovereignty over the Transvaal".* Kruger and Joubert, for their part, now realised the stark reality that there was no other choice left open for them but to fight for the independence of their country....

THE FIRST BOER WAR – 1880/1881

When it came, the outbreak of hostilities was triggered by a seemingly insignificant affair in Potchefstroom. In the process of the execution of Lanyon's tax arrears recovery policy, a tax collector and his armed guard set upon a farmer, Piet Bezuidenhout, who was in arrears of an amount of £27.5.0d and an ox-wagon. The confrontation was a fairly vigorous and noisy one and soon a hundred or so incensed and well-armed neighbours and sympathisers gathered around the office of the local Landrost calling for 'justice' and shouting threats against the 'damned English invaders'. In response to this display the Administrator of the Transvaal in Pretoria, Colonel Owen Lanyon, issued urgent orders for a military force to occupy Potchefstroom to support the civil authorities there. The Boers were incensed over this move, and soon some 4,000 congregated at nearby Paardekraal and voted overwhelmingly to oust the English, and to restore the Republic, by force if necessary. It was also agreed to set up a governing triumvirate consisting of Paul Kruger, Piet Joubert and Marthinus Pretorius, and to create an official republican government administration at Heidelberg, a town straddling the Durban/Pretoria railway. Meanwhile, back in Potchefstroom, the British troops sent by Lanyon to maintain law and order clashed with some Boer demonstrators – a shot rang out – it was returned and the war had begun…..!

Following the meeting at Paardekraal the Boers despatched a commando to Potchefstroom to protect a printing press facility there. A commando was also sent to Heidelberg to assist in the establishment of the new capital, and other commandos were sent to Pretoria to interfere with British troop movements. Matters now began to heat up seriously, and in Pretoria the commander of the British troops in the Transvaal issued orders to recall three outlying garrisons to reinforce the town's defences. The units that were ordered in were a company from the 94th Regiment and a small mounted detachment at Marabastad, the mounted units of the 94th at Wakkerstroom, and the H.Q. and two companies of the 94th based in Lydenburg in the eastern Transvaal. Lanyon also requested General Colley to send up the 58th Regiment from northern Natal to the Transvaal to help prevent any further civil disturbances. Colley acquiesced by assembling the Natal contingent of the 58th at Newcastle, with the intention of marching north through Laing's Nek and into the Transvaal, in order to join up with the remainder of the 58th garrisoned in Standerton.

By the end of December 1880, the Boers had besieging forces surrounding all the remaining British garrisons in the Transvaal and with these units effectively "locked up" Joubert rode south to the Transvaal/Natal border. On the 1st January 1881, he silently crossed over and occupied the heights covering the pass at Laing's Nek, the only practical route into the Transvaal from Newcastle and the south. Thus, the stage was set for the imminent encounter

Barely seventeen months after the conclusion of the Zulu war in 1879, only four battalions of regular infantry remained, distributed through Natal and the Transvaal, and none had any cavalry support. The six 9-pdr.RML guns of "N" Battery, 5th Brigade RA., were also available, but these too, were widely dispersed, with four of the guns situated in the Transvaal and the remaining two in Natal. To supplement this meagre force and to cover his deficiency in cavalry, Colley created a mounted squadron from scratch, the core of which consisted of 35 dismounted members of the 1st King's Dragoon Guard who were awaiting transport back England. They were joined by 25 members of No.7 Company of the Army Service Corps and by 60 men drawn from the 58th and 3/60th regiments. They were all given mounts and hastily despatched to the front, where they were joined by 70 men of the quasi military Natal Mounted Police (NMP) who had been placed under Colley's command.

Efforts were also made to supplement the artillery, and two 9- pdr.guns were released from stores in Natal, and No. 10/7 Battery was taken out of garrison duties in Cape Town and rushed off to Durban to report to Colley. A further two 7-pdr guns were discovered in the stores at Pietermaritzburg, and these were sent to Colley, who in the absence of gunners to man them, ordered volunteers from the 3/60th Rifle Regiment to help. It is sad to think how little Britain had learnt from the Zulu campaign, and how much they under-estimated the resolve of their opponents. The line infantry regiments were still equipped with glaringly obvious scarlet tunics and dark blue trousers with a red welt down the inside seam (the 3/60th, as riflemen, wore dark green uniforms with black webbing). Headgear was still the large white foreign-service helmet, but since the Zulu war these had been dyed khaki or covered with khaki material. The standard infantry weapon was the single shot, breech-loading, mark II, Martini-Henry – the rifle that had proved so effective against the Zulus.

In addition, Colley continued to maintain an arrogant disinterest in the use, or even the value of military intelligence and in his over-confidence felt secure in his belief that, even with his obviously limited force in Natal, he would be able to control, without any difficulty whatsoever, any aggressive moves that the Boers might make. He looked down on the Boers as an "*undisciplined rabble, quite unable to stand up and face a regular force*" and was convinced that there was little if any cause for anxiety. When the news of the annihilation of the detachment of the 94th regiment reached Colley from Bronkhorstspruit on Christmas Day 1880, he was devastated, and rudely shocked into the awareness of the Boer's determination to stand up and fight for their independence and for their freedom.

On the Boer side the supreme commander of the Transvaal forces was Commandant-General Petrus Jacobus Joubert, a descendant of the French Huguenots who had arrived at the Cape in the late 17th century. Petrus (Piet) Joubert was a self-educated man with a strong interest in law. In 1873 he became Chairman of the Transvaal Volksraad, and, later Vice-President of the South African Republic. He had accompanied President Kruger on his fruitless missions to seek the restoration of self-government for the Transvaal after Annexation. Joubert could speak English well and was a shrewd and tough negotiator, but in spite of these qualities, or perhaps because of them, he was not totally trusted by many of his own people, and earned the nickname of "Slim Piet" (crafty Piet). Joubert's second-in-command was the remarkable Commandant Nicholas ('Nicho') Smit, who had an unrivalled natural talent for all matters military, and an uncanny second sense for effective use of cover. He was undoubtedly one of the ablest leaders of the mounted infantry of his time. At the time of the 1880/81 war the most popular Boer weapon was the Westley-Richards falling-block, single-action breech-loading rifle – a weapon, which in the hands of an expert, could become a lethal killing machine.

Bronkhorstspruit

On the 23rd November 1880, orders had been issued from Pretoria to the outlying garrisons at Wakkerstroom, Marabastad and Lydenburg to withdraw to the capital at once in order to consolidate defences there against possible Boer attack. These instructions were received at Lydenburg, some 188 miles to the north-east of Pretoria, five days later on the 28^{th,} but in spite of the urgent tone of the orders, the local commander, Lt. Col. Philip Anstruther, delayed his departure, and only set off for Pretoria seven days later on the 5th December. The cause for this delay was Anstruther's decision to acquire additional wagons to move his men and accoutrement - regulations allowed the column 10 or 11 wagons, but Anstruther sought 29 in total plus 1 mule cart, an ox drawn ambulance, a water cart and an extra ox wagon to carry the regimental canteen – a total of 34 vehicles. The delay in procuring these extra wagons was to have fatal consequences for Anstruther and his column.

When he eventually did set off, Anstruther displayed no sense of urgency, and his column trundled along regardless of anxious signals from Pretoria. To make matters worse, heavy rains had started to fall shortly after his departure from Lydenburg, and it did not take long for the single dirt road to turn into a veritable quagmire. By the 10th December, the column arrived at Middelburg, half way to Pretoria 97 miles ahead. By this time the column from Marabastad, 155 miles from Pretoria, had arrived and was already safely integrated into the overall Pretoria defence plan. After Middelburg the pace slowed down even further, barely managing to cover 60 miles over the following ten days.

On the 20th December Anstruther's column of 9 officer and 259 other ranks, together with some women and children and a few native servants, reached the outskirts of Bronkhorstspruit, a small outpost some 30 miles to the east of Pretoria. In spite of signals from Pretoria warning that the outbreak of hostilities could begin at any moment and that important enemy troop movements in his direction had been spotted, the only scouts that Anstruther posted were four mounted infantry, two in the front and the other two at the rear of the column.

At about 12.30 p.m. the column was about two miles from Bronkhorstspruit, where Anstruther intended to make camp for the night. It trundled on unsuspectingly, the band playing popular airs of the day and the men munching peaches they had gathered from an orchard a mile or so back. At this point the surrounding countryside was mainly flat with a low grassy ridge about 500 yards on the left. Extending from the base of this ridge to within 200 yards from the road was a screen of thorn trees. Behind the ridge was a Boer commando led by Commandant Frans Joubert with orders to stop

Anstruther from reaching Pretoria. Suddenly as if from nowhere, a group of about 150 mounted Boers appeared, lining the crest of the low ridge. At the same time, a lone rider emerged from the thorn trees and rode up to the head of the column under a white flag. A letter was handed to Anstruther informing him that the Transvaal had been declared a Republic, and that until a reply had been received from Lanyon, it was not known whether a state of war existed or not. In the circumstances Anstruther was required to hold his position, and informed that if he chose to continue his march to Pretoria, it would be construed as a declaration of war. The messenger added that only two minutes were permitted for Anstruther to respond to the ultimatum. Anstruther replied that his orders were to make for Pretoria, and that was what he intended to do. He told the messenger to inform the Boer commander accordingly, and then ordered F-Company to form into skirmish order. While they were in the act of complying a murderous volley crashed out from the Boer riflemen concealed in the trees. Within minutes all but one of the nine officers were either dead or wounded, and within fifteen minutes of commencement of fire, 156 men and a woman lay dead or dying – a devastating 58% of the entire column compliment. Anstruther himself was severely wounded in the initial onslaught, and realising that all was lost, gave the order to surrender. He died from his wounds just under a week later, on the 26th December.

The news of the Bronkhorstspruit disaster shocked and appalled the British, and immediately orders were issued to rush reinforcements to South Africa. Two ships had just arrived in Durban carrying a large draft of 148 men for the 58th, 91[st,] and 94th regiments, plus 209 for the 3/60th and 2/21[st.] Later, on the 5th of January, a Naval Brigade was set up in Durban consisting of five officers and 124 petty officers and ratings, with two Gatling machine guns and three 24-pdr.rocket tubes. All these reinforcements were rushed to Newcastle with orders to join Colley at Fort Amiel, just to the north of Newcastle, where urgent preparations were underway to march north towards the Transvaal.

The Road to Majuba

Colley was stunned by this sudden turn of events, and very unsure of what to do next. He regarded the disaster at Bronkhorstspruit as an 'Isandhlwana on a smaller scale' and urged that steps had to be taken quickly to repair the damage done to British prestige. Although he knew that large numbers of reinforcements were on their way, he realised that time was against him; no one knew just how long the isolated Transvaal garrisons could hold out. He decided upon a quick, bold movement into the Transvaal with the force available to him on the spot, prior to the arrival of the reinforcements. This, he hoped would ease the situation for the besieged garrisons as numbers of Boers would have to be called forward to oppose his advance, and, moreover, in spite of the defeat at Bronkhorstspruit he was still optimistic and absolutely convinced of his ability to inflict defeat on the Boers.

Whatever the reason, Colley felt the urgent need to engage the Boers, who in contrast were quite content to sit it out at Coldstream on the Transvaal/Natal border awaiting further developments. They did not have long to wait – on the eve of his departure from Newcastle, Colley sent the Boers an ultimatum ordering them to disperse. Joubert forwarded it to Heidelberg, and did not receive a reply until three days later, during which time Colley was already forging ahead through some horrendous weather, which was making his progress both slow and exhausting. On the second day of marching Colley reached a long, low rocky hill called Schuinshoogte, and pitched camp at the nearby Ingogo River from whence he could command a splendid view of the Drakensbeg and beyond to the dramatic twin buttresses of Nkwelo and Majuba. In the face of relentless rain, Colley continued to push ahead over hostile and difficult terrain, until, finally on the 27th January he halted and set up camp at Mount Prospect, which at 1464 ft altitude offered clear views of the Drakensberg, of Nkwelo and Majuba and of Laing's Nek, the gateway to the Transvaal.

The Boers, encamped at Coldstream, were only a short distance from Laing's Nek. They enjoyed a perfect position, either for launching an attack on Natal or for taking up an impenetrable defence rampart. Here the border of Natal narrows down to a point flanked to the west by the Orange Free State, and to the north and east, by the Transvaal. The road leading from Natal into the Transvaal is over-shadowed in the west by the imposing peak of Majuba from which extends a long spur running west to east and through which the road passes. The end of the ridge curves southwards, and any movement further east is curtailed by the steep valley of the Mzinyathi (Buffalo) River.

As soon as Joubert heard of Colley's forward movement from Newcastle, he advanced some of his commandos down to Laing's Nek to form two laagers on either side of the road on the reverse (Transvaal) side of the slope. On the same day that Colley made camp at Mount Prospect, about a thousand Boers were entrenched at the Nek, and by the 28th trenches were dug and stones piled up to build sangars and walls along the whole length of the Boer positions. Joubert's tactical positioning was superb, with an obvious killing ground over which any attacking force coming through the Nek from the south would be totally exposed to devastating rifle fire from at least two sides.

Laing's Nek
On the 28th January, the British forces at Laing's Nek numbered 1,216 men (58 officers and 1,159 other ranks). There were four 9-pdr.and two 7-pdr.guns plus three 24-pdr rocket tubes. The Boer strength, at this time was estimated to be about 2,000 men within the area, distributed along the whole length of the defence line. At 9.25 a.m. the artillery and rockets opened fire on the Boer positions on the Nek and on the reverse slope of the hill. The Boers took cover in their trenches and behind their breastworks. The British believed that the Boers were terrified of the artillery, but in reality there was no great panic in the Boer lines. A few were observed galloping about a bit, but the majority sought cover and sat out the bombardment While this was going on, Colley ordered forward his infantry on the right to begin the turning movement that would roll up the Boer position. At about 9.40 a m Major William Hingeston led the 58th Regiment forward. Rather unusually, Colley then directed five of his staff, including Col. Deane who nominally commanded the Natal Field Force, to accompany the 58th. Deane, being senior ranking officer, immediately took command of the attack. From their position it was about 1,000 yards to the beginning of the spur that led upa steep hill to the Boer positions.

The 58th Regiment was supported on its right by the Mounted Squadron commanded by Major William Brownlow of the 1st King's Dragoon Guards (KDG). The Mounted Squadron was a scratch force, formed specifically for the campaign, and was quite inexperienced, having had only a very limited time for training together as a unit. At 10.10 a.m., as the 58th began its advance up the spur in a tightly packed column of companies, four abreast, it came under fire from a few Boer skirmishers. The range was about 900 yards and the firing was largely ineffective. Brownlow's orders were to protect the flank of the 58th if they came under attack, and, rather than scouting for a more suitable approach to the Boer positions, he immediately wheeled his men to the right and prepared to attack up the hill. Unfortunately, his impetuosity caused him to lead his men right up the very steepest part of the hill, and most of the horses were blown before they had clambered half way to the top.

Brownlow was the first to reach the crest of the ridge, followed by the remainder of the first troop, with the second troop still struggling up from behind. A volley crashed out from the Boer defenders and Brownlow's horse fell to the ground. Major Lunny, who was just behind Brownlow, fired his revolver in all directions, killing one Boer and wounding another before he was shot dead. The scene on the ridge was one of total confusion, with wounded horses, terrified and exhausted, wheeling about uncontrollably, while unseated riders tried desperately to make good their escape. An attempt was made to rally the shattered first troop, but it failed since half the horses were either dead or dying. Meanwhile, the second troop, disconcerted by the fleeing horses and the firing ahead of them, turned before reaching the crest, and retreated down the hill. With that, the assault petered out, and it was soon all over for the Mounted Squadron. After the battle, the British named the hill 'Brownlow's Kop'.

The impact of Brownlow's failure to clear the Boer position now began to take effect. Those Boers, freed by the retreat of the mounted men, were able to move to a new position and open fire on the 58th Regiment below. Meanwhile the infantry were breathlessly clambering and struggling up the steep and difficult slopes of the spur, and soon, in order to counter the new threat to their flank, a part of the 58th was wheeled to the right to engage the Boer riflemen, while Colonel Deane urged the remainder of the column on up the slope. At 10.40 he reached the ridge where the spur joined the top of the hill. Too late he realised his error in not extending the companies to right and left, because as the panting and exhausted compressed column reached the crest, it found itself confronted with a wide slope which led up to an entrenched Boer position about 160 yards away. Deane immediately shouted out for the men to extend to the right and the left and fix bayonets. The British exchanged shots with the Boers for about five minutes, but in their congested position they were getting the worst of the action, and Deane gave the order for the 58th to charge the Boer entrenchment. He led the charge forward but was soon cut down, and his orderly officer, Lt. Inman of the 3/60th was also shot down just behind him. Major Hingeston, now commanding officer again, urged his men forward into the withering fire, but fell mortally wounded at about the same time that Major Poole and Lt. Elves, both of Colley's staff, were shot dead. Now, of the five members of Colley's staff that had joined the attack on Laing's Nek, four were dead, the only one to survive being Major Essex, who amazingly, had been one of the five imperial officers to survive the crushing defeat at Isandhlwana in the Zulu War two years before.

Incredibly, the men of the 58th had reached as close as thirty or forty yards from the Boer positions in places, but they could advance no further. Keeping close to the ground, they continued their fire, but Boer reinforcements were being fed into the front line all the time, and it became increasingly clear that the British attack was not going to succeed. Just after 11 a.m. Major Essex gave the order for the retreat, and slowly the 58th fell back to the ridge, the three right-hand companies first, followed by the two left-hand companies retired down the hill in good order. The Boers now moved from their cover for the first time and pursued the retreating 58th, and in addition, a party moved against the 3/60th and the Natal Brigade on the British left flank, but they were held off. The retreat down the spur was a very orderly affair, considering what the regiment had just been through. One company had formed, turned and faced the Boers and put up a very effective rearguard action. At the commencement of the retreat two companies of the 3/60th were ordered across to cover the movement in an attempt to pin down the Boer pursuers.

On reaching the foot of the spur safely, the regiment re-formed and marched back to its start position, and the main attack having failed, the whole force then retired to Mount Prospect camp in two sections. Colley had lost 7 officers and 77 men killed, and 3 officers and 110 men wounded. The 58th lost the majority of these casualties, 74 killed and 101 wounded; 35% of their total strength. The Boer losses were 14 killed and 27 wounded.

With Deane dead, Colley assumed official command of the Natal Field Force and moved his camp to a better position some 500 yards forward. The NMP were sent back to Newcastle to bolster the garrison there and to ensure that communication lines with Mt. Prospect remained open. All that was now left to do was to await the arrival of those reinforcements that were already en route for Newcastle.

When word of Bronkhorstspruit reached London, no efforts were spared in getting reinforcements to Natal as fast as possible, and, on the 6th January, General Sir Evelyn Wood was appointed as Colley's second-in-command. Wood was actually senior in army rank to Colley, but, for expediency, agreed to accept the position. On the 25th, the first of the reinforcements arrived from India – the 2/60th Rifles, the 15th Hussars, and an artillery battery. Five days later they were joined by the 83rd and the 92nd Regiments and a second Naval Brigade of 58 men from HMS *Dido* and HMS *Boadecia*, with two 9-pdr.guns.

Schuinshoogte (Ingogo)
Following their success at Laing's Nek, some Boer commandos gained confidence and the more able commandants, such as Nicho Smit, starting taking advantage of the British forces which were now virtually locked up at Mount Prospect and Newcastle. They scoured the countryside in sorties of fifty or more mounted men in order to harass British patrols, and as far as possible, to disable the communication lines between Mount Prospect and Newcastle. The road between these two posts was just less than

twenty miles long, passing up and down through tortuous hills and difficult river crossings. For Colley it was a vital artery because along this single muddy track passed all his correspondence, his food, medical supplies and ammunition. It was not surprising then that he was becoming more and more frustrated with the roving bands of Boers interfering with this more than vital but very vulnerable lifeline.

On the 7th February one of the camp's regular postal deliveries left for Newcastle. On its way it was intercepted by a party of 50 Boers who opened fire. The post detail managed to scramble back to Mount Prospect, except for one man who made his way to Newcastle. The following day Colley received a telegram from Newcastle advising that in view of the situation it would be unwise for them to send forward the wagon convoy that Colley had ordered to set off that very day. Colley was angry and decided there and then to remove for once and for all the threat to his communication lines, and he prepared to make a demonstration of force along the Newcastle road to meet up with the expected convoy and bring it back safely to Mount Prospect. Orders were issued to prepare to march.

The force consisted of five companies of the 3/60th, part of the Mounted Squadron, and a few artillery pieces. The artillery alone, Colley believed, would put the Boers off from interfering with his mission, and he was quite confident that his force would discourage any action from the enemy; he even gave orders for dinner to be prepared for their return to camp at 8.30 that same evening. The column set out at 8.30 a.m. and the first three or four miles were easy going. Colley was so convinced that he would not encounter any resistance on the way that he made no provisions for rations to be issued, nor did he request a water cart to accompany the march. After a short time the column encountered the first of a series of ridges - spurs extending from Nkwelo along the descent down to the Ingogo River. After the Ingogo crossing, the track rose gently, gradually climbing for about 1½ miles up to a low plateau called Schuinshoogte. Before commencing his march down the hill towards the river, Colley prudently detached the two 7-pdr guns and one company of the 3/60th to cover the crossing. He also ordered Mount Prospect to send a company from the 58th to relieve the detachment of the 3/60th and so allow them to rejoin their unit on the road to Newcastle. As a further precaution to protect the river crossing the Mounted Squadron was sent ahead to scout the area around the river fords. Having safely crossed the Ingogo unscathed, the column now proceeded southwards towards Newcastle at a leisurely pace, re-organising slowly on the road up the gentle rise to Schuinshoogte.

Suddenly the peace of the leisurely advance was shattered by the sound of gunfire ahead. Wasting no time, Colley ordered his command up onto the heights, with rifles leading, followed by artillery and staff. The highest point was a plateau roughly tri-angular in shape, very flat and covered with short grass, and a perimeter studded with rough outcrops of rock. The ground below the plateau was also littered with rock and had the added advantage of expanses of long grass, in some places up to four feet high.

As the artillery came up onto the plateau, a body of some 100 Boers was seen on a low ridge about 1,000 yards to the right. They made no move to retire, and the artillery opened fire on them while the rifles extended around the perimeter on both sides of the guns. To Colley's surprise, instead of dispersing, the Boers, led by Nicho Smit, began to exploit the cover provided by the numerous folds in the ground, and to advance towards the British positions. Within a very short space of time, more Boers appeared from cover and began to deploy around the ridge, opening a fierce and very accurate rifle fire on the surprised British. To prevent themselves from being outflanked, those on the plateau extended further until the only open point was on the northeast section of a rough circle. The two 9-pdrs were planted, one in the northernmost sector of the plateau facing north and the other in the southern sector, facing south. The Rifles lay prone behind whatever protection available while bullets relentlessly raked across the plateau. Some of the British riflemen tried to pick off the Boer marksmen, but it soon became obvious that it was suicide to raise a head above the rocks. The artillery also attracted the attention of the Boer fire and soon Capt. Greer on the southern gun was killed, while Lt. Pearson's northern gun also took severe punishment from the Boer volleys. In an attempt to ease the situation Colley ordered Maj. Brownlow to charge the Boer rifles in the north with the depleted Mounted Squadron. Brownlow's men moved forward to the edge of the plateau, but before they could charge a volley crashed out from about 150 yards and decimated the Mounted force.

Casualties also continued to mount in the artillery and soon volunteers were called from the Rifles to take their place. Eventually Colley ordered the guns to withdraw a short distance, but unfortunately this manoeuvre resulted in limiting their field of fire drastically. At about 2.30 p.m. a Boer attempt to outflank the open British left sector was repulsed but with appalling casualties for them. Colley then ordered a half-company of the 3/60th to move out wide on the left to oppose the Boer initiative, and while moving into position the men suffered horribly. Although Capt. J.C. McGregor, the officer in charge of the initiative, was killed, the British managed to hold on to their exposed position, thus successfully preventing the Boers from their manoeuvre of total encirclement.

Around 3 p.m. there was a lull in the battle during which Colley sent a despatch to Mt. Prospect ordering up two further companies of the 58th Regiment to join the units of 3/60th, the 58th and the two7-pdr.guns already in position overlooking the Ingogo. Throughout the afternoon firing continued to flare up and die down, and casualties continued to mount. By now, the situation was worsened by wounded horses galloping about on the plateau in a frenzy trampling anyone and everyone in their way. It was a hot day and the pleas from the wounded for water, were pitiful and without a water cart, nothing could be done to alleviate the suffering. Mercifully, around 5 p.m. a massive storm broke lose, bringing welcome relief to the hot and the thirsty but as the heavy downpour continued, chills set in which led to the deaths of many of the already badly inflicted casualties.

During the latter part of the afternoon the Boers made attempts to thwart the detachment that had been left overlooking the Ingogo, but their thrust was disturbed by the arrival of the two additional companies of the 58th Regiment, which Colley had ordered up from Mount Prospect. At about 6 p.m. the light began to fade, and some of the Boers raised a white flag. At the other end of the perimeter, however, fighting continued as Smit tried to encourage his men to a final attack to bring the battle to victorious conclusion there and then. As the British, with some gallantry, held off these onslaughts, it soon became too obscure for accurate marksmanship, and the firing drew to an end. By 7.30 p.m. all firing on Schuinshoogte had stopped, and Colley was left to contemplate his disastrous situation – he could not expect to be relieved, as there were too few troops available, and Mount Prospect was, itself, very weakly defended and very vulnerable to attack. His men were without food and water, and there was absolutely no chance to replenish ammunition stocks. To stay where he was would surely result in his command being totally annihilated come the dawn, and thus, and thus the only possible chance for survival was to move away from there during the night, because if the rain continued, the Ingogo would be too high to cross in the morning. At 9.30 p.m. Colley started to prepare for his daring night march. The few horses that remained standing were rounded up and attached to the two guns, and to one of the ammunition wagons.

It was at this point that the Boers made their first critical mistake of the war. With the onset of the heavy rain and the cessation of firing, Smit gave the order for his men to withdraw for the night, and they all pulled back to a farm about two miles away. They felt certain that with the bulk of Colley's horses dead, and the heavily swollen Ingogo in his way, it would simply be impossible for him to move during the night, and all that remained for the Boers to do, was to ride over in the morning and finish him off. At 11.00 p.m. Colley was ready to move. He formed his men into skirmish order in a hollow square with the guns in the centre, and, as silently as possible they set off. Approaching the river by a roundabout route, they encountered no Boer patrols. The river had risen greatly and the water reached up to the soldiers' armpits, and in order to cross safely, they linked arms as they struggled across. The force of the current was so strong that seven men and one officer were drowned during this fording manoeuvre. Once across the river the long haul up the hill began, and after a super-human effort Colley's men reached Mount Prospect around 4.00 a.m. on the morning of the 9th February. It had been a miraculous achievement.

Schuinshoogte had cost the British dearly. The 3/60th Rifles lost 58 men killed and 63 wounded. In addition, 1 officer and 7 men were drowned while crossing the Ingogo. The artillery had lost 3 killed and 12 wounded and the Mounted Squadron had 3 killed and 12 wounded plus 14 of their 27 horses. Colley's staff, too, had suffered again with the loss of Capt. McGregor and a civilian interpreter. The Boer losses were thought to have been 8 killed and 10 wounded of which 2 died later.

Smit was angry that an opportunity to inflict a crushing defeat on Colley had been lost, but Colley himself was in no position to consider the battle as anything but a reverse. His demonstration of force had been surrounded and pinned down in an exposed position. Having suffered heavy casualties he was only able to withdraw to safety thanks to extreme gallantry in appalling weather conditions. He felt the loss of his men and staff deeply; almost a quarter of his command had been killed or wounded since his departure from Newcastle only seventeen days before, and now he was left with no choice but to remain inactive until the arrival of Evelyn Wood and his reinforcements.

By the 17th February, the bulk of the British reinforcements had arrived at Mount Prospect, a total of 39 officers and 698 other ranks, the majority coming from the 92nd Highlanders, with 17 officers and 501 other ranks, and the 15th Hussars, with 5 officers and 98 other ranks. Evelyn Wood had joined the reinforcement column on the 15th February, and met up with Colley on the 17th. Colley planned for Wood to take a column from the ranks of the reinforcements and march on, to relieve Wakkerstroom and Lydenburg, while he himself would push on to Pretoria, Potchefstroom and Rustenberg. On the 19th February, Wood led a reconnaissance from Newcastle, and scoured the whole area around Wakkerstroom. Having established that there were no large bodies of Boers in the entire area, he returned to Newcastle on the 21st and then set off back to Pietermaritzburg to expedite the transportation of supplies, ammunition and reinforcements to the front.

During this time, urgent peace negotiations were under way between London and the Transvaal triumvirate, but progress was hampered by the Boers' insistence that any settlement needed unequivocally to include the immediate annulment of the Act of Annexation, and the government proposed to submit the matter to a Royal Commission of Enquiry in order to consider this pre-requisite. While awaiting the outcome of the Royal Commission's enquiry, London agreed to a conditional acceptance of the Boers' request in order to give Colley time regroup his troops. Colley was incensed as he had fully intended to redress, with his recently arrived reinforcements, the defeats of Bronkhorstspruit, Laing's Nek and Schuinshoogte, and had been preparing urgently to launch a fresh initiative against the Boers as soon as possible. To calm him, London gave Colley the authority to impose a suitable time limit for the Boer response to its latest offer. Colley was aware that Joubert, the Boer Commandant-General and principal decision maker, was at this time in Heidelberg, some 100 miles away from the front. He also knew that it would take at least four days for a decision to be delivered and returned so he purposely set an ultimatum of only 48 hours for the Boers to reply to London's offer of conditional acceptance of their request for annulment of the Act of Annexation. Two days after forwarding the ultimatum to Joubert at Heidelberg Nicho Smit learned that Joubert had since moved on to Rustenberg, a further 200 miles away. This meant that he would only receive the letter on the 27th or 28th, long after the expiry of the delay set aside for receipt of the Boer reply. Nevertheless, when he did receive it, Joubert immediately accepted the proposal, but his reply did not reach Smit at Laing's Nek until the 7th March, by which time the ultimatum had long expired and it was too late for any further negotiations.

Amajuba

Amajuba, which in Zulu means "The Hill of Doves", rises majestically some 2,000 ft above Laing's Nek. With its contours etched by ravines, ridges and cliffs, it looms over the Nek and offers splendid views for miles in all directions. Because of the limited combat area on its summit, it was not of much battle significance, being of more tactical rather than strategic importance from a military point of view. But it could certainly

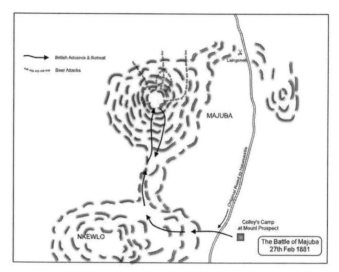

The Battle of Majuba
27th Feb 1881

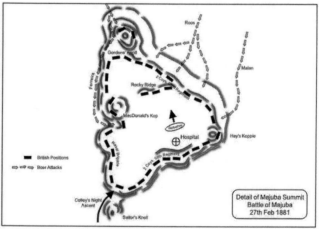

Detail of Majuba Summit
Battle of Majuba
27th Feb 1881

provide a magnificent observation post for any army because from it one would be able to spot any movement for miles around. Colley's decision to occupy Majuba could not be interpreted as an aggressive gesture in defiance of orders from London, nor to be in contradiction of the spirit of the ultimatum, because, technically, it lay entirely within the boundaries of the Natal Province. Moreover it had never been occupied by the Boers on a permanent basis before except for some sporadic ventures of small pickets sent up to spy on enemy activities. The question that needs to be asked is what Colley intended to do once he had positioned such an unnecessarily powerful force on the top. Shelling the enemy from the summit was out of the question since none of his guns had the range to hurt the Boer defences from that distance, even if he had succeeded in getting them up the precipitous and broken slopes of the mountain in the first place. Some writers have suggested that perhaps it was Colley's disdainful attitude to the Boers' military capabilities, even after Laing's Nek and Schuinshoogte, that blinded him to the futility of, and the risks involved, in such a hazardous undertaking. It could have been that he believed that he could easily occupy the summit after a night march with little risk of bloodshed, and that once installed up there, he could overlook the Boer defences and intimidate them with defiant gestures of force into abandoning the Nek altogether.

It is also questionable whether such a massive force was actually necessary to accomplish so simple and small a task. There was always the tremendous risk of a breach of secrecy in moving large numbers of soldiers in difficult and unknown terrain in the pitch dark of the night, and, when once installed, to guarantee the success of any possible ensuing military operation where such large numbers were confined to so small and exposed a battle arena. In the absence of any reasonable answers to these questions, one could only assume that Colley's troops had been lolling around idly since the debacle at Schuinshoogte, and that any sort of activity would provide an excursion for the bored men who had little to do but await the arrival of the reinforcements. The ascent and occupation of Majuba would provide good training in the face of the main objective, which was, once the reinforcements were in place, to make a direct onslaught on Laing's Nek, dislodge the Boers and send them packing back into the Transvaal.

Whatever the reasons, Colley felt fully justified in his decision to take Majuba, especially after having heard reports from two local African scouts that the mountain was easy to scale, and that the summit was like a large saucer-like depression ringed with protective boulders, and with adequate supplies of water not far below the surface. It was, in fact, on the sole basis of this information that Colley, after careful deliberation, decided to go ahead with his plan. It was strange that he paid so much credence to the judgment of two locals who had no military training whatsoever, without taking any time to consider the need to make a proper tactical reconnaissance of the hill and its summit. In fact, he kept his plan so secret that he confided in two persons only, his personal military secretary, Lt. Col. Herbert Stewart, and his friend Major Fraser of the Royal Engineers.

The Night March to Majuba
At 8.30 p.m. on the 22nd February, as the men were preparing to retire for the night, a sudden flurry of activity broke out around the staff tent, and orders were hurriedly give to start preparations for a major night march. Two companies of the 58th Regiment, two

of the 3/60th Rifles, three of the 92nd Highlanders, a company strength of Naval Brigade and various small detachments from other units were mustered. Each man was instructed to carry 70 rounds of ammunition, a greatcoat, a water proof sheet, rations for three days, a full bottle of water and a rifle - a total weight of 58 lbs per person. In addition, each company was ordered to carry four picks and six shovels. The total strength of the force was 595 officers and men, plus Colley, Stewart and Fraser of the staff, three newspaper correspondents, and an unknown number of African guides and servants.

It is said that Colley made up his force from the various battalions under his command and not exclusively from any one single unit, which would have ensured some measure of cohesion, because he was so confident in the imminent capture of Majuba, which, he believed would prove to be the turning point in his fortunes. He wanted all his units to have a share in the glory of the event to make up for the earlier disasters of Bronkhorstspruit, Laing's Nek and Schuinshoogte. This ominous decision was to have a direct influence on what was about to enfold....

At 10 p.m. the column set off into the moonless night – no lights were carried and total silence was ordered. Colley and his staff officers rode at the head, followed by two Zulu scouts and the 58th and the 3/60th, and the Naval Brigade bringing up the rear. The column headed west from Mt. Prospect, crossed the Newcastle-Laing's Nek road and proceeded to climb up the lower slopes of Mt. Nkwelo. After a half hour, it reached a low plateau about half way up the hill, where it halted to re-organise. The column then turned north and followed a track, only wide enough for men in single file, with a steep slope on one side. Soon it reached another plateau at the northern end of Nkwelo where two companies of the 3/60th Rifles were detached and installed to protect the line of march.They were ordered to hold their position but were not informed of Colley's destination. The march continued northwards along a wide ridge between Nkwelo and Majuba, and at the far end the column halted for about an hour while part of the rear, which had lost the way in the dark, was located and brought back in. At this point Colley detached a company of the 92nd Highlanders with orders to dig an entrenchment. The Highlanders were informed that they would be joined later by a company of the 3/60th which had been ordered up directly from Mount Prospect and that in the meantime to take charge of the officers' horses and the reserve ammunition.

By now, the destination was no longer a secret. The main column marched off and began the ascent of Majuba directly ahead. The climb was a tough one with the men, encumbered with heavy kit, struggling up the steep slopes. Occasionally one would slip and clatter to the ground while those around him would freeze waiting at any moment for Boer bullets to go zipping through the air. But they were not discovered. Near the top of the hill the scouts lost their way in the dark, and Colley and his men passed anxious moments while the search for the path was under way. When it was finally found, the men now faced the stiffest part of the climb, a steep grass slope that had to be scaled on hands and knees as the soldiers groped their way up. Colley ordered Maj. Fraser to go forward with a small detachment of the 58th to scout out the area ahead. He soon returned to confirm that the summit was unoccupied, news which Colley was more than happy to receive. He personally allotted the exhausted men to their positions around the summit, and most of the units were finally in place by 5.30 a.m. He was pleased with the situation. The summit, which was lined with rough boulders, had a perimeter of about one-third of a mile. It sloped gently inwards to form a shallow basin in the centre. On the western side of the mountain was an isolated koppie, later named 'MacDonalds Kop', and on the eastern side there was another rather less defined hill called 'Hay's Kop. The basin was bisected by a low rocky ridge, which in the darkness was erroneously believe to be the northern edge of the summit.

Having left three companies behind on the approach march to protect communication lines, Colley's force on top of Majuba now totalled 23 officers and 382 men - 405 in all. They consisted mainly of the 58th Regiment, with 7 officers and 164 other ranks, – the 92nd Highlanders, with 6 officers and 135 other ranks, and the Naval Brigade, with 3 officers and 62 other ranks. The Highlanders lined the perimeter from MacDonald's Kop, named after Lt. Hector MacDonald, along the rocky ridge to Hay's Kop, named after Maj. Hay. The line was continued by the 58th along the southeast face up to the south-west point where the main column had originally crossed onto the summit. From here, the Naval Brigade commanded the western lip up to a steep grassy gulley that extended down the mountain-side below MacDonald's Kop.

The men were spaced at roughly twelve pace intervals along the perimeter, and a mixed reserve of about 110 men made up from all the three major units, formed-up in the hollow behind the rocky ridge close to Colley's HQ. The medical men also positioned themselves in that area, and set up a field hospital. A well was dug, and water was found at a depth of three feet. Later a second one was added nearby. There was no serious co-ordinated effort in place to fortify the positions although some junior officers did encourage their men to create individual defences by piling stones in front of their positions. The Naval Brigade made a serious attempt to produce some strong stone defensive positions, the remains of which are still evident today.

As the skies brightened it became apparent that the 92nd was not actually on the true perimeter of the mountain top, and that beyond the ridge the ground sloped gently away to the north before dipping abruptly onto a wide, grassy terrace below. Orders were quickly issued for the 92nd to move up and occupy this forward brow of Majuba, and a handful of the men also took up an exposed position on an isolated knoll to the north, later to become known as "Gordons' Knoll" in honour of the 92[nd,] who were to become the Gordon Highlanders later that year. This small knoll was an important feature as it enabled flanking fire to be directed across the northern slopes. Having considerably extended their lines, the 92nd were now even more widely dispersed than ever. From the top of Majuba, the men now expected to see the remaining force at Mt. Prospect to march out with the artillery, and prepare an assault on Laing's Nek as part of a co-ordinated attack on the Boer forces. But this was not in Colley's plan. He had been ordered by London not to attempt Laing's Nek until a reply had been received from the Boers regarding the peace proposals that were under way. In fact, Colley had told Wood that he was not to advance until the reinforcements had arrived, and he reported to London that all he intended to do was to 'seize some ground which has hither too been practically unoccupied by either party'

Colley believed that with their flank threatened, the Boers would probably retire, but even if they did not, it would not be a great problem because he had already intended to hand over the command of the force on Majuba to Commander Romilly of the Naval Brigade, and return to Mount Prospect to prepare the advance on Laing's Nek. Then, he believed, the Boers threatened from flank and front, would retire from the Nek permanently and leave the way open for him to move forward for the relief of the besieged garrisons in the Transvaal. Now safely ensconced on top of Majuba Colley failed to investigate, or even to recognise one very critical aspect of the mountain topography – that the slopes on the north and the northeast sides held by the Boer sides, were very different to those that his own men had encountered on their arduous slog to the top. Instead of steep rocky climbs, a grassy slope pushed forward to the north beyond the true summit of the hill, but below this the ground dropped abruptly to a wide flat grass covered terrace, then sloped sharply down again, hiding large extents of the ascent in dead ground. In addition, gullies and ravines choked with brush, ran down the mountain making it possible for any attacking force to advance at least two-thirds of the way up virtually unseen by anyone lining the perimeter of the summit

All was quiet in the three Boer camps down in the valley behind Laing's Nek. At dawn, they became aware of movement on the summit of Majuba, it soon being apparent that the British had occupied the mountain during the night. The Boers immediately hulled down and waited the inevitable arrival of artillery shells. They waited and waited and......nothing happened.

Majuba – The Battle
Checking in the direction of Mtount Prospect, it soon dawned on Joubert that there was no movement at all from that area, so in consultation with Nicho Smit, he decided that there was nothing left but to try and drive the British off the mountain. Volunteers were called for, and shortly groups of fifty to sixty men from various commandos began to gather until a quite reasonable force was mustered. The volunteers that eventually gathered around the leaders came from various commandos in the area, and in the end neither the exact number nor composition was actually established, but it is believed that between 450 and 500 men took part in the engagement, the direction of which was designated to Nicholas Smit. As the men assembled, Smit organised them into groups. One, about 150 strong, was despatched around the western side of the mountain to cut off any British reinforcements or retreat. Two other groups of fifty to eighty men gathered at the foot of the mountain and were divided into individual attacking parties under the respective leadership of Veld-Kornet Stephanus Roos and Commandant Joachim Ferreira. These two groups began a slow and careful advance up the lower slopes of Majuba, keeping about 100 to 150 yards apart, Roos on the left and Ferreira on the right. They took advantage of every bit of natural cover provided by the vegetation and topography of the slopes, and also of a large gully which helped them to climb slowly upwards towards the summit without being spotted. A third group led by commandant D. Malan now joined them, advancing up the slope to the left of Roos. All three groups grew in size as the Boers began to realise that any danger of attack on their positions at Laing's Nek was becoming more and more improbable as time went by. The Boer parties continued their advance up the mountain, zigzagging from boulder to

bush and from bush to boulder, forever seeking cover from above and providing cover for each other as they edged upwards.

Back on the summit, everything was calm, the British feeling secure in their belief that their position was impregnable. However, the level of Boer fire aimed at the summit was gradually building up, and some officers began to become aware that, although everything was fine, things were "hotting up somewhat" During all this time, Colley remained confidently unconcerned. Even when, a while later, the first British casualties started limping into the hospital area, he preferred to busy himself with trivia such as sending unnecessary messages to Mount Prospect concerning matters of supply and reserve ammunition. He even ordered the 2/60th Rifles and three troops of the 15th Hussars, to move forward from Newcastle in preparation for a direct assault on Laing's Nek when the time was opportune.

Shortly after 10.30 a.m. Colley, rather belatedly started thinking about the construction of some sort of defensive redoubts on the summit. He also started preparations for his own departure from Majuba, and arranging for Commander Romilly to assume overall command after his departure. It was just at this time that Romilly noticed two Boers far below, remarking that one of them was 'trying to shoot at us'. Colley asked Stewart to check the distance (it was about 900 yards), when suddenly Romilly let out a cry of pain, and crumpled to ground at Colley's side, mortally wounded - he died from his wounds three days later at Mount Prospect. Colley was shattered when he suddenly realised that his entire position was exposed on all sides to Boer fire.

Meanwhile, the Boers were continuing their slow and methodical advance up the slopes of Majuba, rarely exposing them selves for more than a fleeting moment. Even now, Colley appeared unaware of the terrible situation he was in, believing that everything still appeared to be going according to plan. At 11 a.m. he signalled Mount Prospect, 'the '*Boers* (were) *still forcing heavily on hill but have broken laager and beginning to move away – Commander Romilly dangerously wounded – other casualties 3 men slightly hurt'* The most northerly point of the British defensive perimeter was occupied by about 18 men of the 92nd Highlanders under Lt. Ian Hamilton, who successfully pushed forward five of his men to occupy the isolated Gordon's Knoll, as well as the spur which connects the knoll to the summit. Hamilton survived the engagement, and in 1915, as General Sir Ian Hamilton, led the British forces at Gallipoli. Directly below the knoll the wide grassy terrace narrows dramatically. Soon the Boers grasped the importance of this feature, and Ferreira began to congregate his men below the brow of the terrace at this narrowest point. The edge of the terrace marked the end of the dead ground so that any further Boer advance from there would be in the open and fully exposed to fire from the British lining the perimeter of the summit and from the knoll itself. Consequently, Veld-Kornet Roos's men extended to Ferreira's left, lining the edge of the perimeter as it opened out to its full width.

The Boer fire continued to increase, and every now, and then a particularly heavy concentration of fire was directed towards the Highlanders, forcing them to keep their heads well down while groups of ten or twelve Boers would dash forward across the fifteen or so yards of narrow terrace below the knoll. Hamilton was powerless to stop this build up of men so dangerously close to his position, and when he had estimated that as many as 100 men were hidden below him, he ran the gauntlet of Boer fire to report the situation to Colley, back in the hollow behind the rocky ridge. Hamilton was surprised to find the reserve units very relaxed, eating, sleeping or smoking, while Colley himself just calmly thanked him for the report and sent him back to his men without taking any further action.

Back on the perimeter, Hamilton noticed that the Boer build-up had now increased to about 200 so he reported again to Colley, who continued to appear quite unconcerned. When the build-up reached about 350 men Hamilton became quite desperate, and he begged for reinforcements. Eventually an officer and five men of the 58th was sent over to help him. Around midday the war correspondent Thomas Carter, full of confidence, sent off a telegram informing his readers that - *'firing kept up incessantly by Boers – our men very steady returning fire only when good chance offers....Boers cannot take position from us....they are keeping up average 60 shots per minute...the Boers have inspanned their cattle and are evidently ready to trek at a moment's notice...'*

But, within the next 90 minutes, Majuba was to become the scene of one of the British army's most humiliating defeats ever....

Shortly after noon Hamilton, feeling uneasy, returned once more to alert Colley that he now believed that 400 Boers were extended below him, and were preparing for attack. Colley was asleep! Col. Stewart refused to awaken him, sending Hamilton away with a flea in his ear. Bewildered and exasperated he reported to his senior officer, Major Hay, and returned to his beleaguered troops. Just after 12.30 there was a sudden outburst of firing – a definite volley, concentrated very close by on one spot The Boers directly below Gordon's Knoll stepped out of cover, opening a tremendous hail of fire on the exposed position on the knoll. The bullets, flying fast and thick, swept across the promontory, killing three men instantly, while the remainder fled for their lives back to Hamilton on the perimeter. Ferreira's men now took position on the abandoned Gordon's Knoll, and opened an even more galling sweep of fire on the thinly spread Highlanders on the perimeter.

With the British in that area now totally pinned down, Roos led his men in a dash across the grassy terrace to the dead ground only 100 yards below the brow of the mountain. From here only a stiff climb up the steepest part separated him from the British, while the pinned down Highlanders could do nothing to oppose Roos's move. The startling volley had finally stung the commanding officers into action. Col. Stewart who was on the south side of the summit, came running to the centre with two or three other officers, and ordered the Reserve forward to reinforce the threatened positions on the northern perimeter. Bewildered, the men crossed the rocky ridge and advanced in skirmishing order with fixed bayonets and startled stares. In the face of the fire, they quickly dropped down in the grass and opened a heavy but quite random fire without really being able to pick out any specific targets. The Boers on the knoll continued to fire with terrible intensity and accuracy, while Roos, with about fifty men, clambered up the steep final slope and positioned themselves on the perimeter of the mountain, just below the brow and only yards from the Highlanders. Within minutes, they opened intensive fire and about fifteen men of the Reserve, were instantly killed. The Reserve had had enough – they turned and rushed back towards the rocky ridge while those of Hamilton's men who were still in position joined them, with the Boers on the summit shooting at the panicking British as they fled. The fleeing men crossed the rocky ridge in total disarray, and carried on towards the south side of the mountain nearest to Mount Prospect. Most of them were rallied, however, and brought to the ridge. They clustered around the western end, while the officers tried to separate them into their proper units, and extend them along the ridge. Colley was there too, close by, looking quite 'cool and collected'

While this reorganisation was taking place, there was a lull in the Boer firing as they too consolidated their position on the mountain in anticipation of the next phase of their attack. Colley's force now occupied the original line taken up during the previous night and which still constituted a relatively strong position. The front was now the line of the rocky ridge that offered good defensive cover. On the left, the eminence of MacDonald's Kop, which was occupied by Lt. Hector MacDonald and a handful of men, could provide excellent covering fire as well as threaten any Boer moves against the front. The rear of the ridge was also protected by the men on Hay's Kop, and around the remainder of the perimeter were many men who had not yet fired a single shot. But the weakness of the British now became manifest in the low morale of the men – the confidence of the early morning had been replaced by fear, confusion and shattered nerves – many men had no idea of what was happening, especially those who had witnessed the sudden and dramatic flight of the Reserves earlier on. Widely spread out and away from any direct influence of their own officers, many men grew nervous, some beginning to quit their posts under a variety of excuses.

The Boers now opened a heavy fire from the front against the rocky ridge, having crept up to about 40 yards from the ridge. Boer bullets that flew too high raked among the defenders of Hay's Kop in the rear, where MacDonald's men were unable to respond because they were themselves pinned down by fire coming from the now captured Gordon's Knoll. Meanwhile a group of Ferreira's men were advancing around the west side of the mountain, moving towards a gully that would cover them in their advance up the mountain. Commandant Malan, who had begun his climb behind Roos and Ferreira, had by now, worked his way around the mountain to the east and was firing up the hill at the men of the 58th defending Hay's Kop, who, in turn, were receiving fire in their rear coming from Roos's onslaught described previously.

As the Boers now closed in for the kill from three sides, time was rapidly running out for Colley and his men. The officers were making every effort to rally their troops. Bayonets had been fixed, and it was believed that with words of encouragement from the officers, the men would survive the hail of bullets and drive the Boers from the top.It was in this spirit that Lt. Hamilton on the right was busily preparing for action, gathering some men from the 92nd for the charge. Sadly he was quickly discouraged by his own superior officer, Major Hay, a decision that was later to be endorsed by Colley himself, who curtly informed the subaltern that 'we will wait until the Boer advances on us – then we give a volley and a charge' - alas, it was never going to be that simple....!

Majuba – The Collapse

Casualties were slowly mounting as a new crisis was developing with the advance of Ferreira's men up the large gully on the western side of the mountain – a gully that opened out to the left rear of the rocky ridge, presenting the Boers with very close range fire into the flank of the main British position. Orders were given for the men to extend a further twenty yards to the left to prevent the threatened incursion, but this now meant having to leave the protection of the rocky ridge. Some of the men nearest to this point consisted of a mixed bunch from the 92nd, the 58[th,] and from the sailors, and they showed great reluctance to leave their cover, and follow officers who were not necessarily their own. Others steadfastly refused to budge and discipline was on the wane. In the confusion, more and more men began to leave their positions around the perimeter and slip away to the rocky ridge that offered better protection. It was at that time that Major Hay informed Colley that the Boers were pressing heavily against the kop (that would later bear his name), and that from there the rear of the British positions behind the ridge would be completely exposed. Colley responded by ordering the officers on the summit to hold the position at all costs, and began to direct some men to extend to the right.

At that moment, a piercing yell of terror burst forth from the direction of the gully, and the men, in twos and threes began to panic, with fours and fives breaking rank, and starting to run to the rear. Despite desperate efforts from officers and NCOs, more and more men began to break and run back. Suddenly, the whole line collapsed with each and every man sprinting for his life. Hamilton was hit in the hand, and as he fell, he saw that the whole line had given way. Colley was standing, revolver in hand, urging the men to hold by the ridge, but they just dashed past and continued to flee. Soon Colley himself was shot in the head whilst rallying the troops, dying instantly. Hamilton joined the rout just as the Boers appeared on Hay's Kop and the rocky ridge, opening lethal fire on the retreating infantry.

At the far end of the mountain, the fugitives threw themselves over the steep edge, trusting to luck for survival amongst the jagged rocks, precipices and gullies as they dashed down the steep southern slopes of Majuba. The last stand of resistance came from Hector MacDonald's group of about twenty men, determined to hold position. Soon 8 men were dead and 3 wounded and finally they were all dead except MacDonald and one other man. They were taken prisoner and it was all over for the British on the top of Majuba. It had been a little over 30 minutes since the Boer attack on Gordon's Knoll that Colley's entire force was swept off the "unassailable" and "impregnable" mountain!

Majuba – The Aftermath

Once on the summit the Boers looted the dead and wounded before gathering on the most southerly rim and firing on the fleeing British, who were scrambling down the side of the mountain, searching for safety. The fleeing fugitives soon swept through the lines of the troops left behind to guard the horses and spare ammunition. After some feeble attempts to stem the tide, they too gave way when a group of Boers appeared around the western side of the hill. In the face of heavy fire and in the most difficult of circumstances they eventually found their way back to Mount Prospect.

When the true scale of the disaster finally became known, an incredulous public was stunned. The losses amounted to 240 killed, wounded or taken prisoner - a total of 59% of the entire force engaged on the mountain top. The 92nd suffered most with a loss of 99 men, 70% of those in action. In stark contrast, the Boers had lost one man killed and six wounded one of whom later died from his injuries. Those who had captured firearms claimed that many of the British guns were still sighted at 400 yards even though the bulk of the fighting had occurred at very close range.

For the British, Majuba had been a crushing and most humiliating defeat. The might of the British Empire had been overwhelmed by a small infant republic with no standing army and on the brink of bankruptcy. When the news of the disaster broke in London, there was a wave of outrage and determination to exact redress and to set the matter right at once, before any further 'peace talks' could continue. Orders were immediately issued by the War Office for massive reinforcements to be assembled urgently and shipped off the South Africa without delay. In Natal, Sir Evelyn Wood was sworn in as acting Governor of Natal and High Commissioner of the Transvaal, in anticipation to the arrival of Sir Frederick Roberts, Colley's officially designated replacement.

However, on the 4th March Wood received an invitation from Joubert, proposing a meeting on the 6th to discuss negotiations for peace. Wood, gunning for quick revenge for Majuba, was not pleased, but following instructions from London, he was reluctantly obliged to accept Joubert's proposal and to agree to an eight-day cease-fire. On the 7th Kruger's reply to Colley's original ultimatum which was handed to Nicholas Smit on the 27th February, reached Wood and the British authorities. Surprisingly it was far more conciliatory than had been expected, and suddenly it seemed as if there was a real chance for mutual agreement.

Gladstone, the British Prime Minister, was very much in favour of negotiations, feeling that to shed more blood simply to regain prestige was very wrong. This was a brave stance taken in the face of a lot of opposition – even Queen Victoria was strongly in favour of continuation of the war to regain honour - but Gladstone held fast, and his decision prevailed. Wood was instructed to open peace talks, as distasteful as he personally found the proceedings to be. On the 28th March a formal peace treaty was signed, and ratified in August, granting a quasi independence to the Transvaal. The clauses when published caused outrage and consternation, even to the Boers. But Joubert was a clever man – he felt sure that once the British had confirmed the cease-fire, they would not return to war, and that there would be ample time thereafter to modify the terms of the agreement in favour of the Transvaal in the long run. And he was right – three years later, at the Convention of London, the Transvaal regained full independence. For the Boers it was a great victory but for the British a humiliating defeat which continued to rankle, and when eighteen years later war with the Boers broke out again, the army went into battle with a burning quest for revenge with the cry 'remember Majuba' on their lips and in their hearts.

Vindication eventually did come, when on the 27th February 1900, on the very anniversary of Majuba, Lord Roberts forced the surrender of the Boer forces, with Piet Cronje, General-Commandant of the Boer forces, lamenting, 'you have even taken our Majuba away from us..' Visiting Majuba today one feels and lives the singularly 'brooding' character of the mountain. Setting off from the gentler northern side, a pathway right up to the summit follows the Boer advance. The areas of dead ground are quite obvious as one ascends, and once at the top, the dominating aspect of the summit is overwhelming as one looks back down onto the site of the Boer encampment in the Nek. On the summit a monument has been erected on MacDonald's Kop, while the graves of the British soldiers who fell there, lie still and undisturbed on the windswept mountain top. A few paces away is a small enclosure with a weather beaten cross and an inscription – "This marks the spot where General Colley died". Standing there and looking across the hollow plateau to the rocky ridge to Gordon's Knoll, Hay's Kop and the rest, one's mind is overwhelmed with the ghastly sights and noises of that fateful day, and of the bitter struggle for this forlorn spot where Maj. Gen. Sir George Pomeroy-Colley tragically found his "hill of destiny" !

After Majuba

The Anglo-Transvaal peace treaty that was signed and ratified in the wake of the British defeat at Majuba was an unsatisfactory one both from the British as well as the Transvaal point of view. At this time, South Africa lay far from the minds of the British leaders in London; they had far more serious issues to deal with such as the cankerous Irish Home Rule problem as well as the Egyptian insurrection and Gordon's death at the hands of the Mahdi dervishes in Khartoum. In reality, therefore, the Majuba treaty was almost bound to be a temporary affair, unsatisfactory as it was to both sides, and almost certain to be changed sometime later.

Gladstone, the "Grand Old Man", who was back in the saddle for his third term needed to channel all his energies into the serious Irish problem, and was thus quick to seize a compromise solution to the Transvaal situation. He agreed to withdraw the large British force under Sir Frederick Roberts of Kandahar away from South Africa, and to restore complete self-government to the Boers, subject to one major qualification, namely the right for Britain to reserve for herself the ultimate control over the Transvaal's foreign affairs. Constitutionally it was an unusual, though not unique arrangement whereby Britain continued to claim her status as a paramount power in South Africa, although she did not claim the Transvaal as a colony or even as a member of her Empire. Under pressure from colleagues in the Cape and the Free State, Kruger reluctantly consented to the arrangement, which was given the form of an international treaty by the Convention of Pretoria in 1881, and the Convention of London in 1884. Kruger, who had become President of the restored Transvaal Republic, did not conceal the fact that he was signing under protest, and would be doing his utmost to negotiate a third convention that would forever remove the shadow of British suzerainty from the Transvaal's independence.

In the end, the consequences of Majuba played more on the Boers than on the British, for whom the results, disastrous as they were, did little to change the subsequent course of events, either in Europe or in South Africa. On the larger world canvas, the war of 1880/81 in South Africa represented a relatively insignificant military setback in a most remote corner of the globe. It was the result of the impetuous actions of a relatively inexperienced commander whose contempt for the capabilities of his enemy encouraged him to set upon a totally ill conceived and futile engagement, simply it appeared, to 'exercise his bored troops'

For the Boers, on the other hand, it was a different matter all together. It would be tempting to muse about the history of the Transvaal if Majuba had never happened. If Colley had succeeded in defeating Joubert and Smit, ensuing circumstances would have forced Kruger and Joubert to relinquish control, and the Annexation would have remained intact. Eventually, the Transvaal, the Free State, the Cape and Natal would heave been integrated into a union of loyal provinces within the British Empire. Instead, the overwhelming Boer victory at Majuba imbued Kruger and his fellow Boers into the real belief of their role in Africa of God's chosen people, ordained to rid themselves of the yoke of foreign suppression, and to thrive in their own manner and mores in the Canaan that the Lord had especially set aside for them. The deliverance of the British at Majuba was God's message to His people that He was on their side and that He would protect them from all evil in the same way as He had done at Blood River some 40 years earlier. In deference to this promise, the Boers would vow to fight to the 'bitter end' for the unfettered control of their own destiny!

PART TWO

THE BOER WAR - 11/10/1899 to 31/05/1902

8
GOLD AND MILNER'S WAY TO WAR.

Most historians have emphasised that one of the main reasons for Britain's renewed interest in the Boer republics, and particularly the Transvaal, was the discovery of gold in quantities such as never ever been dreamt of before. It is certainly a fact that in 1886, London once again began to focus its corporate mind on the Transvaal, for it was during that year that the Rand goldfields were officially proclaimed, and the great Stock Exchange boom started, with prosperity surging ahead in London and Johannesburg. The opening of the goldfields presented a new and very lucrative source of revenue and wealth for Britain. Whether the discovery of gold and its ensuing wealth was indeed the cause of war in South Africa or not, it did help to create a disposition for intervention, because, suddenly the Witwatersrand had become a very valuable 'acre of acquisition'. Yet, it does not entirely explain the reasons *why* war did eventually break out in South Africa: after all, there was little danger of Britain being denied the benefits of the goldfields because she was already 'on the spot'. The Transvaal was hemmed in by two British colonies, British capital, financing the goldfields, was provided by British gold magnates such as Sir Julius Wernher, Sir Alfred Beit, and Cecil John Rhodes, and above all, there already existed a quasi-British administrative presence in both Boer republics.

By 1885, Britain was already very seriously committed to the much wider scramble for Empire, not only in Africa but all over the world as well, and there is little doubt that her involvement in the affairs of the two republics was inevitable, regardless of diamonds or gold. After 1815, the dominant influence of France on the dynamic scene of European power politics was crushed, which left Britain an almost free hand in global empire building. Germany, after emphatically driving the last nail into the French coffin at Sedan in 1871, also began to seek her own seat at the carving table, and Bismarck in 1884, called for a conference to regulate the scramble for Africa. At the Conference of Berlin in 1885, it was declared that 'occupation of any territory by a European power gave rights of possession'. It was a decision which was to play a major role in the ensuing frenetic endeavours by all to colonise as much of the African continent as possible.

A feature of latter-half nineteenth century colonisation was that it did not merely mean occupation and economic exploitation of the indigenous inhabitants, but that it brought the entire world into one trading system, which was dominated by the industrialists and bankers of Europe. As conquest turned into possession, the prestige of the empire became the dictates of small groups of men – politicians, entrepreneurs and particularly military personalities, and there emerged a new world where everything was controlled from Cabinet Offices, Boardrooms and Military Headquarters. Military men often used imperial status to boost, and to make 'the Empire' a symbol of national prestige and greatness, and a model justice and liberty.
It is important to note that imperial advancement and struggles for colonial acquisition brought vastly exaggerated prestige for the military establishment. Generals and governmental military planners straddled the late nineteenth century political landscape

like giants engaged in a universal game of chess, while the public stood back in awe of their expertise, courage and hold on the public imagination. The Generals and other elite military brass were left free to devise military plans and strategies, and were unhindered by the constraints of diplomacy or national policies, let alone of common sense! In many instances colonial policies were dictated by military planners rather than by diplomatic considerations, and especially in Southern Africa these dictates would in the end prove to be very costly in terms of human sacrifice and loss of national prestige. Because of all this, or perhaps in spite of it, colonial expansion in South Africa was inevitable and would have happened regardless of whether there was an abundance of diamonds and gold or not. The presence of these precious commodities merely served as a very handy and easy reason when justification was eventually called for. How then did the inevitable confrontation between Britain and the Transvaal Boers eventually come about?

What no one, least of all Kruger, could have foreseen when the London Convention was signed in 1884, was that the Rand would be discovered two years later. The resulting explosion of wealth in the Transvaal had devastating political results. Suddenly the Cape Colony and the Transvaal exchanged roles, as the political leadership of the sub-continent passed from the Cape to the Transvaal. By the mid-1890's, there was a double anomaly-the Cape was a British colony, though the majority of the inhabitants were Afrikaners,   while, although the Transvaal was still a Boer republic, so many British immigrants had been sucked into the rush for gold, that it began to look as if the majority of its inhabitants were British. And, of course, it also provided for the emergence of the so called 'gold bugs', two of whom, the multi-millionaires, Cecil John Rhodes and Alfred Beit, contrived to take possession of the Transvaal for themselves and of course for the Empire. It was in the diamond mines of Kimberley where they had made the fortunes that would eventually bring them to Johannesburg. Rhodes had become Prime Minister of the Cape, and together with Beit, formed a new British colony in the African territory to the north of the Transvaal, which they called Rhodesia.

Gold had made the Transvaal the richest, and militarily the most powerful nation in southern Africa. It also made, for the second time, the fortunes of Rhodes, and especially of Beit, and precipitated a collision between the Boers and the 'Uitlanders', the new immigrants, mainly British, swept along in the gold rush. The situation of the 'Uitlanders' was unique. Although they outnumbered the Boers in the Transvaal, they were, through the means of new franchise laws, starved by the Boers of political rights and a constitutional say in matters of their own concern. It was this political hunger, backed by the Rhodes/Beit millions, that seemed to offer the British a chance of once again taking over the Transvaal from the Boers.

Much was made out of the 'Uitlander' factor that was manipulated to fuel the dissent between the British people and the burghers in the Transvaal. It was even exploited to initiate an uprising in support of Rhodes's attempt to annex the Transvaal as a British colony under the British flag. It is certain that both Rhodes and Beit had hopelessly over-estimated the strength of the opposition by the Uitlanders against Kruger and his government. In fact, a large minority of them were not British at all, but Afrikaners from the Cape and the Free State, Germans, Dutch, Frenchmen and even Americans.

It is a fact that the Uitlanders did have their grievances, particularly their dissatisfaction over the lack of political rights. In the main, however, they were content to earn good money working in the gold mines, and were in no hurry to overthrow a government, which in all other respects, left them free to get on with their own affairs. Even the Johannesburg 'Reformers', those 'cardboard revolutionaries' who were inciting Rhodes, Beit and the British government to intervene in toppling Kruger and his regime, were not entirely agreed to whether the new authority would be self-governed by the Uitlanders themselves, or handed over to British, which de facto meant Rhodes's control.

Whatever the situation, Rhodes, in order to overthrow the Kruger administration, used the Uitlander question to fan dissent and unrest to the point of conspiracy. During the course of 1895, he and Beit hatched a plot to create a revolution in Johannesburg that would be backed by an armed raid from Mafeking under the command of Dr. Starr Leander Jameson, an associate of Rhodes. In a confidential letter to Beit in August 1895 Rhodes wrote: '*Johannesburg is ready, (this is) the big idea which makes England dominant in Africa, in fact gives England the African continent*'

The Jameson raid failed miserably. Inept leadership, bad management and poor intelligence had finally brought the column to a farm called Doornkop, about twenty miles of Johannesburg. For two days, they had carried on a running fight against the Boer commandos, the Boers hanging on to their tail and picking off the stragglers. Now after 171 miles, they found themselves huddled in a rough square formed by ammunition carts, the ambulance wagons and the horses, surrounded by the Boers with no sign of the promised help from the Johannesburg 'Reformers'. As dawn broke, they could see the pit-heads and shacks of Johannesburg, the Golden City, only two-hours ride away. Yet it might have been the moon for all their chances of ever getting there – no help was arriving – Johannesburg had not risen, and the Uitlanders were peacefully at their work in the pits, and continuing to earn their good wages. The leaders of the 'uprising', the Reform Committee, had made their peace with President Kruger and his Boers, and not a single armed volunteer had broken out to join Jameson's column.

Shortly after dawn, the Boers attacked the column, and by 8 a.m. that morning at Doornkop there lay 65 bodies, dead or wounded. Someone raised a white flag and Jameson's bid to conquer the Transvaal was over. The humiliation was complete – those who remained were taken away to the Pretoria gaol, and bringing up the rear was a cape-cart in which a bound and weeping Jameson sat in abject humiliation. Jan Smuts later wrote: '*The Jameson Raid was the real declaration of war in the Great Anglo-Boer conflict, and, in spite of the four years truce that followed...(the) aggressors consolidated their defences and the others had silently and grimly prepared for the inevitable*'

The Jameson Raid disastrously weakened the imperial position in South Africa. In 1898 Kruger was re-elected as President for a fourth term, and he was now the hero, not only in the Transvaal, but amongst his fellow Afrikaners in the Cape and the Free State. Many other foreign powers that were ill disposed towards Great Britain and her Empire manifested overt disapproval of Britain's 'rapacious interference' in the internal affairs of a sovereign independent state. Rhodes himself, was severely censured and forced to resign, both as chairman of the Chartered Company as well as Cape Prime Minister, and in 1897, Sir Alfred Milner was appointed High Commissioner for South Africa and Lieutenant-Governor of the Cape, with orders to restore the world that Jameson had destroyed. His first problem, however, was how to deal with the Rhodes and his partner, Sir Alfred Beit.

As Governor and High Commissioner it was Milner's job to be on good terms with all the pro-British parties, particularly those ex-German, naturalised British multi-millionaire 'gold bugs' such as Sir Alfred Beit, Sir Julius Wernher, Sir J.B. Robinson and others, even though he could not trust any of them an inch. He had no doubt of the lessons of the past – the Jameson raid was Rhodes' private attempt at a shortcut to solve the Transvaal problem, and it had failed as abjectly as the forward policy of the imperial government. However, that did not prove that intervention was wrong, especially for Milner, who was as anxious as anyone else to engineer as quickly as possible the total subjugation of the Transvaal to the sphere of British imperial dominion. Milner based his intervention policy on three pre-requisites: agreement with the Cape loyalists, agreement with the Colonial Office, and the support of British public opinion on both sides of the political fence. For him the issue was clear and concise – there were only two ways out of the abyss in South Africa- either Kruger made profound political reforms in his ramshackle republic, or there must be a 'row'. In other words, a choice between reform or war. Of these two Milner believed war to be the more likely.

During this time, matters in the Boer camp had not been standing still either. In the Transvaal Volksraad Kruger's reputation had suffered badly during the years of peace that followed Majuba, and by 1893, his stock had fallen so low that he almost lost the Presidency to Joubert. Joubert openly accused Kruger of unethical personal enrichment through his control and connivances in the granting of State concessions and monopolies in dynamite and engineering production for the mines and railway construction contracts. By 1895, Kruger was reaching the end of his tether, when all of a sudden the Jameson raid changed everything for him. The first debt Kruger owed to Jameson was that the raid had united the volk behind the Transvaal government, and at a stroke the fumbling old President became a national hero. The second debt was that the raid rallied the volk outside the borders of the Transvaal, especially in the Free Sate. Finally, and perhaps most importantly, the raid highlighted the deplorable state of the Transvaal burgher army. It brought to light the fact that almost one third of the burghers had no rifles, and that a large percentage of the remainder could only muster antiquated and dangerously inefficient weapons. Moreover, there was only sufficient ammunition in the state armoury to make war for a fortnight.

Kruger immediately set about modernising and re-equipping the Transvaal militia at a cost of well over a million pounds. He made provisions for some 37,000 state of the art Mauser rifles, to be purchased from the Krupp Works in Germany. These were to be in addition to a second, backup, rifle for every fighting burgher. At the same time he established an excellent artillery corps, providing it with 22 of the most modern field-pieces from Creusot in France, 4 of the latest 155mm heavy guns (Long Toms), 14 75mm Creusots, 4 Krupp 120mm howitzers, and 25 Maxim-Nordenfeld 1pdr Pom-Poms. As a result, Kruger could mobilize, within a week, 20 fully armed and fully equipped commandos; an effective fighting force of over 25,000 men plus a further 15,000 that he could call on from his allies in the Free State. This made a combined army four times the size of all the British garrisons in the two republics, and the largest modern fighting unit in the entire sub-continent.

But Kruger still had one more problem to overcome – to modernize the Republic without alienating his deeply conservative burghers, and to make concessions to the Uitlanders without risking his country's independence. To do so he appointed Jan Smuts to sweep clean the 'Augean Stables' of the Transvaal administration. Smuts flung himself into his work with single-mindedness, working ceaselessly to reform the shortcomings and corruption of the administration. All this effort and zeal brought Smuts face-to-face with a new political problem, namely that of the coloured people who were British subjects. In a conscientious attempt at settling the matter effectively and amicably, he arranged to discuss the matter with the British Agent in Pretoria, Edmund Fraser. Smuts had been encouraged by reports in the press about a most conciliatory speech delivered in Grahamstown by Gen. Sir William Butler, who was holding the fort while Milner was on leave in London. Butler was quoted as saying *'Unity is strength, but it should be a union of hearts, not a union forced under pressure. To my mind, South Africa needs no surgical operations – it needs rest and peace'*

With these sentiments in mind, Smuts discussed his problems openly with Fraser, when suddenly, to Smuts' intense surprise, Fraser launched into an extraordinary outburst, which Smuts later recorded as follows:
'Fraser: We have now sat still for two years because our own officials put us in a false position in the Raid. The time has now come to take action.
Smuts: Action? Could you explain what you mean?
Fraser: Well, you see, Gladstone made a great mistake in handing you back the Transvaal after Majuba and before (instead of) defeating your army. It encouraged your idea of a great Afrikaner republic throughout South Africa. If you ask my opinion, the time has now come for us to end this nonsense by striking a blow. We've got to show who's the boss in South Africa.
Smuts: But whatever would give you occasion for this?
Fraser: England's fed-up with the administration of this country, and especially with the mal-treatment of British subjects. This is the point on which England will take action. I know perfectly well that England won't go to war over abstract subjects like suzerainty – that means nothing to the man in the street. She'll go to war over things that everyone can understand'

Smuts was left gasping by the interview – what was the meaning of these threats? Was it the opening of a new and extremely dangerous phase in the endless wrangle between the two giants? Were the British seeking a 'causus belli'? He did not have to wait too long to learn the meaning of the puzzle - already reports were coming in of protest meetings in Johannesburg – the British 'Uitlanders Reform Committee' was in an uproar again, and intending to petition the British government to intervene on its behalf. And the cause of all this was that an Englishman called Edgar had been shot dead by a trigger-happy ZARP (Zuid Afrikaansche Rijende Politie or South African Mounted Police). In itself it was a small event, but it proved to be the pebble that started the avalanche.

In the fifteen years since the opening of the goldfields, Johannesburg had grown into a city of more than 50,000 inhabitants, with perhaps as many again living in the many townships scattered over the Rand. They had arrived from all over Africa and the world, a huge pool of white, black, brown and yellow workers from every continent and from every corner of the world. Under these vast and composite layers of Brits, Boers, Dutch, German, French, Americans, Africans, Asians and the rest, Johannesburg felt just like a British colonial city, far more so than Cape Town, Port Elizabeth or even Durban. It was this feeling of 'British-ness' that lay close to the hearts of the Uitlanders, those foreign workers who had flocked to the Rand in search for gold.

The Uitlander leaders had a grievance that added seriously to the antagonism they bore against the Transvaal government. In 1898, nearly fifteen years after the rush, very few of them were enfranchised, although many of them felt that they were legally eligible for it. Under the original Transvaal franchise law they had had this option after five years residence, so by now the majority of the 60,000 male Uitlanders would have been able to exercise it if they so wished. This would have given them political equality with the 30,000 Boer voters, and collectively they could have taken over the control of the state. For very obvious reasons Kruger had changed the franchise law in 1888, raising the residence qualification from five to fourteen years. The aggrieved and disgruntled Uitlanders decided on a 'franchise now' priority in an effort to force Kruger to disgorge the vote and so let the control of Johannesburg, and in consequence the Transvaal, pass on to the British. Percy Fitzpatrick, a leading protagonist in this movement was an important employee of the Wernher-Beit mining house, and a confidant of Milner. Fitzpatrick had made the most of the Edgar affair in order to foster discontent amongst the Uitlanders. His efforts were richly rewarded when on Christmas Eve 1898 about 5,000 demonstrators marched to the Standard Buildings in the heart of the city's business area, where the British Consul had his office. On the balcony the leaders of the Edgar Relief Committee, the 'Reformers' and the 'Leaguers' stood bare-headed and listened to the reading of a 'humble petition' to Her British Majesty Queen Victoria, from her loyal Subjects resident on the Witwatersrand Goldfields. The petition '*begged Her Majesty to extend Her protection to their own lives and liberties and to take such action as might be necessary to terminate the present intolerable state of affairs*'

It was now that Jan Smuts, Kruger's new and brilliant young States Attorney, in a dramatic bid to forestall imperial intervention, made a dazzling offer of a 'general settlement' with the mining companies. It was named 'The Great Deal', and it was a difficult stroke to counter because the 'Deal' offered important concessions to the mining industry which consequently found favour and full support from the huge mining houses in Johannesburg and London. With the 'Great Deal' Kruger offered direct inducements to the mining houses such as preferential mining rights and more acceptable mining taxes. To the Uitlanders he offered a major concession by promising to recommend to the Volksraad that they should restore their right to vote after five years residence in the Transvaal, although this was only to date from the time they applied for Boer citizenship. In exchange, the Rand firms were required to make some concessions on their part such as their acquiescence on the continuation of the hated dynamite monopoly. From Britain pledges were sought on some political matters such as backing the Transvaal's stand against claims from the 'Cape Coloured' and the 'Coolie' traders, the clamping down on the agitation of the anti-Boer press, and the repudiation of 'the political mischief-makers amongst the more radical Uitlander leaders.

Fitzpatrick, now more determined than ever to invoke British occupation, prematurely leaked the contents of the 'Great Deal' to the London press, resulting in the total collapse of the negotiations and the alienation of the gold bosses. This left him free to go to Cape Town and hand over a petition signed by 21,000 British subjects on the Rand calling on the British government to intervene. What Fitzpatrick was offering Milner, was in effect a powerful triple alliance – Britain, the Uitlanders and Wernher-Beit, the giant of the Rand. In Fitzpatrick Milner had found a soul mate, sharing in every respect the burning desire for formal British military intervention in the Transvaal. They now agreed that they would, together, each in his own sphere of influence, make every possible effort to sway the British government, the Press and the Public to come round to their own way of thinking. Milner in particular, was aware that it was going to be a long and arduous road to travel, but felt certain that if he went about it carefully and methodically, he would succeed in the end.

However, the fact was that in England at this time, the threat to British supremacy in South Africa was still only 'a matter of faint interest', and that the British public took little or no interest in any South African issue, and that certainly included the question of franchise. Consequently, Milner had to work hard to get the British cabinet to consider the contents of the petition, and his best chance of success was via his powerful and influential friend, the Colonial Secretary Joe Chamberlain. Chamberlain himself, was becoming increasingly concerned - even disturbed - over the lack of interest displayed by both the British government as well as the British public, in the state of affairs in South Africa, so to stir matters up a bit, he asked Milner to publish a Blue Book for consideration by the Cabinet. This was at last the chance that Milner had been waiting for, and within a few days, he cabled one of the most flamboyant despatches ever sent by a Viceroy; it was to become known as the 'Helot Despatch'. In it Milner wrote –'The case for intervention is overwhelming....The spectacle of thousands of British subjects kept permanently in the position of helots... calling vainly to Her Majesty's Government for redress... a ceaseless stream of malignant lies about the intentions of the British government'. In reply Milner received a despatch from Chamberlain – it read.. 'The Despatch is approved. We have adopted your suggestion...'

Matters now moved swiftly, and a fortnight later Kruger's moderate allies in the Cape, Hofmeyr and Schreiner, leaders of the Cape Afrikaners, proposed that Milner should meet with Kruger to try and settle matters face-to-face. President Steyn of the Free State offered Bloemfontein as a neutral venue for the meeting.

The Bloemfontein Conference – 31/5/1899 to 5/6/1899
The proceedings opened on the morning of the 31st May, and throughout the first day Milner played his part admirably, telling Kruger that he had no wish to apportion any blame, but that in the existing deplorable situation it was his personal opinion that the increasing tension was being caused by the Transvaal's policies towards the Uitlanders. If this could be cleared out of the way satisfactorily, then all the other outstanding questions of contention could be settled swiftly, effectively and amicably. He then put his hand on his heart, and told Kruger that Britain had no designs on the independence of the Transvaal. If only the Transvaal would treat the Uitlanders better, they would cease to call on Great Britain to intervene, and that would in turn strengthen the independence of the Republic, as well as re-establish the cordial relations that everyone desired.

Kruger's reply was the expected one – the political demands of the Uitlanders conflicted with the national rights of the Transvaal because of the serious threat of the new burghers outvoting the old burghers, and in so doing turn the laws topsy-turvy to the benefit of the newcomers and the detriment of the established way of life and law. In short, he, Kruger, and his fellow Boers would lose their independence. *'If we give them the franchise tomorrow, we may as well give up the Republic'.* Notwithstanding this, Milner then urged Kruger to go the whole hog – give the Uitlanders back the 5-year franchise, and make it retrospective, to which Kruger replied in the same dogged refrain – 'no chance at all of a 5-year franchise – it would be political suicide for the volk'

On the third day of the conference, Kruger sprang a surprise, layimg on the table a 'complete Reform Bill' including its clauses, and even its sub-clauses - *'he must have had it in his back pocket all the time'* Milner cabled London. Kruger was offering a deal on the franchise question, which was considered to be 'a great advance' on the existing position. He was prepared to slash the residence qualification from fourteen to seven years. It would not give substantial and immediate representation to the Uitlanders because it was only partially retrospective, and the length of delay could vary according to a sliding scale. He also offered the gold mining districts five out of the twenty-eight seats in the Raad. In return he wanted Milner to meet him on three outstanding questions – the Raid indemnity, the Boer control of Swaziland, and most important of all, arbitration on rival interpretations of the 1884 London Convention.

If Milner truly wanted to do business here was the golden opportunity. On the question of franchise the gap was well-nigh bridged – seven years for five and five seats against seven – and as far as the other demands were concerned Milner had been given a remarkably free hand from Chamberlain, who had already agreed in principle for considerable damages for the Raid, and the arbitration question was not an insurmountable one. The question of Swaziland was more complicated, but it was possible that some kind of compromise may eventually be agreed. It was now that the path to reconciliation could have been smoothed out if only Milner was disposed to negotiate. But it was not peace, nor even voting rights for the Uitlanders, which he sought – his goal was the total conquest of the Transvaal by any means whatsoever, even war. As a result, he proceeded to 'screw' Kruger as Chamberlain had put it, and brushed aside the Reform Bill, calling it a 'Kaffir Bargain'. He then goaded Kruger by asking for 'some form of self-government' for the Rand, to which Kruger replied, his weak eyes watering profusely, 'It is my country you want'. Milner's response was to close the proceedings without further ado with the chilling words – *This conference is absolutely at an end and there is no obligation from either side arising from it'*.

After Bloemfontein
The breakdown of negotiations at the Bloemfontein Conference left many matters hanging in the air. It was obvious that both Kruger and Smuts were troubled at the 'inevitability' of armed conflict, while Milner was frustrated at being out-manoeuvred by Kruger. He expressed the 'fear' that war was now inevitable and made three proposals to London – Britain to send at once an 'overwhelming force, perhaps as many as 10,000 men' to South Africa. Secondly, to replace General Sir William Butler, the Commander-in-Chief in South Africa, with a British general, politically and militarily capable of doing the job, and finally to push most of the reinforcements forward to the frontier land of northern Natal. Wolesley, the Commander-in-Chief of the British Army reacted favourably to Milner's suggestions, even to the extent of increasing the number from 10,000 to 35,000. However, instead of the troops leaving immediately for South Africa, Lord Lansdowne, the Secretary of State for War, an 'Indian' rival to the 'African' Wolesley, frittered about for months without doing anything positive in this regard.

The failure of the Bloemfontein Conference had greatly increased the risk of war, and no one, not even Lansdowne, could now deny it. He and his advisors at the War Office were reluctantly obliged to face the three military proposals made by Milner. Yet even now Lansdowne's prevarication was typically characteristic - his immediate reaction to Wolseley's demands was insipid and rife with meaningless and ineffective counter-proposals. Wolseley was furious and countered with a triple salvo of minutes proposing a 'forward' policy. He repeated his previous request - equip Buller with 35,000 men and exercise them on the Salisbury Plain in order to 'terrify Kruger'. Secondly, procure transport for South Africa of 11,000 mules at the cost of £500,000, and thirdly, send out a first instalment of 10,000 troops to South Africa at once.

There was now no doubt at all, regardless of what was happening that Britain was preparing for a war to annihilate the Transvaal Republic and to bring it into her empire. It was obvious too, that Kruger was also preparing for war if that was what was required to safeguard the freedom and independence of his Volk. Yet during all this time Kruger's allies in the Cape, the Free State and even among the more forward thinking 'Young Turks' in the Transvaal, Smuts, De la Rey and others, were pressing him hard to find an equitable solution to the Uitlander problem, and so to stave off the looming threat of war. Chamberlain, Wolseley and Milner were by now too far down the road to armed conflict to be swayed or even influenced by 'side issues' such as the franchise question. This became clear when, on the 19th July, Kruger once again offered substantial political concessions, including a fully retrospective 7-year franchise. But Wolseley had by now convinced himself that Kruger was irredeemable, and just 'buying time' to complete his preparation for the war that was bound to come.

In South Africa, Milner continued to pursue his ultimate goal – to provoke a war and thereby annexe the Transvaal for the Empire. So intent was he about the total downfall of the Kruger regime that he had made it widely known that the President could in no way be trusted, and that all his attempts at conciliation were pure 'sham'. He warned that Kruger's sole aim was to put the British off their guard, and to gain time for the final and irrevocable showdown between his Volk and the British Empire.

Even while London was ostensibly seeking, for political and logistical reasons, all possible means of putting off an immediate confrontation, Milner and his allies in Johannesburg and London were stoking tension throughout South Africa. On the Rand, the Uitlanders, who had in early June, declared them selves in support of the Bloemfontein franchise offer, now stiffened their terms. They formed an 'Uitlander Council', a sort of Uitlander parliament, dominated by members of the Reform Committee, which proceeded to make new demands of the most provocative kind; Kruger must dismantle the forces and disarm his people; immediate and radical reform of the franchise, and redistribution of seats in the Raad; in other words, a political take-over.

On the 18th July, details of Kruger's latest offer - a retrospective 7-year franchise - were revealed. It came as a result of strong pressure on him from his allies throughout the country – Abraham Fischer, the State Secretary of the Free State, Schreiner, the Cape Prime Minister, Hofmeyr and other sympathetic Afrikaners in the Cape and the Free State. Chamberlain, influenced by Milner, believed that Kruger was 'trying it on', and that, whenever an overt display of a mighty military presence was made, he would capitulate unconditionally. He suggested to Lord Salisbury, the British Prime Minister, as well as to Milner, that the diplomatic screw be turned tight on Kruger until the details of the settlement were finally and satisfactorily concluded. They demanded to know exactly what the effects of the 7-year franchise would be – how many Uitlanders would immediately be offered the vote – how many would take it – how would the new voting power be distributed in the Raad, and so on. Chamberlain insisted that a joint enquiry be held to establish whether the new franchise would meet the principle of giving the Uitlanders 'immediate and substantial' representation. It was a cool, rational attempt at ending a century of wrangling between Britain and the Transvaal, and if the two had trusted each other just a tiny bit, it may very well have succeeded. In reality however, by now, Kruger and Chamberlain were so suspicious of each other that neither remotely believed in any form of diplomatic or political solution and it came as no surprise when Kruger bluntly rejected Chamberlain's proposal on the grounds that it posed a threat to his country's independence.

Then, out of the blue, some extra-ordinary news reached Chamberlain. Kruger, under extreme pressure from his Afrikaner friends in the Cape, had made 'another climb-down' - and this time it seemed to be 'really complete'. And so it was, for on the face of it his offer went beyond the Bloemfontein minimum – a 5-year franchise and ten seats in the Raad, a quarter of its Members, for the Goldfields, which made it three more than that offered at Bloemfontein. In Britain, the news was not only welcome, it seemed that at last 'peace had broken out'. But once again peace was not what Milner wanted. He was now more than ever convinced that Kruger's offer was a sham and that, at the final count, the matter would only be resolved if and when Britain took to arms and forcibly removed Kruger and his cronies, killed the Volksraad and took over the Transvaal as a Crown Colony within the British Empire.

On the 31st August Milner delivered an impassioned appeal to Chamberlain arguing that Kruger would 'bluff his way up to the cannon mouth', and implored him to expedite the long overdue 'big expedition' to South Africa as he was convinced that this would 'bring Kruger to his knees'. He solemnly warned Chamberlain that, unless the troops were sent in soon, there would be a 'break-away of our people'; meaning the Uitlanders and the Wernher-Beit Corporation. Milner's *cri de coeur* was answered – Chamberlain was sufficiently influenced to swing back to his support for armed intervention, and in Britain, the pace of events leading in that direction was perceptibly accelerated. The impetuosity which he for so long kept in check, now found public expression in a return to the caustic language of his earlier days – '*Mr. Kruger procrastinates – he dribbles out reforms like water from a squeezed sponge – but now the sands are running down*'

Chamberlain's utterances and correspondence concerning South Africa was criticised at this stage as being devoid of diplomatic tact and ethical content, especially in contrast to Gladstone's plea for 'righteousness in foreign affairs'. But for Chamberlain the ethic was now no longer a matter of the suppressive treatment of British subjects, nor the economic advantages of territorial gain. It was now that of 'British Paramountcy', For him that <u>was</u> an ethic – it meant '*British paramountcy is good – its overthrow is bad*'. Chamberlain added, '*I believe that the British race is the greatest of governing races that the world has ever seen, and in South Africa there is now no way out except total reform in the Transvaal, or war. And of the two, the latter would be most effective and most desirable*'

And that was it – now there was no turning back. There followed a frenetic race to get all the pieces on the board as quickly as possible. Wolseley consulted his old colleague, Gen. Sir John Ardagh, Director General of the Intelligence Department at the War Office, with a request to assess 'the Boer's capacity for war'. Ardagh replied that he was inclined to believe that the Boers would adopt a raiding strategy, and not confront the British in pitched engagements. He then listed a number of Boer military characteristics based on his Department's recent research deductions as printed in an eighty-nine page booklet entitled: 'Military Notes on the Dutch Republics'

Ardagh predicted correctly, that the two republics together would field a potential invasion force of 34,000 men armed with the latest in guns and rifles. Then, after that, he got it all wrong. He assured Wolseley that the Boers were not to be feared as a serious military adversary. As fighting men, they were inferior to their compatriots, who had beaten Colley's small force at Majuba. He then went on to say that:

(a) Boer generals, used to fighting Kaffirs, knew nothing about handling large bodies of men.

(b) The officers would be unable to cope with the problems of transport and supply.

(c) Boer efficiency would be seriously impeded by indiscipline.

(d) Their new artillery, the Krupp and Creusot field-guns were inferior to Britain's Armstrongs and that their guns would seriously hinder them if they tried to adapt them to any of their guerrilla tactics.

(e) They had a 'fearful' dread' of British cavalry and had yet to taste the effects of a modern artillery shrapnel barrage.

(f) Far from the Boers being able to invade successfully, an 'adequate' force of British infantry, supported by artillery, would, itself, have no difficulties in invading the Republics.

Just how did the Intelligence Department come to these conclusions, so astoundingly incorrect in the light of subsequent developments? The answer is given in the Military Notes itself, which stated – *'The Boer is not regarded as a serious military adversary..'* and which concludes, majestically, *'It appears certain that, after one serious defeat, they would be too deficient in discipline and organisation to make any further real stand'*

The Cabinet was informed on the 8th September of Britain's intention to go to war, and that urgent sanctions would be sought from the House to put into effect a substantial armament programme as soon as possible. They were informed that there were some 12,000 British soldiers scattered all over South Africa, and that authorisation had been received to raise a force of 10,000 men from India under Sir George White, which was to be sent to South Africa immediately. Orders were also issued for the mobilisation of an Army Corps of 50,000 men under the command of Gen. Sir Redvers Buller. This activity in London was the final signal for Kruger to move quickly. His strategy would be to strike hard, far and fast, before the arrival of White's reinforcements from India. On the 27th September he was ready to telegraph the 'commando order' to set in motion the assembly of fully armed and ready for combat burghers from across the nation under their local elected commandants and veld-kornets. War was now a matter of weeks, days, even hours. Britain had prepared a 'final ultimatum' which was being held back because the Natal Governor, whilst alerting the authorities of commando activity in the region of Laing's Nek in northern Natal, did not think that they would be 'so crack-brained as to strike the first blow'.

On the 2nd October the Volksraad officially approved war and agreed to send their own ultimatum to the British. In the meantime, White and his reinforcements had arrived in Durban just in the nick of time, for on that very same day the Boer ultimatum was drafted, calling on the British government to withdraw its troops from the frontiers and send away all reinforcements. Chamberlain received it of Tuesday 10th October 1899 at 6.15 a.m. and was angered because he never expected Kruger to assume the onus of aggression so clearly. That evening the British government cabled the Queen's rejection of the Boer demands, and Chamberlain informed the House of the Boer's declaration of war and, speaking for nigh on three hours, defended his own position and that of the Government, finally carrying the day triumphantly by 362 votes to 135. *'Very, very good,'* commented the Queen, when the speech was read to her at Balmoral, *'I am delighted with it'*. And so was Milner who at last had got his war for which he had strived so assiduously, and even as he rejoiced the echo of rifles was cracking sharply and loudly across the South African veld...!

9
OPPOSING FORCES and STRATEGIES

At the outbreak of hostilities, the combined forces of the two Boer republics amounted to a little more than 40,000 men. Although these included small contingents of professional soldiers, the bulk was essentially a civilian militia. The Boers decided to opt for an aggressive strategy, especially since the majority of the British reinforcements was still on the high seas. The plan was to strike swiftly against the existing British garrisons, inflicting serious damage on them, and thus drawing them to the negotiating table in order to conclude a favourable political resolution to the situation; and all this before Britain could bring her full might to bear. The invasion took place across several fronts – in the west at Kimberley and Mafeking, and in the Northern Cape at Stormburg. But by far the biggest thrust was in the east where the main forces of the Transvaal Republic where gathered. The commander of the Transvaal contingent was Commandant-General Piet Joubert. He was supported by several Free State commandos who had gathered along the passes through the Drakensberg, between the Orange Free State into Natal. Joubert rapidly moved into Natal at Laing's Nek, under the very shadow of Majuba, Colley's "hill of destiny".

In spite of the years of tension leading up to this moment, the outbreak of hostilities found the British Army singularly unprepared. The commander on the spot, Sir William Butler, had steadfastly refused to admit the inevitability of armed conflict, and failed to make any contingency plans. His successor, Gen. Penn-Symons, was of a more aggressive state of mind, but Britain had scarcely more than 12,000 troops in South Africa at the time of the Boer invasion. In London, the Commander-in-Chief, Sir Garnet Wolesley, had energetically urged the government to mobilise the army and its reserves immediately, but by now he was aging and in bad health, and had lost his one-time 'thrust and vigour of the very model modern Major General'. In addition, the army of that time was rotten with petty jealousies and rivalries at the very highest level, and it took several weeks for an Army Corps to be raised in Britain. In the meantime, whilst awaiting the arrival of White's reinforcement from India, the local commander, Penn-Symons, planned to check the Boer advance below the Drakensberg before it could threaten the larger settlements and towns further south.

Shortly after the outbreak of hostilities both Kimberley and Mafeking were quickly surrounded by the Boers. The British were, however, very reluctant and unwilling to risk the heavy cost of a direct attack and just bogged down instead. As a result, unlike their comrades in Natal, they were virtually out of the war until the arrival several months later of British forces under Roberts and Kitchener.

The Boers
As at Bronkhorstspruit and Majuba some twenty years before, the Transvaal possessed no established 'army' in the conventional concept of regiments, officers, non-commissioned officers, barracks, and parade ground discipline. Instead, they went into battle as an armed citizen militia consisting of individual fighting units emanating from all the administrative districts of the Republic. In times of crisis, every region was

required to provide a mounted commando under the leadership of a 'commandant' and to take to the field within forty-eight hours of announcement of mobilisation. The task of bringing the men together fell to the "veld-kornets", two or three elected men from each district. All able bodied males from sixteen to sixty were obliged to turn out, fully equipped with a horse, a saddle, a rifle and ammunition, and rations for eight days.

The commandos varied in strength according to the size of the population of any particular area. At the start of the war most averaged about 1,000 men apiece, but figures as low as 200 and as high as 3,000 were not uncommon. In civilian life, each district was broken down into "wards" administered by a "veld-kornet" who served as a local magistrate, and in war doubled as a junior officer in the commando where he was serving. A commando would, therefore, have an elected commander, the Commandant, assisted by veld-kornets. The only other officials were "corporals", individuals elected to represent informal groups of burghers camping together Neither commandants nor veld-kornets possessed any legal power to discipline the men under their command – most had to count on the strength of their personality to ensure disciplinary compliance. A commandant could issue orders, but he could not oblige his men to obey them – if they disagreed with any order, the burghers were quite at liberty to ignore it. Nor could they be prevented from taking leave whenever they chose to do so: with farms and families at home to attend to, it was quite understandable that periodic absences from the front were necessary and inevitable.

Every burgher was by nature an expert rider, and because he was accustomed to hunting for provisions, a superb marksman. They fought in their everyday farming clothes with no bright uniforms or insignias to distinguish them from the natural colours of the veld. For them warfare was a necessary business to be accomplished as quickly and effectively as possible and at a minimum cost to one's self. Their fighting was best done at long range with the rifle, while hand-to-hand combat was to be avoided at all cost, for death in battle carried too heavy a penalty for the burgher's family left to fend for itself back home on the hostile veld. The highly mobile Boer commandoes traditionally lived off the land, and required very little in the way of a baggage train. The Boer was, in short, the forerunner of the hit-and-run guerrilla soldier of modern times.

The Boers made extensive use of black Africans; as they had no formal supply and commissariat departments, each man had to forage for himself. As a result, many took their black servants with them to the front. Known as "agter-ryers" (rear-riders), their duties were to lead spare horses, drive wagons, cook, and wash-up, and, as the war progressed, they were increasingly used for scouting and spying purposes.

By 1899 both republics had made some attempt to add a professional element to their forces. In 1880, the Orange Free State had created the "Free State Artillery", commanded by a German volunteer soldier, Maj. Albrecht, and by 1899, it had over twenty guns manned by well-trained and efficient men. The Transvaal too, had a regular artillery unit, the "Staatsatillerie", which at the start of the war, boasted a personnel of 650 men servicing four heavy 150mm Creusot siege guns, plus about fifty other Creusot and Krupp 75mm guns with a range of over 8,000 yards. They also had numerous quick firing 1lb Maxim-Nordfelt "pom-poms" The gunners wore fine military uniforms based on Austrian and Dutch styles. The Boers did not deploy their guns "European style" in batteries and detachments, but used them instead singly behind emplacements, moving about swiftly from place to place to command a better field of fire or to avoid enemy detection. Both Republics also fielded police units trained to fight as soldiers. In 1899, the Transvaal fielded about 400 "ZARP's" (Zuid Afrikaansche Rijende Politie), while the Free State had about 150 white men and a number of black auxiliaries. The Boers were also assisted by a small number of foreign volunteers consisting of individuals and units from Ireland, the United States of America, Italy, Germany, Holland, Scandinavia, and many fellow Afrikaners from the British controlled Cape Colony and Natal.

.

On the eve of the conflict, the Transvaal had imported thousands of modern weapons. In the early 1890's Joubert had ordered a large number of single-shot Martini-Henry rifles, but by 1895 they were already becoming obsolete. At Kruger's insistence, they switched to the 1896 model German 7mm Mauser, which was a highly efficient and accurate weapon, sighted to a maximum range of 2,000 yards and equipped with a magazine containing five rounds of ammunition loaded into the breach with a clip, making it singularly fast and simple to re-load. The bullets were primed with smokeless powder, which made it impossible to be detected when it was sited in a concealed position, and very often, it was just the distinctive double crack of the shot that provided the only indication of the user's presence.

At the time of the outbreak of the war, Piet Joubert held the five-year post of Commandant-General. There was no Staff, nor Intelligence Services to support him; he merely out-ranked the other local commandants. To assist him in critical situations the government maintained the right to appoint "Vecht-Commandants" - field or fighting generals - selecting them in accordance with their combat and tactical abilities, and giving them a command whenever a particular situation demanded it. Most command decisions were taken at a "krijgsraad", or council of war, at which anyone had the right to speak – individuals could refuse to endorse the decisions of the council, but if they did give it their support they were then morally bound to follow it's actions. Because of this general absence of formalised discipline and obedience, the British tended to disregard the Boer as an inefficient and ill-disciplined fighting entity, often sadly to their very dear cost, as it turned out.

The British
The British Army in contrast, was a well organised, a disciplined and well- equipped regular force of men under arms. At the outbreak of the war in October 1899 it boasted a total of 106,000 men with the colours, and a further 78,000 men with the reserves. It was an army geared to the needs of policing the Empire at its zenith, and during Victoria's reign there was scarcely a corner of the world in which it had not fought, from Ashante on the Gold Coast to China, from Afghanistan and India to the South Island of New Zealand. Yet at the close of the nineteenth century, the practical legacy of all this action totally eluded the comprehension of the British military establishment, whose ingrained attitudes in respect of battle drill and tactics precluded any deviation from their unimaginative and drearily traditional methods of warfare. As a result, instead of drawing from sorely tested lessons learned from the new mobile, open

skirmish type of warfare as that recently experienced in Afghanistan and elsewhere in the Empire, they stubbornly continued to adhere to the age-old attitudes of parade-ground precision, and close order frontal encounters on the battle arena. As a consequence it was widely held that the most effective tactic of engagement was that of a heavy bombardment followed by a close-order marching advance, with the troops pausing occasionally to deliver volley fire. It was reasoned that these 'well tested' formations were not only the easiest to teach the men, but allowed the officers to maintain maximum mass control. Independent firing was frowned on, not only because it lacked the frightening effect of volley fire, but also because it wasted valuable ammunition. Sometimes open-order formation was permitted, as well as the use of cover, but both were strictly subordinated to the need to maintain formation and impetus. These tactics had served admirably in recent campaigns in the Sudan, but they had made no provision to allow a soldier to act on his own account or initiative, and certainly did nothing to develop individual marksmanship.

However, on the surface all this was deemed to be of little significance because there were few on the British side in 1899 that did not believe that the Boer farmers would not quail before the steady line of bayonets advancing towards them in disciplined formation. Alas, in due course they would be proved horribly wrong, for despite their enormous superiority in man-power and military hardware, the mental rigidity and over reliance on discipline and blind obedience prevailing at that time in the British army made it singularly unsuited to the impending clashes with a foe whose abiding characteristics were independence and agility of mind.

Since the Zulu Wars in 1879 and the first Boer War in 1880, the army had abandoned the scarlet and blue uniforms in favour of the drabber and less conspicuous sandy coloured khaki field uniforms, and standard khaki foreign-service helmets. The officers, too, who initially went into battle with shoulder pips, brown Sam Browne belts, revolvers and swords, duly abandoned all outward trappings of rank, and fought with rifle in hand like the men around them.The infantry carried bolt-action .303 magazine rifles, either the Lee Metford or the newer Lee Enfield. Both were sighted up to 2,800 yards but with an effective range of between 500- and 800 yards. The magazines contained ten rounds but these had to be loaded individually, which rendered it much slower than the five-round clip magazine of the Boer Mauser. The infantry also carried a knife-bladed bayonet, whilst cavalry regiments were armed with short Lee-Enfield carbines and swords, and for the Lance regiments, a 9-ft bamboo lance. Both infantry and cavalry regiments had Maxim machine guns attached for support, but they were never fully utilised or appreciated as a weapon of assault or defence, and consequently were hardly ever integrated into a plan of tactical thinking

The backbone of the British regimental system was the infantry battalion – 800 men divided into eight companies of a hundred men apiece. Since the 1st Boer War, the old system of identifying units by number had been replaced as part of a territorial unit – for example, the old 58th regiment which had so badly been mauled at Majuba, was now known as the 2nd Battalion, Northamptonshire Regiment. A cavalry regiment usually consisted of 600 men, and artillery batteries, both Royal Horse and Royal Field Artillery, consisted of 6 breach loading guns, 12-pounders for the Lighter Horse and 15-pounders for field artillery. The 15-pounder could fire a shrapnel shell that exploded with an airburst, showering the target with lead balls to a range of 4,000 yards, and the high explosive shell somewhat further. Nevertheless it was still out-ranged by many of the Boer guns At this time artillery theorists were still committed to the concept of massed battery fire across open sights –communication systems had not yet been fully developed to allow for indirect fire – yet despite this the guns had no shield to protect them or their crews from return fire.

The Army Corps assembled in Britain during the crisis of 1899 consisted of thirty-three infantry battalions, a cavalry division of seven regiments, nineteen artillery batteries including three howitzers and four Horse Artillery batteries together with a Supply Corps, making a total of 47,000 men, almost half of whom were reservists. The Corps was divided into Divisions and Brigades but few of these had any experience of serving together. The Corps was placed under the command of General Sir Redvers Buller, one of the most highly regarded soldiers of his day. He took with him to South Africa only his personal staff, since the Corps was very short of adequately trained personnel, and they had to learn the lesson of working together in the painful school of active service.

At the time of the Boer invasion of Natal, he so-called "Indian" contingent of 10,000 men was already garrisoned in Natal. The Commander of this army was Lt. Gen. Sir George White, an associate of Lord Roberts, Wolesley's chief rival. Both White and Buller were light on cavalry – few in the establishment realised the extent to which cavalry would come to dominate a war which would be fought over huge areas, some still un-mapped, and most lacking roads. To some extent both Buller and White would eventually be able to rely on existing volunteer forces raised locally in the colonies, in particular the Cape Mounted Rifles (CMT), the Natal Carbineers (NC), and the Natal Mounted Police (NMP), all of whom had been trained in a more disciplined military version of the Boers' fighting methods. Other voluntary units came from the ranks of the "Uitlander" refugees the most important of them being Thorneycroft's Mounted Infantry (TMI), the South African Light Horse Infantry (SALHI) and Bethune's Mounted Infantry (BMI) and the "Uitlander Volunteers Contingent". Although they all proved to be remarkably successful, they could not match the skills of their Boer counterparts in the field.

Throughout most of the war the British Army's pace was limited to that of its infantry, and the huge trains of baggage-wagons required to sustain it in the field. This impediment would eventually prove to be a near fatal handicap in a war against a will-of-the-wisp enemy, consisting principally of extremely mobile mounted infantrymen.

10
BULLER'S WAR IN NATAL

The Invasion

In anticipation of the imminent outbreak of war, the Transvaal Commander, General Piet Joubert, strategically deployed his main force close to the Transvaal/Natal border astride the Pietermaritzburg/Pretoria railway line, positioning the left wing under the command of General 'Marula' Erasmus and the right under General Kock. A back-up force, under General Lukas Meyer, took up a tactically sound position away to the east in the area around Wakkerstroom in order to present a serious threat to the British right flank. Joubert's force totalled some 14,000 burghers and included the Staatsartillerie and units from the Dutch, German, and Irish Volunteer Corps. A further accumulation of about 6,000 Free State burghers under General Marthinus Prinsloo lay on the west of the Drakensberg mountain-range, in the area around Van Reenen's Pass, where they poised a serious threat to the British garrison in Ladysmith.

In October 1899 the commander of the British army in Natal was Sir George White, who had recently arrived with a last-minute reinforcement muster, which together with General Penn-Symons's original garrison of 4,000 men plus some volunteer units, raised locally from amongst the colonists, and some Uitlander refugees, constituted a well-equipped and sizeable army of more than 14,000 men. However, the effectiveness of this force was impaired by the fact that it was spread about at various places in the colony, and notably at Ladysmith where White sat with 8,000 troops and at Dundee, about forty-five miles to the north, where Penn-Symons had, in defiance of orders, previously moved with 4,000 men in order 'to be nearer the enemy'

On the night following the expiration of the Boer ultimatum, all the Boer forces were on the march, and advance units soon crossed into Natal. Within a few days, they were at Newcastle, while Joubert's forward wing under Erasmus moved on towards Dundee, where he established contact with Lukas Meyer, who had closed in from the left. The other wing, under General Kock, advanced on to Ladysmith from the north, while the Free State burghers crossed the Drakensberg, and were approaching Ladysmith from the west. White became increasingly anxious over the Boer incursions, especially as his own forces were divided between Dundee and Ladysmith, and both were in danger of being cut off from the rest of Natal. It was imperative for him to prevent the Boers from coming between himself and his force in the north, so he asked Penn-Symons to fall back at once and return to Ladysmith. The request was hesitant and vague because White was not quite sure of the exact strength or whereabouts of the Boer forces and because Penn-Symons had often openly aired his confidence in being able to deal successfully with the situation in the Dundee sector. In the event it all turned out to be too late because on the 19th October, before any further developments could take place, an advance guard of Kock's force poured into Elandslaagte, between Ladysmith and Dundee, captured a supply train, and completely severed all road, rail and telegraphic communication between White and Penn-Symons. The war in Natal had begun.

Dundee - Talana - Impati

Neither the threat of Elandslaagte nor that of Erasmus and Lukas Meyer ruffled Penn-Symons in any way. He informed White that he felt 'perfectly safe and dead against retreating' He rejected all reports about the skills of the Boers as 'ridiculous', and refused to listen to any reports about the proximity of the enemy forces. Dundee lies in a long shallow valley surrounded by low hills, excepting the flat-topped Impati that reared up some 1,500 ft on the north side of the town. Although it dominated the valley and the town and also contained the town's water supply, Penn-Symons made no effort to place any pickets on it. Nor did he bother about a pair of low hills much closer, some two miles east of Dundee – the nearest one called Talana. He discounted any possibility of the Boers occupying such positions, let alone hauling up artillery, and declared that no number of Boers would ever dare take on an entire brigade of the British Army.

The Boers were inundated with a constant stream of reports flowing in from loyal Afrikaners living and working in Dundee, and had very exact intelligence of the situation. They planned for Erasmus to occupy Impati, and Meyer to take Talana, thereby locking Dundee in the jaws of a nutcracker. On the night of the 19th October, in heavy rain, the two hills were occupied. During Meyer's ascent, he stumbled on a British patrol at about 2.30 a.m., but the sergeant of the patrol managed to get away and carry the alarm to the garrison. Penn-Symons was not disturbed in any way - it was merely a Boer raid, not worth bothering about, he said. When the mists lifted from the hills around 7 a.m. the whole crest line of Talana and the adjoining hill was crammed with Boers, and the next moment two shells came screaming into the town, the second landing in soft earth only a few yards from Penn-Symons's tent. His reaction was swift, and soon the infantry was lined up and at the same time the guns burst into action to rake the top of Talana. Not only were the Boer guns silenced but about a thousand of them fled down the hill and made away on their ponies. Others, however, stayed back and spreading themselves out strategically, they prepared for battle. Penn-Symons then ordered a frontal infantry assault on Talana, and sent the cavalry down the valley between Impati and Talana to cut off any Boer retreat. He ignored Erasmus and his 4,000 men on Impati, deciding that, if they were still there, he would deal with them later. Meanwhile he hurried his men on to Talana through a dry watercourse running from the town up to about a mile from the hill. The town was left defenceless and exposed on the left against Erasmus who was poised on Impati.

Beyond the watercourse a plantation extended to about a hundred yards from the foot of Talana, and the heavy fire plunging from the hill above, stripped the trees of their leaves, leaving the air heavy with gun-smoke, and the pungent smell of eucalyptus resin. The troops, in the face of this heavy fire, wavered before finding protection behind a wall at the end of the plantation, while the artillery, which was ordered to come in closer, systematically and relentlessly pounded away at Talana. The inexperienced Boer gunners were quickly subdued, and unfortunately for them, Lukas Meyer had led most of his troops with him up the hill adjoining Talana, leaving only some 400 to 500 Boers to defend Talana. Like Erasmus on Impati, he made no attempt to help the Boers on Talana, by for example, sweeping down on the British flank or into the town. Even so, the ferocity of the fire from the men on Talana continued to hold off the British from the foot of the hill. Penn-Symons grew impatient – he galloped up to the wall and stepped over to view the situation on the hill for himself. Suddenly he was struck in the stomach by Boer fire, and mortally wounded he was carried off the battlefield. This left General Yule, his second-in-command, to launch the assault. The Boer defence of Talana was a desperate one, and successive British attempts to rush the hill left dozens of prostrate khaki figures spread all over the slope. However, the artillery continued to pound the crest, while reinforcements painfully crept up to the top, and when the King's Royal Rifles eventually succeeded, they launched a fierce bayonet assault that thrust them forward until they crashed into a blinding barrage of Boer bullets. Incredibly more and more soldiers managed to haul themselves to the top, and eventually the British succeeded in sending the Boers flying. In the silence that gradually descended over the battlefield, all that was heard were the muffled and painful groans of the wounded.

Then suddenly, hell broke loose again as the crest of the hill was once more raked with gun-shrapnel, only this time it was British shells which burst amongst the troops. Their guns below, unaware that the hill had been won and invested by their own men, had resumed the assault, not only managing to clear the Boers off the hill but, unwittingly, their own comrades as well. Ironically, had the burghers discovered the mistake sooner, they could have re-occupied the hill without any problems at all but, instead, they continued their withdrawal from Talana and the adjoining hill, and streamed back over the valley and on to the distant horizon. The cavalry that Penn-Symons had posted specifically to deal with just such an eventuality, engaged with the fleeing Boers, but soon got themselves split into two groups. The smaller section finally managed to get safely back to camp, but the other, led by Maj. Moëller, thundered on towards Impati, and after a two hour engagement with Erasmus, was captured and became the conflict's first prisoners-of-war. They were led away to Joubert's encampment near Newcastle.

The battle of Talana, or Dundee, as it was sometimes called, was considered by the British to have been a splendid victory. However, the situation was now more critical than ever - the Boers were still in possession of Impati and the town's water supply, and were relatively unaffected by their casualties of about 150, and most important of all, they knew that they could attack again as a united force, at any place or at any time of their choosing. On the British side, in spite of the "victory", their commander lay dead, their force had been depleted by almost 550 casualties and their chances of direct escape to Ladysmith were nil since the Boers had captured Elandslaagte the day before the battle of Talana, and had cut off all means of escape, either by road or by rail. At Elandslaagte itself, Kock's force had now grown to over 1,000 fresh and fully rested men.

Back in Ladysmith, White's cavalry commander, General French, having just arrived, promptly captured a Boer patrol. This success lulled White into an unfounded confidence, so he ordered French and his chief-of-staff, Maj. Douglas Haig, to recapture Elandslaagte at dawn the following day.

Elandslaagte

Although French's dawn attack came as a total surprise, the Boers were too quick to be caught. They leapt onto their ponies and made for some nearby hills where they had two guns in position. Now it was French's turn for surprise. He was totally unprepared for the strength of the Boer counter-attack, and for the accuracy of their artillery fire, and he signalled Dundee for instructions. White resolved, in response, to strike hard at once, and rushed guns, horses, and infantry up to the front by road and rail. In charge of this reinforcement was Colonel Ian Hamilton, the third commanding officer at Elandslaagte that day who would go on to fight at senior command level in the 1st World War fourteen years later. The last of the reinforcements reached French by 3 p.m. when three 6-gun batteries began a preparatory bombardment. The force comprised 3,000 infantry, the Manchesters, Devons, Gordon Highlanders, and mounted troops, including the Imperial Light Horse made up largely of men from Johannesburg. The ridge behind the settlement was shaped like a huge horseshoe with the British occupying one arm and the Boers the other, and between the two, some three miles of flat and open veld. The Boer arm was shaped like a hogs back, with, at the open end, three small koppies clustered together, on which their guns were cradled.

Before the attack Hamilton addressed his infantry, and ordered the Devons to attack the hogs-back across the open veld directly below them, and the rest of the infantry to work along the curve of the horse-shoe extremity from their right front, and when reaching the beginning of the hogs-back, to roll up the whole of the Boer line. Contrary to the traditional close order battle tactics of the infantry, Hamilton made the Devons advance across the veld in an open formation never before seen in European warfare. He deployed his men at intervals of nearly a yard thus enabling them to advance unscathed, firing in volleys. Presently they were forced to crawl for cover behind the anthills, and finally at about a quarter of a mile from the enemy they came to a halt. The Boer gunners, out-numbered by eighteen to two were often silenced, but they stuck to their posts inflicting serious damage on the advancing British lines.

Meanwhile, the Manchesters led the flank attack along the curve of the horseshoe. They reached the hogs-back but could not gain a foothold. Then, taking advantage of a torrential downpour they rushed forward to the boulders strewn along the lower slopes. There the I.L.H. dismounted, and were reinforced by the Gordon Highlanders. However, the fury of the Boer fire checked them, but they rallied until a barbed wire fence, erected for farming purposes, again stopped them. As they cluttered around in groups, they were mown down by the intensity of the Boer fire, but one small group finally managed to   clear a way, and the Boers started to waver. Then the German detachment, which had been sheltering at a nearby farm, hurled itself recklessly upon the British right. In spite of their gallant efforts, they were soon forced to a halt by the I.L.H., but this assault did serve to give the Boers fresh spirit. A fresh attack was launched against the British that ended their advance and soon half their officers lay dead or wounded, and the slope was strewn with casualties sodden in blood and rain. However, with encouragement from Hamilton, the Gordons and the Devons renewed their efforts, and the men on the hogs-back gripped their bayonets and surged forward – faltered – rallied again and finally over-ran the crest, even over-running the still smoking guns as the Boer gunners continued to fire right up to the end. Suddenly, fifty Boers, who had been concealed in the rear of the crest, led by General Kock himself, forced the British back a hundred yards. The British commanders made forceful efforts to rally the men, Hamilton, French, and many others coming into the line to try to stem the panic. The colonel of the I.L.H. was mortally wounded during this onslaught, but gradually the men rallied and were joined by the Devons who emerged at that time from the plain. A wild three-minute combined assault finally overwhelmed the Boers, and the cease-fire rang out over the battlefield. The surviving burghers made their way back in the gloom on their ponies and into a trap that the Lancers and the Dragoons had set for them. The onslaught was too heavy for the fleeing Boers as the cavalry rode through them for a mile or so, piercing and hacking without quarter. When it was dark, the charge mercifully came to an end, but sadly for the Boers, not before their commander, General Kock was fatally wounded. He was gently lifted off the battlefield by the cavalry and carried back to Ladysmith.

The British victory at Elandslaagte was complete. The Boer general lay dying, half his force was killed, wounded, or captured, his two guns were taken as well as his laager, his supplies, and equipment. In addition, the Boer thrust to Ladysmith was thrown back, and the road and railway were once again safely in the hands of the British. Nevertheless, White was still very concerned. His forces had sustained serious casualties during the course of the battle, and worse by far, a messenger had just brought news that the Free State commandos were poised to attack Ladysmith, and that Joubert had resumed his advance with his main forces. As a result of these reports White decided to abandon Elandslaagte and retire his army to Ladysmith.

Back in Dundee Yule waited anxiously while the Boers sporadically shelled the town from the summit of Impati. He had asked White for support, but White was unable to oblige, so he found himself grappling with an important final decision - withdraw the troops and run the gauntlet of a gruelling and dangerous march of sixty-four miles over a bad, hostile and very difficult roundabout route at the height of the rainy season, or surrender to the enemy. As an option, submission was galling and unacceptable, so on the 23rd. Yule fell in his men and silently slipped out of Dundee into a providentially black night. The column slowly and painfully made its way over the hills, fearful of pursuit or ambush, and at dawn it had reached a spot some twelve miles to the south. During the ensuing day, the column continued to push on slowly, battling with storm-swollen rivers and nigh on impassable mud. Fortunately, for the British, during the night of the escape, a thick mist had descended on the surrounding hills and had blotted out Dundee from the Boers ensconced on Impati, and it was only late in the morning that they became aware of Yule's departure during the night.

On the second day of the march, White attempted to distract the commandos' attention from Yule's column. Four of his infantry battalions supported by artillery and mounted troops, attacked a party of Boers from the Free State dug in on some hills at Rietfontein, eight miles north of Ladysmith, to prevent them from joining up with the Transvaal commandos and cutting off the line of Yule's retreat. The outcome of White's foray was insignificant because, apart from achieving its limited objective, the Boers were still in command of the ridge of hills around Rietfontein, having hardly suffered any loss. The

British, on the other hand, had suffered 114 men killed or wounded, including the C.O. of the Gloucesters, Colonel Wilford, who inexplicably broke his cover at the height of the action to lead an entire company plus the battalion's Maxim gun, forward to destruction. Around noon of the fifth day after leaving Dundee, the escape-column arrived in Ladysmith in a dreadful state, with Yule critically ill, Penn-Symons dead and the entire national force of 14,000 men now locked up and effectively out of the war until Buller's army eventually relieved them 118 days later.

With the British army bound up in Ladysmith and the whole of the Natal midlands open to roam, the Boers rapidly approached Ladysmith with confidence, and on the 29th October they occupied the heights surrounding the town. On Pepworth Hill, the central and highest of the hills that formed a semi-circle around the town, they dug in one of their fearsome 94 pdr. Long Tom guns and set its sights on the centre of the town.

Ladysmith
Looking out from the town, to the right of Pepworth Hill, broken country sweeps around, via Long Hill, to a series of ridges on Farqhuar's Farm, lying some four miles to east of the town. On the left of Pepworth a valley leads from the plain to a hill called Tchrengula, continuing the semi-circle around to the west of the town. Somewhere in this western sector, the Free State commandos had taken up positions.

White decided first to tackle the Transvaal Boers whom he believed were occupying a line from Pepworth to Long Hill. He sent Col. Grimwood with a brigade, under cover of darkness to the ridges on Farqhuar's Farm. He ordered Grimwood to swing north at daybreak and, with the support of French's cavalry, attack the Boer flank on Long Hill. After that, he was to push on to Pepworth where a frontal assault by a force under Hamilton would burst in at the same time. To distract the Free State burghers and to cut off any retreat by the Transvaal commandos, White sent a column up the valley between Pepworth and Tchrengula to occupy the pass at Nicholson's Nek and so "lock the back door to the hills above". The column consisted of 1,000 Dublin Fusiliers and Gloucesters, under command of Colonel Carleton, and a string of mules carrying guns and spare ammunition. The mules, just recently arrived and unbroken, were restless, and with inadequately trained drivers, created a chaotic delay before they finally set off.

Grimwood reached Farqhuar's Farm safely, then wheeled to face Long Hill, and waited for dawn to start his surprise attack. In fact, there were indeed to be several surprises that morning, but they were all for Grimwood! At first light, he discovered that half his brigade had failed to keep up with the rest, and that French's cavalry was in the wrong position. Then, suddenly, 4,000 Mausers tore the dawn apart, raking his position with a storm of bullets that came, not from the supposed Boer flank on Long Hill, but from *his own* flank. For, while the bulk of the Transvaalers were indeed around Pepworth, none of them were on Long Hill, and those fighting under Lukas Meyer had all this time been skilfully deployed a little way back on the very same ridge that Grimwood was occupying.

Hastily Grimwood wheeled his men to the right while French's men dismounted to help him. The artillery also opened up but for a long time they wastefully pounded away at the deserted Long Hill. Early that morning the Long Tom on Pepworth Hill opened a salvo on Ladysmith, the first shell landing near the railway station with a tremendous explosion. Other guns scattered around the hills also opened up while the British guns covering Hamilton's advance on Pepworth Hill pushed forward to engage in a sustained gunnery duel with the Boers. The frontal attack, intended to combine with Grimwood's would-be flank assault, was slowed down by the artillery battle, during which the Long Tom was hit by a British salvo. Nevertheless, the Boer guns concealed on the surrounding hills, using smokeless powder continued, with telling accuracy, to the distress of the British forces. White's anxiety was further increased when new problems broke out in the mule train. Loose mules and straggling gunners began to arrive back in Ladysmith. Apparently, Carleton, fearing that his delayed departure would expose him at daybreak in the valley between Pepworth and Tchrengula, decided to spend the night on the latter rather than risking Nicholson's Nek in the dark. But, while climbing up the slopes of Tchrengula, the mules broke again in a stampede, running off with the spare supplies and ammunition. The noise, augmented by some panic firing by some of the men, brought the Boers swarming to the position, and in the confusion Carleton's situation was turned into chaotic disorder.

White, in the meanwhile, was trying desperately to make contact with Carleton by heliograph, and failing to get any response at all, was unable to send any of the reinforcements which were steadily arriving from behind, because he was not quite sure where Carleton's forces were actually situated at that time. Instead, he diverted the reinforcements to Farqhuar's Farm where Grimwood's position was fast deteriorating. The troops were pinned to the edge for hours under the blistering sun, and were unable to advance. Boer tactics, deployed by the newly appointed vecht-generaal, Louis Botha, were superior to those of the British and their determination turned them into a formidable and dangerous foe. Botha's instinctive grasp of leadership was such that his men threatened at any moment to sweep Grimwood clean off the ridges.

Growing tension and unrest in Ladysmith was threatening to turn into panic and White eventually gave the order for all troops to "retire as opportunity offers" His signals to Carleton on Tchrengula continued to remain unanswered, but Hamilton's men in front of Pepworth started to retreat in good order. However, when the men at Farqhuar's Farm at last moved from their ordeal, Botha's men opened up on them with the full power of their 4,000 Mausers, forcing them to flee in panic. The Boers rushed to the edge of the ridge with the fleeing men at their mercy but, as the infantry fled wildly past, the gunners of two batteries stood fast and drew away the Boer fire from the retreating infantry and, in so doing, denied the Boers that vital quarter-hour which enabled the infantry to escape to safety. At this time, too, the Boers were shaken by the arrival of two naval guns, which had hastily been brought into action against Botha and his men on the ridges.

At Tchrengula, after the mules had stampeded, the column climbed to the top of the hill and hulled down. At dawn, the Free Staters, attracted by the noise, crept up to the summit at about the same time as Carleton who, to his horror, discovered that he occupied only one of the two portions into which the mile long crest was divided. On the Boer side, Christian de Wet, second-in-command of the Free State commandos, had perceived that the unoccupied part of the hill was in fact, higher than the one occupied by the British, and that he, consequently, held the key to the whole situation. He gathered sufficient burghers to gallop round to the unoccupied side, which he invested. Pushing his men forward slowly he engaged with the enemy wherever and whenever possible, and for several hours in the blazing heat the British fought back as best they could until they were slowly forced back with heavy losses by the deadly firing from all around them.

Soon their ammunition started running out, and when they eventually became aware that the main army was already in retreat back to Ladysmith, they realised that their position was a helpless one. When the Boers began to overrun the crest, the men started to surrender in groups, and Carleton ordered the general cease-fire. A white flag was raised and the troops walked towards the burghers with their rifles at the trail. Over 800 prisoners were taken and the remainder of Carleton's men were either dead or wounded. The prisoners were treated with kindness and dignity by their victors, and a message was sent by Joubert to White telling him of Carleton's surrender and granting an armistice to bury the dead.

So ended the battle, variously called 'Ladysmith', 'Farqhuar's Farm', 'Pepworth' or even the place that was never reached, 'Nicholson's Nek'. The British losses totalled 1,200 men – those of the Boers, 200, and to the British public back home this sad day became known as 'Mournful Monday'. Behind the scenes in London, Chamberlain was angry. He wrote a note to a Cabinet colleague concerning the Secretary of War: *'Do you remember Lansdowne telling us that modern guns required elaborate platforms and mountings which took a year to consolidate? The Boers apparently find no difficulty in working their Long Toms without these elaborate precautions. On the whole I am terribly afraid that our War Office is as inefficient as usual'* The essential message of Mournful Monday was summed up by the Times History, as follows: *'The battle of Ladysmith was the first engagement on a large scale between British and Dutch burghers and the first in which the two military systems were fairly matched against each other. It showed inconclusively that in an open field 1,200 British troops were not a match for an equal number of Boers'*

The public's reaction to this statement ranged from 'absurd' to 'incredible'. But above all, there was hope that all this would soon be properly redressed, for now none other than Sir Redvers (Bulldog) Buller had been appointed to go to South Africa to 'teach Kruger a sound lesson'

Colenso - The Prelude
With White neatly bottled up in Ladysmith, a magnificent opportunity now lay before the Boers – between Botha and Durban, along the railway line, were small hamlets pocketed by military garrisons of little significance – Chiveley, Frere, Estcourt and others. There was no concentration of troops anywhere between the Boers at Ladysmith and the provincial capital itself – Pietermaritzburg, or indeed, the vitally strategic port of Natal, Durban. A determined advance on either would seriously undermine British

resolve, especially since it would deprive them of the main harbour through which they intended to land all reinforcements and military equipment destined for the impending action against the Transvaal and Free State republics. But Joubert was a cautious man and lacked the resolve and vigour to push forward for the knockout blow. He believed that the investment of Ladysmith itself would be sufficient to force the British to the negotiation table, and his reaction to pressure from his younger and more dynamic subordinates was '*when the good Lord offers you His finger do not try and take the whole hand for it will severely try His patience*'. In spite of this, he did agree, at the insistence of Louis Botha, his young second-in-command, to undertake a tentative raid into the deep south and Botha took 2,000 men with him to reach the Thukela River. In front of him lay the entire Natal Midlands – wide open and aching for occupation. Earlier the small British garrison at Colenso had pulled back to join a stronger force at Estcourt further south, and Botha was reluctant to pursue the British beyond the Thukela at Colenso for fear of Joubert's wrath as well as for White's troops in his rear. He did however, organise lightning strikes with small patrols aimed at disrupting the British supply lines from Durban to Ladysmith. In fact, on one of these hits on the 15th November, he succeeded in de-railing a British armoured train and capturing some prisoners-of-war among whom was a young journalist, one Winston Churchill, who was taken and sent to Pretoria for incarceration.

It was at this time that the first of Buller's Army Corps brigades started to arrive in Natal, and to push on to the front as quickly as possible to stop Botha's progress. There was a short encounter at Willow Grange on the 27th November, and although the outcome was inconclusive, it was bad enough for the Boers to persuade Joubert to call off Botha's initiative and order his return to the Ladysmith lines. Buller had arrived in Cape Town at the end of October ahead of his Army Corps. It had been decided that the best way to win the war would be for him to strike directly on the western front, right into the heart of the Boer republics, firstly taking Bloemfontein and then straight on to Pretoria. This would cut the heart right out of the Boer resistance, and force their urgent withdrawal from the Natal theatre in order to strengthen their support for their comrades in the west.

It is interesting to pause at this stage, and to examine Buller's attitude and performance in Natal during the first few months of the war. From the onset the mind is assailed by a myriad of questions to which answers become more and more difficult to fathom as his campaign progressed through the ensuing months until his eventual recall to Britain. There is little doubt that the enthusiasm which accompanied his departure from Southampton and which continued on his arrival in Cape Town on October 31st 1899, was well justified. Buller had displayed great acumen and courage during his previous service in South Africa during the Zulu campaign on 1878/9. He was an inspiring and able leader and had been awarded the Victoria Cross for valorous conduct at the Battle of Mount Hlobani in November 1878. His tactical prowess during the whole campaign earned him great praise even from that most taciturn of soldiers, Lord Chelmsford, whose disastrous encounters against the Zulu impis at Isandlwana and Rorke's Drift were to an extent mollified by Buller's contribution to the successful outcome at Mount Hlobani, and later at Ulundi. Chelmsford had later written of Buller as a '*leader of exceptional qualities*'.

113

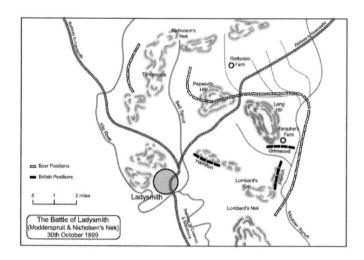

The Battle of Ladysmith
(Modderspruit & Nicholsen's Nek)
30th October 1899

114

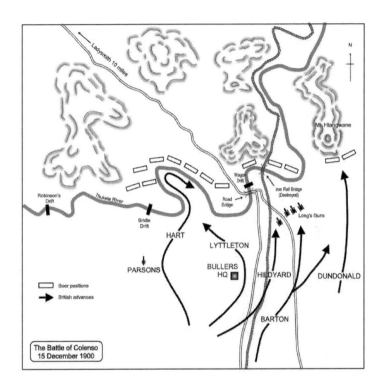

The Battle of Colenso
15 December 1900

During the Zulu campaign, Buller had fought side-by-side with South Africans and had learnt a lot about their attitudes to war. He had commanded a force of 800 locally recruited irregulars that had been formed into a mounted infantry unit and which even included a small contingent of Boers led by Piet Uys, son of a prominent original Voortrekker leader. Buller later wrote, after the First Boer War in 1880/1, '...*the Boers have no strategical point, the occupation or destruction of which would render a continuation of the struggle hopeless. We should have to reduce them by harrying their farms and burning their homesteads'*. This was an astute perception of the Boer psyche, and a profoundly prophetical assessment of the events which were about to enfold. But, it failed completely to influence in any way whatsoever, not only Buller's tactical strategies in South Africa, but the entire British military establishment including Field Marshal Lord Roberts, who would replace Buller in South Africa after the Natal campaign. Instead of the British leaders sitting up and re-assessing their early failures, they continued to press on with the traditional close formation tactics as exercised on the parade grounds of Aldershot. It was only after one disaster followed another that they were forced to abandon pitched-battle encounters and resort to a scorched-earth campaign against woman, children, fields and farms, a tactic which would eventually lead them to a costly and ignominious cessation of hostilities at Vereeniging on May 31st 1902.

On Buller's arrival in Cape Town, he was confronted with strong political pressures to free White at Ladysmith, because it was considered most undesirable to have some 12,000 fighting men locked up indefinitely by a handful of Boers. Buller could not divert the entire Corps to Natal, because, in the meantime, Cecil Rhodes had foolishly allowed himself to be trapped inside besieged Kimberley, and was using all his financial and political influence to cry for help and for protection of his assets invested in diamonds in that town. Buller was also under pressure from Milner who, while having no particular sympathy for Rhodes, nor any thoughts one way or another for Kimberley itself, was concerned about the security of the Cape. With the entire army away in Natal, he felt a serious danger of some of the Cape Boers openly supporting their brothers in the northern republics, and thus constituting a real danger for Cape Town itself.

It was for all these reasons that Buller was reluctantly obliged to split his Corps by diverting sixteen infantry battalions, 8 artillery batteries, and 2 cavalry regiments to Natal. Once Ladysmith had been relieved, he reckoned, the Corps could move rapidly through the Drakensberg passes directly onto Bloemfontein, and join up with the main western force for the final onslaught on Pretoria. The Natal detachment was nominally under the command of Lt. Gen. Sir Francis Clery, but Buller proposed to accompany it himself. By the time Buller arrived in Natal, Botha had retreated north of the Thukela, but it was still worrying for him, especially since small parties of Boers were rampaging along the vital railway line, and were deploying large numbers across the Thukela barrier with White still bottled up in Ladysmith beyond. White's supplies could not last forever, and since the Ladysmith force now seemed paralysed by inertia, Buller had little choice but to try to dig them out. This would mean punching through the Boer line on the Thukela, that very barrier that the British themselves had regarded as formidable, and beyond which Buller had previously urged White not to venture. In spite of 'hindsight criticism', Buller's plan was a sound one because he had a very realistic idea of the difficulties that faced him. Immediately south of the Thukela the country was open and undulating but beyond the river, which in itself was a significant barrier, 100 yards wide and swollen by early summer rains, the hills rose in a line of rocky terraces scattered with boulders and bush, some reaching heights of over 1,000 ft above the plain.

As has already been mentioned, through his experience fighting alongside the Boers in the Zulu wars, Buller had learned to respect their field craft and prowess. He realised that, properly entrenched on the heights, they would be a considerably difficult force to dislodge. But he had very few options open for him – the very string of minor Boer successes had made it politically imperative for him to force his way through the nearest and quickest door which, regrettably lay at the foot of the most hostile military terrain in which to attempt a break-through. The main road and railway to Ladysmith crossed the Thukela at Colenso, and then wound through a maze of rocky hills before emerging into the open country beyond. The little settlement at Colenso offered a real practical route with a road and a railway bridge over the river. Yet it was so obvious a point of attack, that Buller was convinced that the Boers would very adequately have entrenched it, and he had therefore to find another, safer way over the river. He concentrated his troops at Frere, just north of Estcourt, and contemplated on his way through to Ladysmith. Fifteen miles upstream from Colenso was a crossing point called Potgieter's Drift, from whence a track ran on to Ladysmith through hills beyond which were known to be higher but not as dense as those along the Colenso route. Buller opted for Potgieter's Drift, and on December 10th ordered an infantry brigade, Barton's 6th (Fusiliers) Brigade, forward to Colenso on a feint move to mask his own imminent departure for Potgieter's. It was at that point that fate intervened. News reached Buller of two disasters on the western front. On the 10th December, Lt. Gen. Gatacre had mounted a daring night attack to deny the Boers a strategically important railway junction at Stormburg in the Northern Cape, but the plan went badly wrong and in the darkness Gatacre lost his way as well as 96 men killed or wounded and 600 captured.

Farther north, on the Kimberley front, Lord Methuen had advanced before dawn across an open plain to attack a Boer force, which he believed had dug in on the Magersfontien Heights. At first light, the Boers suddenly opened killing fire from well-concealed trenches, not on the heights but in the very veld right before the approaching British troops. The day ended in disaster for Methuen's troops, and almost 1,000 bodies lay wounded or dead when the final order to retreat was sounded.

Both battles deeply shocked British pride and the public was outraged. Far from running at the first sight of a bayonet as was predicted, the Boers had in fact stopped the cream of the British army dead in its tracks. Pressure was now on Buller to make immediate and effective headway in Natal in order to retrieve the initiative, and spurred on by this imperative, he decided, after all, to make a headlong assault and attack by the most obvious way. He would in fact, take on Colenso.

Colenso – The Battle

The Thukela winds in great loops below the Drakensberg, and the tiny village of Colenso lay in one of them. With a few tin buildings, a hotel and a station, its significance lay in the fact that it commanded two substantial bridges across the river, the most impressive one being the iron railway-bridge, which Botha had destroyed previously during one of his raids towards Estcourt in order to deny it to the British troops. The other bridge, used to convey wagon traffic across the river, was left intact as part of a deliberate ploy on Botha's part. There was nothing particularly sophisticated in the concept of Botha's defence plan, but its virtue lay in the skill with which it was carried out.south of the river, the terrain sloped gently down to the river, and there was virtually no cover to obscure the British movements. On the Boer side however, there was a basin of undulating country immediately north of Colenso itself, broken here and there by several rocky outcrops, collectively called the Colenso Koppies, one of which, known as Fort Wylie, commanded the demolished railway bridge. North of the Colenso Koppies the land rose in several terraces to a line of steep hills, slashed through here and there with deep gorges. Botha made no attempt to defend the river but hoped simply to use it as a barrier to concentrate the British force, and to funnel them into the open spaces just below the Colenso Koppies. Here, with a point of retreat so narrow as to be impractical under fire, he intended to cut them off and destroy them with his artillery, which even now was being set up, piece-meal, on the heights above. He deployed his 4,500 men in a broken line between the foot of the hills and the river.

The total number of Boer troops in the entire Natal sector at that time amounted to 14,000 men, half of whom were committed to the siege of Ladysmith, leaving Botha no more than 7,000 men to guard a line that reached from the Drakensberg to the hills east of Colenso, a distance of over 50 miles. He had little choice but to screen the most obvious points of attack, and patrol the sections in between, trusting on the slowness of the British advance to give him ample time to concentrate his forces. In selecting a suitable assault point for an invading force, Botha estimated that Colenso would be the obvious choice, and in the event, Buller did not disappoint him. He placed the Free State men and the Johannesburg and Middelburg commandos upstream of Colenso to cover a crossing called Robinson's Drift. The Ermelo, Zoutpansberg and Swaziland commandos were deployed along the edge of the great loop in the river between Robinson's Drift and Colenso. The Boksburg, Heidelberg, Vryheid and Krugersdorp commandos, together with the Johannesburg ZARP's held the Colenso Koppies and Fort Wylie, whilst the Wakkerstroom and Standerton commandos secured Hlangwane Hill on Botha's extreme left. The Boers were protected here and there by natural cover or existing stone walls, and they linked the rest of their line with carefully concealed trenches, where they remained hidden until the proper battle began.

Botha's position not by any means invulnerable. In fact, his left flank gave him great concern because just downstream from Colenso, the Thukela bends sharply north, leaving the Hlangwane ridge isolated on the southern bank. Since it covered the flanks of Fort Wylie and the Colenso Koppies, any British force that could capture it, would be able to enfilade an important section Botha's line. It was crucial therefore, that Hlangwane be held, but the Boers showed reluctance to occupy this dubious post of honour since the river behind them effectively cut off their line of retreat. The men originally stationed there had abandoned their post in the face of the obvious British assault preparations and it took all of Botha's persuasive powers, backed up by a telegram from Kruger himself, to cajole and bully the burghers back into line. The Wakkerstroom and Standerton men only agreed to re-occupy the hill as late as the 14th December, the very day before the battle.

To attack the Colenso position Buller had four infantry brigades, each of four battalions, a cavalry division, five batteries, and some assorted naval guns – heavy ships' guns landed at Durban off four vessels, mounted on improvised carriages and dragged up from Durban by ox-wagon. The largest of these 4.7 inch guns had a range of 10,000 yards and represented a significant addition to Buller's arsenal. Maj. Gen. Sir Geoffrey Barton's brigade (The Fusiliers) was already in position between Chiveley and Colenso, and in the second week of December cavalry patrols were pushed up to the river itself to feel out the Boer positions. Botha kept his men well in hand and gave no clues to the British of his whereabouts or strength. The 4.7 guns were advanced to a line near Barton's position and on the 13th they began to shell the heights some 5,000 yards away but with little if any affect. By the evening of the 14th Buller had concentrated all his forces nearby, and laid plans for a dawn attack the following day.

Buller's plan was a simple one – he needed to force a way across the river – the intact road bridge was all to obvious a trap – and according to his incomplete and inaccurate maps there appeared to be at least one good drift upstream from the loop in the river named 'Bridle Drift'. If Buller was aware of another infinitely more suitable drift, Robinson's, which was situated further upstream, he took no account of it in his planning. Instead he decided to launch one brigade, Maj. Gen. H.J.T. Hildyard's 2nd Brigade, directly against Colenso itself whilst the other, Maj. Gen. A. Fitzroy ("No Bobs") Hart's 5th Irish Brigade would strike at the drift on the right of Colenso. Both brigades would be supported by artillery whilst the two remaining brigades, Maj. Gen. Neville Lyttleton's 4th Light Brigade and Barton's 6th, would remain in support. The heavy naval guns would shell the Heights from a rise in the rear.

Buller had no clear idea of how he would proceed if he did in fact secure a crossing, and he dreaded, once over the river, the inevitable engagements in the gorges further north on the way to Ladysmith. He also believed that Ladysmith itself was too far away to organise and launch a diversionary sortie by White, to draw some of the enemy strength away from the Colenso defences. One of the most surprising omissions was Buller's failure to take account of the vulnerability of the Boer line from Hlangwane. It is conceivable to believe that he failed to appreciate the extent to which the hill dominated the Colenso hills, since the course of the river was obscured by bushes and trees. It is also probable that he was a victim of his dismally poor Intelligence services, and he may have believed that the Thukela flowed in front of Hlangwane, which would then have placed it entirely on the northern side of the river. Whatever the reason, Col. Dundonald's Cavalry Division, supported by a single battery of artillery, was given the task of attacking Hlangwane, but this was intended merely to support the British right flank and in no way to establish a significantly strategic objective in its own right.

Colenso – The Attack

The attack began before dawn on the 15th December. Hildyard's, Lyttleton's and Hart's brigades were assembled to the left of the railway line, opposite Barton's, and as the long lines of infantry advanced, they threw up a cloud of dust which hung at waist level for a long while in the still morning air. The attack began to go wrong almost from the start. Hildyard's brigade was slow in setting off, and so its supporting artillery, commanded by Col. Long, rapidly drew way ahead of the brigade. Buller later claimed that he had specifically ordered Long to deploy at a particular spot on the map well away from the river. But the maps were unreliable, and Long's guns crossed to the right of the railway line, and were soon abreast of Colenso itself. Perhaps Long thought that the Boer positions were further down than where they actually were, but whatever the reason, his two batteries of field artillery, the 66th and the 14th, were eventually deployed no less than 1,000 yards from the river bank. Long also commanded six Naval 12pdrs under Lt. Gilvry, but these, being ox-drawn, had fallen behind, and were further delayed when crossing a deep donga several hundred yards behind Long's rear. So, when Long's gunners deployed and fired their first salvo to test the range they were almost entirely unsupported, and very conspicuously isolated right in the middle of the open veld, and within easy killing range of the deadly accurate Mausers which lay hidden straight ahead of them.

From a position on the opposite side of the river Botha gave the signal to reply, with a single shot from his Howitzer. Immediately the Boers concealed in their trenches below Fort Wylie opened fire, and a storm of Mauser fire broke over Long's men. The air hummed with bullets and although at 1,000 yards the fire was not as accurate as would have been desired, the sheer volume of bullets swept like a scythe, raking the veld. Almost at once, two of Long's Battery Commanders were killed, and Long himself lay badly wounded, having been struck by a piece of shrapnel through his liver.

On the left, Hart's brigade was also in serious trouble. He had set off for the river in fine style – his battalions were lined up as if on parade, in close order with the Dublin Fusiliers in front and the Inniskillians behind them, and the Border Regiment and the Connaught Rangers in support. Lt. Col. L.W. Parsons covered Hart's left with the 63rd and 64th Field Batteries, whilst beyond him two squadrons of the 1st Royal Dragoons skirted the flank. The cavalry was the first to spot the Boers concealed in trenches just across the river, seriously threatening Hart's flank. The commander sent a message warning Hart of this danger, but Hart chose to ignore it and continued to advance in tight close-order formation, replying that he intended to take no notice of the enemy unless they interfered directly with his advance.

As Hart approached the river, his position became confused. He had been searching for the 'Bridle Drift', but some of the dongas he crossed did not appear to be in the places that had been shown to him on the map. He consulted an African guide, who insisted that there was only one drift in that area and that it lay further to the right. This was bad news because on Hart's right was a tight loop in the river, and to enter it would expose his entire brigade to close-range enfilading as well as frontal fire. In spite of the cavalry's warning of this danger, Hart refused to falter, and dismissing all advice, he pressed on into the loop with three of his four battalions trapped in a noose. A fierce storm of Mauser fire swept down, devastating the first ranks and lashing away at the flanks. Several companies tried to protect themselves by moving into a more open order, but Hart angrily insisted that they close up again into tight formation.

The vanguard of the Dublin Fusiliers was pushed into the apex of the loop, where a native homestead provided some sort of cover. A handful of men reached the bank of the river, and searched for a way over. Any drift that may or may not have been there, lay submerged beneath the rush of the summer flow, and with no cover available, most of the men were either shot up or washed away. The remainder lay down in the open grassland as the Cruesot guns, concealed on the slopes of Grobelaar's Kop, added their own quota to the firestorm.

Buller, back on Naval Gun Hill, appeared 'surprised' at the disastrous turn of events. In spite of the massive fire that was being laid down, neither the Boer guns nor the trenches could be detected because of the smokeless powder that they were using. During all this time the naval guns were relentlessly pounding away at the distant heights, although there was little if anything for them to fire at. So far, only two of his four brigades had been committed and Buller was angry that Long had exposed himself so far forward. Now, with the news of Hart's disaster on the left, Buller quickly rode forward in an attempt to sort things out in a situation that he referred to as "a devil of a mess!" When he met Hildyard's brigade, still ponderously shuffling forward towards Colenso, it was no later than 6.30 a.m., barely a half-an-hour after the first shots were fired. He ordered them to come up faster and relieve the pressure on Long's guns. By now Ogilvy's guns were also been deployed and supporting the attack. At this stage, a further crisis developed as the second supply of ammunition ran out. The chances of bringing up a third supply rapidly were nil because the ammunition reserves were such a long way back, that it was taking ages to move them up to the front. Soon Long's guns fell silent and the gunners retired to shelter in a small donga nearby. It was here where Buller found them, and he stayed with them from then on to direct the battle from the donga.

It was also now that the severity of Hart's position dawned on Buller, and he ordered Lyttleton's brigade forward to support Hart. Lyttleton soon came under heavy fire himself even before he could reach Hart, so he deployed his men in open order, giving whatever covering fire he could. By now, some of Hart's companies had realised the hopelessness of their situation, and were trying to move away from the loop. Others were reluctant to do so – indeed, for many retreat simply meant openly exposing themselves even more to the devastating enemy fire, so they just lay down and did nothing. The whole situation soon developed into a chaotic farce, and when at the bitter end, the official withdrawal order finally came the exodus was a shambles.

Adding to Buller's miseries Dundonald, on the right, had also run into trouble at Hlangwane. After his initial onslaught, he had dismounted his men and deployed them in a wide curve, the S.A. Light Horse on the left, the Composite Regiment in the centre and Thorneycroft's Mounted Infantry on the right, with the 7th Field Battery supporting in the rear. On the slopes of Hlangwane they ran into heavy Boer fire from the summit, and the attack bogged down in the maze of boulders, strewn folds and gullies that scored the sides of the hill. Dundonald's call on Barton for help was refused because he had initially been ordered, "not to move"! Now, without reinforcements, his initiative gradually petered out and finally collapsed. Ironically, it could have been the turning point of Buller's fortunes, because had Dundonald succeeded at Hlangwane, the British forces would have commanded a superb advantage over the entire left flank of the Boer lines including Colenso itself and all the way up to the drifts.

Buller was rapidly losing the initiative. He had been busy trying to redress the problem of Long's guns, which were standing in the open surrounded by dead and dying gunners. He was also facing set-back upon set-back including the loss of Lt. Freddy Roberts, the son of Lord Roberts, Buller's long confirmed adversary, who had been mortally hit during an abortive attempt to retrieve the guns. On top of this, Hildyard's advance into Colenso had petered out dismally and with Hart locked up in the loop and Dundonald's failing efforts on Hlangwane, Buller, in despair, called off the attack and ordered the retreat. Most galling for Buller was the loss of the 14th and 66th Battery guns. When the gunners temporarily retired to the donga to await the arrival of the ammunition they believed that they would be returning to their guns to resume action, so they had made no attempt at disabling them. But now, acting on Buller's specific orders, they were made to quit the field leaving the ten remaining guns abandoned in the open veld. Later that day a party of Boers jubilantly dragged them away intact and unmolested, and subsequently used them in future battles against the British.

The entire engagement lasted a little over an hour and it took just two hours more for most of Buller's men to withdraw from the stage. By 10 a.m. it was all over, including the disorderly retreat of Hart's and Lyttleton's men from the loop. British losses were severe – apart from the loss of the guns, which represented more than half of Buller's entire Natal artillery contingency, he counted seven officers and 178 men killed, forty-three officers and 719 wounded, and twenty-one officers and 199 men missing or captured. Over 500 of all the casualties came from Hart's brigade, and Long's two batteries lost two officers and seven men killed, six officers and twenty-seven men wounded, and a further five officers and forty-four men missing. The Boer losses were few – perhaps forty killed or wounded in total. Buller later complained that Long had 'spoiled his entire plan' - 'sold by a damned gunner' were his exact words. But in reality Hart's headstrong march into the loop called for serious consideration as well as did Dundonald's failure to capitalise on Hlangwane, and finally Barton's refusal to assist him there

Colenso – The Aftermath
First Stormburg on the 10th then Magersfontein on the 11th and now Colenso on the 15th - almost 2,750 men killed, wounded, missing or captured, and all in the space of six days. For the British, it was indeed a "Black Week" and back in England the Parliament, the Press and the Public vociferously displayed their shock, their disgust and their disapproval. The people of Britain had enjoyed war on the cheap for nigh on fifty years – small wars fought against savages – the big-game rifle against spears and the rawhide shield – small, heroic casualties for the troops, massive losses for the enemy. To lose more than a hundred soldiers in a single battle was a disaster suffered

only twice since the Indian Mutiny. Yet now, in 1899, they had sent out the biggest overseas expedition in British history, to bring to heel and subdue one of the world's smallest nations, with shattering consequences. Within three months there were more than 700 killed in action or dead from wounds. Even more galling was the list of those who had surrendered. In the British Army there was no precedent for this humiliation – yet to the two white flags at Majuba and Doornkop were now to be added Moëller's cavalry at Talana, White's infantry at Nicholson's Nek, Gatacre's infantry at Stormburg, and never to forget the 20,000 plus soldiers bottled up for months at Ladysmith, Kimberley and Mafeking.

Almost as unbearable for British pride was the delight displayed by some foreign powers over the deficiencies of her military machine, so suddenly and so spitefully exposed. The Germans were particularly scathing as they wrote, *'the vast majority of German military experts believe that the South African war will end with complete victory for the Boers and complete defeat for the English'*. The ultimate humiliation at the hand of the Germans came when Chamberlain's proposal for an alliance with Germany was scornfully rejected. Everywhere the Boer victories were taken by most of the powers, to mean the imminent dissolution of the British Empire. In the storm of anger and frustration that followed in the wake of Black Week, it was the Opposition leaders, Asquith and Campbell-Bannerman, who adopted the most statesmanlike attitude and tone. Asquith warned that it would be 'grotesque' to get the reverses out of proportion. The struggle now, was not one of Jingo-like 'revenging, asserting and maintaining our position in South Africa', but the need to protect and uphold our status as a world power'.

Back at Frere, Buller received a signal from London informing him that he was to be superseded as General Officer in Command – South Africa, and relegated to the command of the Natal Forces only. As GOC he was to be replaced by Field Marshal Lord Roberts, assisted by Lord Kitchener as Chief-of-Staff. Buller was also requested 'not to proceed beyond the Tugela'. In Britain and across the Empire, serious recruiting drives now took place. A wave of colonial patriotism was set in motion all over the world; all the white British Dominions, except the Cape Colony, unanimously took sides with Britain and started recruitment campaigns for volunteers to assist her in South Africa. Soon it would bring some 29,000 white colonial troops to swell the ranks of the British forces in South Africa. At home the initial provision of £645,000 which had been set aside to cover essential war preparation costs was increased to nearly £10 million, and plans were set in motion to mobilise the 7th Division, the last organised Division of regulars in the Home Army, and also to enlist civilian volunteers. The aim was to reach a total of about 45,000 extra men, thereby almost doubling the fighting force in South Africa. The civilian volunteer scheme proved a big success and eventually served to provide great assistance to the regulars in combat on the veld. The original requirement was for 8,000 irregulars, equipped as mounted infantry, to be 'able to shoot as well as possible and to ride neatly'. These units would be amalgamated with colonial irregular M.I. units to make up an invaluable addition to the fighting force of around 20,000 men.

123

Platrand

In retrospect, Colenso may not have been as disastrous for the British as it first appeared. In fact, it could be considered a turning point, because until then the war had been fought very much on Boer terms, at venues and in conditions of their choosing. After Colenso the Boer tactics of advance and attack ceased, and from then on it would be the British who would advance and attack, slowly, methodically, and relentlessly. The change came shortly after Colenso in the aftermath of a relatively minor skirmish on an insignificant hill called Platrand. Botha's victory at Colenso, together with the British setbacks at Magersfontein and Stormberg, had a profound effect on the Boers. In Natal, Commandant-General Joubert, as cautious as ever, saw their success as a gift of divine providence, and advocated quiet thanksgiving and praise to the Lord. Botha supported Joubert, but not for the same reasons. In spite of his success against Buller, he was concerned over the welfare of his men and their horses, and was anxious to welcome a short period of rest and refurbishment. On the other hand, Kruger and other leading members of the Volksraad in Pretoria, saw the British setbacks as an indication of weakness, and urged the reluctant Joubert to press the Boer advantage to the limit, and 'drive the English into the sea!' In the face of opposition from Joubert and Botha, Kruger successfully pressurised the Krijgsraad in Pretoria to resume the Boer offensive in Natal, and orders were issued to attack and occupy the Platrand. The reason for selecting this target was obvious. The Platrand overlooks Ladysmith from the south, and if the Boers occupied it they would effectively lock-in the town on all quarters. The Krijgsraad argued that with Buller out of the way, and the Platrand in their possession, the fall of Ladysmith was imminent. The capture and incarceration of General White and his army of 14,000 men would force the British to the conference table.

Platrand is a flat-topped ridge to the south of Ladysmith, about 300 feet high and a quarter-of-a-mile wide on the top. It extends some four miles to the west and east in a succession of three hills, roughly in a straight line and linked with shallow bolder- and brush-strewn hogbacks. The British had named the three hills 'Wagon Point', 'Wagon Hill', and 'Caesar's Camp' The Boers believed that the British occupied the Platrand in strength. In fact, White had steadfastly refused any of his officers to occupy and fortify any positions on the outskirts of the town, but had recently allowed Ian Hamilton to locate some heavy naval guns and other artillery pieces on Wagon Hill, in order to support a possible break out or to cover Buller whenever he decided to liberate Ladysmith. In reality, Hamilton held the Platrand with a force of 1,000 men, which not being strong enough to guard the entire four miles of the summit, was used to build a row of small forts strung along the back of the crest. Because these men worked at night in order to maintain security, the Boers were quite unaware of their presence. They planned a simultaneous attack on all three hills, Wagon Point, Wagon Hill and Caesar's Camp, with 2,000 men, and in concert with a Boer artillery barrage from the nearby heights, as well as a strong demonstration by the remainder of the besiegers on the plains around the town. As a reserve, Botha would bring up a force from the Thukela area

Platrand – The Battle

At 2.40 a.m. on the night of 16th January, the burghers, while climbing up the hill, suddenly came upon a party of thirteen naval gunners assisted by twenty-five sappers and an escort of seventy-five Gordons, digging in a huge 4.7" naval gun, affectionately named the 'Lady Anne'. In the dark the startled Boers immediately opened fire, and bullets buzzed wildly through the air. Soon some pickets, who had been posted on the same side of the hill, also joined in the fray. The pickets were men from the I.L.H. who ordinarily wore slouch hats very similar to those of the Boers, and this added to the wild confusion.

The Boers succeeded in pushing the pickets back, and poured onto the hill, but the I.L.H. had previously built a small 'fort', a loop-hold ring of stones about twenty feet around, and some of the pickets managed to occupy it and hold back the Boer attack. Others took shelter in a gun-pit that had been dug for one of 12-pdrs, and as the bullets flew around, and the men called out in confusion, the Boer attack was eventually beaten off. Meanwhile, two-and-a-half miles away, on the eastern edge of the hill at Caesar's Camp, other wild scenes were taking place. Here the pickets had had a quarter-of-an-hour warning before the Transvaalers stormed over the ridge, but while they managed to establish some kind of foothold on the crest, they were completely out-numbered, and forced to give way. When dawn came the whole of the hill was swarming with Boers. In the 'ring defences' on the plain, White's outposts were coping well with the Boers' 'diversionary demonstration'. Two miles to the north, at Convent Hill, Robinson, and Hunter, the Chief-of-Staff, were awakened by the sound of gunfire below, and before long alarming messages were being received, because the Boers, disregarding their conventional tactics, were storming in from all sides of the perimeter under cover of a bombardment from every gun they possessed.

The perimeter defences held out well against the Boer attacks, but up on the summit of Plat rand the situation was more serious for the British. At Wagon Hill, as well as at Caesar's Camp, the confusion still reigned, and attack after attack by Hamilton's men failed in the face of determined Boer fire. It was at this critical stage that events took a bizarre turn. The gradually blackening skies suddenly burst forth into a massive storm, which temporarily brought to an end all manner of activity. Later, when the storm had abated, things on Plat rand were in a very confused state. The Boers, fearing that the British might charge through the storm, resumed their fire, assisted by many of their kin on the plain below. At Wagon Point the British wavered, but rallied again to hold their own, and at the other end, at Caesar's Camp, their counter-attack was renewed and maintained, and then started making headway. As the rain finally lifted at 5.30 p.m., the British broke through, and the Boers dropped their guard, and fled headlong down the slopes, many drowning in a flooded rivulet below. By now the Devons, who had been sent out to reinforce Hamilton, arrived at the rear of Wagon Hill. Hamilton joined them and urged them to charge – they climbed up the hill, and rushed out into the open. The Boers emptied their magazines into the advancing line of Devons, but still they rushed on until, when darkness fell, the Boers ceased firing and quietly slipped away and so ending sixteen hours of gruelling warfare on the top of Platrand.

The following day a cease-fire was called to collect the dead and wounded. The casualty toll was high on both sides – fifty-two dead Boers were counted at and around Caesar's Camp but the total number could have been much higher – as many as 200 dead and wounded. On the British side the losses were 424 – seventeen officers dead or dying, and twenty-eight wounded – 158 men killed, 221 wounded. The brunt of the casualties was borne by the Manchesters, the I.L.H. and the Devons, whose gallant charges had cost them every one of their officers except Col. Rawlinson the commanding officer.

Platrand –The Aftermath

For the Boers the exercise had been a pointless and fruitless one. They had suffered heavy and unnecessary casualties, and in addition, during the storm, their tents and belongings washed away for upwards of a mile. Moreover, they were not able to light fires to dry their clothes. Miserable, wet and cold, and in the dark, they had only their future to brood upon, and the memory of the dead and wounded comrades lying back there on top of that hill. Under a flag of truce their wounded and dead were collected, and carried away the following day.

The Boer defeat at Plat rand brought about changes in Pretoria as well. From now on Kruger and the other Transvaal politicians would busy themselves solely with matters of state, and leave the conduct of the war to the generals in the field. Colenso and Plat rand had demonstrated that any small and well-disciplined force could successfully withstand any attack by a force many times its own size and strength.

From Colenso to Spioenkop

Following the disastrous performance at Colenso, Buller fell into a state of profound meditation. He retired his troops to Frere to lick their wounds and build up their morale, while he contemplated his own predicament. He believed that the set-back at Colenso did not warrant his relegation of command of the army in South Africa, nor that it justified the appointment of Roberts, his close rival and 'old enemy', as G.O.C. (S.A.) in his place. After all, the Boers' 'success' at Colenso had only come about as a result of blunders by Long and Hart, and in the final reckoning, more than half of his force had not even been fully committed in the battle. In fact, the fighting was all over even before Lyttleton's brigade could fully engage Colenso, or before Hildyard could be of any real help to the beleaguered Hart, while back in reserve, Barton's brigade had hardly moved at all before the battle was over.

Buller remained convinced that the Boers were not invincible – in fact, he truly believed them to be very vulnerable to the impact of a well co-ordinated frontal assault in force, and the success of White's troops at Plat rand, rekindled his desire for a renewed effort to relieve Ladysmith. His optimism was further fuelled by the arrival at Frere, on the 11th January of Lt.-Gen. Sir Charles Warren's 5th Division, which now increased his total strength to over 30,000 men. There was therefore, no excuse at all for not attempting a second advance on Ladysmith, but to do so, Buller needed to act quickly and set off before Roberts's arrival in Cape Town. Technically of course he was still G.O.C. (S.A), and directly responsible for the Thukela operation. Caught up in the fever of his haste, Buller also irrationally argued that the War Office signal for him not to attempt Ladysmith until the arrival of Roberts was made as a 'request' and not as a 'direct order'. Thus, as the G.O.C. on the ground, he believed he could exercise his discretion whether to move on to Ladysmith or not. When it came, Buller's decision was decisive and irrevocable, and on the 10th January, the day before Roberts landed in Cape Town, he marched his army out of Frere on a flank advance on Ladysmith via the village of Springfield, some twenty-five miles to the west of Colenso.

At this point it would be interesting to speculate on the extent to which the conduct and the outcome of the war in South Africa was affected by White's ill-conceived confidence, and his failure in assessing the true depth and value of the Boers' determination and their martial capabilities. It would certainly be safe to assume that the course of the war and its eventual outcome would have been very different if he had not caused the confinement at Ladysmith of 14,000 apt and very able soldiers who needed to be liberated and returned to active duty as quickly as possible. As we have seen, when Buller had arrived in Cape Town, he had a plan – that of the War Office - to start a counter-invasion against the two Boer republics straight through the western front. It was not possible for the plan to be put into action because of the situation at Ladysmith that had obliged Buller to go to Natal instead. It is ironic then, that on the very day that Roberts arrived in Cape Town, he too had a plan, and he too received a telegram from London, which forced him to change everything, and hastily to take alternative action to redeem the situation. It is easy to imagine his anger and frustration on receipt of this news, because prior to setting off from Southampton, he had sent a cable – it was repeated at Gibraltar and for a third time at Madeira. The message was for Buller, asking him firmly to remain strictly on the defensive and await further instructions. The telegram that awaited Roberts on his arrival in Cape Town stated that Buller had, notwithstanding, set off once again on a renewed campaign to relieve Ladysmith. As a result, Roberts, in order not to offend Buller's sensibilities, was obliged to abandon Natal, and proceed, instead, to the western front, and from there, to launch a thrust directly on Bloemfontein, and eventually Pretoria.

It was incredible too, that during this period there was someone else who was not very happy either. Since his landing at Cape Town, Lt. Gen. Sir Charles Warren had also been messed about by orders and counter-orders, to such an extent that he eventually burst out in rage: '*am I a shuttlecock to be ranged about up and down on this wretched line?!*' He could hardly be blamed for this outburst, because when he arrived in Cape Town on the 13th December as commander of the Vth Division, and had been charged with orders to serve with Buller as his second-in-command, he was met with different orders from London - to join the Kimberley Relief Force, and replace the discredited Lord Methuen. The very next day he received further contradictory instructions. He was now ordered to put himself at Methuen's disposal instead of replacing him; it appears that it was Buller's doing, having prevailed upon the War Office to retain Methuen in command. Then Warren's anger and indignation was really fuelled to fury, for when he arrived by train at DeAar, some 500 miles north of Cape Town, he received new orders to return to the Cape forthwith, and from there to proceed to Natal to join Buller. Buller had persuaded the War Cabinet to agree to a further attempt at Ladysmith; the War Cabinet had also agreed to reinforce this latest rescue attempt with the Vth Division, and this of course included its commander, Warren.

Buller had good reason to be alarmed at the prospect of Sir Charles's close company, because for a long time these two men had not got on together. Warren was noted for his tactlessness and peppery temper, as well as his stiff pride, which made it difficult for him to act in a subordinate capacity, particularly to someone like Buller whom he disliked intensely, and privately considered beneath him. To make matters worse Warren was carrying a dormant commission to replace Buller as commander of the British troops in South Africa, if for any reason he would became incapacitated or dismissed from his command. Warren eventually reported to Buller at Frere with very bad grace. Buller had already been snubbed by the appointment of Lord Roberts as supreme commander in South Africa, and perhaps one can sympathise with his irritation at having Warren, who had such an excellent opinion of himself and his own abilities, thrust upon him as second-in-command, and possible successor of the Natal Field Force. It had even been suggested that it was at this time that the idea started to germinate in Buller's mind to put Warren in charge of the next attempt to break through the Boer lines – if it succeeded the overall commander would get the credit, but if it failed Warren would surely be left to carry the blame.

The Move to Springfield

The arrival of the Vth Division was the last peg in Buller's scheme. He had given great thought to the renewed advance on Ladysmith, and Warren, soon after his arrival, was fully briefed of Buller's plans. However, instead of Springfield, Warren suggested the capture of Hlangwane, followed by an attack via Colenso. In principle this appeared to be an excellent plan, one with which Buller had been toying with himself. However, exasperated with Warren's elated opinions of his own intelligence and ability, Buller emphatically decided to stick with the original plan of forcing the Thukela at Trichardt's Drift, some sixteen miles upstream. Warren clearly did not like the idea, and explained that he was full of forebodings about the army being over-exposed to a flank attack from the Boers hidden behind the Thukela Heights. Throughout the campaign, Warren was haunted by this dread of flank attacks, and on more than one occasion he was to throw away good opportunities to turn the Boer lines with his own flank manoeuvres, due to his lack of the confidence to undertake them.

In addition to Buller's personal dislike for Warren, he also had no confidence in his military capabilities, and he was not going to allow himself to be influenced by Warren, the 'Sapper' who had trained at the Royal Military Academy, Woolwich, and who had no practical field experience of commanding infantry, cavalry, or artillery. Buller's plan for shifting his army to a sector of the Boer line that was less strongly defended than the obvious Colenso area, was in fact quite a sound one, providing the flank march was executed swiftly, and that the Thukela River and heights beyond could be forced without delay before the enemy had time to move reinforcements in quantity.   Not surprisingly however, Buller had no intention of moving swiftly or of taking his enemy by surprise. It seemed as if he only intended to shift his massive Army Corps, with ponderous deliberation from one base at Frere to another at Springfield. Buller moved so slowly that at first the Boers suspected the flank march simply to be a feint designed to cover another attack on Colenso. Because of this Botha actually strengthened his forces there, but after a day or two of perplexity, he finally decided that it may be worthwhile and wise to take the precaution of increasing the number of Boers covering the drifts of the upper Thukela.

The move to Springfield began on the 10th January. However, even the task of getting the troops from Chievely to Estcourt to rendezvous with the main force encamped at Pretorious's farm, was to prove a difficult operation. Heavy rains had turned even the most insignificant spruits into torrents, and there were so many of them, they proved to be a serious obstacle for the 650 ox-drawn wagons in the column. At one drift, the men were obliged to improvise a bridge of wagons over a stream, and in middle of all this, Warren, the 'engineer general', was in his element, rushing to-and-fro and tackling sticky situations with a 'roll up your sleeves' hands-on enthusiasm. Some of his officers felt that he could have put his energies to better purpose at the head of his column, where he could have taken advantage of any opportunities that may have arisen to surprise the enemy. In fact, by now the Boers had awakened to Buller's intentions, and were moving parallel to the centipede crawl of the British Army, on the other side of the river

In Warren's absence, it fell to Lt. Gen. the Earl of Dundonald, commanding an advance screen of 1,700 horsemen of the cavalry brigade, to exercise the only initiative undertaken during the entire march. Moving quickly ahead of the column, he soon took the village of Springfield on the 10th January without a fight. The country ahead appeared to be clear of any enemy, and he now decided to exceed his orders and attempt the capture of Spearman's Hill, some nine miles further on. This hill, about 700 ft high, is made up of two parts, later christened by the troops as Mount Alice and Naval Gun Hill, and by evening the cavalry brigade was in possession of both these important features commanding the Thukela crossing at Potgieter's Drift, directly below.

On the next day, the 11th January, the infantry tramped into Springfield after a gruelling march. Some of Lord Dundonald's men had, by that time secured the ferry at Potgieter's Drift, and crossed over the river onto the north bank without a shot being fired. The Boers on the other side, afraid of being cut off by the torrential rain of the preceding days, had evacuated the south bank. Five days later, after the swollen waters had receded, Lyttleton's brigade managed across and that night the British forces were on both banks of the Thukela in strength without having fired a shot.

From Springfield, the advanced troops were soon pushed forward to Spearman's Hill, which they began to fortify. A tremendous view spread out below them – immediately opposite lay a comparatively low section of the Brakfontein ridge, and over it ran the road to Ladysmith, some seventeen miles away, where roofs could be seen glistening in the bright sunlight. It soon became obvious to them, however, that this direct route was blocked, for below them the summit of Brakfontein was alive with Boers digging in, and throwing up entrenchments and stone schanzas. Buller set up his HQ on Mount Alice, and soon busied himself with studying the terrain ahead with great interest. From his position, he had a splendid view across to the river below. Beyond that, he could see the range of hills that ran from the Thukela heights in the east, all the way to the point where they merged in a blue haze with the high peaks of the Drakensberg. Directly before him was the Brakfontein ridge, and on both sides of it were stretched ridges of steep saw-like hills, or 'ry-koppies', bound together by narrow saddles, or 'neks'. On the east of Brakfontein, the ridge grew into the stern outline of a craggy hill called Vaalkrantz, whilst on the left lay the even more formidable whale-back hump of Spioenkop, standing out from the Heights like a massive salient. Beyond Spioenkop lay a ridge called Thabanyama, three miles long, with its southern face indented by alternating spurs and ravines. It appeared to terminate in a bold promontory, which, because of its shape, the British named "Bastion Hill".

Buller soon realised that Brakfontein, directly opposite him, was heavily manned by burghers and that Thabanyama, way over at the western end of the heights, might be less strongly held, and could perhaps offer a better way through. It also looked that it could be turned quite easily beyond Bastion Hill to cut the Boer rear on the northern side of Brakfontein. He also saw from his map that there was a farmstead called 'Acton Homes', from which there was a fairly good road all the way to Ladysmith. The road ran through a low pass, and from there, directly on to Ladysmith, over a wide, rolling, grass covered shallow valley. Buller knew that this road must have been an extremely sensitive one for the Boers since it joined the Free State laagers situated outside Ladysmith, with Bloemfontein, their capital.

From Trichardt's Drift to Thabanyama
Buller appeared quite content to spend the next few days poring over his maps and staring at the hills in front of him, contemplating with his staff officers the technicalities of continuing the flank march. It was only on the 15th, that he sent Warren to reconnoitre a reported ford called 'Trichardt's Drift' about four miles up-stream. Warren returned later that day to report that it was a perfectly feasible place for the army to cross the Thukela, and it was decided that on the following night, a flying column would seize the drift preparatory to a wide turning movement around the Heights. The command of the operation was given to Warren, while Buller decided to remain at Spearmans with half of his army to cover Brakfontein. Warren's "flying column" comprised 15,000 men of the 11th Division, plus one infantry brigade, Dundonald's cavalry brigade, and six batteries of artillery.

By appointing Warren to lead the Trichardt's Drift operation, Buller had in effect, shifted the responsibility of the forthcoming action four square onto the shoulder of his subordinate, while he himself was happy to sit back and take credit for its success, or to let Warren take the blame if it went wrong. His instructions to Warren were clear – he was to 'refuse his right,' and advance his left wing around Bastion Hill, and on to the Ladysmith plain, while General Lyttleton would mask the initial stages of the operation by demonstrating in force in front of Brakfontein.

Warren's troops moved out of camp near Springfield on the morning of the 16th and by 12.30 on the following day, his vanguard reached the hills immediately above Trichardt's Drift. In front of him lay, wide open and enticing, one of the finest opportunities any general may ever have wished for, because, at that moment, there were barely 500 burghers guarding this threatened sector of the heights, and Warren was at that decisive point with a concentration of overwhelming force. A direct crossing here was perfectly feasible for mounted men to cross, and lines could then also have been rigged up rapidly to allow the infantry to pass over. Thereafter a quick push could hardly have failed to capture Thabanyama, only four miles away. Even a hard cavalry gallop at first light could have seized the heights, and hold them until the infantry arrived. Warren however had no intention of exploiting this golden opportunity. In his mind, it was the time to demonstrate to his troops his maxim of 'a few days introduction to the enemy'. The Boers, baffled by this procrastination, speedily took advantage of shoring up the defences at Thabanyama, and by the evening of the 17th, Warren's God-given opportunity to end the war was lost.

Spioenkop – The Approach
If Warren's actions baffled the Boers, it totally mystified his own troops. He opened the engagement with a slow bombardment on the scanty enemy field works in the vicinity, whilst the infantry wasted golden hours in a formalised ritual of throwing two pontoon bridges over the river - an operation that Warren superintended in person - and in pushing a bridgehead onto the northern bank. From the depleted and scanty Boer forces, only a desultory firing emanated, but they had not wasted away the breathing space that Warren's antics had allowed them; reinforcements were being hurried in to the threatened part of the line opposite Trichardt's Drift, and Botha himself rode up to assume command. Even at this stage the scene was incredible – on the top of Thabanyama the Boers were in a flurry of activity, urgently digging in, whilst Botha himself, gazing down on the valley below, observed Warren's men leisurely setting up camp as though they were on a peace-time exercise instead of fighting a war.

Chance after chance was slipping rapidly from Warren's grasp. Over and above the advantages that the Boers had grabbed while he dallied on the plain, another, and perhaps final golden opportunity to outflank the Boer and roll up his rear, was rudely quashed and wasted by Warren's lack of vision. For, while Warren was occupying himself unnecessarily with hands-on management of transport, communications and logistics, Dundonald had managed to shake himself free, and was riding ahead with the cavalry brigade straight for Acton Homes. They stampeded past Bastion Hill without meeting any opposition, and were soon cantering on to the direct road to Ladysmith. He sent a message to Warren urging him to follow up this success with some assistance from the infantry, but Warren refused and ordered Dundonald to withdraw at once from his forward position. In the meantime, Dundonald had dismounted his men and taken up a strong position in the hills above Acton Homes. He was in a winning position and he knew it – the road below led up to a gentle slope, and could be seen surmounting an easy pass through the heights. The slope was broken up by gullies and small ravines which would make it easy for troops to work up to the summit under cover. On the far side of the pass, Dundonald could see the road entering the broad, shallow valley leading straight to Ladysmith, a bare twenty miles away. He sent a second rider back to Warren urging him yet again to send support to envelope the entire enemy lines from this vantage point, and open the way for a rapid relief of Ladysmith, and thereby an end of the Thukela campaign.

This time Warren responded by sending one-and-a-half squadrons of the 1st Royal Dragoons to assist Dundonald. At the same time, Dundonald was ordered to send more than half the cavalry at Acton Homes, back to the base on the pretext that he '*had to make certain that the mounted troops did not, in their zeal and exuberance, get themselves into a position where they could not be extricated.*'

In truth, Warren never did regard his cavalry brigade as a fighting unit, but rather as a screen to protect the infantry, and he was very nervous, as ever, of a devastating flanking counter-attack. In his strong reply to Dundonald's second request, he even went as far as to add, '*there was no cavalry around the camp and an attack on his position might cause the trek oxen to stampede while grazing and so immobilise his column*'. It is needless to say that Dundonald was dismayed by Warren's refusal of support.

Warren then spent the following five days at Trichardt's Drift, 'consolidating the bridgehead' while the Boers were frantically busy in perfecting their defences on Thabanyama and elsewhere along the ridge. During this time, the only positive activity on the British side was at Potgieter's Drift where Lyttleton made another demonstration against the Boers at Brakfontein. Although Warren was being criticised for his obvious lack of activity, he oddly believed that things were going 'very well'. Finally, on the 19th January, he decided that his troops had become sufficiently familiar with the enemy to allow him to begin feeling his way on their flank, and to get them on the move once again. Yet even now, the march was not pressed. There had been a good deal of confusion when the head of the long column reached Venter's Spruit, but at least Warren could enjoy his handiness with a wagon train. Dundonald, who had ridden out to plead in person for reinforcements, subsequently reported that he had found the General at the crossing, '*taking an active part with his voice in urging the drivers to do their best*' If Warren really intended to turn the Boer flank that Friday morning, he soon lost heart, for after he had managed to get only half his forces over the spruit, he suddenly decided that his column was particularly vulnerable to an enemy swoop from the hills, and turned them back again to their old camp at Trichardt's Drift.

With all the time in the world at his disposal, Botha had by now succeeded in entrenching more than 2,000 burghers on Thabanyama, which had been virtually unoccupied a few days earlier when Dundonald had first investigated this area, and made his vain plea to Warren for infantry help to invest the hill. Now, from the heights of Thabanyama the burghers watched the British column's movements with interest and amusement. A frustrated Buller paid a flying visit to the column, and made no bones about hiding his impatience at the way Warren had been actively milling around for three days on the Upper Thukela, and getting absolutely nowhere. Warren was full of explanations and excuses, but at the end of a rather unpleasant interview, he failed to impress Buller who informed him that he 'seriously considered removing his second-in-command from control of the operations'. '*On the 19th I ought to have assumed command myself*', Buller wrote later – '*I saw that things were not going well – indeed everyone saw that*', and he added contritely, if not sanctimoniously '*I blame myself for not having done so*'

132

Buller told Warren that he believed that, due to all the procrastination, the Boer positions opposite Potgieter's Drift had been so strengthened that it would no longer be possible to overcome them by means of a 'direct attack'. He then said to Warren, '*I intend to try to turn (them) by sending a force across the Tugela, from near Trichardt's Drift and up the west to Spion Kop. You will, of course, act as circumstances require, but my idea is that you should continue throughout, refusing your right and throwing your left forward until you gain the open plain north of Spion Kop. Once there you will command the position facing Potgieter's Drift and, I think, render it untenable…I shall endeavour to keep up heliograph connection with you from a post on the hill directly in your rear…*' The order was confusing and indecisive, its intentions were vague, the method was obscure, and the lack of adequate provision for proper communications would prove to a vital factor in the debacle that was to ensue. Yet it appeared that Buller's admonishment did have some good effect on Warren, who, after Buller's departure, called a conference of his senior officers that very same evening, and dealt briskly with the problems facing them. There were two ways to reach Ladysmith- they could either go by Acton Homes - imagine Dundonald's scornful disgust at this - or they could take the more direct track over Thabanyama, which passed by two farms called Fairway and Rosalie.

Thabanyama
Warren was not particularly happy about the Acton Homes route because he feared that it would dangerously stretch his communication lines. It would be better by far, he thought, to attack along the shorter Rosalie road, but only after softening up the Boer positions astride it with a prolonged artillery bombardment. What he was suggesting, of course, was to make a frontal attack on a prepared position instead of following Buller's orders to turn the enemy's flank. However, most of his officers, whether sycophantically or just being desperate for some action at last, agreed with him, and thus it was arranged. However, there is little doubt that Warren was somewhat apprehensive about Buller's reaction to this change because the message he sent Buller showed more than his usual penchant for obfuscation – '*I am going to adopt some special arrangements which involve my staying at Venter's Spruit for 2 or 3 days*'

Warren put in his long-delayed attack on Thabanyama at dawn on the 20th, approaching it with an elaborately contrived flanking fire. The infantry skirmished forward in long lines to a spur called Three Tree Hill, projecting from the main ridge. It came as something of an anti-climax when their objective was found to be unoccupied, and was taken without loss. An understanding of the shape of Thabanyama is fundamental to the comprehension of the fighting that was to follow over the next two days. From the northern plain to the south, the ridge swells out of the Thukela plain presenting an easy slope to the top. From the summit towards the southern slope, the ground drops sharply to the plain below. Several spurs project from the southern face, like fingers of a hand, with the main mass as the wrist. The Boers had made trenches in two semi-circular lines along the rolled crest of the ridge, their trenches facing out on to a grassy glacis fully 1,000 yards across, and quite devoid of cover until it reached the sharp drop of the 'fingers'.

The next British attack, mounted by Maj. Gen. Hart's brigade, went up the third and the forth fingers, and so on to the glacis. The choice of terrain was unfortunate; a far better opportunity awaited Warren had he extended his attack to the left, for by now his artillery barrage had driven the Boers out of their trenches on the western half of Thabanyama. In any event the attack was made in the good old British style, led by a brigade general waving a naked sword, and followed by soldiers charging their enemy and accepting inevitable casualties until they could get amongst them with the bayonet. But, it did not quite work that way across open ground against a foe as brave as themselves, and who were armed with high-powered automatic rifles. The attack simply stalled at about 600 yards short of the Boer trenches, and by the afternoon in gruelling conditions, the column had halted, and had succumbed to a feeling of hopeless stalemate.

Yet even now, in a haphazard sort of way, the fates suddenly gave Warren another good opportunity to win the Natal campaign with one single blow, and once again he failed to grasp it due to his intolerant attitude towards his subordinates. Once more it was Dundonald who was behind it all, for whilst patrolling on the flank, he had heard the gunfire, and had come riding in from Acton Homes to investigate. As he passed Bastion Hill, he saw Boer riflemen on the ridge beyond, enfilading the British infantry attacking up the slopes of Thabanyama. Hoping to reduce the pressure, he detached a handful of dismounted men to climb up Bastion Hill. The few burghers nearby were too intent on the main attack to prevent Dundonald's men from effecting a secure lodgement on the crest of the hill. Without support, the troopers could go no further,r but he had provided Warren with another splendid chance to roll up the entire position. But, exploitation on his left flank did not fit in with Warren's tactical plans, even if he had any, so he ignored Dundonald's toehold on Bastion Hill. One wonders at this time whether Warren recalled an interview with Sir Garnet Wolesley in London, when he expounded that *'flanking movements had no effect, and the only way to deal with the Boers was to sweep over them with long lines of infantry attacking all at once and pounding away with the guns until they quailed'* Whatever his thoughts, the following day after a vigorous bombardment by the six field batteries he resumed the frontal assault on the eastern end of Thabanyama. What followed was as pointless as the previous day's fighting – in spite of severe casualties the soldiers found it impossible to reach the Boer trenches. Buller rode over from Spearmans to see how Warren was getting on, but by that time it was obvious that the attack on the Boers had failed, so Buller returned to Spearmans, avoiding what he described as 'an embarrassing encounter with Warren'.

Despite all Warren's mistakes so far, he had in fact, come nearer to a breakthrough than he could have imagined. The burghers, having faced fierce shelling for a number of days, had started to pull out here and there, and those that remained were getting nervous and jumpy. An observer in the Boer ranks had been reported to have stated that *'if things continue like this any longer we will be forced to break and run...'* Of course, all this was unknown to Warren when he called off the attack, which had he only realised it, was on the very verge of success.

Spioenkop – 'The Dress Rehearsal!'
The morning after Warren called off the attack on Thabanyama, Buller rode over to Three Tree Hill to see how matters were progressing. On finding everything quiet again, he made no secret of his dissatisfaction, and the meeting between the two men became as strained as ever – in fact, even more so when Buller threatened to replace Warren if the situation continued to drift any further. What followed between the two men after that was almost too incredulous to be true. Warren was so startled by Buller's threat, that he promised another assault on Thabanyama, although he thought two more days would be needed 'to soften up the position with shellfire'. At the same time he sternly rejected the idea of advancing from Bastion Hill – *'If successful'*, he told Buller, *'it would mean attacking and taking the whole line of the enemy's position which we might not be able to hold.'* It was no surprise that this reply only served to make Buller angrier than ever, and strong words were exchanged. The two men's accounts of what ensued do not agree, but it seems that an evil fate had made Warren mutter, perhaps for the want of some 'face-saving' thing to say, that anyhow it would be impossible to get up the Fairview road without taking Spioenkop first. Immediately, and without any thought, Buller, as if it was the most obvious thing in the world, shot back – *'Of course you must take Spioenkop.'*

It had been difficult for the two men to agree about anything during the past week, but here now, was something about which they concurred, even if only in the most casual of fashions. Warren believed that Buller had replied so sharply 'because he had evidently not thought the matter out'. However, the damage was done, and in this haphazard sort of way a decision was made to attack Spioenkop that very same night. Buller was soon to regret his assent to the operation, and later wrote – *'I did not like the proposal and wanted to warn Warren off by stating that I always dreaded mountains, but after some considerable discussion I had to agree to his suggestion'*. *'That'*, he concluded, *'was why I allowed Warren to have his own way'* Warren's account merely states that, on second thoughts, he said that he favoured an attack on Green Hill, and then only after a thorough military operation, but that this did not meet with Buller's approval, and that rather than retire once again, he undertook to attack Spioenkop that very night instead. He further arranged for the operation to be carried out by Maj. Gen. Coke and the Lancashire Brigade.

Pausing here for a moment to consider how strategically important the capture of Spioenkop actually was, immediately brings us to the fundamental weakness of the plan so casually concocted by Buller and Warren. The seizure of the hill could have little significance other than if Buller had it specifically in mind as being the *'hill directly in your rear'* mentioned in the vague order, which he had previously given to Warren. If this was in fact the case, it would have made more sense to attack Spioenkop *after* Warren had set off, via Three Tree Hill and Rosalie Farm, on his assault of the Boer positions. Otherwise, the occupation of Spioenkop would only have been significant if the ascent had been part of a bigger plan to drive a two-prong hole into the Boer lines, first of all via the hill itself and secondly via Rosalie Farm. However, neither Buller nor Warren appear to have intended the operation to be anything else but an isolated thrust involving a single brigade only, without any consideration to following up the capture by widening the scope of the offensive. In fact, this would have been quite feasible since any troops, securely dug in on the summit, could have been put to very effective use to enfilade the Boer trenches on Thabanyama. In addition, most military authorities also maintain that with some artillery on the summit, the Boer trenches would not have been tenable for more than an hour or so. In short, Buller and Warren had set themselves a very limited objective, hoping it seems, to break *into* the Boer line, but giving no thought as to breaking *through* it. It seems as if Warren had cherished some vague hope that the loss of the hill would somehow make the Boers panic and abandon their whole line. It is doubtful whether Buller's discernment had reached even as wistful a conclusion as that, because when he was later asked by a staff officer what Woodgate's force should do after it had captured the summit, he pondered over the problem for some time before muttering -...*it has got to stay up there...!*

In hindsight, it is obvious that the capture of Spioenkop could have been used as a lever to wrench the enemy line wide open, particularly through the skilful deployment of artillery. Unfortunately, here one touches on perhaps the most tragic lapse in the British plan, for although there had been some vague intention to get guns onto the plateau after its seizure, no one had thought of providing the necessary weaponry. The most suitable guns for the purpose were those belonging to a Mountain Battery attached to Buller's army, because they were capable of being dismantled for transporting on pack-mules, making it easy for getting them up even the most difficult of mountains. Unfortunately, they were left behind at Frere when the troops had moved out to Springfield a fortnight earlier, and no one had thought of bringing them up to the front since then, and nor had anyone remembered they were available, and would be useful on the day that the Spioenkop operation was decided upon. It was in this casual and haphazard manner which characterised the methods of the Ladysmith Relief force that it was only on the day following the ascent, that the Mountain Battery was belatedly remembered, and a message sent to Frere to get it up to Trichardt's Drift without delay. Quite inexplicably, the vital message failed to reach Frere!

Following Buller's departure, Warren again succeeded in wasting time. He concurred with Coke's request to take a day to reconnoitre the hill's approaches, but he forgot to inform Buller about this 24-hour delay. For his part, Coke set off for his own camp nearby but promptly lost his way in the dark and had to spend the night out in the open veld. It would also not be the last time that Coke would lose his way in the dark – it happened again two nights later, but that time the consequences would be infinitely more serious. Meanwhile, fully expecting the Kop to have been invested during the night, Buller rode over to Three Tree Hill the next day and was furious to discover that nothing had been done at all. The blame, obviously, was laid on Coke's shoulders, and Buller in his anger, informed Warren that he had his doubts about Coke's staying power in view of his 'lame leg', and desired that the assault column be led by the more energetic General Woodgate. Coke, he added, should take command of the Vth Division while Warren would be the over-all commander, with a small, improvised command staff to assist him. He then returned to Spearmans and signalled London that Spioenkop 'would be seized' that night. Now, at last, there was no going back - the 'dress rehearsal' was over.

The Battle of Spioen Kop
24th January 1900

The Battle of Spioenkop – The Ascent

With uncanny instinct, the British had chosen to tackle the most formidable hill in the whole line of the Thukela Heights. It was as if there was something pre-ordained about the choice. They first toyed with the idea of attacking to the right of it, then around it from the left from Spearmans, and then they then made half-cock of it on the left, at Thabanyama. Yet, all along, it had stood aloof, as if it had been reserved for the hour when it alone would be destined to provide the climatic battle to these past three months of struggle across the whole expanse of the very country, which was visible from its summit. From its top, one can see the hills of Ladysmith, across to Elandslaagte and Dundee in the north, to the hills of Colenso in the east and Estcourt in the south, and brooding on the vast western rim, the massive range of the Drakensberg. Spioenkop rises to 1,470 ft above the Thukela, and is four miles long. The right, or eastern end, near Spearmans, consists of two eminences called Twin Peaks. From these a long narrow passage leads westward to a small rise, whose spiky aloes earned it the name of Aloe Knoll. From there a slight saddle-shaped dip leads on to the main summit on the west. This summit, which overlooked Trichardts and Warren's army, is hump-backed. Its exact delineation was obscure to the British, and therefore unknown to them, which was a pity, because no attempt had been made to find out anything about it. It was an unfortunate omission, which was going to cost them dearly. From the summit, the sides fall away precipitously except for a spur on its southwest corner, which was near to where the British were situated. This spur provided. a reasonable way up for the assault group. There is a second spur on the farther corner, on the northwest, from which arises a hillock called "Conical Hill", and close by this is another knoll called "Green Hill". From Spearman's, Buller had an unbroken view of the entire profile of the mountain, and could follow every phase of the battle on it. On the other hand, from Warren's H.Q. at Three Tree Hill, the entire eastern half of Spioenkop - the most elevated part, as well as Aloe Knoll and Twin Peaks, were hidden by a spur of Three Tree Hill, and could not be seen at all.

A survey of the southern face of Spioenkop from Three Tree Hill revealed the broad spur running out from the southwest section of the Kop, offering a reasonably easy ascent to the summit. The spur was marked by three successive step-like ledges, the lowest one situated about half way up, heart-shaped and comparatively expansive. The intermediate shelf adjoined the hill's southern cliffs, and was no more than a narrow ledge. The highest shelf was much larger and pocked with about half-a-dozen bushy mimosa trees.

Buller's insistence that the assault be led by the more active Maj. Gen. Woodgate rather than Maj. Gen. Talbot-Coke displeased Warren immensely, for it seriously altered the structure of command of the Lancashire Brigade, and did indeed add greatly to the confusion which followed. Warren did eventually succeed in restoring Coke as Task Force Commander, but this only served to worsen the ultimate confusion. Woodgate's assault column consisting of 1,700 men, included the 2nd Battalion Lancashire Fusiliers, the 2nd Battalion The Royal Lancashire Regt. (The Kings Own), two companies of the 1st Battalion of the South Lancashire Regt., plus half a company of Royal Engineers. In addition, there were 200 men from Thorneycroft's Mounted Infantry, made up from an

"Uitlander Volunteers Contingent" which had been recruited in Johannesburg and Natal, and which was dismounted for this particular operation.

The Task Force set off from Three Tree Hill at dusk on the 23rd on its six-mile approach to Spioenkop. General Coke stood at the roadside to see them off. It was intended that each soldier would carry one sandbag up the hill; these were left in a large heap by the side of the road, but no one had remembered to pass on the order to the soldiers. As a result, the sandbags, which may have spared many casualties during the coming massacre, were left behind – a forlorn little pile standing alone in the veld. The column reached the foot of the Kop around mid-night, and there was a brief halt while the officers searched in vain for a section of water-carriers who had failed to put in an appearance. Eventually the ascent proper set off, and the troops, led by Thorneycroft's MI, moved up in single file, zigzagging up the steep slopes of the mountainside.

Thorneycroft, at the head of the column, was a giant of a man, just a few days off his fortieth birthday. He weighed well over twenty stones, and had an uncanny knack for leadership, and he was admired and respected for his enthusiasm and driving pugnacity. The ascent grew more and more difficult, and the men had to struggle to keep going. When they stopped briefly on the successive shoulders of the spur, some were so tired that they simply rolled over and fell asleep where they lay. Any fit man would have scaled the slope in a bit over an hour, but it eventually took the column four-and-a-half hours to make the ascent. At 3.30 a.m. Thorneycroft noted that the slope was beginning to flatten out, and it was then that they heard voices in the dark ahead – "Wie Daar?" It was a challenge from a small party of Boers who had been sent up the hill to dig some gun emplacements, and overtaken by the dark, had decided to stay up there and finish the job in the morning. A brief encounter ensued and the Boers rushed down the other side of the hill, but not before one of them was killed and two others wounded. The British, with the cost of three men wounded, were masters of the Kop!

The charge had carried the soldiers to the raised central dome of the plateau, and it was there that they paused to regain breath. Woodgate called for three cheers, the agreed signal, to inform Warren below that the summit had been secured, and at once the British artillery opened fire, with a crash, onto the rear slopes of the Kop to harass any Boer reinforcement that might be coming up on the counter-attack. Taking meticulous care not to repeat Colley's mistakes at Majuba, Woodgate ordered the Engineers to lay out a trench system along the summit on the line where his men had halted, which appeared to be the near crest of the hill. Unfortunately, Woodgate omitted to explore the ground slanting gently away in front of him, and he assumed that the slope continued for some distance in the same way as it did on the top of Thabanyama. In fact, he had no idea at all that only a mere 200 yards in front of him, there was a crest line from which the ground fell away almost precipitously down towards the Ladysmith plain and the Boer positions.

The soldiers did what they could to help the Engineers with the trenches, but for all their efforts the trench was disappointing – there was very little topsoil, and they soon struck hard solid rock. At the end of three hours, they had merely managed to raise a flimsy wall of stones and rubbish some eighteen inches high in front of a shallow scooped out ditch. The low wall was irregular and only provided cover for a man lying prone. The ground was particularly hard on the right where the soldiers piled rocks around likely clumps of boulders to make rough sangars. A few yards to the rear, a second support trench was started, but progress was slow because by now the men were very tired, having worn themselves out completely on the hard and rocky ground. The main trench extended a bit further than 400 yards, and centred on the dome- shaped summit of the plateau forming a shallow V-shaped pattern with the apex pointing northwards. The 200-yard section on the left faced northwest and was terminated by a prominent group of boulders. It was occupied by the Royal Lancashire's, while the two companies of the South Lancashire's scooped out some form of cover behind the boulders to the rear of the T.M.I. The Lancashire Fusiliers on their right shared the central, 180 yards-long portion of the trench, which faced due north. On the right of that, was the Fusiliers section of the trench, which angled back sharply for a further fifty yards, and was then extended to the south by a few inadequate sangars, echeloned, one behind the other, and extending almost as far as the steep slopes leading down the hill's precipitous southern face.

At 7 a.m. the mist lifted momentarily and it became obvious that the trench was badly situated. Directly in front, the field of fire extended for a mere 200 yards up to the plateau crest-line, whilst at the far right it, was even worse, with the trench only eighty yards from the crest. The mist was still thick enough, however, to conceal the saddle which joins the two halves of Spioenkop, and the soldiers were still unaware that only 400 yards away it humped up into Aloe Knoll, high enough to command and enfilade their exposed position, and close enough to bring them into a deadly rifle-fire range.

From this moment onwards, and for the ensuing twenty-four hours, a disastrous sequence of errors and omissions were to have a fateful and deadly affect on the Battle of Spioenkop. Not only had the sandbags been forgotten, but in addition, the mountain battery had not arrived. Furthermore, between 3.30 and 7 a.m., not one of Woodgate's 1,700 soldiers had been sent out to reconnoitre the forward summit of the hill. The folly of this omission became obvious with the melting of the morning mist, the British soldiers had unwittingly dug their own graves when they entrenched in the centre of the plateau. They had ignored the well-established military principle that on a tabletop hill there are only two places to hold - either the forward crest or a position immediately behind the rear crest. As it was, their entrenchment could hardly have been situated in a more dangerous position, because a large part of it aligned directly on the commanding position of Aloe Knoll, which the Boers had already occupied.

At 3.30 a.m., Botha, in his H.Q. on a hillock a little north of Spioenkop, was awakened by the sound of rifle fire and the "three cheers" of the soldiers on the summit of the Kop. He knew at once that his positions were under serious threat, and he resolved to recapture the hill at all costs. He summoned two of his most able subordinate officers, commandants Opperman and Prinsloo who's Pretoria and Carolina commandos had been laagered behind Green Hill and Twin Peaks respectively. The significance of the fact that these two commanders had spontaneously positioned their forces at each end of the battle arena was a credit to the military strategy of the Boer commanders. After briefing Opperman and Prinsloo, Botha sent riders to Acton Homes, Vaalkrantz, and the

Boer laagers around Ladysmith, with messages calling up reinforcements. He sent three men to accompany Opperman up Aloe Knoll, to 'spy out the enemy position' and not only did they do this, but went one further, and crept through the mist to the crest of Spioenkop itself, where they found the plateau swarming with soldiers digging in. In the meantime, all available Boer guns were directed into positions from where they could shell the summit of the Kop, and before dawn, Botha had mustered a large number of burghers at the foot of the hill, and despatched them post-haste up the slopes to assault the plateau. It was a fantastic effort indeed, and was all accomplished with incredible speed and efficiency. Commandant Hendrik Prinsloo, already a battle veteran at the age of thirty-eight, commanded the crack Carolina commando, which was considered as something of a "corps d'elite" amongst the Boer forces. He was ably supported by his own very efficient subordinate officers such as Abraham Smit, Jan Grobelaar, and Louis Bothma, a teacher who was particularly expert as a heliograph signaller.

On the night of the 23rd, the Carolina commandos were encamped immediately under Spioenkop and as soon as they became aware of the movement on the summit, they set about manoeuvring into favourable assault positions along the crest by extending themselves to the left on Aloe Knoll. By this time they were joined by some burghers from Heidelberg under Veld Kornet Steenkamp, as well as a few who had recently arrived from Boksburg and Germiston. By the time the mist lifted, an impressive battle force was in position on and about Spioenkop to execute Botha's order 'to clear the British from the plateau' Later these forces they joined by Sarel Marais and fifty additional men from Heidelberg, who scrambled up to occupy the saddle connecting Aloe Knoll to Twin Peaks. At about the same time, veld-kornet Sarel Alberts's Germiston commando occupied Conical Hill, while a strong force from Pretoria under Opperman, climbed the northwest slopes of Spioenkop itself. Other groups of burghers from Heidelberg and Utrecht were stealthily taking up positions on Green Hill, where they could enfilade the British left flank. It fell to these men to open the Boer counter-attack with long-range rifle- fire. Rather than attempting a hasty storming of the Kop, Botha used the milky obscurity of first light to secure strong points commanding Woodgate's position, and by 7 a.m. he had succeeded. The right wing of the Carolina commando was, hidden behind the crest less than 200 yards from the unsuspecting British soldiers. Aloe Knoll and Green Hill were strongly held, and as soon as the sun appeared, Botha was immediately in direct contact with his forces, Bothma having got his heliograph into action on the slope of Aloe Knoll. It was with great relief that he learned that the British had no artillery on the summit of Spioenkop.

At 7.30 a.m.the mist lifted again, and the soldiers realised that the Boers intended to dispute their possession of Spioenkop, as a murderous fire swept the summit, and the British were taken completely by surprise. The British recovered well from their first shock, as their officers led spirited rushes to the crest, and after some hard hand-to-hand fighting, they succeeded in dislodging the Boers. There was little chance of consolidating by digging in – the ground here was even harder than on the plateau, and in any event the R.E. had taken the heavy picks and spades to make a road up the hill for the expected guns to come up. The only cover for those on the crest was that provided by some boulders fringing the edge.

Communication between the summit and Warren at Three Tree Hill was pathetic, and it was only at 7.45am that Woodgate sent Col. a'Court down the hill with a written report – *'We have entrenched a position and are, I hope, secure – fog is too thick to see'*. He went on to –*'suggest that 12-pdrs. be hauled up'* in the place of the missing Mountain Battery, and also requested that Lyttleton's brigade might ease pressure by making a demonstration against Twin Peaks. a'Court reached Warren sometime after 9 a.m., and was in an optimistic mood. He gave the General a description of the situation, and Warren was relaxed. They had no idea that by 8.15 a.m. the situation at the summit had changed, and that a message by the acting British commander on the plateau had been sent reading *'reinforce at once or all lost. General is dead'*. When the message finally reached Three Tree Hill, after having been relayed via Spearman's, Warren was overwhelmed.

Spioenkop – The Battle ("an acre of massacre")

Compared to Botha's communications and battle control, both the British liaison and signalling were deplorable. From Spearman's Hill, Buller had a particularly good view of the action on Spioenkop; through his telescope, he could even recognise individuals. Unfortunately for the British, Warren, who of all people should have made sure that he was in the best position to assess and control the action, was in fact in the very worst one. His camp faced onto the southwest spur of Spioenkop, some two miles away, and he was too short sighted to see the summit as more than a blur, while neither Aloe Knoll nor Twin Peaks were visible from Three Tree Hill. Also, from a tactical point of view, Warren was much too far away to be able to direct the battle personally, especially in view of the particularly poor signalling arrangements. Of the two heliographs on the summit, one was destroyed soon after the fighting had begun, while the other was too exposed to be used effectively. Flag signals were almost impossible to read in view of the distance, and Warren had to rely on messengers to carry messages to and from the firing line, and this method who could take anything up to three hours to accomplish. Most damning of all, no-one had though of running a telephone line from H.Q. to the top of the hill, regardless of the fact that all the equipment was available and at hand. Of course, there was nothing to prevent Warren from moving his H.Q. forward to cut down the time lapse, and to give him a clearer view of the theatre of action, but bizarrely this obvious solution never seemed to have occurred to him nor to anyone else. Episode by episode, the accumulation of errors and omissions continued inexorably to unfold.

The Battle of Spioenkop – First Phase

The real battle, which started around 8.30 a.m. and lasted over the following fourteen hours or so, could be broken down to four stages. The first stage was the struggle for the crest-line, followed by the Boer siege of the main British trench and their attempt to storm it. The third phase was the struggle for possession of the slopes of the hill to the right of the trenches, and finally, the fourth, Botha's attempt to destroy the British with intense shellfire. Hell burst upon the British when at 8.30 a.m. the sun finally burned away the mist, and the soldiers on the crest line as well as those in the shallow trenches immediately behind, were suddenly swept by continuous rifle fire, mainly from the flanks – Green Hill, Aloe Knoll and Conical Hill. The wide arc of fire covered every inch of the summit, and under its storm, the Boers were able to scramble up the northern slopes and regain the crest line.

Fierce hand-to-hand fighting broke out, with both commanders feeding reinforcements into the melee, which would swing from the crest in a wide line to the trench, and then back again. Initially, and at close quarters, the British would gain the advantage, and move forward to the crest. Once they had reached it however, their ordeal would become even worse, as they crouched behind a thin necklace of strewn boulders, and suffered the terrible clamour of rifle-fire from Aloe Knoll. As a result, nearly all of them were killed, except for a few survivors who found their way back to the doubtful shelter of the trench. It was at this time that Col. Bloomfield, at the western end of the main trench, observed large numbers of Boers streaming up Spioenkop's northwest slopes, and called over Gen. Woodgate to investigate. As soon as Woodgate arrived, he immediately caught a burst of shrapnel above the right, eye and was carried away to die shortly thereafter. Bloomfield took over command, but soon after he too was badly wounded, and the command passed on to the next in line of seniority, Col. Crofton. Crofton decided to send an urgent message to Warren for help. As a heliographer was nowhere to be found, a crawling search discovered a certain private Goodyear, who claimed to be able to signal in semaphore. Crofton ordered him to signal Warren: 'General Woodgate dead – reinforcements urgently required'. Goodyear, in his excitement, thought it necessary to improve on Bloomfield's original text, and signalled *'Reinforce at once or all is lost. General dead.'* A few moments later poor Goodyear was blown to bits, but his panicky message had made a significant contribution to the tragedy of Spioenkop, because although the British forces were in a serious situation, it was by no means as desperate as the message suggested. Admittedly, it did look as if the whole of the western extremity of the crest would have to be abandoned to the Boers, and that the soldiers were being subjected to heavy shelling and rifle-fire as well, but the main trench was still being firmly held, and the Boers were also sustaining serious casualties. The damage inflicted on the Boers could have been heavier if the British artillery had been anything as enterprising as the enemy's was. In the event, their only success was when a burst of shellfire succeeded in driving the burghers off Conical Hill.

The British guns, although ten times more numerous than the Boers, were very badly handled, and they frequently fired on their own troops. On only one other occasion did the field guns seriously hurt the Boers when they opened heavy fire on Aloe Knoll. By an unlucky chance, Warren saw their shells bursting on a position, which all through the fight, he assumed to been held by his own men, so he sent off a message to the artillery commander: *'we occupy the whole summit and I fear you are shelling us seriously. Cannot you turn your guns on those of the enemy?'* The batteries at once wheeled to other targets, and the Boers continued to remain in possession of the knoll, quite unscathed. Perhaps the most absurd facet of this incident was that Buller from Spearman's could see that Aloe Knoll was in fact held by the Boers, but he failed to overrule Warren's request. It is said that he was 'too courteous' to interfere with his subordinate's handling of the battle. Indeed, it seemed as if Buller purposely wished Warren to lose it!

The Boers had fewer guns than the British, but what they had they used brilliantly, and after 9 a.m. their shells, as much as their rifles, inflicted serious damage on the British troops on the plateau. Botha had skilfully sited his guns behind hills, and by using smokeless powder they were never spotted by counter-fire. Two 6" Creusot and "Long Toms" were placed on the rear slopes of Green Hill, only 4,200 yards from the summit, while even closer to the western edge of the battle-field, he concealed a Krupp gun and a pom-pom. Another Krupp and pom-pom were set up near his own H.Q. and a third Krupp was concealed behind Twin Peaks, some 2,800 yards from the summit, while a pom-pom was pushed further forward on this flank. All these guns commanded an arc of 120 degrees, and the Boer gunners handled them so efficiently, that their shells consistently dropped on the British soldiers, who were only 50 yards from their own positions.

The action on the summit, at this stage, had developed into an ebb and flow pattern, "like a perilous game of see-saw". By approaching the burghers more steadily, and moving from rock to rock, the British soldiers would reach the crest without any due loss, and from there, touch off flurries of hand-to-hand fighting. But then they would be driven back to their trenches by super accurate Boer fire from Aloe Knoll and Conical Hill on the flanks. This to-and-fro action persisted all through the first half of the morning, with the disputed crest line as the prize for both sides. The British troops spent most of their time crouching in their trenches, or lying prone on their bellies while bullets whip-lashed over them and shells burst all round. Then three or four times in every hour, they would respond to their officers' call for another counter-attack. By 11 a.m., the Boers' hold on the crest had become firm, except at its extreme western sector where a handful of the T.M.I. maintained their position during the remainder of the day. The T.M.I. salient was protected by a fold in the ground, which ran at a rectangle from the crest line towards the entrenchment giving them shelter from enfilading rifle- fire.

Back at their respective HQ's, both Buller and Warren appeared to remain impassionate and aloof from the activity on the top of the Kop. Through his telescope on Spearman's, Buller had a better idea of what was going on, and would, from time to time, send a casual bit of 'advice' or a 'suggestion' to Warren. Warren, on receipt of these 'recommendations', reacted to them as if they were orders. The situation on the summit was already chaotic, and Warren's reaction to Buller's suggestions exacerbated an already disastrous position.

At 10 a.m. Warren, after receipt of Crofton's despairing message, was aroused into a spate of activity – he had already despatched two supporting regiments, the Imperial Light Infantry (I.L.H.) and the Middlesex Regt., up the hill, but now he ordered Gen. Coke to go up with the Dorset Regt., and assume command at the summit. He then addressed himself to the technicalities of getting water, food and ammunition to the soldiers on the top, and then....had a nap! He made no effort to relieve pressure on the summit by deploying any of the additional 10,000 men he had available, but he did make a lame appeal to Lyttleton for help. The whole aspect of Coke's interventions at Spioenkop seemed quite pointless, and it is sure that his presence there had no effect on the battle whatsoever. He began his ascent some time before 11 a.m., and reached the mimosa ledge about an hour later, where he then un-explicably remained for the next

145

three hours. He finally appeared on the southern edge of the plateau, though not the summit proper, at 5.30 that afternoon. He stayed there about an hour, and then returned down the slope to the mimosa ledge. He did have one good idea which may even have won the battle if it had succeeded – he took a machine gun with him when he began his climb but, later 'unfortunately it over-turned'

By now things on the top were making less and less sense – the British were subjected to continuous rifle and shell fire from an invisible enemy, and events seemed to have been overtaken by an inexplicable and irrational futility – message after message was being sent down to Warren, yet no response ever appeared to be coming back. Water carriers at the base of the hill wept in despair because the containers needed to carry the water to the top, had been left behind on the other side of the Thukela. Thus, the tally of mistakes and misunderstandings continued to increase from hour to hour. There was no direction to this battle – just a grim hanging on to a broken down trench while errors and blunders occurred in plenty. While the bungling lack of leadership given by Buller and Warren may have added up to something in this situation, it simply did not add up enough to account for all that went amiss, and one cannot help feeling that there remains some inexplicable and mysterious element in the battle which had so far not been recognised.

The Battle of Spioenkop - Second Phase
Despite all these lamentable failures, there were some rare oases of hope, and one was in Thorneycroft who became the kernel of the British defence. He waged his fight with frenzy, importing to the soldiers his own frenetically aggressive spirit, propping up their courage with his own. At 11 a.m. he fell heavily and twisted his knee badly, yet still he pushed on and on. At this stage all the odds were favouring the Boers. The main British trench was under siege, and assault - reinforcements were reaching the Boers in a steady stream. At one stage 200 fresh men under Tobias Smuts joined the burghers on Twin Peak, and the threat from Aloe Knoll also increased as the Carolina commando began to advance to the right extremity of the British trench and infiltrate under cover of the southeast slopes of the hill, around its rear. By midday, the Boers slowly began to gain more and more of the plateau, and the British rifle-fire was withering. In some areas, a few feeble attempts at a forward push with fixed bayonets were crushed from the start. The Boer commanders eventually got some 600 men crouching behind the boulders in front of the trenches, and a heliograph message called on their guns to cease-fire as they moved themselves for the final assault to overwhelm the right flank of the British position. When it came their charge carried them right up to the main trench, and the Fusiliers, who were nearest, began to crumble with white handkerchiefs at bayonet-end and with soldiers staggering up with hands in the air. It was at that this moment that total victory for the Boers was only ten minutes away!

But, now there occurred one of the most extraordinary events in a most extraordinary battle! *'We should have had the whole hill'*, lamented veld-kornet de Kock – *'the English were about to surrender when a great big, angry-faced soldier, ran out of the trench on our right and shouted – 'I am in command here – you take your men back to hell, sir – I allow no surrender'*. There was a mixture of the ridiculous and the epic about the incident, described by de Kock. Thorneycroft, a little further down the trench had seen the Fusiliers giving up. He rushed up in limping, stumbling haste, overwhelmed the Boer command with a torrent of shouted words, while the burghers and the soldiers stood around with gaping mouths. Thorneycroft, 'in order not to get mixed up in any discussions' withdrew, taking with him those soldiers who would listen to him, and before de Kock had a chance to protest, he got them under cover of the southern crest. The right half of the trench was now in Boers hands and in the end, only 180 of the Lancashire's were led down the hill on the Boer side. At precisely that moment when Thorneycroft had intervened and had got his soldiers safely back to the crest, a company of the Middlesex Regt. came up from the rear, and Thorneycroft took them into a line with his own men, and led them all back in an irresistible bayonet charge which ended in regaining the trench.

From his viewpoint on Spearman's, Buller had seen it all, and it now occurred to him that the mettlesome Thorneycroft would make a far better commander than the faint-hearted Crofton. He telegraphed to Warren, '*now that Woodgate is dead I recommend you put Thorneycroft in command*'. Warren immediately signalled to Crofton that Thorneycroft had been promoted to the rank of Brigadier-General in charge of troops on the summit, but in true form, he omitted to inform Gen. Coke who never heard of Thorneycroft's appointment until the following day, and a tragi-comedy of utter confusion regarding the identity of the senior British officer on Spioenkop now began.

A while later Buller had another chance to interfere fatally in the course of the battle. Three line battalions of Lyttleton's command concentrated around Spearman's were aching to get into action when the shooting began, and around 10 a.m. they got their chance. Lyttleton had received a message from Warren asking for help, and he grabbed the chance to intervene in the battle. He ordered his three battalions to Kaffir Drift, midway between Potgierter's and Trichardt's, and crossed the river around 1 p.m. His leading units, the Scottish Rifles under Col. Cooke, and Bethune's Mounted Infantry, were ordered to move directly on Spioenkop. After they had set off, Lyttleton saw other reinforcements climbing up the hill on the far side, so he decided that his third battalion, the King's Royal Rifles, would march straight across the plain and on to Twin Peaks. Buller was furious in the way Lyttleton was interfering in Warren's battle, and he thought the move he was making was dangerous in the extreme, and feared that the KRR would be annihilated. He sent an urgent message ordering the recall of the KRR, but it was ignored by Buchannan-Riddell with Nelsonian disobedience, and the KRR opened out in skirmishing order and continued their advance. Col. Buchannan-Riddell, the battalion commander, had constantly "hidden" Buller's orders, but after he was fatally wounded his second-in-command, Lt. Col. Wilson, could no longer risk disobeying any more of Buller's orders, and was forced to withdraw the battalion.

The attack was, brilliantly conducted; while all attention remained concentrated on the struggle on the plateau, the riflemen doggedly clambered up the slopes of Twin Peaks, encountering only nominal resistance. By 5 p.m., both the peaks were in their possession, and Gen. Schalk Burger's commando, which should have been defending them, was in full flight towards Ladysmith. The panic of Schalk Burger's burghers quickly communicated itself to their neighbours on Aloe Knoll, and Prinsloo had great difficulty in preventing the Carolina commando from abandoning the knoll. At the price of twenty men killed and seventy wounded, the KRR had punched a hole into the Boer position, and now it seemed that nothing could prevent the British winning the battle. This success was something of a miracle, and one can only marvel at the prowess of the riflemen. Their efforts deserved, and should have ensured a notable victory, because once they had secured the Peaks, there was nothing to prevent them from turning westwards along the crest line and linking up with the soldiers on the Kop – nothing, that is, except Buller!

One can only wince at the folly Buller now displayed. He was determined to get the Rifles back, and pelted Lyttleton and the beleaguered Wilson with angry instructions, ordering them back. Wilson ignored these, until in the end, even he could not afford to disobey any longer, and disgusted and heart-broken, he was forced to remove his Riflemen from the Peaks, and back again down to the river!

The Battle of Spioenkop-Third Phase
The arrival of the first companies of the Middlesex Regiment on Spioenkop during the early afternoon enabled Thorneycroft to restore the position in the main trench. The enemy effort had reached its climax at about 1.30 p.m.and from then on the danger of the British being driven of the hill receded as more and more reinforcements were fed into the fight.   The third phase of the battle now opened with Botha's attempt to outflank the trench along the hill slopes. Thorneycroft had by now set up a proper battle H.Q., and signalled Warren for reinforcements. His attention remained riveted on the plateau, and he was quite unaware that a separate battle had now flared up a mere 200 yards away on the southeast slopes of Spioenkop. For while the 2,000 men he now commanded were busy keeping their heads down among the 500 dead and dying on this "acre of massacre", the Boers were trying to envelope the plateau by pushing round the right flank below the southern lip of the mountain.

More British reinforcements were coming up the hill, and were being directed to the right before reaching the lip. From there they moved east, just above the southern precipice of the Kop, until they reached a place where the slope becomes more gradual, onto a fourth southeast spur. It was here that the third phase of the battle was being fought out, amidst pure chaos on the hillside, as fresh companies of the Middlesex Regt., the I.L.H., Bethune's Mounted Infantry, and finally the Scottish Rifles were sucked into this separate struggle. Confused attacks and counter-attacks surged across the slope in a wild reprise of the earlier fighting on the summit, and there were desperate struggles for positions consisting of no more than a few rocks or a shallow ledge in the ground. Thorneycroft on the summit, and Colonel Hill, office-in-charge of the Middlesex Regt. on the slope below, both believed that they were fighting the main battle and were so engrossed that neither was aware of the other's existence. For his part, Coke had no idea at all of what was going on in either sector of the struggle. Around 4 p.m. the battle for the south-eastern slopes was passing its crucial stage – repeated efforts by the Boer flank had been beaten back by the timely arrival of reinforcements, and the tide was now beginning to turn against them as the British, in their turn, were counter-attacking in an attempt to outflank Aloe Knoll.   The British movement was unsuccessful, but it made Botha give up all hope of driving the British off the plateau – his burghers were by now no less exhausted than the British were. Yet

148

he would not admit defeat, and instead decided on a plan to contain and destroy them with non-stop shellfire, thus opening up the fourth stage of the battle.

The Battle of Spioenkop - Fourth Phase
The burghers were recalled to withdraw behind the crest of the hill, and the Boer artillery opened up a sweeping bombardment of the summit of the Kop in continuous drum-fire. At 5.30pm Coke finally ventured from his sheltered shelf on the hillside and climbed up to where the Middlesex Regt. was taking cover on the upper slopes of the hill. There he was surprised to find 'a scene of considerable confusion', with mixed-up units not quite sure from whom to take orders because officers had removed badges of rank to avoid detection in action. Coke eventually made contact with Col. Hill, but he made no attempt to reach the summit proper or to see Thorneycroft, whom he regarded as a junior brevet Lt. Col. in command of a small unit assisting Col. Crofton in a portion of the front line.

It was one of the strangest aspects of the battle of Spioenkop that at this time there were four British Acting General Officers on the hill, three of whom at least believed himself to be the supreme commander. Coke had good reason – he was, after all, by far the most senior, and had been personally entrusted with the command by Warren. Hill was acting Brig. Gen. of the 10th Brigade, but knew nothing of Thorneycroft's sudden promotion, while Thorneycroft had been notified of his promotion by a message from Warren, and like Hill, had no idea that Coke had come three-quarters of the way up the hill. Even Crofton was uncertain where he stood, having been 'deeply hurt' at being superseded during the engagement by 'an officer so much (his) junior'. To add to the confusion, Col. Cooke of the newly arrived Scottish Rifles demurred at taking orders from Thorneycroft. Coke, on the slopes, was aware that Twin Peaks was now in the hands of the British, and he was in a perfect position to order a determined attack, which would have punched out Aloe Knoll and so secured that British position, but no such thought had entered his mind. Instead, he solemnly ordered Hill to hold the summit through the night, and then returned to the signal station on the upper shelf of the southwest spur, from where he received a message from Warren tentatively suggesting withdrawal from Spioenkop.

Yet, as the sun was going down over the distant Drakensberg, in spite of the slaughtering, the confusion and the Generals' muddling, the British had virtually won the battle of Spioenkop. They had held the summit against repeated attack and had beaten off Boer attempts to envelope them along the southern slopes. Twin Peaks was firmly in their hands and threatened the vital salient of Aloe Knoll, and immense reserves were available to reinforce or relieve the troops on the plateau. By now, food, water, and ammunition were coming up the hill in a steady stream. All that the soldiers needed to do was to hang on to their positions during the night and Spioenkop would go down in history as a glorious British victory. It only needed a single spasm of initiative by Warren or even a short message of encouragement from him, to give Thorneycroft and his men the resolve to hold on. But neither came and the mistakes and blunders continued to occur as though they had attained an irresistible momentum of their own. As the light faded most of the Boers had admitted defeat and many were withdrawing quietly back to their laagers. Botha was exhausted, but refused to admit defeat; his instinct told him that the British would throw away their victory and abandon the hill during the night. He was determined that, if necessary, he would resume battle in this morning. For his part, Warren at last started displaying some concern over the state of affairs on the hill, and ordered Coke to come down and report in person on the conditions at the firing line. The order went out, and Coke, the only man who could have prevented the final consuming tragedy of Spioenkop, then proceeded to spend the next few hours stumbling about in the darkness on the steep hillside, totally lost and unable to control events.

The Withdrawal

It was truly an ironic twist of fate that the one person who had fought all day like a lion, whose leadership and tenacity, courage and encouragement had virtually won the battle, and who in the end, in spite of the stupidity and indifference of his superiors, would be the man who was to lose it all! Soon after 7 p.m. Thorneycroft's nerve suddenly snapped; darkness had set in, the shooting had died away, and the 5,000 men on the mountain had settled down for whatever rest or relief they were able to muster. Suddenly, a flurry of rifle-fire flared up on the right flank, and in the darkness, the southeast slope was lit up with spurts of flame. It came from a small handful of Prinsloo's burghers who had come up to recover the body of a comrade before abandoning the Kop, but it sounded and looked much more serious than what it really was, and it was just enough to push Thorneycroft over the top and break his spirit.

He had had enough, and his men had had enough, and he gave the order to abandon the hill. It was a sudden decision – the snap decision of a man overcome by the horror, the futility, and above all the wanton waste and suffering that had taken place on the top of that hill that day. From that moment onwards, Thorneycroft acted like a man who had admitted defeat – he was determined to get his men off the hill at any cost, and no amount of persuasion or argument was going to make him change his mind. He called for a council of his senior officers, and he put the proposal to retreat to the vote. The result was a stalemate, until after a search, they found the missing Crofton, who cast his vote in favour of quitting the summit.

It is regrettable for the British that Col. Hill was not present, for despite his belief that he was the senior officer in command, he had inexplicably made no effort to exert his authority, even though earlier he had received an order from Gen. Coke that the summit had be held for the night. It was a pity therefore, that he was nowhere to be found when the council was assembled, for he most surely would have come out strongly against retreat. It is easy to understand the reason for Thorneycroft's breakdown – few men could have endured a day like Spioenkop without experiencing revulsion for the unnecessary suffering and death that had taken place there. No one can blame him either, for feeling an overwhelming sense of betrayal, for apart from one brief message appointing him to command, he had heard nothing further from Warren all day. For twelve mortal hours, he had gallantly held a vulnerable position, which the military incompetence of his superiors had forced upon him, and during all that time, he had watched the remainder of Buller's army making no effort at all to relieve the pressure on him and his troops. From his position on the summit, he was not even aware that Twin Peaks had been taken by the K.R.R., and not a single word had reached him at any time about arrangements to bring up artillery during the night. He had not even been told about the preparations to supply him with food, water, and ammunition. He was disgusted to learn that Coke had reached the plateau that afternoon, and had not made any attempt whatsoever to make contact with him. Now he was determined to make no more sacrifices of his exhausted and shell-shocked men to the incompetence and ineptitude of his seniors. Once he made his decision, his resolve to abandon the Kop never wavered.

Around 8.15 pm Thorneycroft formed up the leading ranks, and marched them down the southwest spur. He soon encountered serious opposition to the withdrawal from Col. Hill, who was startled to encounter the retreating troops a little below the summit. There was an angry altercation between Thorneycroft and Hill, and Hill only gave way when Thorneycroft assured him that he now held the rank of Brigadier-General, and took full responsibility for the withdrawal. It was not exactly clear what Hill was actually doing on the slopes of Spioenkop and indeed, why he was there at all when he should have been using his resources and experience to assist with the disastrous situation on the plateau itself. It is also true that throughout the entire battle he had shown a marked reluctance to expose himself to the slaughter on the summit, and never seemed to be anywhere near where he was supposed to be at times of crisis.

When the column reached Gen. Coke's command post 600 yards further down, Coke, the last person who had the authority to countermand Thorneycroft's orders, had just set off for Three Tree Hill in response to Warren's request for him to 'come down for consultations'. Before he left, Coke's last words to his aide, Capt. Phillips, were -'the hill must be held'. Regardless of the fact that it had never occurred to Coke that he should have been on the hill himself to give orders, he failed to specify exactly how, and to whom Phillips was to transmit the message. In the event, Phillips responded by falling asleep very shortly after Cokes departure, and it was a full two hours after the first of the retreating column had filed past the command post, that he eventually awoke, and by then, despite his sleepy efforts, it was too late to stem the downward flow. When he arrived at the foot of the hill, Thorneycroft met Col. Sims, with 200 men of the Somerset Light Infantry, carrying a written message from Warren, urging that the summit be held at all costs. After further altercations Thorneycroft retorted *'I have done all I can and am not going back and my troops have been ordered to retire'*. Sims, after consultation with his own officers, eventually set off behind Thorneycroft.

Around 2 a.m., Coke, who had once again succeeded in losing his way, finally limped into Warren's H.Q. at Three Tree Hill, after stumbling around for a number of hours trying to find it. He had scarcely made his vague report of the situation on the top as he had left it nearly six hours before, when Thorneycroft trampled into the faint haze of light cast by the hurricane lamp where the two men were standing. Weariness and defeat were glazing in his eyes, as he announced in flat tones that he had abandoned the Kop.

"Lost and stumbling around" is the legacy of Coke's contribution to the fatal battle of Spioenkop. The indictment may be a cruel one, yet it is a fact that on numerous occasions the course of the battle was jeopardised by the ineptitude of this senior British commander. Although there is little direct evidence that Coke was at any time under the influence of alcohol or opiates, his actions and reactions seriously point in that direction. Countless precious hours were lost, here and there, while he was stumbling around on his injured leg, trying to find his way from one point to another. Perhaps his painful injury was the reason why he appeared to shy away from direct encounter with the enemy, spending the bulk of his time on the slopes of the hill, some 600 yards away from the crest, and only presenting himself on the summit for a very brief period in the late afternoon of the battle. Whatever the reason, it was a grave and costly mistake on the part of Warren, to bestow so serious a command on a person so weak and physically distressed as the aged Maj.-Gen. Talbot-Coke.

Yet, even now, at this dramatic hour, all was not lost because another opportunity to save the situation had presented itself. Col. Cooke, whose two battalions had arrived on the upper slopes just when the main retreat began, turned his own men around and joined the downward march. When he passed Coke's H.Q., Phillips with difficulty, managed to persuade Cooke to stem his withdrawal until orders arrived from Warren. Cooke agreed to signal for specific instructions, but after a frantic, but fruitless search for oil for the signal lamps, he could wait no longer, and as daylight approached, and with his troops dangerously perched on a vulnerably exposed slope, he had no alternative but to give the order for withdrawal to the plains below. In the end there were no British troops left on Spioenkop apart from the dead and the wounded, and for them the battle was over....

Warren was stunned by Thorneycroft's report, and his only concern at that moment, was to shift the blame of the debacle onto someone else's shoulders as quickly as possible. He scribbled a message to Buller announcing that 'Thorneycroft has abandoned Spioenkop on his own responsibility' and ended it with a puerile request, 'can you come at once and decide what to do?' It is difficult to understand why it had taken a mounted orderly nearly three hours to ride the eight miles from Warren's H.Q. to Spearman's, because it was not until 5 a.m. on the 25th that Buller first read Warren's timid message. It took him less than an hour to ride over to Three Tree Hill to listen to Warren's news with something akin to complacency, bordering on indifference. In fact, he almost appeared to exude a smug gleam of satisfaction that Warren, like himself, had failed to defeat the Boers. As it was, the meeting balanced on the edge of strained courtesy as Buller tried to make it clear that he held, not Thorneycroft, but Warren himself responsible for the debacle. He then dismissed Warren from command of the Task Force, and briskly ordered a general retreat back to the far side of the Thukela.

After darkness fell that Wednesday night, most of the Boers were in no better shape than the British were – the same fatigue, the same numbness, and the same despondency. The day had ended without anyone really knowing what was going on, with most of the Boers expecting some sort of action by the British to sweep them off the hill. Ammunition was growing short, and hopes of victory were faint, and many burghers silently sneaked off to find rest and shelter in the laagers below. Here and there, some determined fellows did band together with the resolve to have a fresh go the following morning. Commandant Opperman, the commander of the Pretoria Commando, did not retire very far that night, and he too, soon became aware that the British were moving out en masse. Elsewhere, at least 40 burghers remained on the top under the command of Sarel Oosthuizen, and it is certain that a number of Caroliner's stayed up there with Prinsloo when they made that last attack which had so demoralised Thorneycroft. Prinsloo stationed his men just below the plateau, and rode down to rally some more of his commando, as well as to raise food and water for the men who stayed behind at the top. Back on the summit, he positioned his men for an ensuing battle, and then sent some of them on a brief reconnaissance down the other side, with orders to monitor and report on the British withdrawal. Twin Peaks remained abandoned during the night but the newly arrived Standerton commando continued to man the trenches further east to provide a stable hinge on which the Boers could pivot if and when the fighting resumed. Back at his H.Q. Botha, unaware of Prinsloo's actions, thought that the Boers had abandoned the Kop. He rode out on the Rosalie road to rally some of the men moving towards Ladysmith, because instinct told him that he could still win the battle if he could only rally a few score of the burghers. It was in this mood that he succeeded in rounding up a number of commandos before he eventually allowed himself to seek some rest.

Down below in the Boer laagers, some 450 men had collected, and were preparing a counter-attack. In the event, it turned out that there was no need to do so, because, by 4.30 in the morning, the Carolina commando had already re-occupied the summit, who in the grey light of dawn could be seen on the skyline, waving their slouch hats affixed to their rifles to announce the victory of the battle of Spioenkop. When Botha arrived on the summit, sickened by the scenes of carnage, he signalled Joubert by heliograph that he was standing amongst at least 1,500 English dead and wounded. By this time, Schalk Burgher had re-invested Twin Peaks, and now there were more than 500 Boers on the summit. The British army was in full retreat back to Chiveley, and the Boers were once again, in charge of Spioenkop.

The Cost
The first official figures of the Boer losses appeared in the evening press in London, stating 'Boer loss is 200 certain'. The first official Boer release reported their casualties as '58 dead – 140 wounded' It is universally believed however, that many more were killed on or around Spioenkop during the week's operation. On the summit of Spioenkop today, stands a monument recording the names of 106 men who died nearby, and according to one account, the number of dead may have exceeded 150. Casualties were particularly severe in the Carolina commando - of its 88 men who went into action, 57 were killed or wounded.

The British losses were reported as being 322 dead, 583 wounded and 300 captured. According to the Boers this is an understatement, and Van Everdingen writes that the Boers 'found between 1,200 and 1,500 dead' An American, Webster Davies, said he counted '400 English dead even after 620 had been buried'. Probably the most authoritative figures are those given by Commandant Pretorious, who appointed by Botha to make an accurate account of the casualties, reported that he had found 650 dead soldiers on Spioenkop and estimated a further 554 men wounded and 120 made prisoners-of-war. The Lancashire Fusiliers went into action 800 strong, but only 553 survived, while of the 194 men of Thorneycroft's MI, a mere 74 came down the hill unwounded.

On the summit, Botha insisted on making prisoners of Col. Bloomfield and several of the injured British officers, but allowed the remainder of the wounded men to be removed by the Medical Corps and the 25 volunteers of the Natal Ambulance Corps, which included Mohandas Ghandi making his first appearance on the stage of world history. Botha also granted a 24-hour truce to allow the British to bury their dead. By the 27th January, no British soldiers remained on the north bank of the Thukela, and the Boers did not interfere with Buller's retreat, Joubert fearing to tempt 'divine providence too far'. In fact, the truth of the matter was that the Boers were too exhausted to hassle the British withdrawal.

The Indictment
Where, when, and why did it all go so badly wrong for the British? – Napoleon once said that the 'general who makes the least mistakes wins the battle', and it is a probability that any one of the errors or omissions committed by Buller, Warren and other senior British officers, could have been overcome and disaster averted. But it is an irrevocable certainty that by no manner or means were they ever going to cope successfully with the mountain of mistakes and gaffes which marked their performance during the Thukela campaign and in particular at Spioenkop. The campaign was doomed from the very moment Buller set off from Frere in the first week of December 1899. The slow and lumbering progress of the so-called 'flying columns', not only revealed their strength and intention to the enemy, but also allowed the Boers ample time to follow their every move. It also enabled the Boers to dictate their battle strategy and to set up secure and adequate defences whenever and wherever it was appropriate. The 'milling around' and massive traffic-jams during the advance to Springfield, and subsequently at Thabanyama, were acerbated by Warren's attempts at hands-on logistics and by his queer notions of "getting to know the enemy', and the so-called 'dress-rehearsals'. Did he truly believe that a mere parading of strength would scare the Boers into upping sticks and fleeing? By now it should have been obvious that hackahs and similar pre-match confrontations, which may have made effectively awesome impressions on the 'natives' and other primitive forces whom the British had successfully overwhelmed during the past ten decades had little if any effect on the Boers. They, instead, simply ignored the posturing and demonstrating and used the time to reinforce and entrench, and in urgently setting about manoeuvring and digging impregnable defences during those precious hours that Warren wasted.

The list of British failures is a long one, but it might be interesting to highlight just a few. Firstly, there was Warren's disdainful dismissal of Dundonald's highly successful action on the left flank at Acton Homes, which, if it had been followed through, would undoubtedly have turned the Boer front, thereby exposing their rear to an assault by Buller from Potgieter's Drift via Vaalkrantz. Instead of help and encouragement, Warren's response was an admonishment, and an order to return more than half of the Cavalry Division to HQ to police the draught-oxen in order to prevent them from stampeding.

But not only Warren was guilty of making tactical errors. Buller, who held the fate of the summit at Spioenkop, and a glorious British victory, in his hands, was, instead, the hangman who sprung the trap that turned the whole shambles into a humiliating failure.

At one of the most critical stages of the battle of Spioenkop, the K.R.R. from Lytlleton's brigade had successfully sent the Boers scurrying from their vital offensive position on Twin Peaks. Buller, instead of reinforcing the hold on Twin Peaks and launching an assault over the saddle towards Aloe Knoll, thereby enfilading the entire Boer flank on the plateau, and up to Conical Hill, Green Hill and beyond, ordered the K.R.R. to withdraw to base because he 'did not want to interfere with Warren's battle'!

In addition to the incidents cited above, the list of other failures is endless. The contemporary training philosophy of the British army rendered it impossible for its officers, even at highest level, to make bold decisions or to take any individual action, without prior orders from higher authority. Then there was the matter of Buller's abdication of command and responsibility at Spioenkop, Warren's insistence on setting up his own H.Q. miles from the scene of the battle, and in a position where a large portion of the action area was hidden from his view. The situation was acerbated by the poor marksmanship of, not only the infantry but the artillery as well, by the failure to take the sandbags up the hill, and by the bad positioning of the main trench on the summit due to the absence of proper reconnaissance before the assault. Effective use of artillery may have saved the day for the British, but their marksmanship was bad. On the one occasion when their intervention may have saved the day for the British, Warren, from his far away H.Q., ordered the cessation of some damaging shelling on Boer positions on Aloe Knoll, because he erroneously believed that the hill was occupied by the British!. In fact, the role of the artillery could have been fundamental to the outcome of the battle, if only matters had been appropriately co-ordinated. Instead, one of the key pieces of the jigsaw was the ill-fated Mountain Battery, whose efficacy was totally negated by the absence of its guns that had been left behind at Frere.

Proper communications were non-existent, yet this aspect of the campaign was critical due to the distances between Buller's and Warren's bases and the battle arena. There were no telephones in use, in spite of the fact that the necessary equipment was available distances were too vast for adequate semaphore signalling, heliograph facilities were inadequate and vulnerable, and hand-carried messages were delayed due to the distances to be covered. One of the worst gaffes of the battle was the confusion over who was in command on the top the hill. On one occasion there were four persons on the summit who believed that they were in charge, and who were unaware of the existence of any of the other legitimate claimants to the title. Then, there was Gen. Coke's bumbling and his reticence to show himself at the battlefront. There was also Col. Hill's reluctance to assert himself, but worse than this was his absence from the action when it was needed most. Finally, there was Warren's failure to make direct contact with Thorneycroft during the entire battle, other than the initial message ordering him to take command on the summit.

Dozens of other omissions may be cited, such as for example, the mystery of the missing water-containers, the shortage of oil for signalling-lamps, and so on, but at the end of the day it all added up to an indictment of incompetence and negligence on the part of the British military establishment.

Ladysmith – The Final Round
Back at Chieveley, Buller's army slowly recuperated and regained strength, and the morale of the men improved greatly. In Ladysmith, however, the situation was rapidly worsening, both for the townsmen as well as for the troops. Outbreaks of dysentery, typhoid, and other diseases increased, mainly due to under-nourishment, as stores and stocks started running out with little if any fresh supplies coming in. The breakdown of morale, was seriously threatened by the daily bombardment of Boer guns, which wore the nerves bare, and friction caused by stress and deprivation further frayed the relations between the military and the townspeople.

Roberts, on the Western Front, was not pessimistic and refused to be dismayed; he was quietly assembling his forces and contemplating his strategy with the minimum of publicity. He resolved that he would only strike when he was reasonably sure of success, and he boosted White's spirits by sending his warm congratulations upon the 'heroic splendid defence' of Ladysmith, and confidently asserted that the impending campaign would significantly reduce the enemy strength by the end of February. Meanwhile, he asked White to sit it out as best he could, and strongly urged Buller, for the same reasons, to stay on the defensive until further notice. But Buller was not impressed – he signalled White informing him that he doubted Roberts's forecasts coming off, and suggested 'playing his own hand alone'. White was terrified that another failure by Buller would fatally postpone the relief of Ladysmith and seal its doom, and he urged Buller to keep up a bold front with harassing tactics and remain on the defensive until Roberts's intervention started to tell on the enemy.

Buller was not convinced; it was as if Ladysmith had become an obsession with him – an irresistible urge to subdue it and bring a lasting honour to his career. Whatever the reason, Buller disregarded Roberts's advice, and on January 28th, the very day on which he received Roberts's signal, he announced at a church parade, that he now really held 'the key to Ladysmith', and that he would be there within a week. The key he believed to possess for unlocking the Thukela defences was a break in the hills to the right of the ford in front of Spearman's Hill. Between two koppies, Vaalkrantz and Doornkop, was an open space – a gateway to the Ladysmith plain itself. He had only to seize these hills, and he could march safely through. Buller spent the following few days confidently preparing his offensive which he finally launched on the 5th February.

On the Boer side, the situation had changed a great deal since Spioenkop. Many burghers had left, including Botha who was on leave. The 4,000 men remaining in the area were strung out in small pockets along the whole of the Thukela Heights, from Thabanyama to beyond Colenso. Less than half were on Vaalkrantz and Doornkop, confronting Buller's army of over 20,000 men. The commandos on Vaalkrantz were mainly from Johannesburg under Ben Viljoen, who when he saw the bustle at Spearman's Hill, called for help. General Botha, who was on leave, was immediately ordered to return to the front and block Buller's attack on Vaalkrantz. On his arrival he discovered that he was too late and that the British advance had already started. A feint in front of Spearman's Hill had enabled them to throw a pontoon bridge across the river, and the first wave of troops under Gen. Lyttleton had already reached the slopes of Vaalkrantz in the teeth of Viljoen's fierce defence.

Inexplicably no attack on Doornkop followed. – Buller had lost heart. Lyttleton's men were now unable to retreat for fear of serious loss, and he begged Buller at least to continue the attack on Vaalkrantz. Buller agreed reluctantly, and ordered over reinforcements. At the same time, he opened up with all his 66 guns at Spearman's to turn Vaalkrantz into a huge cloud of smoke. A lyddite shell burst above Viljoen's head, stunning him and killing his comrades around him. He had scarcely regained his senses when the British were charging with fixed bayonets, sweeping up the slopes, and for half a mile along the crest. Viljoen escaped, dragging along a Pom-Pom with him, but over half his comrades on this side of the hill were wiped out. Then Boer reinforcements and artillery checked the British advance, but Buller would still do nothing to help. Night came with Lyttleton's men entrenched amongst the rocks. He pressed Buller to complete the original plan in the morning for they now held the important end of Vaalkrantz and had only to secure Doornkop to leave the road open to Ladysmith.

Buller postponed his decision until the next morning when he set about sending a string of messages proposing first one course of action and then another. During this time, the Boers, taking advantage of the inactivity, poured reinforcements into the gap, and on Doornkop itself. Buller, now confronted with this new threat, telegraphed Roberts, telling him that to get through the gap he had already all but forced, would cost the lives of 2,000 to 3,000 men, and he asked '*do you think the relief of Ladysmith is worth the risk? Is it the only possible way to relieve White?*' Then he added, despairingly, '*if I give up this chance I know no other.*' Roberts replied with patient fortitude – '*Ladysmith must be relieved even at the loss you anticipate*'. Buller did not react immediately, but pondered for a long while over the message while the two sides kept up an artillery duel. On the Boer side, Botha arrived at noon, and infused a fresh initiative into his men, and at 3pm, the grass in front of the British lines was set ablaze by pounding shellfire. The Boers made a charge through the smoke, and nearly overran their opponents, until a half battalion of the 60th Rifles, lying in reserve, sprang forward with fixed bayonets and checked the stampede. Towards sunset fresh troops arrived to strengthen the British entrenchments. Buller was still undecided about how to proceed, and remained so throughout the night while the guns thundered on resolutely. At 4 a.m. he called a council of his generals, and decided to pull out. He telegraphed Roberts that the present engagement would uselessly waste the lives of hundreds of his men, and that he would try again elsewhere. He then spent the following three days marching the troops, guns and nearly 600 wagonloads of stores back to Chieveley. In the end a total of 400 casualties had been incurred in this attempt of monumental fatuity, Buller's third unsuccessful effort to force the Thukela Heights.

The Boer leaders were delighted, and imbued with an aura of invincibility. Joubert alone was acutely aware of the British determination not to let go, and it was this unrelenting persistence that he feared most of all in the British. He urged Kruger to take advantage of the current state of affairs to make peace overtures. Kruger refused - large British reinforcements were undoubtedly arriving, but wherever one looked, the Boers seemed secure – on the Western Front, in the Cape and in Natal. Things could not go wrong for the Boers at this stage especially since they stood astride every railway route;

the British dared not advance a yard without it, to bring up their food and supplies, and even their essential water. What Kruger did not appreciate, or even realise, was that it was precisely this problem of transport and communications, which Roberts and Kitchener were contemplating day and night in their H.Q. in Cape Town. The news that Buller had broken off the engagement at Vaalkrantz, and his emotional messages that followed, reached them at this critical moment, just when they had believed that they had found a solution to the matter. Roberts and Kitchener's priority since their arrival in South Africa, was exactly how to conquer the veld without total dependence on the railway routes. The War Office plan for an invasion from the Cape Midlands was scrapped, and Roberts worked on his new 'grand design'. His plan would be to assemble his army on the western railway sector, at Orange River station. Then, instead of continuing north along the railway line as originally planned, he would set out towards the east, over 80 miles across the veld, until he reached the central railway line, at Bloemfontein. In so doing, he would draw back the Free State burghers in defence of their homeland, and thus weaken the forces surrounding the besieged town across the country, as well as their defences at the Thukela Heights.

Ladysmith – Buller's 'Desparate Dash'
Following Cronje's defeat at Paardekraal on the western front, the Boer defences in Natal were seriously weakened, as thousands of Free State burghers streamed back to defend their capital and their country. Encouraged by this, Buller telegraphed Roberts that he was now ready to make a 'desperate dash for Ladysmith, and he signalled White that he intended to set off on the 10th February. Buller then put his 'desperate dash' into action by providing one of his most remarkable performances of indecision and shilly-shallying ever. He barely managed to finish assembling his troops by the 11th, and then for the next five days, he left White waiting anxiously for further news, while he kept changing his plans from one hour to the next, unable to decide whether the weather was too hot to move, or too wet or too windy or too whatever! At the end of that first week Buller eventually succeeded in 'desperately dashing' his army forward for a distance of six miles only.

Nevertheless, he remained determined to press on with his fourth attempt at Ladysmith. His confidence was boosted by a series of discussions with his staff and his senior officers, which resulted in a conviction that that the true key to Ladysmith lay in an entirely different approach to the problem - one which entailed a radically new system of offensive warfare. After numerous defeats, at the cost of over 3,500 casualties in Natal since the start of the war, Buller had begun to realise that the old 'one-day, three act' battles of the past had been killed stone-dead by the combination of trench and magazine rifle fire. To win modern battles, troops should now be committed to a series of inter-locking engagements, spread over a great number of miles as well as days. In addition, to counter-act the deadly effectiveness of Boer marksmanship and mobility, new infantry tactics needed to be adopted, such as better use of terrain, more individual initiatives, and more skilful use of cover. The role of the artillery also needed to be revolutionised - instead of merely supplying the first act in the 'one day-three-act' strategy, it would now be required to engage day after day, harassing the enemy by continually throwing a creeping barrage ahead of the advancing infantry.

It seemed that the British were at last beginning to see through the restrictions imposed by the exigencies of their traditional and rigid parade ground battle training, and Buller's officers, in particular, cautiously displayed support of this innovative thinking of new offensive tactics. Hildyard, the Staff College expert, Warren, the Sapper, and many of the younger officers and artillery commanders, were enthusiastic over these new views, and some of them, including Warren, even complained about Buller's caution in not putting the new innovations into practice immediately. They all now agreed that the real 'key' to success against the Boer, was in effect, the efficacy and tenacity of the British infantry. In his book 'The Boer War' (BCA1999), Thomas Pakenham writes: *In the simple, geographical sense, there was not so much a 'key' as a double combination lock, whose first sequence of positions centred on a hill nicknamed 'Monte Christo', a hill on the British side of the Tugela'.* Just east of Colenso, the Thukela is abruptly diverted to the north by a six-mile long gorge cutting through the hills east of Colenso, and in so doing, completely isolating the entire Boer left flank along the south bank of the river. Hlangwane, the first of the hills south of the gorge, was well known to the British, Dundonald's Mounted Brigade having previously attacked it during the early phases of the first Battle of Colenso. Hlangwane is pitted with ravines, and was completely hidden in a tangled maze of mimosa trees. It is barely 500 feet high, and is commanded by a series of wooded ridges further east, which culminate in the imposing 1,000-foot hill at Monte Christo.

Initially Buller made lukewarm proposals in favour of an attack on Hlangwane, and the matter was considered in depth at his staff meetings. The suggestion was met without enthusiasm by his officers, even Lyttleton commenting that an attack on Hlangwane would 'achieve little'. A reconnaissance of the area revealed that since the Battle of Colenso, the Boers had greatly strengthened their trench lines there, and were well prepared for an assault in that sector. Nevertheless, Buller, for once thinking like a commander of strategy, responded with the question, 'what other choice is left?' They had tried the frontal attack at Colenso, and two flank attacks to the west. A flank attack to the east was the last 'forlorn hope' of ever reaching Ladysmith, he argued. He encouraged his officers to trust in their immense superiority in heavy guns, and in the new tactical skills of both gunners and infantry, hammering and squeezing out the enemy, step by step, hill by hill, crumpling their line from Hussar Hill to Cingolo, from Cingolo to Monte Christo, and from Monte Christo to Hlangwane. It was a ponderous style of fighting, but the concept was undisputedly correct – it was, in fact, the painful prototype of modern warfare.

The Breakthrough
Hussar Hill was the first target. It was dubbed 'Hussar Hill' after some of the 13th Hussars had been surprised and forced off it some six weeks before, with the loss of two men killed. Buller's new field intelligence, supplied by Lt. Col. Arthur Sandbach ("Sandbags"), and forty well-paid African agents, was now greatly improved, but still hesitant about the best line of advance. He therefore recommended that a probe be launched to test the Boer defences in the area. On the 12th February, a group of Dundonald's irregulars', together with Lt. Col. Julian Byng's S.A.L.H, set off to assess the possibility of an attack on Hussar Hill. At midday, Buller followed behind the

reconnaissance detail, and personally surveyed the countryside around him. The results were discouraging, the project was called-off, and the entire force ordered back to Chieveley.

During the following seven days, the advance, in typical 'old Buller' fashion, was resumed – faltered – recalled – set off again until eventually, on the 14th February, Hussar Hill was captured by Dundonald's men after a daring rush and a lightning strike. The following day Buller threw his right, pushing up Lyttleton's division crabwise onto Green Hill, the ridge linking Hussar Hill and Cingolo. Heavy guns were dragged onto Hussar Hill and soon the infantry marched forward under cover of gunfire, for by now, 34 guns had hastily been positioned on Hussar Hill, including two 5-inch Royal Garrison Artillery guns. In total, Buller had 50 guns heavy and field-guns concentrated on the Thukela, compared with the Boers' eight. On the 16th February, the men received some good news. Kimberley had been relieved after a daring dash by Gen. French's Cavalry Division, and on the 17th, as if encouraged by this success Buller's men consolidated their finger-hold on Hussar Hill, and established a firm grip on four miles of tangled ridges east of Colenso.

The struggle for Monte Christo on the 18th was rather tame compared to Colenso or Spioenkop – it was Hildyard's 2nd Brigade, the West Yorkshires, the East Surreys and the Queen's Own, who stormed the skyline in a thick mass. On the opposite ridge, Green Hill, Barton's 6th Fusilier Brigade picked its way over the scarred and pock-marked ground to the skirl of the pipes of the Scots Fusiliers. A thin cheer arose as they joined the other men on Monte Christo. The hill was theirs! Following the capture of Monte Christo and the other ridges, the Boers fled across the river, leaving everything behind them. Buller was now master of the south bank, giving him an unchallenged six-mile arc of ground east of Colenso. With Monte Christo firmly in British hands, the occupation of Hlangwane on the 19th was an easy affair, and after rapidly installing some batteries of heavy artillery on its summit, Buller opened the way to Colenso. It was a sound tactical victory even if he, perhaps mistakenly, failed to take the risk of sending some of his troops forward to cut off the fleeing Boers. British morale was high as 15 battalions of infantry surged north over the hills. Buller heliographed White – it would not be long now, he predicted.

The Relief of Ladysmith

Buller now found himself faced with his next problem - how to open the second part of the combination lock, represented by the area between the Thukela and Ladysmith. His first priority was to consolidate his hold on Colenso, and on the morning of the 19th two infantry companies marched into Colenso unopposed, followed the next day by Thorneycroft's Uitlander unit, which splashed across the Thukela and occupied the hills at Fort Wylie. There was no sign of the Boers anywhere, but their presence was keenly felt. Buller knew they were there somewhere, and that it would be quite easy for them to block his advance to Ladysmith on any one of the two outlets from Colenso to the north. There was the new road, traversing a relatively flat plain to the northwest, and the old one, winding northeast through the hills along the railway line. Both were heaven sent for an ambush, the surrounding hills providing tier upon tier of natural defence and attack positions.

One can never be sure whether it was the mauling that the Boers had, until now, inflicted on Buller's army in Natal, which caused him to be so over cautious, and to make some very doubtful decisions. For example, it is surprising that he had opted not to follow up his advance while the fleeing Boers were on the run after Monte Christo but, instead, decided to double back to Colenso, in spite of his original plan to bypass it altogether. When Buller had surveyed the surrounding region from the summit of Mount Christo after it was occupied, he could actually see Ladysmith, and his staff officers urged him to press northwards, either by swinging round to the northeast of Monte Christo, or by cutting through the great gorge to the northwest. Buller appeared eager to follow one of these routes, but Col. Sanbach, the Intelligence Commander, reconnoitred both areas and reported it to be *'out of the question'*. It was on the strength of this report that Buller decided that he had no other choice but to fall back on Colenso.Whatever the reason, the decision to occupy Colenso served little purpose other than to provide the Boers with sufficient time to prepare and consolidate their new and very effective defence positions in the hills to the north

On the 21ˢᵗ February, the order to set off for Ladysmith was given. The sappers immediately floated out a pontoon bridge, (the same wood and canvas one that had already carried the army four times across the river), and anchored it across the swift current where the Thukela turns north to avoid Hlangwane. On the 22ⁿᵈ, the main advance resumed; Maj. Gen. Arthur Wynne set off with the Lancashire (11ᵗʰ) Brigade to seize the koppies three miles north of Colenso, and a mile above the falls. Earlier, Gen. White signalled, from Ladysmith, that the main Boer position was at Pieter's Hill, two miles further north. Beyond Pieter's Hill, it was downhill all the way to Ladysmith. Buller was optimistic – Roberts's successes in the Free State had pulled away many hundreds of Free State burghers from around Ladysmith, and Roberts had called Buller and White to report that *'lots of special trains'* were taking the burghers from Natal to the Free State and other parts of the western front. On the 23ʳᵈ Buller heliographed White – *'I am now engaged in pushing my way through by Pieter's – I think there is only a rear-guard in front of me.* But it was not a rear-guard opposing him. It was in fact a force of 5,000 Boers ensconced in the hills in front of him. These hills range one behind the other in a row beyond Colenso, running parallel with the northward bend of the river. Between the hills and the river lies a shallow valley through which ran the road and railway to Ladysmith. Buller's plan was to reach this road by crossing the river westward from the foot of Hlangwane, by way of the pontoon bridge which had previously been thrown over the Thukela on the 21ˢᵗ. After crossing the river, the leading troops and transport reached the other side without incident, but when they started marching up the valley, the Boers opened fire from the flanking hills, and brought them to a halt, with some hundred or so casualties.

In spite of the hold-up, Buller continued the whole day, that night and into the following morning, to pour men, ammunition, supplies, guns and baggage across the river, creating a monumental pile-up which caused chaos behind the immobilised troops ahead. It soon became obvious that something had to be done to alleviate the situation, and a brigade was despatched to attack Wynne Hill, one of the flanking hills on the left of the blocked column ahead. No provision was made, however, for flank cover and the brigade suffered severely from Boer fire from the adjoining hills, Horse-Shoe Hill and Hart Hill, as well as from the Boers directly in front of Wynne Hill itself. However, by nightfall, Wynne's Lancashire Brigade, in spite of severe casualties, had succeeded in establishing a precarious toehold on both Horse-Shoe and Wynne hills. Throughout the night, the men were swept by shell and rifle fire, and the Boer attempts to brush them off the hills were only held at bay by frantic bayonet rushes. During the night, some reinforcements arrived, but after another day of fierce fighting their casualty list had exceeded 500.

With the Boers clinging to their line of ramparts and barring the corridor to the Ladysmith plain beyond Hart Hill, Buller realised that it was no longer a 'retreating rearguard' in front of him but a solid crest-line very much in the hands of the Boers. He also realised that in the narrow crowded corridor between the hills and the river, he had no elbowroom to exploit effectively his five-to-one advantage in manpower and his ten-to-one superiority in artillery. To regain the initiative it was imperative that Buller remove the barrier in front of him in order to absorb the pressure from behind. To achieve this it would be necessary to clear the flanking hills, particularly Hart Hill. The British would then be in a position to attack the main Boer force on Pieter's Hill, not head-on, but from their vulnerably exposed right flank.

The attack on Hart Hill was ill conceived and doomed to failure even before it started. The two principal reasons for the disaster were obvious – the urgency with which it was set up and the impatience and inflexibility of its commander, General Hart. In view of the urgency of the situation, no serious thought had been given to the fine-tuning and the logistics of the assault. The Irish Brigade was far from ready when the urgent marching order was given, and Hart hastily pushed the men forward as and when they could muster. The result was that the two battalions of the Inniskillings arrived at the foot of Hart Hill while the next two battalions, the Connaughts and the Dublins, were spread out across the valley, at least two hours behind everyone else. In addition, no support could be expected from Wynne, who at the time of the start of the attack, was himself still precariously balanced on the adjoining Wynne and Horse Shoe hills.

After an exacting march across the veld, the Inniskillings arrived at the foot of Hart Hill shortly before dusk. The terrain ahead of them was hostile, and the steep slopes of the hill covered with rocky outcrops and ragged ravines, presenting an exhausting challenge to the already spent soldiers. Without waiting for the other battalions to arrive, and giving the Inniskillings no time to rest, Hart ordered them up the slopes and as he had done before at Colenso, compounded the agony by pushing his troops forward in columns of four, in full view of the enemy's firing line on the hills, thus once again playing up to his nickname– "General No-Bobs". The Inniskillings scaled the ragged hillside with extreme difficulty, and were totally winded when they eventually arrived at the crest. Then, without any pause, they were ordered to charge at once, and as they appeared over the skyline surging forward in rows, the Boers in front of them stood up and fired from trenches on the true crest-line some 250 yards back, across an open grassy plateau as flat and storm-swept as the summit of Spioenkop. Hart continued to push the men to the top, company after company, and soon the Connaughts followed by the Dublins, found themselves in serious difficulties. Regiment after regiment was driven back with heavy losses, and the summit of the hill was strewn with several hundred dead or wounded bodies, all crammed together in 'a space the size of two tennis courts'

The following morning the Irish Brigade drifted back to the valley, dazed and humiliated. Some of the men had fled, abandoning both their officers, and also their wounded, who were left to their own fate on the top of the hill. The disastrous encounter cost the Irish 500 casualties in less than twenty-four hours. The colonels of both the Dublin and the Inniskilling battalions were killed in the battle, and in all, the Inniskillings lost 72% of their officers and 27% of their men – the highest proportion of any regiment in the war so far It was inconceivable that Hart could not wait until all his battalions were gathered together before he committed them to battle in such a very dangerous and hostile environment. Had he rested his men overnight, and then sent them forth the following morning in bright daylight, he would at least have been able to count on effective support from the artillery. But most damning of all was his insensitive pride that was to restrict initiative and deny his troops the benefits of appropriate strategy and adequate cover, and by so doing, unnecessarily sacrificing hundreds of lives. Although Buller was, understandably, very displeased with Hart's performance, he was nevertheless imbued with a satisfying glow of optimism. There was growing evidence that, in spite of some individual battle successes, the sting had gone out of the Boer threat, and that the futility of further action against the British army was slowly dawning upon them.

The Transvaal burghers were now beginning to realise that Roberts's massive army in the west was poised to strike at the Transvaal. They believed, therefore, that they would be of more use defending their own land and protecting their own kith and kin, than in fighting a string of successive retreating battles in Natal, which was, for them, technically a foreign land, against a highly mobilised army six times their own strength. At the height of the Thukela campaign, Botha's force numbered up to 12,000 burghers. After the departure of the bulk of the Free State commandos and the increasing number of Transvaal Boers trickling back to their homeland every day, he could now barely muster more than 6,000 men to face the might of Buller's army of 30,000. Although they were still able to win individual engagements, there was no question of following them up, and the Boers were doomed to fall back from hill to hill, until they would eventually, be forced out of Natal altogether.

Buller was confident, even though he had by now, managed to get into as fine a jam as he had yet contrived. He found himself with 25,000 troops strung out four miles along the river with no room to focus effectively on any one point of the Boer defences. The units were inextricably mixed up, and the artillery too crowded together to be of any effect, and during all this time, droves of men on Wynne Hill and on Inniskilling Hill were clinging for dear life, without any water or rest from the continuous Boer fire.

Then, on the morning of Sunday 25th, some unexpected relief came when Botha proposed a 24-hour armistice to deal with the wounded and the dead. Although the offer was welcomed by the British, and particularly by the soldiers stuck on Inniskilling and Wynne hills, it was Botha, more than anyone else, who needed the respite. His own depleted force was exhausted after a week of continuous fighting, and because of it he had been unable to exploit the vulnerability of the distended British lines and the shambles down in the valley below. Buller's first priority was to find a way around the hills, and taking advantage of the armistice, he sent Col. Sandbach out to take a second look up the Thukela gorge for a possible outlet. This time Sandbach reported that it would be possible for a pontoon bridge to be floated over the river, and a track for the guns to be hacked along the line of a narrow path on the opposite bank. In the shelter of the deep gorge it would also be possible to push fresh brigades all the way up to the end of the corridor, without running the gauntlet of the Boers located on the ramparts. By the 27[th,] the arrangements were finalised. The plan, a two-handed manoeuvre, was ingenious. The left hand, Lyttleton's division, would maintain its grip on the hills at the lower end of the corridor, and so pin down the main part of Botha's men to their trenches along the line. The right hand, Warren's division of three brigades under Barton, would make a three-pronged attack on the upper part of the corridor, while being protected by the artillery. The three hills commanding this upper section, Hart's, Railway and Pieter's, would then be attacked in reverse order, from east to west, and so outflanking the entire Boer line from the left.

Botha was relieved when he saw Buller using the armistice to withdraw his forces back across the river. Unknown to him however, it was simply a manoeuvre to set up Barton's planned attack along the gorge. At 10 a.m. on February 27th, 'Majuba Day', the new pontoon bridge over the Thukela was finished, and a signboard marked "To Ladysmith" was nailed to its parapet. As the leading battalions stepped onto the bridge, news of Cronje's surrender at Paardeberg was announced, and Buller's massed artillery, machine guns and rifles shook the earth, while the infantry, safely concealed from the Boers, crossed over, and swarmed onto the opposite bank. After months of blunder and disaster, after chance upon chance had been wasted and nothing gained but more killed and more wounded, things suddenly started to go right. The British offensive unfolded with textbook efficiency, as for the first time Buller used the whole of his army against the whole of the Boer line. As soon as the attack on one hill got under way, the attack on the other began. The execution was perfect and as wave upon wave of khaki swept over their defences, the Boers had no earthly chance of redeploying or of reinforcing. In a mere six hours Buller at last found himself master of the Thukela.

Around 2 p.m. on the 27th, Pieter's Hill, the furthest one east, came under attack from Barton's Fusilier Brigade. Botha, believing the terrain too rugged for Buller's troops, had left Pieter's Hill virtually unprotected. When he became aware of Barton's attack, he suddenly realised that if his flank was turned at Pieter's Hill, his entire line would be in danger. In desperation, he threw in as many reinforcements as he could muster, and succeeded in establishing a hold on the northern sector of the hill. At 2.30 p.m. Barton responded by sending forward a company of Scots Fusiliers and two companies of the Dublin's to storm the Boer strongpoint on the northern knoll of Pieter's Hill. The British were beaten back with severe losses, and in the meanwhile, the Boers on the next hill a mile away to the west, Railway Hill, also succeeded in pouring a violent cross-fire onto them. Mercifully for Barton's men, this barrage from Railway Hill did not last for long. Around 3 p.m. small dots began to emerge on the rocks and scree of Railway Hill – Walter Kitchener's brigade, the West Yorkshires, and South

Lancashires, previously commanded by Gen. Wynne, had launched an attack from the Pieter's side of the hill, and gradually worked their way along the series of terraces. Then, with a shout, they stormed the hill with bullet and bayonet, stabbing and jabbing and winning the nek between Railway Hill and Hart's Hill to the west, taking some forty Boer prisoners in their wake - the first since Elandslaagte some four months ago. Meanwhile Norcott's 4th Brigade had fanned out successfully in the third and final phase of the attack, and the eastern positions in the Boer lines – the trenches in front of Pieter's and Railway Hills – had fallen in turn like skittles. All that was now to be done was the storming of Hart Hill. The 4.7 Naval Guns doubled their efforts, and the ensuing bombardment was terrible. This onslaught saw the last gallant moments of Botha's four-month-long defence of his Thukela line as the burghers silently slipped away amidst the lyddite bursts and shrapnel, throwing up earth and stone at each trench.

The capturing of Pieter's Hill, Railway Hill, Hart's Hill, finally opened the door to Ladysmith. Although the British had sustained heavy casualties in the final assault, it was a victory so sudden and so overwhelming that it seemed a remarkably tame anti-climax to the long months of fighting along the river. In all, Buller's casualties since he first set out to relieve Ladysmith, totalled more than the entire strength of the Boer force opposing him. But Joubert had been right in fearing Buller's persistence, because Botha's force was now totally broken. He still had hopes of making a stand before Ladysmith, but wherever he looked he now saw his burghers in full flight. In addition, as soon as the news of Cronje's surrender reached him at Ladysmith, Joubert ordered the siege abandoned, and retired his men to Elandslaagte, twenty miles to the north. Buller ordered the cavalry to keep an open eye on the fleeing Boers, and when a forward section of Dundonald's mounted brigade approached Ladysmith, a challenge rang out - "who goes there?" The reply came back - "The Ladysmith Relief Column" When it reached the town, the moment was an emotional one as the entire settlement came out to welcome them. The siege of 118 days had ended and the victory was complete – the Boer retreat did not stop at Elandslaagte – by the time Botha arrived there, Joubert had already left, and the tide was sweeping irresistibly on. The huge quantities of stores, which had constituted the main Boer supply base at Elandslaagte, had been piled up and set alight, making a pyre visible for fifty miles around.

The war in Natal was over.

11
ROBERTS'S WAR – (a) THE WESTERN FRONT

Setting the Stage
As we have seen when Buller first arrived in Cape Town at the end of October 1899, the War Office had a tactical plan all set out for him. He would entrain his men, and send them off to the rail junctions in the Cape Midlands, from whence they would strike along the central railway for the heart of the Boer Republics – first Bloemfontein and then Pretoria. In addition, as a supplementary commission, Kimberley and Mafeking could be relieved on the way. It was a good plan whichever way one looked at it. In Natal, Penn-Symons and White had 12,000 men north of the Thukela, plus 2,000 at Durban and Pietermaritzburg, and together, they would be quite able to deal effectively with any Boer incursions from the Transvaal. In addition, those Boer forces already in Natal, would be sorely depleted as soon as the central column neared the capital cities of Bloemfontein and Pretoria, for when that happened, their men in Natal would surely be forced to withdraw in order to defend their countries and their homes.

But Buller was in for a surprise, for on his arrival in Cape Town, he had been greeted with the details of Penn-Symons's death and of his 4,000 men retreating to join White's 8,000 troops in Ladysmith. There, Joubert would bottle them up, rendering them ineffective, and exposing the whole of southern Natal to the mercy of the Boers. It was obvious, even to Milner, the British High Commissioner in Cape Town, who could not care two hoots about the fate of Natal that this state of affairs could not be allowed to continue. Something very drastic would need to be done to relieve White and his 12,000 men, and just as importantly, to ensure the safety of the port at Durban. Buller made a desperate decision – he threw the War Office plans to the winds and split the Army Corps into three uneven parts – the largest would relieve Ladysmith, the next Kimberley and what was left would contain the direct threat of invasion of the Cape from the Orange Free State. When these goals had been attained, he would re-assemble his Army Corps in the Cape Midlands, and then proceed with the execution of the original plan.

At the outbreak of the war on the 11th October, 1899, the Boer commandos had assembled on the Transvaal borders with Natal and the Cape Province, and crossed over with the intention to hit out hard before Buller could affect the situation. In the northwest area of the Transvaal's boundary with Bechuanaland the Boer commandos immediately focused their attention on Mafeking, where Lt. Col. Baden-Powell had arrived in September with a body of colonial irregulars who he had been training in Rhodesia further north. These troops, together with the town guard of clerks and shopkeepers made up a force of about 1,200 men. Half a mile outside the town was a native township with a population of 7,000 from which Baden-Powell raised 500 cattle guards and watchmen, armed with elephant guns and similar ironmongery for their own defence. His artillery consisted of half-a-dozen 7-pound muzzle-loaders and seven maxims. He created a defensive perimeter nearly eight miles long to keep the Boer guns as distant as possible, and at the same time, protect the native township, the grazing, and the town's water supply.

A complicated system of redoubts, trenches and forts was put in place, all linked by telephone. Minefields were laid, streets barricaded for house-to-house fighting, suspected spies were goaled, and bombproof shelters for the town's 650 women and children constructed. Clad with railway ties gathered from up and down the railway line, a train was effectively armoured. Baden-Powell had prepared thoroughly, and well he might because 10,000 Boers had massed on the Transvaal border some 13 miles to the east. Fear of a British attack from Mafeking similar to that of the Jameson Raid a few years earlier determined them to neutralize Baden-Powell and his build-up of forces on their western frontier

The Boer commander was General Piet Cronje, widely considered at that time to be one of the ablest of the Boer leaders. Under his command were some very worthy militarists including General J.P. Snyman and the redoubtable warrior from the western Transvaal, General Koos De la Rey. Moving rapidly across the border on the night of 11th October, Cronje's men cut all communications with Rhodesia in the north. At the same time, others moved south of the town, where they not only tore up the railway line, but way-laid an armoured train bringing up supplies of precious guns and ammunition intended for use in the defence of the town. After preliminary skirmishes in which Baden-Powell took the offensive, the Boers called on him to surrender. When the invitation was declined, the Boers closed in and formed their laagers on every side of the town, and the siege of Mafeking had begun.

With the bulk of Cronje's men comfortably settled around Mafeking, some of the commandos under De la Rey rapidly moved southwards along the railway, capturing stations and villages all down the line. Village after village along this 300-mile western border surrendered without struggle, including the important settlement of Vryburg. Only one town other than Mafeking did not submit immediately, and that was Kimberley, the biggest and most important of them all. Kimberley was the centre of the fabulous diamond industry, and stood only a few miles from the high wire fence, which marked the Orange Free State border. Added to the richness of this prize, was the presence of Cecil John Rhodes, who had arrived two days after the start of the war, on one of the last trains to get through from Cape Town.

It was only a few weeks earlier that Col. R. G. Kekewich and his 1st Loyal Lancashire Regiment had occupied Kimberly. On his arrival, Kekewich reported that the town was "dangerously unprepared", and he immediately set about to repair the situation. He hastily succeeded in raising a defence force of 3,000 infantry and 850 horse men, of whom the bulk were townsmen and the remainder members of his own regiment. Eventually eleven machine-guns and fourteen 7-pdr guns became available, but they were not only feeble, but were muzzle-loading to boot. On the 11th October, while Kekewich was talking to Milner on the telephone, the line went dead, and at the same time, some burghers appeared on the skyline. This was the vanguard of some 5,000 men with superior artillery, and after encirclement of the city, the siege of Kimberley began – with the great Cecil John Rhodes locked up in it.

The British
Robert Stephenson Smyth Baden-Powell – Following a liberal arts education, Baden-Powell, one of seven children of an Oxford clergyman professor, chose a military career, and became an expert in reconnaissance and scouting. After some time in India he was posted to Natal in 1884, and returned there in 1886 when he participated in the Dinizulu campaign. After spells of duty in Malta, Ireland and East Africa, he returned to South Africa as brevet Lt. Col. and staff officer at Bulawayo, where he took part in the Matabele campaign of 1896. This action brought him promotion to brevet Colonel and the appointment as Commander-in-Chief, North West Frontier Forces. Transferred to India he published his "Aids to Scouting" in 1899. At the approach of war he was he was posted once again to South Africa, to recruit the Rhodesia Regiment for defence of Bechuanaland and Matabeleland. During his service in India, and later in Matabeleland, he had learnt to become a good rider and an excellent teacher of men. He developed a consuming passion for scouting, moving unseen through enemy country, drawing miraculous deductions from spoor and leaf. Here was a man to whom the public had ascribed an almost supernatural ability in field-craft, and he would undoubtedly be the best person to match his skills against the prowess of the Boers.

Robert George Kekewich- Kekewich first saw service in Malaysia in 1875, and then as a captain, in the Sudan ten years later. In 1897 he became military secretary to the Commander of Madras, after which, on the eve of the South African war, he was promoted Lieutenant Colonel, and transferred to Cape Town, where he was given command of the Loyal North Lancaster Regiment. In November 1899, he set off on a secret mission to organize the defences of Kimberley, and to take command of all the British forces in Bechuanaland and Griqualand-West. After he arrived, he telegraphed Milner that Kimberley was a 'sitting duck', and he was instructed to remain there while Milner arranged for reinforcements to be sent up to garrison the town. Kekewich was given a half battalion of his own, the Loyal North Lancashires, plus six semi-obsolete 2½- inch guns. Three weeks later the war broke out, and on the following day, the Free State commandos crossed the border, and cut the railway and telegraph lines linking Kimberley to Mafeking in the north and to Cape Town in the south.

Lord Paul Sanford – 3rd Baron Methuen of Corsham
Methuen was born into nobility and wealth. A great English landowner, he was raised at Corsham Court in Wiltshire, and after studying at Eton he served in the Royal Wiltshire Yeomanry and in the Scots Fusilier Guards. By 1882, he was a major, and between spells of military service in Africa, he was military attaché in Berlin. His early military activity in South Africa was in 1884 to 1885, when he had raised a troop of Light Horse to fight with Warren in Bechuanaland, and again from 1888 to 1889. At the outbreak of the Anglo Boer War, he was in command of the 1st Infantry Division, and arrived with it in South Africa in November 1899. Methuen was never thought of as a 'great soldier', but a rather reclusive and 'painstaking' one, as his friends described him. He was tall and big-framed with a tendency to stoop. An abstemious and taciturn man, he was too independent and detached to belong either to Roberts's 'Indians' or to Wolesley's 'Africans'. He was well respected by his troops, and amongst his peers he was suspected of having a 'soft spot' for the Boers of the backveld, and for blaming the war on 'those rascals in Pretoria'

168

The Boers

Commandant-General Pieter Arnoldus Cronje

A farmer in the Potchefstroom area, Cronje saw some military service under Kruger during the Civil War. He was politically active during the British annexation of the Transvaal from 1877 to 1881, and during the 1st Boer War he commanded the burghers at the siege of Potchefstroom, where he displayed 'little evidence of sound military leadership'. This, together with his interference in political and military affairs, led to reprimands from the Provincial Republican government. Nevertheless, after the war he was elected to the Volksraad as member for Potchefstroom and in 1884 he was elected acting Commander-General. He also resumed the leadership of the Potchefstroom commando, taking part in the Battle of Mamusa against the Korana chief, David Massoni, at Schweizer-Reneke on the 2nd and 3rd December 1885. Later he resigned from the Volksraad, retreating to the 'quieter life of farming', only to become a hero for the efficient way in which he forced the raiding party of L.S. Jameson to surrender at Doornkop on the 1st January 1896. In that same year, he became Superintendent of Native Affairs, which brought him a seat on the Executive Council, and when pre-war tension was building up in the middle of 1899, he was appointed to the post of Assistant Commandant-General and Commander of the Transvaal forces in the Western Front. After having failed to reduce Mafeking, he laid it to siege with an initial force of 10,000 men. As a soldier, Cronje demonstrated little talent for leadership and military skill, and he certainly had no dash. He forever tended to over-estimate the enemy strength, and committed large numbers of his men to besiege small garrisons and insignificant posts such as Potchefstroom and Mafeking.

Jacobus (Koos) Hercules De la Rey

Koos De la Rey came from a family in which all the male members played prominent roles in the history of the Transvaal. Although he had had very little formal education, he filled, very early in his life, important public offices such as Government Surveyor, Bantu Commissioner, and others, and from 1893 was a member of the first Volksraad of the South African Republic. His military career started at the age of nineteen when, as veld-kornet, he took part in the Basuto campaign in 1865, the Sekhukhune War of 1876, and the First Boer War of 1880/81. He was also at the Battle of Mamusa in 1885, by which time he was commandant of the Lichtenburg Commando. In 1886, he was present at the Jameson Raid encounter at Doornkop. De la Rey was a liberal, in favour of the franchise for British subjects in the Transvaal, provided it did not threaten its independence, and he openly opposed a war with Great Britain. However, when it did come in 1899, he proved to be a most able and astute soldier with absolute loyalty and fervour for the cause of his country's independence. On the eve of the war, Commandant-General Joubert appointed the 52-year old De la Rey as Combat General, and advisor to Piet Cronje. Unfortunately, Cronje very seldom heeded De la Rey's very sound advice, and his consistent slighting of De la Rey's counsel led to many Boer reverses in the months to come, eventually culminating in Cronje's disaster at Paardeberg.

De la Rey succeeded in becoming a very able soldier, and delivered the first engagement of the war at Kraaipan. Much more important was his success at Modder River, where his skilful deployment checked Methuen in his tracks, earning a vital ten days preparation period for the Boers at Magersfontein. Unfortunately, for him, he was denied a complete victory at Modder River by Cronje's untimely decision to withdraw, and more importantly at Magersfontein where he delivered a total victory over Methuen's forces, only to be thwarted, once again, by Cronje's reluctance to follow up and close in on the enemy in retreat.

Later guerrilla strategy was to demonstrate De la Rey's military genius to the full, and he was to emerge from the war undefeated. His courage, sense of duty and humane treatment of prisoners made him the most respected of all the Boer commanders in the eyes of the British. Lord Milner described him as 'a man, every inch of him, and one of whom any country in the world might justly feel proud'. A master of the three basic principles of mobile warfare – good reconnaissance, speed and surprise, his control of situations was such that he never refused a battle, and could rely on bold frontal charges at the right moment as an infallible means of achieving the upper hand.

The British Campaign - The Plan
By the time of his departure from Cape Town to Natal, Buller had done much to bring about a marked improvement to the imperial fortunes in South Africa. Lt. Gen. Clery had been rushed to Natal with his 2nd. Division of 8,000 men, and was already established at Estcourt and Mooi Rivier, shielding Maritzburg and Durban from Botha's drive south. On the western borders, Lord Methuen had set off from his base at De Aar with rations for only five days. He had crossed the Orange River in a bid to be in Kimberley within a week. In the Midlands and Eastern Districts, where the Boers were still advancing towards the Cape, a shield was established in the very nick of time, with Lt. Gen. Sir William Gatacre's 3rd Division occupying Queenstown in the east and Maj. Gen. John French's Cavalry Division successfully holding the line at Colesburg in the south.

Methuen was in his element. He had with him at the Orange River line his own 1st Division ('Methuen's Force') totalling 8,000 men from the Guards Brigade and the 9th Brigade, whilst the Highland Brigade lay further back to guard Methuen's communication lines. His task was to march his men across the Orange River, and over 74 miles of sandy veld to relieve Kimberley. After that, he would head due east and capture Bloemfontein, the capital city of the Free State Republic. Methuen had signalled Buller – '*I intend to set out before dawn tomorrow. It will probably take six days and at least one battle – I shall breakfast in Kimberley on Monday.*' Methuen's orders were simply to relieve Kimberley, but not to garrison it. He was to throw in a few troops and guns, with full supplies, and take out those of the inhabitants who were reported to be giving trouble - the women and children, 10,000 Africans, and one very notable Englishman, Cecil John Rhodes.

By now, the defences around Kimberly were well established; the De Beer Company had supplied labour and materials in sufficient quantities to enable the construction of a formidable defence system that covered the 20-mile perimeter around the town. Kekewich had erected barbed wire entanglements between a series of redoubts, made in the dumps of tailings, and connected by telephone to his "Tower" on top of the 160-foot mine headgear. The guns and five searchlights, known to the Boers as 'Rhodes's Eyes', were strategically placed between minefields, real and pretended, which were sown across the outskirts. The perimeter was manned by town volunteers, and the regulars and horsemen were kept in reserve in the botanical gardens. Food stocks were controlled efficiently, and when the Boers cut the town's water supply from the river, it was replaced by water tapped from springs within the mine. To reduce the number of mouths to feed, Rhodes sent away 3,000 Natives, who were immediately returned by the Boers. Later, some 8,000 natives did succeed in getting away bringing welcome relief to the town's feeding problems.

But there still remained many thousands of mouths to feed plus one special personage, causing Kekewich problems far more worrying than the threat of direct assault by the enemy. When Kekewich rejected their surrender demand, the Boers started a sporadic shelling of the town, causing little real damage, but rubbing raw the nerves of the populace. But, more frustrating than all was the mounting agitation between Rhodes and Kekewich, with Rhodes fulminating with fierce impatience against the delay of the arrival of the relief force, and Kekewich in the unhappy position of being the direct target of much of Rhodes's 'squeaking and squalling'.

Belmont
On the morning of the 21ˢᵗ November, Methuen set off from the Orange River station on his march to Kimberley, some 75 miles to the north. He was in a very confident mood –'My dear fellow...' he said to one of his colonels, 'I intend to put the fear of God into these people'. His optimism was indeed well founded because between him and his goal there was only one Free State commando of 2,000 burghers, led by a very nervous and hesitant commander; General Jan Prinsloo, whose orders were simply to delay the British advance until adequate reinforcements had arrived from the north. However, whilst Methuen's confidence ran high, his combat intelligence facilities were practically non-existent. He had very little notion of what lay ahead of him. Devoid of any reliable reconnaissance reports, he actually believed that there were well over 4,000 burghers with Prinsloo, and he had no idea at all of any Boer reinforcements scheduled to arrive from the north. To compound the problem, the quality of his combat maps was appalling – they were all very inaccurate and devoid of any contour lines. In fact so unreliable were they that his officers were obliged to base their very complex strategic plans on rough sketches, hastily drawn-up only minutes before engagements. Nevertheless, Methuen's confidence was in no way daunted. Before he set off, he had already sent a message to Kimberley with the glad tidings that he would be there within a week – by the 27ᵗʰ November latest, unless delayed at the Modder River.

The Modder is the only sizeable river between the Orange and the Vaal, and was crossed by the western railway some twenty-two miles south of Kimberley. Steadily advancing up the line of the railway, Methuen's force had by now increased to 12,000 men – Grenadiers, Coldstream and Scots Guards, his famous regiments in Lancashire, Yorkshire and Northumberland, and a few hundred troopers from Australia - the New South Wales Lancers. In addition, there were droves of transport animals and long lines of guns and wagons, an armoured train lumbering ahead, and finally a detachment of the Naval Brigade, scheduled to join Methuen before his arrival at Belmont. By easy marches, the column soon reached Belmont, and on the closest of a small cluster of hills just beyond the station, some breastworks revealed Prinsloo's presence. Methuen ordered his brigade of Guards to despatch the burghers with a dawn assault, to be launched after a night-march. But the maps were faulty and misleading, and in the absence of wire-cutters, axes had to be used to chop down an un-marked railway fence. This not only alerted the Boers to the whereabouts of their enemy, but also delayed the manoeuvre, so the Guards found themselves still some distance from their quarry, and dangerously exposed in the open veld between them and the burghers hidden in the hill ahead. In the end, it was only a resolute and gallant charge, regardless of casualties, that enabled them to shift Prinsloo and his men.

In the action, the Boers lost about 100 men and they were not happy at all. Their position had been a very strong one, and yet the British were able to storm it from across a sizable distance of wide-open terrain. In the end, it was Prinsloo's poor leadership which was largely to be blamed for the setback, and for the low morale of many of his men. On the British side, in spite of the loss of over 300 casualties, Methuen was pleased with the performance, and congratulated the men on their success. However, regardless of this outward show of satisfaction the officers were shocked by the realities of battle on the South African veld. The Guards had suffered 36 men killed or mortally wounded, a total of 137 casualties in all – the highest of any unit engaged to date.

In a search for reasons, it was a worrying thought that most of the tactical errors could be traced back to very basic handicaps, such as weak intelligence and poor mobility. Methuen had marched his men from the Orange River to meet the Boers at a place of their own choosing – he could not by-pass them, but was forced to clear them from his communication line – the railway – in addition to which he had failed to reconnoitre the enemy positions satisfactorily.

It was not yet over at Belmont. Ahead of him, Methuen still had the remaining koppies to deal with. The Boers were few in number, but their position was a secure one on a mass of broken ground, and three strong points astride the hills. Methuen's plan was for his two infantry brigades to attack the first two hills simultaneously from the west flank, approaching under cover of darkness, and then to work round to the third koppie. Once again, his poor intelligence denied him an effective result. His sketch map was so defective, that he soon discovered to his horror, that the two brigades were diverging, and that they were heading straight for the foot of a jagged hill. Fortunately, he did not lose his head – he saw that he was committed to a frontal attack, and organised the Guards to straighten up, and for the 9th Brigade to join them and push forward with the aid of the guns covering the troops with shrapnel fire. Thus, with heavy losses, they succeeded in seizing the three hills in turn, and were relieved, but at the same time shocked to see the Boers trotting away over the veld, seemingly unhindered by the artillery or the cavalry.

Graspan

Three days later, the battle of Graspan repeated the pattern, but on a smaller scale. Methuen had driven the Boers from the next line of ridges, but what he did not realise however, was that De la Rey had joined the Boers after Belmont, and had immediately assumed command. With the defection of so many Free State burghers after Belmont, the forces facing the British at Graspan amounted to only 2,000 burghers. This time Methuen did not make a night move, but again succeeded with a resolute charge led by the small Naval Brigade. Once again, the Boers broke, leapt onto their ponies, and made away across the open veld. The British troops were too parched to follow up, but the cavalry did attempt a pursuit, only to be cut-up by the Boers' skilful covering tactics, which enabled them to get their wagons, clean away. Methuen was furious, and dismissed his cavalry commander. He was, in fact, hopelessly short of mounted infantry against such a mobile force as the Boers, but his successes at both Belmont and Graspan gave him confidence for his next target – the settlement at Modder River, a few miles ahead of his advancing army.

Profound despondency marked the Boer discussions at their head laager. They had given better than they had received, but could see no hope of trying to resist an infantry charge, however strong their position. In addition, there had been more defections among the Free State commandos, who had by now, totally lost confidence in Gen. Prinsloo, their leader. At the krijgsraad following the Graspan encounter, De la Rey listened attentively to the complaints of the burghers. When they all had had their say, he spoke his mind, quietly and deliberately. He consoled them that in no way had they failed for want of courage or marksmanship, and he praised their overall conduct during the engagement, and particularly commended them on their perfect tactical disposition on the hills. Then he dropped his bombshell – alas, it was those very same hills that were responsible for their failure! He demonstrated how, when firing down upon an advancing enemy, a bullet had only one chance to hit the target before it buried itself in the ground. Later, when the foe eventually succeeded in reaching the foot of the hill, and started to scale it, its steep slopes actually became a cover for him, and not for the man firing down upon him from above. In fact, the person firing from above needed to rise and lean over in order to fire his rifle accurately, and in so doing expose himself to those below by creating a perfect target against the skyline. De la Rey then explained that if the burghers placed themselves below the surface, while firing at veld-level, not only would they be concealed and the enemy caught out in the open, but a bullet's flat trajectory would ensure that if it missed one soldier it had many chances of hitting a companion in the ranks behind him. Persuaded by the simple logic of De la Rey's arguments, the Boers dug themselves into the southern bank of the Modder River, on either side of the dynamited railway bridge, and quietly awaited Methuen's arrival.

Modder/Riet Rivers

By the night of the 27th November, Methuen, having successfully covered 50 of the 74 miles to Kimberley, was only a few miles south of the Modder River. He planned to make a flank march the following morning, intending to turn the enemy's left flank by leaving the railway, and marching the final 25 miles to Kimberley in a broad arc to the east. During the night, the Rimmington Tigers and the Lancers brought him news that made him cancel his flank attack plan for the time being. He learnt that some of the enemy was digging in along the banks of the Modder and the Riet, on either side of the railway bridge. Major Little of the Lancers estimated their numbers to be in the region of 4,000 men. Metheun doubted this figure – he was still unaware of the arrival of the Boers from the north, and going by the numbers of Free Staters he had seen returning to their farms, he put the figure at Modder River to be around 600 Boers. However, he decided to deal with the problem at the Modder River before carrying out his flank march. Leaving an enemy force, small as it was, astride his communication artery would be far too dangerous.

In fact, the Boer strength was 3,500, and their position along the Modder River and its tributary, the Riet River, which joined the Modder just before the bridge, was effectively concealed by trees and bushes. In the distance, beyond, were the blue outlines of the Magersfontein hills, which Methuen argued, would be the only feasible position from which the Boers would make their final stand before Kimberley. If he had seen a few odd biscuit tins, or white stones lying about, he might just have recognised that they had been left there by the Boer artillery as aids to sighting their guns!

It had taken some urging and lots of influence in high places for the Boers to muster such a substantial force at the Modder River in so short a while after Belmont and Graspan. It was no surprise therefore, that Methuen had found it nigh impossible to accept the fact that there could hardly be more than six or seven hundred Boers in the area, despite intelligence reports to the contrary. Of course with the benefit of hindsight, we know that De la Rey had already arrived with about 700 of his Lichtenburg commando, and that Cronje, too, had now joined the forces with about 2,500 burghers from the Mafeking area. Relations between De la Rey and Cronje were strained, especially after the investment of Mafeking and Kimberley. De la Rey disagreed both with Kruger's all-out offensive strategy and in particular with the wishy-washy and half-hearted way in which Cronje was conducting it. In the event De la Rey's anxieties were well justified, because soon all the advantages of Cronje's tactical and numerical strength were to crumble and disappear in the wake of his reticence and caution, and in the meantime Methuen had already succeeded in brushing aside Prinsloo and the Free State commandos at their very first encounters at Belmont and Graspan.

But De la Rey's endeavours were not in vain. As a result of his urgent supplications at top levels, there were 3,500 men along the Modder and Riet Rivers, lying in wait for Methuen. These included the three major groups of burghers - Prinsloo's Free State, Cronje's Transvaal burghers, and De la Rey's own crack Lichtenburg Commando. In support they had 7 Krupp field guns, plus four 1pdr Maxims "Pom-Poms". Against these, Methuen had at his disposal, a force of 8,000 soldiers and a battering ram of sixteen guns. The two rivers, Modder and Riet formed a natural line of defence of remarkable strength. The rivers had gouged out of the plain a broad shelter trench, donga-like, with steep banks up to thirty feet high. The rivers themselves were deep and muddy, and now that the burghers had dynamited the railway bridge, the only place of crossing in the centre was the drift beside it. There were only two other areas where the attackers could cross – a pair of drifts at Bosman's Drift a few miles to the east, or by the drift beside the dam at Rosmead, two miles to the west of the confluence of the two rivers.

De la Rey and most of his 800 Lichtenburgers had dug themselves in on the southern bank of the Riet. On his left, straddling two miles of the same river, east from the junction point with the Modder, was Cronje with the bulk of the other Transvaal commandos. They tethered their horses behind them in the shelter of the banks of the Riet, while beyond them on the island between the two rivers, other burghers lay concealed in the undergrowth in the event of the British turning their east flank at Bosmans Drift. Dug in to the right of De la Rey and extending to as far as Rosmead Drift, were Prinsloo and the Free State commandos.

The positioning of the Boer guns was left to Cronje, who concentrated most of the field guns on the north bank of the Riet covering De la Rey's trenches. Four of the Krupp 75mm field-guns were close to the railway line, commanding the central drift, and the other two, plus the three 1-pdr Maxims, were scattered along the island, including one field-gun opposite Bosmans Drift at the extreme east of the line. Cronje had made no provisions for any guns to cover the Free Staters at Rosmead in the west, and this omission proved to be a monstrous mistake on his part, and soon to have disastrous repercussions.

Early on the morning of the 28th November, the men of Methuen's 2nd Infantry Brigade began to tramp down across the open veld towards the clump of trees marking the line of the Modder River. They were told that they would breakfast at the Modder River. '*They* are not here' said Methuen to Maj.Gen. Sir Henry Colvile, pointing to the tall poplars on the river bank less than a mile ahead. '*They are sitting uncommonly tight, if they are, Sir*' replied Colvile. Ahead, in the earthworks along the Modder, hidden in every hole and crevice along the banks of the four miles of the winding river, 3,000 Boer riflemen were preparing to deliver the most concentrated rifle barrage yet fired in the war. The Guards and the 9th Brigade led the advance, the Guards on the east of the railway line led by Colvile, and on the west of the line, the 9th Brigade led by Maj. Gen. Reggie Pole-Carew. The Guards were slightly in advance of the rest of the force, which altogether covered a front of over three miles on either side of the railway track. The deployment over such a wide area was deliberate, 'in order to facilitate a rapid forging of the river'. The main line of the British advance lay towards the eastern side of the bridge. This tactic was exactly what De la Rey had anticipated and he had placed his main strength at that very spot, leaving the western sector of the line to the weaker Free State commandos under Prinsloo.

Within minutes of the British infantry's advance, De la Rey, still concerned over Cronje's omission to protect the western flank with gun cover, realised that Cronje on the banks of the Riet River further east, had committed a second serious error. De la Rey had agreed with Cronje that all his men, as well as all the other burghers along the entire defence line, were to hold fire for a long as possible. The nearer the infantry approached, the more crushing would be the effect of the Boer fusillade, and the harder it would be for Methuen to extricate his men. Alas for De la Rey, and the ultimate outcome of the entire battle, just as the Scots Guards, who were the nearest lines of infantry, were marching towards a tall clump of poplars, and were within a 1,000 yards of the Boer entrenchments, Cronje's nerve failed, and his men opened fire, and the

Guards fell flat. And so it was that in that fusillade, fierce as it was, the burghers had lost all chance of a decisive defensive victory, for the battle now became an affair of blow and counter-blow, an endless struggle between two gladiators, differently armed yet evenly matched – the spitting, drumming hailstorm of mausers against the thunder of the 15-pdrs. This ensuing dual was to last for the following ten awful hours.

The soldiers lay flat on their faces, hungry and thirsty, nibbled by ants in a temperature that rose to 90 degrees in the shade. Any smallest movement, even the twitching of a kilt in the breeze, brought down a hailstorm of bullets from the Mausers ahead, hidden and unseen. The Boer's little 1-pdr Maxims squirted amongst the prone troops, like a water-hose –'pom-pom-pom' they went and it was from then that they were referred to as 'pom-poms' for the duration of the war, and on many other international battlefields thereafter.

Despite Cronje's error in allowing his men to fire prematurely, the advantage of the battle seemed at first to tilt to De la Rey's side. Through their field glasses the Boer leaders could see disaster overwhelm the two leading companies of the Scots Guards, their solitary machine-gun smashed by a pom-pom. Then an anxious time followed for the Boers, and De la Rey angrily blamed Cronje for doing to little to cope with the overall situation; he was after all, nominally the senior ranking Boer leader at Modder River. The cause of De la Rey's concern was that under heavy fire, the Coldstreams had successfully managed to work their way along the bushy banks of the Riet to the east, and some had even managed to wade across to the island. However, it was not a proper ford and Colvile ordered them back. After that the Guards were well nigh pinned down, and made no further threat to the Boer defences.

It was now the turn of the British artillery to take up the cudgel, with the 12-pdrs of their 18th and 75th batteries firing just over the heads of the prostrate Guardsmen. An armoured train soon arrived from the south with four Naval Brigade 12pdrs, which significantly added to the strength of the bombardment. In reply, the Boer artillery performed prodigies of improvisation. Their artillery commander, an ex Prussian NCO called Major Albrecht, moved his guns, out-numbered three-to-one, all day from one emplacement to another, and wrought havoc on their British counterparts, openly exposed in the veld without sandbags or rocks to protect them. The Boer guns, in spite of the continual re- positioning, were so skilfully concealed, that the British gunners were unaware of their presence throughout the entire battle.

Now alarming reports were reaching De la Rey from Prinsloo and his Free State commandos, who had dug-in in the riverside village of Rosmead, a mile or two to the west of the railway line. Cronje had omitted to put sufficient men there to cover the Rosmead Drift, or to protect it with guns, or later to provide it with reinforcements when required. Now they were beginning to pay the price for this negligence, because opposite the Drift, part of Pole-Carew's 9th Brigade, who for three hours had been nailed down in the veld, could now be seen creeping forward in rushes, with Prinsloo's men unable to hold them. A fold in the veld gave the attackers better protection, and as they moved nearer the Boer lines the Free Staters, their morale already dented by Belmont and Graspan, started giving way. Some of them sought shelter in a nearby farmhouse, which made a perfect target for the gunners. This was the last straw – the wretched Free State commando could take no more, and started fleeing back over the north bank, followed by the British who captured the farm and used it as a strongpoint to cover their further advance.

It was Kekewich's half-battalion of North Lancashires, who had stayed behind in Cape Town when he had set off for Kimberley, who led the action. Now they seized the honour of being the first across the Drift and up on the other side. Other men of various units, including the Argyll and Sutherland Highlanders, followed on their heels, and some soldiers even managed to scramble in single file, across the dam wall just above the Drift. By one o'clock, the British had dug themselves into the north bank, and driven the Free Staters out of Rosmead. They were soon covered by four guns of the 62nd Battery, and with Pole-Carew leading, the British now began to push through the hedges of prickly pears towards a building behind the Boer's central position. Cronje did nothing to cope with this threat, and it was De la Rey who was left to organise the counter-attack. Having re-crossed the river, he sent the men of his Lichtenburg commando who remained in reserve on the north bank, westwards to block Pole-Carew's advance. They gave covering fire to Albrecht's hard-pressed gunners, and pinned down the leading men of the North Lancashires and Argylls, who were crawling forward through the reeds and bushes along the riverbank, and succeeded in driving them back into Rosmead. Assisted by a deluge of British shrapnel from the field guns across the river fired in error at Pole-Carew's men, De la Rey's burghers then held on to their trenches until darkness put an end to the fighting.

It was at that time that De La Rey's son, Adriaan, was mortally wounded. De la Rey himself had also suffered a slight wound earlier on, and in the darkness, he wrapped his son in a blanket and carried him down the road to Jacobsdal some nine miles away. At about 8 p.m. he met Cronje, his men were now in full retreat, and it was De la Rey himself who made a record of their bitter exchange: Cronje" – *'How did the battle go?'* – De la Rey - *'Why did you leave us in the lurch? – We saw nothing of you all day!'"*
By now De la Rey had reached a decision almost as painful as his bereavement – they could no longer keep a grip on the line of the Modder and the Riet – Cronje and Prinsloo had betrayed them. Had the Free Staters held on to the west flank, De la Rey believed that Methuen would have been forced back all the way to the Orange River, but they had fled, and now Methuen would have no difficulty in reinforcing Pole-Carew's bridgehead on the north bank, and then continue to push forward. Sadly for De la Rey, he had to accept that his own men too, would have to abandon the Riet and retire to the north.

When the moon rose at 10 p.m., the night was bright and clear. Along both sides of the river lay 460 British and 80 Boer casualties. Opposite Rosmead, British forces lined up in the darkness and splashed over to join Pole-Carew. At dawn, the British guns resumed their bombardment, but there was no reply and when the infantry approached De la Rey's positions, they found it deserted. The Boers had withdrawn to the north and to the east, and now there was only Spijtfontein Ridge, ten miles further north, that lay between Methuen and Kimberley.

Black Week – Stormberg

In the days following Joubert's successes in Natal, many previously hesitant Boers were now saddling-up and riding to the front to 'take on the English', and in the northern Cape a number of the 'Cape Dutch' were crossing the Orange River from the colony to throw in their lot with President Steyn's Free State commandos strung along the Cape border. On the 1st November, these Free State commandos began crossing the Orange River into the Cape Midlands, and throwing back handfuls of police guarding the bridges, and advancing into village after village. This action forced Buller to face the sombre fact of a third front seriously threatening the vital rail junctions of De Aar on the western line, and Naauwpoort and Stormberg on the Port Elizabeth and East London lines. These vital junctions were the fulcrum points from all the principal Cape ports, Cape Town, Port Elizabeth and East London, and before leaving Cape Town Buller had ordered a campaign of 'holding tactics' in the Cape Midlands area – one to operate towards Naauwpoort, and the other towards Stormberg. In command of this operation was Lt. Gen. Sir William Gatacre, who, with the Boers approaching Stormberg, urgently set off from Queenstown, and moved up the East London railway line to thwart them.

In the last Sudan campaign, in 1897, gaunt Sir William had won a knighthood and promotion to Maj. General, even though his restlessness had made him 'the exhausted victim of his own vitality'. He had a mania for imposing physical exertion on others as well as upon himself, thinking nothing of a twenty-mile ride before breakfast. General 'Backacher', as his troops nicknamed him, made plans to capture Stormberg Junction by first making a surprise dawn attack directly on the pass through which the railway and the road entered a ring of koppies around the junction. Guarding the pass was the Boer commander, General Olivier with 2,300 Free State burghers and some Cape rebels.

Besides a reserve force, Gatacre had 3,000 men available for this attack, and in preparation for his dawn assault, he ordered them, on the 9th December to entrain for Molteno, the nearest up-line station to the junction. The men were aroused at 4 a.m., but teams of mules blocked the line, and arrangements in general were so jammed up that the troops had to hang about in the scorching sun for hours, the last of them only arriving at Molteno after 8.30 that evening. By then Gatacre received news that the railway pass was strongly guarded by the Boers. As a result, he gave up the idea of a direct attack along the main road, and decided instead, to make a diversion attack from the rear. The entire western wall of the basin consisted of a range of koppies called the Kissieberg, and Gatacre reckoned that by taking the nearer end of this range, he would dominate the pass and make his entry into the basin a very simple matter. To accomplish this, a detour would be required, which meant a longer march on a secondary track in the dark. To advance over this rough and unknown country at night made skilled guidance essential. Although he actually did have on his staff a very accomplished captain of intelligence who new the terrain well, Gatacre, for some obscure reason had ordered him to stay behind with the reserves, and he set off on his perilous night march making shift with whatever alternatives he could lay his hands on.

At 9.15 p.m., the Irish Rifles and Northumberland Fusiliers led the way out of Molteno, less 400 men who were supposed to join them from an outlying post; these howver, mysteriously failed to appear - apparently, a clerk at the base telegraph office had forgotten to send the order! Nevertheless, Gatacre was determined to press on by the light of a full moon, and although not expecting any action until dawn, he ordered the troops to fix bayonets, forcing the already exhausted men to port their rifles in a fixed position throughout the long march. After the moon went down the tired soldiers began to flounder about on the rough terrain in seemingly perpetual darkness, and in response to Gatacre's increasingly anxious inquiries about their exact whereabouts, the guides returned comforting replies. However, the one fact they carefully kept to themselves was that they, having completely lost their way, had themselves no idea at all of where they were!

By now, twenty-four hours had passed since the troops were aroused, so a brief rest in the dark and sinister valley was ordered. Unbeknown to all, and by pure chance, they were exactly on the spot where Gatacre wanted to be for his dawn attack, namely along the foremost portion of the Kissieberg. But the guides had misunderstood Gatacre's intentions, and continued to lead the force right along the western front of the whole range, so that in the pre-dawn light, Gatacre found himself on the wrong side of the hills from which he had was actually behind the hills he was supposed to be in front of. By now, he had lost all sense of direction and actually thought he was bearing down upon his objective, the railway pass. Up on the heights, at the rear end of the Kissieberg, some Boer pickets suddenly became aware of the British force winding through the shadows below. At once, the alarm was raised, and the burghers opened fire. It was a small detachment, and the firing was blind and panicky, the Boers neither knowing at what nor where they firing. Had Gatacre realised that it was only a mere token force confronting him, he could have entered the basin and captured the junction simply by marching on around the hill. Instead, the troops panicked and rushed up the slopes of hill. The three leading companies of the Rifles managed to reach the summit by going around the left of the hill, but the bulk of the force panicked and set about grappling with the steepest part of the Kissieberg. Carried forward by their impetus, they had moved well up the slope before they came upon some solid cliffs of jutting rock, which were quite impossible to scale except at a few widely separated spots. Barred by the cliffs and by now absolutely exhausted, the men began to dribble back down to the foot of the slope in scattered groups, and the commanding officer of the Northumberlands took the initiative and ordered the retreat.

It was barely a half-an-hour after the first shots were exchanged when Gatacre saw the demoralised infantry streaming back across the valley. Powerless to prevent the debacle, he marched the men back to Molteno, and while he was doing so, a Boer commando arrived from the rear causing the infantry to degenerate into a huge mob of stragglers. Despite a brisk rear-guard action by the Mounted Infantry and artillery, scarcely a man would have escaped had not the Boers shown an ineptitude matching that of the British. So wild was the Boer fire that the British troops sustained only ninety casualties by the time that they had reached Molteno and safety. Unfortunately a little later, a check-up revealed that some 600 men had not heard the call to retreat, and had been left behind on the summit of the Kiessieberg. Hours later when they realised that Gatacre had gone, they came down the hill and gave themselves up to the Boers.

The situation in the Cape Midlands was now a desperately critical one. Back in a London horrified and aghast, the news published the following day suggested that Gatacre had been treacherously led into an ambush, an accusation which may or may not have been true, but which does not justify the inexcusable abandoning of 600 soldiers back on the slopes of the Kissieberg. The disaster at Stormberg was to be the first of three horrifying defeats that would mark the 'Black Week' of December 1899.

Black Week – Magersfontein
The death of De la Rey's son after Modder River had one immediate effect. De la Rey had stayed back at Jacobsdal to bury him, and consequently missed the krijgsraad on the day after the battle. He was furious and strenuously objected when he heard the decision of Cronje and Prinsloo to withdraw ten miles to Spijtfontein instead of digging in at Magersfontein, only six miles back. In despair, he telegraphed President Steyn, over Cronje's head, with an urgent request for his views be heard. Steyn passed his message on to Kruger, who in turn asked Steyn to go to the front in person, and sort out the matter. Kruger also informed Steyn that Prinsloo's cowardice and bad leadership was the cause of all the Boer setbacks to date, and urged Steyn to take over the command of the Free State commandos himself. Steyn drove from Bloemfontein in haste, and on arrival he summoned the generals to a second krijgsraad, where De la Rey put his case against Spijtfontein. His proposal to repeat the tactics, which had been so successful at Modder River, was accepted for the next stand at Magersfontein. In addition, in order to prevent the Free State commandos from packing up and running away as they had done in previous engagements, it was agreed to un-mount them, and put them at the centre of the trenches to such purpose that reconnaissance at a hundred yards would not have revealed them. De la Rey discouraged any of Methuen's scouts who ventured to within a thousand yards of the well-concealed trenches and earth-works, by driving them away with rifle fire. The end result of all this camouflage and caution was that, even when the British scanned the plain through their field glasses from sites out of rifle-range, they still had no inkling of the trap that had so meticulously been set.

On Saturday 9th December, eleven days after the battle at Modder River Methuen set out on his last bid for Kimberley. His forces were by now not only well rested and restored to full strength but reinforced by the arrival of a brigade of Highlanders, a balloon observation section and an extra cavalry division. The artillery was also strengthened to a total of twenty-four field guns, four howitzers, and a huge 4.7" naval gun, nicknamed 'Joe Chamberlain'. During the days following his setback at Modder River, Methuen spent many hours contemplating his strategy for the impending advance. It was imperative that the dynamited railway bridge was repaired before he dared to venture further north. Indeed, the railway was the lifeline of the whole campaign, and any breach could result in fatal consequences for the entire army. On the other hand, the Boers had been in total disarray after the Modder, and the ten days of grace provided by the delay in repairing the bridge, allowed them to rebuild their morale and their defences. In the end, it turned out to be a sacrifice for which Methuen was to pay dearly at Magersfontein.

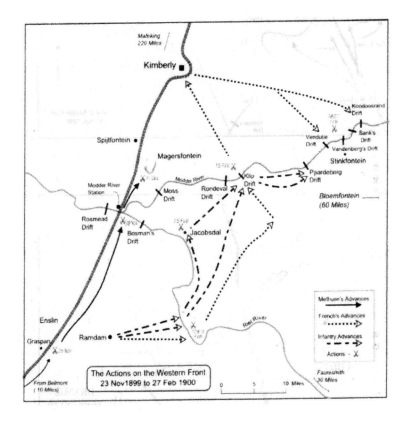

The Actions on the Western Front
23 Nov1899 to 27 Feb 1900

181

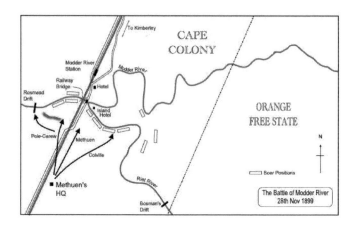

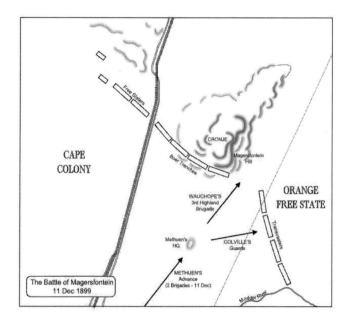

From the Modder River, the ground rises gradually, all the way to the Magersfontein hills, some six or more miles to the north. The flat plain stretches away in the distance with no treacherous riverbeds to hinder an advance, and there was only the odd patch of scrub or mimosa sprinkling the sparse grassy veld ahead. The hills are clustered together in the shape of a triangle, with the prominence of Magersfontein itself, rising out of the veld for nearly 200 feet, and out-topping all the other peaks. On the slopes of Magersfontein, standing stark above the plain, the Boers made themselves obvious to Methuen's scouts by visibly appearing to be digging themselves in. These activities were closely observed by British cavalry patrols, sent out regularly to keep a wary eye on the Boers.

Encouraged by the nature of the terrain between him and the Boers, Methuen decided to revert to a night march followed by a dawn assault. In addition to the daily cavalry patrols, he commissioned a qualified Royal Artillery surveyor, Major Benson, to reconnoitre the best route to follow for a night approach. Benson reported that a night march would be very feasible, there being no hilly areas to flounder across, no faulty maps to confuse and mislead them, and that their target lay clear across five miles of open flat and unhindered ground straight ahead of them. To spearhead the attack, Methuen selected the redoubtable Highlanders, generally regarded as the finest fighting brigade in the British Army. He ordered The Guards and the 9th Brigade to be held in reserve. Commanding the Highland Brigade was Maj. Gen. A.T. (Andy) Wauchope, who happened to be not in favour of an attack on Magersfontein. He believed it more strongly defended than supposed by Methuen, yet, although he openly made his views known, once he became committed to the task, threw himself with vigour into the execution of the plan.

On Sunday, 10th December, Methuen unleashed one-and-a-half hours hours of terrifying bombardment with every gun he had. Magersfontein was consumed by massive spurts of red earth, yellow lyddite fumes and boulders flying fifty feet into the air. He was satisfied at the end, that any Boer defence works on the hill would have been pulverised, and the Boers severely shaken, if not entirely dispersed. In fact, the Boer losses during the barrage only amounted to three burghers wounded. Shortly after midnight, Wauchope set off with the Black Watch in the lead, followed by the Seaforths, the Argylls, and the Highland Light Infantry. They marched into a driving storm that made the darkness impenetrable except for vivid flashes of lightning. The Highlanders advanced, shoulder-to-shoulder in ninety-six successive lines making a solid rectangle of 4,000 men marshalled on each side by rope-connected guides. The massive square was made up of thirty companies in ninety-six files all condensed in a column 45 yards wide and 160 yards long.

After three hours of marching, Wauchope, at the head of the column, dimly perceived the shoulder of Magersfontein in the greying light. It was at this time that Benson suggested that the brigade deploy into open-order advance, but Wauchope, wishing to leave as little ground as possible between him and the hill before the enemy became aware of his presence, ordered the men to continue forward in close-order formation. He reasoned that to extend his line now would not only eat into precious time, but would be greatly slow down the impetus of his advance. As a result, he continued to push forward a further several hundred yards, encountering on the way, a small delay in getting his force through a belt of thick bushes. At 4 a.m. Magersfontein, faintly outlined in the dawn's early light, appeared to be only a half-mile ahead, and Wauchope gave the order to deploy. As the men moved forward in the dark, the silence was suddenly shattered by a blast of fire that shrivelled them in their tracks. They had walked into a terrifying trap – thousands of rifles opened fire from point blank range – not from the slopes of the hill as expected, but from the very feet of the leading Black Watch.

What followed for the next nine hours was a dual on the same pattern as the previous battle. The sun rose to find the Highlanders pinned down on the plain, the movement of a hand, even of a twitch of ankle being attacked by ants, brought down a hail of Mauser bullets. Once again, the British artillery saved the infantry by bringing the field guns to well within rifle range of the foe, which did not respond with any of their own guns excepting for some fire from their three pom-poms. Encouraged by this and by the calm weather conditions, Methuen ordered the launch of the aerial reconnaissance unit, a large balloon manned by Capt. Jones and some of his engineers. Jones reported that Cronje had somehow left a gap of about 1,500 yards wide in the eastern sector of the Boer lines, between the end of the great trench at the foot of Magersfontein koppie, and the beginning of the defences on the ridge running down to the river. If Methuen had now, pushed his reserves up into this gap, the Guards could have punched a hole into the Boers' left, in the same manner that Pole-Carew's brigade had broken their right at Modder River. Instead, he desisted because there were handicaps here, which had not existed at the Modder. Firstly, it was not the weak Prinsloo commanding the vulnerable sector, and secondly the Transvaal leaders had mustered over 6,000 riflemen for this battle and not just 2,000 as at the previous encounter. Thirdly, he now had three brigades instead of two, and he had posted the third, the reserve brigade, in the rear to be ready to parry any blow against his base camp. Because of all this Methuen failed to seize the chance, and before any of the Guards were able to fill the gap, some Boers, who had arrived in that area quite by accident, hastily galloped over and sealed it.

Methuen now found himself in a serious quandary, and could not decide what to do next. To prevent the Highlanders from being over-run, he sent some Gordon's forward to reinforce the centre, and some Guards to block the Boers on the east. At this stage the British were fortunate, because Cronje, like Methuen, was now over-cautious in seizing opportunities, and as the mid-day shadows shortened, the battle passed into stalemate with the men falling asleep over their rifles where they lay, with terror once more giving way to boredom. Up to this moment, most of them had withstood their ordeal with stoicism and courage. Inching forward, some 200 men of the Black Watch and Seaforths had succeeded in reaching the eastern face of the Magerfontein koppie, where they were suddenly confronted by a party of Boers. In the ensuing confusion, they were decimated, not only by the Boer marksmen, but also by their own artillery which had mistaken them for the enemy. A few of the soldiers, quite by chance, managed to trickle through the gap in the Boer lines, but there they stumbled upon a party of seven Boers, including Cronje himself, who opened fire and rounded them up.

Then, suddenly, like a frayed steel cable, the nerve of the Highlanders snapped! In waves of despair, the will of the men finally broke. After nine hours of horror and terrifying boredom, baking in the scorching sun without water or food, the Highlanders just could not take any more. About 1 p.m., Lt. Col. James Hughes-Hallet, commander of the Seaforths, became aware of some Boers working around his right flank, and he ordered two of his companies to trickle back a few hundred yards. Lt. Col. George Downman of the Gordon's gave similar orders. It was at this moment that the foray with Cronje's small group shattered the calm, and suddenly, the trickle became a flood, and the flood became a deluge as the entire brigade gave way, and went on the run for all they were worth. The troops in the rear were soon caught up in the stampede, and despite desperate and valiant efforts by their officers to stem the tide the men ran on and on and melted away into the veld behind them. When the ambulance-men went out the next day to collect the wounded and the dead, there were 902 on the British side and 236 on the Boer side. They found the gallant Wauchope, dead within 200 yards of Cronje's trenches.

From his H.Q. Methuen had witnessed the destruction of the Highlanders, and bitterly saw his dream end with (in his own words) 'bad luck and Wauchope!' being the causes of the debacle. Yet, even now, there was a sliver of a hope. Methuen opined that the Boers might well have withdrawn during the night as they had done after their victory at the Modder, and soon after dawn the next morning, he sent the balloon up to check the situation. As it rose out of the line of shadow, Capt. Jones's telephoned report shattered the last of Methuen's illusions – the Boers, masters of the new art of warfare on the western front, were still holding fast in their trenches.

Methuen now found himself beset with conflicting counsel – to retreat or to renew the conflict. Most of his staff favoured retreat – gun ammunition was short, water supplies were low, and a large part of the army was shattered. In sadness, Methuen agreed to withdraw. The retreat began at noon with the Boers, cautious as ever in following up an advantage, using only their artillery to harass the retreating troops. At 4 p.m. the soldiers were back again in their camp on the Modder River. Upwards of 2,000 men had been killed, wounded, captured or were missing. Three-quarters of them were Highlanders whose leading companies had lost 60% of their officers. The Boer losses, about a quarter of those of the British, testified to the intensity of the struggle, and ironically, the chief architect of their victory was absent on the day of the battle. De la Rey had gone back to his wife to break the news of the death of their eldest son.

Details of the Magersfontein disaster and of Methuen's defeat were released in London on the Thursday. Monday's news about Gatacre's mishap at Stormberg had been a misfortune, but now the galling news of 13,000 of her finest troops routed in the open veld, struck Britain numb. The shadow of "Black Week" was lengthening over the shocked nation.

Black Week - The Aftermath – Political and Strategical
The phenomena of Black Week owed much to the daily press, which brought to the majority of the British for the first time, the naked reality of sudden death, with detailed descriptions of yellow lyddite fumes, the thud of a Mauser bullet, and the horrifying

hiss of a snaking pom-pom shell. The 'man in the street' suddenly became aware of a new type of warfare – no longer fought against primitive "savages" or "fuzzy-wuzzies", but against an enemy as brave, skilful and chivalrous as their own, and with a new style of war with modern battle tactics which included superior mobility, superior armaments and superior field-craft. After the immediate shock waves of Black Week dulled down, there followed an intense resolve and closing of ranks. A hysterical patriotism emerged, coupled with increased hostility to the conduct of the war so far, and particularly against the generals responsible for it.

Four days after Magersfontein, Buller, on the Natal Front, provided the third catastrophe to make up Black Week. On the 15ᵗʰ December General Louis Botha had whipped the cream of the British Army at Colenso, sending Buller reeling back to Chieveley to lick his wounds and restore the shattered morale of his defeated troops. In the west, Methuen, forced back to Modder River, was too stunned to contemplate any immediate action against Cronje and his triumphant commandos.

On the Boer side Kruger and Steyn spent hours, pondering the possibilities of following up the Boers' military successes on the western front and in Natal, and their enthusiasm was fanned, in no small measure, by the ardour and impatience of the new generation of young Boer leaders such as Smuts, Fischer and Grobler. The more cautious Boer commanders however, questioned the practicality of such a strategy. Cronje, for example, urged caution. Even when President Kruger himself, asked to block Methuen's lifeline by capturing Belmont and turning it into a Boer stronghold, he resisted on the grounds that the terrain was too flat for successful offensive action. He also warned that there was not enough water there, and that his burghers and their horses, were too exhausted for any further immediate action. Still Kruger was anxious for some form of immediate action against the defeated British or else the impetus of victory would be lost. Turning to Natal, he asked Botha after Colenso, to '*smite the enemy while the terror is still so great in their minds*'. '*Impossible,*' Botha replied, just as Cronje did, '*there are no hills around to offer cover and the burghers' morale was too volatile to attempt such a risky venture*'.

If Botha, the very boldest and most level headed general in the entire Boer force, believed that Buller was too strong to attack head-on, who then can say that Cronje was wrong to adopt the same attitude in regard to Methuen, or that the Boer governments were remiss in not insisting on an all-out general offensive against the British? In the end, the outcome of all this was that the two republics' military activities were now restricted, limited to blocking the progress of the British relief columns, and to squeezing slowly to death the three beleaguered garrisons at Ladysmith, Kimberley, and Mafeking. Ironically, it was the fate of these three towns that was also the principal concern of the British in spite of the relative unimportance they held in strictly tactical terms. If the Boers had succeeded in capturing them, it would have dealt an exceedingly humiliating blow to British pride and prestige, not only at home but throughout the Empire as well. On the other hand, by leaving these garrisons to the Boers, the British, in strictly military terms, would have made their task in South Africa much easier, for neither Buller nor Roberts would have been encumbered with the entanglements of relieving them. It would have left the road wide to make straight for Bloemfontein right up the Cape Midlands and over the flat open plains of the Free State.

Whatever the attitude of both the British and the Boer leaders after Magersfontein and Colenso, it was obvious that they had failed to recognise the new conditions of warfare. They did not grasp the reality that smoke-less long-range magazine rifles used by mobile infantry concealed in carefully prepared slit trenches, tipped the tactical balance in favour of defence. By the same token, they also under-rated the difficulties and problems related to the employment of offensive strategy, and it was this obfuscation that would cause the conflict to drag on painfully for yet a further two-and-a-half bitter and costly years.

In the days following Black Week, Roberts and Kitchener were fraught with anxiety and concern. The big question was, how quickly would the successful Boers press their advantage over the weakened British forces in the Cape Midlands? A rapid and telling thrust southwards could not only spark off the expected rebel uprising in the Cape itself, but would send the dazed Gatacre reeling back to Cape Town. This would leave the field wide open for the Boers to turn on French in Naauwpoort, a hundred miles to the west, and to take De Aar and so cut Methuen off from the Cape. Roberts need not have been so worried, because as it turned out, the Free State generals in command of operations in that area were both unimaginative and ineffective. At his base in Colesburg, General Schoeman had scarcely budged since crossing the Orange River, and was sitting overcautiously tight. At Stormberg, General Olivier left Gatacre unmolested, giving him ample time to recover his strength, and to send out small forces to take control of the surrounding countryside, even as far as Dordrecht in the extreme southeast.

The timely arrival of General French consolidated the tenuous advantage gained from the Boer generals' indolence. When French was with White at Ladysmith during the siege had no intention of being incarcerated for the remainder of the war, and succeeded in escaping and immediately making for the Cape Midlands, where he rightly believed the real action would soon be taking place. He brought with him his two very able assistants, his Chief-of-Staff, Douglas Haig, and the exceedingly efficient E.E.H. Allenby, who had previously seen action in Bechuanaland under Warren, and in the Zulu Wars of 1888. Moving swiftly and effectively, French conducted enterprising and harassing operations, which succeeded in confounding the Boers. His crowning achievement was the recapture of Naauwpoort, a vital rail junction on the Cape Town-Kimberley railway line. French's dash and élan baffled Schoeman, rendering him torpidly moribund. More than anything else, the successes of French and Gatacre had a resounding bearing on the military and political situation in the Cape. Apart from the very positive 'morale boosting' effect on the British military establishment, it undoubtedly influenced the outcome of the much feared 'Cape Rebellion'. The Boers had depended heavily on the successes of Black Week, together with their invasion of the Cape, to stir up the rebellion. However, the ensuing deadlock played very much to the advantage of the British, and in the event, out of the 40,000 Cape Dutch Boers hoped for, only 7,000 rebels eventually emerged. Nevertheless, no one was under any illusion about the Colony's safety, especially the 'young lions' amongst the Boer leaders who were seriously agitating for quick and effective thrusts to the south, not only in Natal but, especially in the Cape Midlands. A clear indication of this very fact came when Steyn appointed Christiaan de Wet's younger brother Piet, to assist and ginger up the torpid Schoeman at Colesburg. In some areas, the Boers did make feeble attempts to stir up the rebellion in the surrounding Cape territory, but apart from half-hearted preparations for an attack on the isolated little settlement of Kuruman, far to the northwest of Kimberley, everything just seemed to come to a halt. Farther north, on the banks of the Modder River, Methuen sat helplessly tight. Having strengthened his guard at the railway line with 11,000, newly arrived, British, Australian and Canadian troops, he brought up supplies on a daily basis, bombarded the Boers, and pushed forward his advance patrols to within a mile of the Boer entrenchments. Yet he neglected to attack their communications, which were strung out eastwards at right angles to his own very vulnerable and exposed right flank. Thus, the year dragged to a close. In Natal, things were once again going badly for Buller, and at Mafeking, Baden-Powell had his fingers scorched while trying to seize a Boer outpost at Game Tree Fort, in an over-ambitious attempt to punish them. During the course of this futile attempt, he lost 50 of his men, either killed or wounded. A few days later Olivier, at Stormberg, stretched out a tentacle, and forced Gatacre's right flank to give up Dordrecht, and by so doing exposing the entire Eastern Cape area as far as the vital eastern seaboard, to the danger on invasion.

New Years Day brought music to British ears. News arrived that French had gradually edged forward, and now strongly reinforced, was attacking those very enemy positions on which any hope of invasion of the Cape depended, namely Schoeman's stronghold near Colesburg. The town was open to the north, but protected on the other three sides by some hills, of which those facing French to the south were particularly formidable. French launched his attack from the west, moving up by night in order to open his initiative at first light. The situation was ominously similar to that at Stormberg except that this time the troops arrived fresh, either on horseback or wagon, and careful reconnaissance had brought them to within yards of the anticipated point of attack. Encouraged by his run of successes, French fully expected to enter the town within hours. His western assault had overwhelmed the hills commanding the Boer defences on the right in spite of stern opposition by Piet de Wet and his new command. But the British attack ground to a halt by early afternoon, and French decided to await reinforcements before resuming the initiative. The Boers' morale, on finding their lines threatened with imminent encirclement, sunk even lower than the point to which Schoeman's leadership had already reduced it, so when his reinforcements eventually arrived, French decided he would make one more push to apply the coup de grace.

However, the Boers in the meantime had also been receiving significant reinforcements. With Christiaan de Wet now promoted to command over all the Boer forces around Magersfontein, Koos De la Rey was despatched post-haste to Colesburg to stir up the torpid Schoeman, and to shore up the Boer defences against French. Now fully reinforced he decided that the moment had come to take the town and planned to start with the night capture of a hill to the north, and launch a day attack from three sides. However, the assault, undertaken with more optimism than forethought, was doomed for disaster. The men, setting off at midnight, donned soft shoes, and to preserve absolute secrecy, received strict orders to hold all fire and to use their bayonets only. As they climbed up 700 yards of rocky slope they were suddenly halted by an outburst of fierce fire out of the darkness. Acting on orders not to return fire, confusion and panic sent half of them running off in the darkness, and the rest failing, after repeated attempts, to close with the enemy. At dawn, the remnants of the attacking force surrendered to the Boers. For French, this unexpected setback meant the loss of morale-boosting superiority his so far unbroken run of successes had achieved. With the arrival of De la Rey, the Boer force had now grown to over 6,000 men, which presented a severe check on any aspirations he may have had for further progress. Unfortunately for the Boers, they too were unable to gain any advantages from French's setback. The frustrated De la Rey, in an attempt to advance against the retreating British, was denied support from his Free State allies. With an unbelievable lack of faith in their own capabilities, they repeatedly shied away from any open confrontation with the enemy. In similar vein, the Free State commandos, operating in the other battle sector near Stormberg, refused to give chase to Gatacre and his army, with the result that now, along the entire Cape Midlands front, a state of deadlock had set in, similar to that on the Western Front.

In the far north, Kuruman finally surrendered in the face of an artillery barrage, so ending an episode of valorous, but pointless defence. With the fall of the settlement, tens of thousands of square miles of the far Northern Cape opened up to the roaming commandos, which in the end, proved to be boundless space dearly bought for very questionable advantage from any point of view. In Methuen's sector a rebel commando, northeast of Belmont, came under attack from a British column sent out to surprise them, resulting in the loss of their laager. This setback, at last stung Cronje into action, and responding to pressure from De la Rey and De Wet, he agreed to a limited foray to blow up the railway line behind Methuen, and to seize a supply train. The end-result of Schoeman's timidity and French's enterprise was that the British succeeded in staving off, both a thrust on De Aar to cut off Methuen, as well as an invasion of the Cape by the Boers. French, in addition to his successes, also succeeded in distracting attention from the yawning gap between himself and Gatacre, giving his men invaluable experience and confidence. Most of all, he resuscitated British morale, and successfully drew off Boers from other fronts to commit themselves to the pointless defence of Colesburg.

Roberts and Kitchener – Plans and Preparations
Frederick Sleigh Roberts, son of an Irish general, was considered one of the greatest soldiers of his time. This lofty status belied his diminutive stature, and the blindness in one eye, which had been caused by a childhood fever from which he had almost died. Neither was there any convincing soldierly promise in his heart and digestive ailments, which obliged him to keep, for medicinal purposes, a bottle of sherry at his bedside. He joined the Indian army as an artillery officer, and emerged from The Mutiny at the age of twenty-six, with seven mentions in despatches and the Victoria Cross. After that, for the next twenty years, staff work and marriage kept him absorbed in routine and mundane activities, relieved only by a single, bloodless expedition against the mad King Theodore of the Assam tribe. When fame eventually came, it came with a rush. A routine staff paper, written in the course of regular duties, was spotted accidentally by

the Viceroy, who was so impressed with it, that he singled out Roberts for command of a column at the outbreak of the war in Afghanistan. For three successive years, Roberts went on marches against Amir, the dissident Mullah, and his name soon spread across the North-West Frontier. Finally, he was cut-off from the world for three weeks, while he marched from Kabul to Kandahar, where he spectacularly rescued a beleaguered garrison. He returned to England a national hero. Roberts was a much-loved leader, brave and humane to his men, temperate in habit and speech, modest, simple and secure in married life, until his only son's death on the last day of Black Week, fused the nation's grief with his own.

The man towering behind Roberts seemed to be someone from another world. Horatio Herbert Kitchener's handsome face, clean-shaven except for a great moustache, is best remembered from the recruiting posters of World War 1, with the glittering emotionless stare of his wide-set blue eyes summoning the manhood of Britain to slaughter on the fields of Flanders. Kitchener was born and schooled in Ireland, but both his parents were English. His father raised his children as masters in a foreign land, and he adored his mother who died when he was only fourteen years old. He never married, and there was no real evidence that any woman ever claimed his romantic interest. On entering the army, he served with the Engineers, and before joining Roberts at the age of forty-nine, he had spent the whole of his military life in the Middle East, first land surveying and then helping to train the Egyptian army. During his stay in Egypt, he had commanded an outpost, and often dressed as an Arab whenever he went spying alone. He exercised a fascination over highly born women, and spent his home-leave in their stately mansions, where he manipulated them to exert their influence in his interests. Kitchener succeeded in making himself detestable in the army for many reasons. His rapid promotion to Sirdar of the Egyptian army after the abortive Gordon Relief expedition, his intolerance with officers who failed through no fault of their own, and his disdainful indifference to the corporate life and graces of professional soldiering did little to endear him to the military and social hierarchy of his day. Nevertheless, on leading the Sudan Expedition, he became, through his methodical advance and decisive victories, a hero in the public eye, and a grateful parliament voted him a grant of £30,000 and a peerage as Lord Kitchener of Khartoum and Aspall, the latter being his mother's home in Suffolk.

Kitchener was a truly remarkable soldier, forever lusting for victory, and delighting in raining down blows of violence on his enemy. He had no scruples about means to attain a desirable end, and practised oriental barbarities to overawe oriental barbarians. His harshness towards his own Sudanese army left it in a state of mutiny, causing the men much suffering and hardship. Yet his personal life was one of inviolate purity and self-control, with a strict adherence to an exalted moral code. And now, 'Bobs and K', together, had the veld to conquer. Beyond the coastal mountain ranges, the South African veld stretched away for mile upon endless mile, beyond the distant horizon and far into the bare and hostile hinterland. Flat and featureless, except for the occasional isolated rocky outcrops of flat-topped, mesa-like hills, or oddly domed conical, bee-hive 'koppies', the veld was sparsely populated, with only here and there, the odd ramshackle outpost with its three or four mud and tin structures. There were no roads in this vast landscape, and the sole means of access was the solitary, single-track railway line, reaching ever further from the major costal towns, for hundreds and hundreds of straight and featureless miles, deep into the northern interior of the African sub-continent. The railway was the umbilical cord that fed and sustained the vast interior, and it was for this reason, more than any other one, that it was imperative for any advancing army, or defending foe, to maintain contact with, and control it. It was natural, therefore, that, at the outbreak of the war in October 1899, the Boers would immediately lay siege to the most important settlements along the existing railway network such as Mafeking, Kimberley, Ladysmith and Naauwpoort. It is also significant that most of the main pitched battles took place at major railway settlements such as Dundee, Ladysmith and Colenso in Natal, Stormberg in the Cape Midlands, and Graspan, Belmont, Modder River and Magersfontein on the western railway line.

At the start of the war in 1899, a well-established rail network was already in place in South Africa. The 'western railway' ran from Cape Town northwards through De Aar, Kimberley and Mafeking, to Bulawayo in Rhodes's Matabeleland. From Port Elizabeth, the 'central railway' went northwest to Naauwpoort, and then north through Bloemfontein and on to Pretoria and beyond. The 'central' and the 'western' lines were linked with a spur from Naauwpoort to De Aar. The 'central railway' was also joined at Naauwpoort, by a track running from East London, via Queenstown and Stormberg. Another important line ran from Durban to Pretoria, via Ladysmith in Natal, and finally, there was the Delagoa Bay Railway that ran due east from Pretoria, via Komaatipoort, to Lourenco Marques, in Portuguese East Africa.

After setting off from Southampton, Roberts and his staff spent much time aboard the Dunnottar Castle, working on feasible alternatives to the prosaic and obvious 'thrust up the railway' invasion tactic as recommended by The War Office. In the end, Roberts decided to scrap it, and arrived in Cape Town to reveal his new "grand design". In his new invasion plan, Roberts decided to assemble an army on the 'western railway' at Orange River station, from which Methuen had so hopefully, set out to relieve Kimberley. Then, instead of continuing north along the railway, he would strike eastward to cover eighty miles across country to the 'central railway', at a point somewhere south of the Free State capital. This would compel the Boer invaders to fall back in defence of their homeland, and so draw the besiegers away from all the beleaguered towns. It was a daring plan, ignoring all the traditional conceptions of reliance on the railways for communication and sustenance. Instead, enormous numbers of supply wagons and draft animals were to be used to transport and maintain the huge army as it moved across eighty miles of bare and barren veld. Buller's failures in Natal had highlighted the uselessness of massive infantry numbers plodding across the plains at the speed of an ox-wagon, so Roberts needed a substantial portion of his new army to be mounted and mobile, and securely welded into a highly efficient fighting machine.

To provide adequately for all the logistics involved in such a massive move, it was vitally important to ensure an efficient and well-coordinated system of transport and supply, especially since the bulk of the new troops came from the Indian, the Egyptian and the home armies, each with its own methods and materials. The task of creating an efficient 'distribution-on-the-move' scheme fell to Kitchener, who casting all tradition aside, came up with a sweepingly revolutionary plan. In essence, it boiled down to a system whereby the bulk of the army's needs would be provided for from a central 'supply-park' of ox-wagons, which would be replenished from the nearest of a number of 'stock depots' dotted along the length of the closest railway line. Kitchener's new scheme was a fundamental change to the traditional methods of transport and supply, and would soon turn out to one of the greatest blunders of the war. It is strange that the two most famous soldiers of the war, Roberts and Kitchener, knew so little about the workings of the British Army. In a way they were both 'outsiders'; Roberts had lived most of his life in India, and Kitchener had served for a great number of years in North Africa. Neither had a clear understanding of the War Office system of transport and supply as used in South Africa, namely the 'regimental' or 'decentralised' system, which provided for each battalion commander to be responsible through his battalion transport officer, for his own day-to-day food and other supplies.

In his vision for his 'grand new plan', Roberts seemed to be oblivious to the conventional War Office and 'British' way of running an army. His goal was to create a finely honed and efficient fighting machine, unhampered by the trappings of traditional means and methods. His aim was for a disciplined force in which each branch would be required to expend all its efforts and resources on the task for which it was best skilled and talented. In this way, soldiers had to kill, engineers to dig, and transport units to carry and supply, and so on. In all this Roberts was fortunate to have Kitchener, the loner and the maverick, as an able and willing lieutenant. It is incredible how they were both so unhesitatingly anxious to abandon at a stroke, well-tried and successful methods, for complex and unmanageable alternatives.

Kitchener set about his task with enthusiasm, and his first action was to replace the effective 'first line regimental distribution-on-the-move' method with the cumbersome and impractical 'central supply park' alternative. He then threw out the 'non-regimental' transport system, supplied by the brigade supply columns, and replaced it with a creation entirely of his own. He called it the 'general transport system', which entailed the use of largely untrained officers hustled into ox-wagon and mule-cart transport companies, to cater for all the various requirements and needs of the army as a whole. The scheme was a blueprint for confusion, and it was not take long before the professionally trained transport officers to prophesy disaster. In fact, they did not have long to wait, and soon 'K of K' became known to all and sundry, as 'K for Chaos'! It is surprising that an officer as meticulous as Roberts was so slap-dash in his anxiety to get his 'grand army' mobile and on the road. Simple logistics were swept aside, unrecognised and unattended. In his haste to get as many men as possible on horseback, Roberts had overlooked the critical problem of supply of adequate mounts for the numerous converted colonial corps and infantry regiments from foot to horse. In the end, horses became almost impossible to procure, and local Cape farmers were reluctant to part with their own beasts that were to be used as a means of pursuing and slaying their own kith and kin on the battlefronts. As a result, horses had to be imported, 12,000 and more from as far a field as England, Australia and even Argentina, involving long and exhausting sea voyages at great expense.

In spite of Roberts's apparent disregard to details, there were many aspects of his plan which were well thought out, well prepared and well executed. Unlike Methuen and Buller, he was not going to leave anything to chance, and he paid special attention to his military intelligence department. In order to gain truly authentic information about the terrain over which he was going to conduct his campaign, he set up an Intelligence Dept. under the command of Col. George Henderson. Henderson was widely considered to be one of the foremost British military thinkers of his day, and Roberts had head-hunted him away from his desk at the Staff College, to appoint him as his Director of Intelligence, with funds, staff and status on a scale hitherto unheard of in the British Army.

As the moment for Roberts's push up the western railway approached, it became increasingly vital for him to maintain the advantage of surprise. Although he only confided in a handful of his senior officers, it was becoming impossible to conceal the massive build-up of troops and supplies in the area around the Orange River station. In an attempt to lead everyone off the scent, he diverted a large number of reinforcements to French, standing by to move over to the Orange River section at a moments notice, and in this way, he succeeded in bluffing the Boers into thinking that his counter-offensive would be coming from the Colesburg area. Yet, in spite of all his well-laid plans and the urgency of his preparations, events were beginning to pile up against Roberts. When he had first arrived in South Africa, he had been amazed to discover the immense prestige value attached to Kimberley by both the Boers and the British South Africans alike. Now, on the very eve of his intended advance, Roberts was receiving increasingly ominous reports, the most alarming of which was that the new Boer siege commander, Gen. J .S. Ferreira, aware of Roberts' activities since his arrival, had intensified the bombardments on the city, and moved his men closer in. This new offensive greatly increased the already miserable conditions in Kimberley, causing a serious deterioration of the health situation, the food and supplies crisis, and above all, the acrimonious friction between Rhodes and Kekewich.

To compound Roberts's anxieties, was the news that the situation in Natal had seriously worsened, and that the outlook for Ladysmith was bleaker than ever after Buller's disaster at Spioenkop. Urgent signals were coming in from London and Cape Town that something drastic needed doing in Natal, and that Roberts, as Commander in Chief of the South African Army, should attend to it as quickly as possible. Then, to cap it all, Henderson, Roberts's Intelligence Officer, brought even more alarming news. The dry conditions in that part of the Karroo through which Roberts had planned to march, had worsened due to a severe three-month drought, and he would need to react urgently, and come up with a new plan if he wished to succeed. Roberts hurriedly came up with new plan that was even bolder than the first one. He would stick to his eastward flank march, not however from the Orange River, but from behind Methuen's position on the Modder, from whence he would strike eastwards, directly at Bloemfontein itself, pausing only to outflank Magersfontein with his mounted troops, in order to relieve Kimberley. With additional tracks hastily laid at various sidings on the western railway, complicated arrangements were set afoot to move an entire army up to various points along the single track behind Methuen. Engineers probed for water along the way, and troops and transport mules urgently moved in from Colesburg and other areas.

When Cronje became aware of all this fevered activity, he surmised that an attack against his Magersfontein defences was being planned. Then another, quite fortuitous incident put him right off the scent. Recently the Boers had been renewing their efforts to raise a rebellion westwards, and to clear that area, Methuen had sent out the Highland Brigade, now led by Hector MacDonald. When news of this assault reached Cronje, he became convinced that a major flank attack on that side was under way. He rushed De Wet off to deal with it, and after a brief clash, MacDonald quietly withdrew, leaving Cronje satisfied that the danger was over. The entire incident blinded Cronje's reasoning and he had no idea at all that Roberts was actually planning a full frontal attack of the Boer positions. At the same time the Boers at Colesburg, were being made to believe that the British preparations in that region were being made for an attack against them. Even while the bulk of the British forces were withdrawing to join Roberts's army in the west, French kept up an illusion of strength with a series of strategies aimed at hiding the true British movements on that front.

In due course, the grand plan was completed, and Roberts was ready to move. However, there were many who were decidedly less enthusiastic about the current state of affairs. For example, back in Cape Town, Milner viewed the situation with dismay, and for good reason. His concern was that Roberts was concentrating his main strength some 600 miles from Cape Town, leaving only a skeleton force along the central front to face any threats against the capital. At Colesburg, there was a concentration of between 700 and 800 Boers, revitalised by the arrival of De la Rey and Piet de Wet, and it would be very easy for them to seize Naauwpoort Junction in front of them, or even De Aar only sixty miles to the south-east. The capture of either, or both of these vital rail junctions would sever Roberts from the Cape, which itself would then be at the entire mercy of the Boers. Roberts was not to be swayed – he had staked everything on the flank march, and for him the die was cast.

The Road to Kimberley
Roberts had made a bold, perhaps even reckless decision, but he was determined to go ahead with it. He recalled French from Colesburg, and ordered him to forge ahead and relieve Kimberley by making a right flank around Magersfontein. On the evening of February 10th he sent French to seize the drifts across the Riet and the Modder rivers, and flank the Boer positions before Cronje could realise what was happening. Then, at midnight, he gave the order for the great flank march to begin. Over 25,000 infantry, nearly 8,000 cavalry and MI, over a hundred guns and thousands of ox- and mule-wagons, set off across the veld towards the Modder- and Riet rivers. Behind them were 7,000 men with Methuen, ordered to stay back and confront the Magersfontein defences. Then there were a further 18,000 soldiers to guard the railway down to the Orange River – a grand total of 58,000 men plus French's cavalry division, which was poised at the Riet river to set off on its dash for Kimberley. At last, the advance was on its way and steamrolling across the open veld.

When Cronje eventually learnt about French's departure, he wrongly deduced that the British were making demonstrations towards Fauresmith in the southeast. He sent Christiaan de Wet to check them, and French, at that time making towards the northeast, ran into De Wet coming the opposite way. He succeeded in distracting De Wet's attention by making a feint across the river upstream of him. As the Boers were confident that the British objective was Fauresmith, Cronje consequently sent De Wet higher up-stream. By the time French arrived at the Riet River, his horses were exhausted, having ridden hard and fast in the gruelling heat, so he rested and waited for the main army to catch up. He then spent his time in preparing for an early start on the morrow. It was Roberts's intention to cover twenty-five miles of waterless veld and to reach the Modder River by crossing Cronje's flank almost under his nose, and in so doing, finally revealing the true direction of the British march. However, as the first supply wagons reached the Riet, a pile up, miles long, brought total chaos, until Kitchener eventually diverted some columns to another drift further up-stream. The result was that supplies reached French too late for the early start he had planned, and by the time he eventually did set off on the 13th February, Roberts had already arrived.

French's delay had seriously increased the risks to the opening phases of the campaign, and Roberts watched anxiously as the 6,000 horse men set off across the veld. Roberts was not the only person who was watching with concern. Unobserved, De Wet had arrived at a nearby hill, and when he saw the great army in front of him, spread across a front of five miles, he immediately sent word to Cronje. Surprisingly and quite inexplicably, instead of harrowing French until Cronje could send reinforcements, De Wet now withdrew to a safe position twenty miles upstream. French swept on and soon the Modder River came into view. His whole force charged the crossing while groups of Boers in the vicinity fled before them. The British forded the river without mishap and occupied some of the hills beyond, securing their bridgehead. Meanwhile, the vanguard of the main army trudged on towards the position that French's cavalry had secured. Although he was ready to set off at once, French could not leave the Modder until sufficient of the infantry had arrived to hold it in strength. The leading divisions did not arrive until two days later, during which time the truth finally dawned upon Cronje that despite their distance from the railway, it was not only the cavalry but the infantry as well, that were marching round his flank, and that they had already reached the Modder River, only ten miles from his main laager.

Once again, the hapless Cronje made a wrong decision. He believed that the British were trying to draw him eastward away from the Magersfontain defences, which they would then attack with a main force from the south. It was wishful thinking encouraged by his reluctance to abandon his superb defences and to move eastward to save his force and cover Bloemfontein at the same time. Because of this, Cronje stayed put, although he did move his main laager to a position a little to the north of Jakobsdal. As soon as the leading British infantry divisions arrived at the Modder and covered the drifts, which French had secured, he set off on the ride, which he hoped would end twenty miles away in Kimberley. It was 8.30 on the morning of the 15th February and ahead of him, and directly in his path, Cronje with 800 burghers awaited his arrival at Abon Dam. The burghers held two miles of koppies around a broad valley, blocked by a low ridge at its farther end. French decided to breach this valley with speed and break clean through the Boer defences.

The stage was now set for one of the last great cavalry charges – the 9th and 16th Lancers were first up the valley and thundered forward in a huge cloud of dust into which the Boers poured their fire. Wave after wave of cavalry followed into the valley, while behind them the artillery pounded away at the Boer defences until the very last minute. When, at the far end of the valley the horse men thundered over the ridge, the Boers finally broke and fled leaving behind them a score or so of their men either captured or speared. French paused only an hour to recover wind and strength, and then made on towards Kimberley. He passed close to Cronje's head laager at Jacobsdal, and had he known about the panic there he would have seized a rich prize. However, his target was Kimberley, which he could now see in the distance, so on he rode.

The cavalry charge at Abon Dam, whilst spectacular, achieved little intrinsic gain other than the relief of Kimberley, which, in truth could well have held out a bit longer until a more appropriate moment presented itself. As it was, it was entirely because of Rhodes and his antics that the charge took place in the first instance. At the time of reckoning it had become obvious that it had done no real damage to Cronje's force, and that French's 5,000 men, constituting Britain's only large mobile force in South Africa, a unique instrument for hunting down a mobile enemy and their siege guns, was now quite ineffectively stuck in Kimberley. Moreover, the cavalry's magnificent, but unnecessary, dash across the veld, expended them to the point of self-destruction, and the massive effort of recklessly galloping for all those miles proved to be the death of a large number of British horses. It was not only the horses that suffered – their riders too, many of them still raw recruits, had yet to learn the cost of over-straining their mounts in such a frenetic hunt. So heavy was the toll in dead or exhausted horses after the charge, that the cavalry division virtually destroyed itself as an effective fighting-force.

Away to the left rear, Magersfontein was aflame with a sustained bombardment unleashed by Methuen, which kept Cronje's main force fully occupied. Meanwhile, French's tumultuous breakthrough badly affected the morale of the Boers who were besieging Kimberly. Already being inferior in number, these lessened further, as many started to sneak away from the front. Shortly after 4 p.m., a patrol of Australian Horse rode into the town, and towards evening French, himself, arrived. Thousands lined the streets to cheer – Kimberley had been relieved and the four-month siege was over. It had cost 1,500 deaths from wounds and disease, and it was rumoured that many women had their minds permanently impaired by the strain.

The Road to Paardeberg
While French was making his break-through after leaving the advance infantry division behind at the Modder River, the long procession of infantry and transport continued to move up from behind. Part of it wheeled into Jacobsdal, the City Imperial Volunteers (CIV) going into action for the first time, and, after overcoming stern resistance from a small party of burghers, they occupied the former Boer H.Q. for use as Roberts's own and as a new base for the army. On the 15th January, Roberts arrived at Jacobsdal with the main column, and set up camp at Waterval Drift on the Riet River, where he awaited the outcome of French's dash to relieve Kimberley. Later that morning he rode out with Colvile's 9[th.] Division to reconnoitre another crossing at Wegdraai Drift on the Modder River, a few miles north- east in the direction of Paardeberg. Before setting off with

Colvile, Roberts ordered the main column to cross the Riet River, and follow in the direction of Wegdraai Drift. From the moment the column set off, it ran into serious difficulties. The riverbed at Waterval Drift was steep and broken up, and seeped in deep, soft and sticky mud, causing appalling problems for the crossing wagons. Very soon, hundreds of supply wagons had piled up all over the place, milling around in utter confusion. In the end, Roberts, anxious not to lose any more time, sent orders for the main column to follow on immediately, and for some 200 wagons to be left behind on the north bank of the Riet to enable the 3,000-odd draught animals to rest and recover. These wagons constituted the main mobile supply park for the entire division, and proved too big and enticing a target for the Boers to ignore, and it was not long before De Wet rode up with a party of burghers, ambushed the convoy, stampeded the cattle and ransacked the wagons. In less than an hour, a third of Roberts's supply system sat stranded beside the Riet River with the contents of its wagons entirely at the mercy of the Boers.

Roberts's decision to abandon the stranded supply wagons was hasty and ill conceived. It was as if his panic to save time and press forward, overshadowed his reasoning and clouded his judgement. In reality, instead of rushing forward at all costs, he would have been far better served by tarrying a day longer at Waterval Drift and confronting De Wet, instead of allowing him to get away unscathed, and in full possession of all his booty. Later, it emerged in evidence supplied to the Royal Commission of War that Roberts had acted as if he seemed to have 'lost his head momentarily and consequently not reacting to the disaster with the unflinching spirit of a great general' He was now obliged to adopt stopgap measures to bolster his critical supply requirements. Refugees, streaming in from outlying districts, had their wagons commandeered, Red Cross vehicles were stripped of their markings and converted into pack wagons, and emergency supplies were hastily hauled up from the nearest railway sidings. Fortunately, the situation was to some degree alleviated by French, who once again came to the rescue. Previously, due to the speed and mobility of his cavalry division, he had managed to prevent the sacrifice of his own 'regimental supply system' to Kitchener's 'central park supply' Now, thanks to this action, the cavalry division's untouched supply park could come to the rescue for long enough to enable sufficient emergency supplies to reach the battlefront.

Roberts need not have been so anxious about Cronje, because by now the Boer leader had become a confused and broken man. He was confounded by Roberts's show of massive strength, and mortified by the ceaseless pounding of Methuen's guns. When he learnt of French's break through at Abon Dam, he was stunned into dejection, and gripped by a paralysis of will. He scarcely moved from his tent, where he sat in utter dejection, while his wife gently patted him on his head and comforted him with whispered texts from the Old Testament. Burgher after burgher came to him, imploring him to act before the semi-circle of steel, which was closing in on them, would crush them all and render impossible all hope of flight and escape.

At last, to the relief of all in the Boer laager, Conje roused himself out of his torpor, and urged a retreat to Bloemfontein before it was too late. He told his generals that it was their only hope – there appeared to be no British yet between Roberts's forward division at the Modder, and French in Kimberley, and before this gap did eventually close, there was a slim chance for the Boers to slip through if they moved quickly. It was, unfortunate for the Boers, and particularly frustrating for De la Rey and De Wet, that of all the options open to him, Cronje'e decision to break out and retire to Bloemfontein was the very worst possible one to take. De la Rey pressed Cronje to consider the possibility of withdrawing along the railway line to the safety of Mafeking in the north. On the other hand, De Wet suggested that the Boers lie in wait for Roberts's ponderous wagon columns, and conduct a guerrilla war against his communications and supplies.

Cronje, in desperation elected to go for the most difficult and dangerous option of them all, namely that of retreating, in the face of the British army, across miles of open veld to the dubious safety of Bloemfontein. At midnight on the 17th February, the Boers abandoned their encampment at Magersfontein, and 5,000 burghers, with their families and several thousands of cattle and horses, set out into the veld in a convoy of 400 wagons. In defiance of his decision, fortune seemed to smile on Cronje, because at dawn on the 18th the British unit set off from the Modder River to join up with French. An infantry division and a brigade of MI under the command of O. C. Hannay went ahead to close the gap before the Boers could escape. To add to the urgency of the operation, Kitchener himself rode with the column to ensure speed. Miraculously Cronje's convoy narrowly succeeded in breaking out, and it was in the grey light of the morning that a huge pall of dust in the northeast announced the news that Hannay was too late and that the bird had flown. It would be unjust to lay the blame for the disaster at Hannay's door. He did everything he had been ordered to do, and he had executed his mission with diligence and alacrity. On the other hand, the British scouting methods were so defective that not a soul even suspected that Cronje, together with his vast and cumbersome convoy, had successfully fled clean across their lines. In fact, even after the Intelligence learnt of the escape, they were not quite sure whether it was the main Boer convoy, or perhaps a secondary one sent out by Cronje as a decoy to mask a major Boer attack on French in the north.

Hannay's MI. immediately rode off in pursuit of the Boers, while Kitchener sent an order to the infantry - 'objective changed – go for convoy'. As the MI. advanced eastwards to get between the river and the convoy, an unauthorised and mysterious order brought them to a halt, offering a sitting target to the Boers' rear guard posted on a hill a half a mile away. Swept by accurate Boer fire, men and horses plunged down the steep riverbank, where there was inextricable confusion as they struggled in the water and the thick mud. When the infantry division eventually came up, they were held-up by skilful Boer rear-guard tactics, during which time the Boer convoy succeeded in drawing further and further away. Roberts was in a quandary – there were no fresh troops near enough to join in on the attack, and he hesitated to divert any of the troops strung out south of the Modder. This was because he was still uncertain, at the time, both of Cronje's whereabouts, and his intentions; and this was not withstanding the fact that Methuen, at about midday, had discovered that Magersfontein had been abandoned.

The Boer column managed to get away far enough to laager safely near the river. The MI, having by now recovered from the confusion, rode up along the opposite bank, and with a battery of guns, successfully harassed the Boers until the burghers drove them off with a sharp and well executed counter-attack. Meanwhile French, unaware of Cronje's break out, was trying to round up the Boers who had been besieging Kimberley. One body, under General J. S. Ferreira had already moved northeast, but the main force, together with a Long Tom and some loaded wagons, was now twenty miles away to the north. French set off after it, and his vanguard reached the sandy dunes where the Boers had posted themselves to protect their convoy. In a hard-hitting action, the British gained the advantage but could not exploit it because of lack of water for their exhausted horses. The remainder of French's force did not come up because it was being tenaciously detained by less than 200 rebel Boers, and French had the galling experience of watching his prize trek away not more than five miles in front of him. He gave the order to withdraw while the horses still had the strength to carry the men back to Kimberley.

Roberts's problems were not over. News now arrived from the central front that General R. A. P. Clements, French's successor at Colesburg, had run into serious difficulties. The arrival of De la Rey in that sector encouraged Schoeman into launching an all-out offensive against Colesburg, and Clements, after staunch resistance, failed to stem the attack and had to withdraw to Arundel, further south. This left the central midlands railway network and the vital rail junctions of De Aar and Naauwpoort, unprotected and vulnerable to attacks by the Boers. Roberts now needed to make important decisions, and he needed to make them quickly. On balance, the situation ahead of him was far more critical than that at Colesburg, so he decided to leave Clements and the rail junctions to their own fate for the time being. He realised that the success or failure against Cronje depended on the vital prerogative to stop Cronje and the Boer forces from reaching Bloemfontein and digging in there. In order to achieve this, Roberts needed to act quickly and decisively to prevent his already sorely taxed supply and communication lines from collapsing completely. Orders were issued for the whole army to move as fast as possible in pursuit of Cronje's convoy, and in an attempt to slow down the Boers, he ordered French to ride swiftly and cut off the Boer advance at a point about fifteen miles ahead of its present position, in order to allow the main army to catch up.

French's task was a well-nigh impossible one because his cavalry division was in a shocking state. In scorching mid-summer heat, the futile expedition north of Kimberley had been the sixth since the flank march had set out. He could barely muster 1,200 sound horses to attempt the thirty-mile dash to the designated point, yet although he knew that the mission was a forlorn one, he allowed his men and horses just a few hours of rest before he set off. Fraught with anxiety, French prepared his men for the monumental task of halting a force of 5,000 Boers, little realising that between him and his goal, General J. S. Ferreira's force, several hundreds stronger than his own, was at that very moment, riding in from the north and descending right across his own path. Cronje continued to push on eastward, knowing that all he needed to do was to keep going to out-distance any pursuit. Just before noon, after passing a hill called Paardeberg on the north bank of the Modder, he prepared to cross over in order to pick up the Bloemfontein road. The banks of the river were steep, often quite cliff-like, and it was a great struggle to get across. Once over the river, the convoy out-spanned in the shade of some trees to recover. Suddenly, there was a violent salvo of shells, and panic ensued as hundreds of oxen were scattered, men women and children scurried for the shelter of the riverbanks, without anyone pausing to ascertain the size of the force that was attacking them. It was French, who had skilfully eluding Ferreira, followed up with a remarkable ride of supreme endurance, arrived unseen and unmolested, and had halted only a mile and a half north of Cronje's position. However, in spite of these achievements, French was still in a position of extreme precariousness, even after some MI. reinforcements did eventually reach him. The Boers on the Modder out-numbered him four-to-one, and he was safe only if they did not turn on him. Fortunately for him, a few hours later the infantry at last came into view, after Kitchener had forced it to cover thirty miles in twenty-four hours of scorching summer heat. It was only after they eventually encamped some two miles from the Boer laager that Cronje at last realised that he was cornered.

It was now that Roberts suddenly fell ill at Jacobsdal, and Kitchener was appointed to assume command during his absence. The infantry commanders were furious over this appointment. Many of them, including Lt. Gen. T. Kelly-Kenny, were Kitchener's superior in rank and had far more campaign experience than Kitchener had. In the end, this unfortunate appointment was to cause much confusion and unnecessary bloodshed, both on the side of the Boers as well as the British, for Kitchener proved to be quite unsuitable for such a high profile command. In the Boer laager, Cronje's commandants urged him to break away before Kitchener could surround them. But Cronje was by now a broken man Realising that his convoy was too weak to break out, he knew that his only hope lay in help from reinforcements from Bloemfontein, from Ferreira standing nearby with 1,500 men, and from De Wet's burghers. It was on these hopes that Cronje finally decided to make a stand at Paardeberg, face the enemy and fight it out.

The Battle of Paardeberg – The Stage
At Paardeberg the Modder flows sinuously from the north east cutting its way between high banks two to three hundred yards apart. The Boers were encamped on the northern bank, opposite and upstream from Kitchener, with their wagons parked in a straggling line along the top of the steep bank, and a concentration about midway to form a laager. Below, on the rocks and sand that bordered the water, and to some extent screened by foliage, were the women, children and oxen. In addition to their wagons, the burghers had hastily dug out some shallow trenches on the veld on both sides of the river, as well as in the banks themselves. Upstream and downstream from the central laager they occupied a stretch of the river of about fives miles in total. On both sides of the river, the ground rose gently in a gradient to a ring of low ridges and koppies. The river, therefore, appeared to be like a deep crack across a shallow saucer with the laager in the centre. On the northern rim, French's force was reinforced by the men who had been left behind in Kimberley. On the western rim was Kitchener's force, opposite from where the Modder twisted in a sort of elbow. From there, the river flowed on to the west in a comparatively straight line. Units of Hannay's MI, with infantry support, had worked their way along the south bank, well past the laager. There they crossed the river and began approaching the Boer positions from upstream.

The Battle - Day 1

Shortly after seven o'clock on the morning of the 18th February, 1900, the main assault was launched from downstream against the Boer positions around the 'bow' (or bend). To do this from the south meant entering the crook of the elbow, and so draw the fire from three sides. In spite of warnings from the other senior commanders of the dangers involved by exposing the troops to accurate and very fierce cross fire - they cited examples of the destruction of Hart's Irish Brigade at Colenso - Kitchener resolved not to delay a minute, but simply to overwhelm the enemy by sheer brute force... 'We'll be in the laager by half-past ten', he exulted, as he brushed aside the advice and warnings of the other generals.

Kitchener's behaviour at that time was an embarrassment to his fellow commanders. He was enflamed by the extent of the bombardment his guns had unleashed on the laager, and his killer instinct resolved him on storming tactics, which filled the other commanders with horror and foreboding. They would have preferred to surround the laager and reduce it with a minimum of loss, but they had to obey orders dutifully, and it was in sadness and disgust that they sent their men forward into a devastating hail of rifle-fire. An hour of desperate fighting followed before the leading troops reached part of the bank within their side of the bend. By then they were too exhausted, and their losses too great for them to continue. For Kitchener it was essential to clear the whole of the bend so that he could move along both banks into the heart of the laager, so he threw in the Highland Brigade, who immediately also suffered very badly. Eventually, a lone Cameron piper leapt into the river just below the bend, and found a safe crossing for reinforcements of Seaforths and Black Watch. With the Canadians and other units joining this thrust from the west, and with the troops sent in from the north, it was now the Boer's turn to face fire from three sides. Yet they bitterly contested every one of the British attempts to advance, and for hours the bloody struggle raged. Still they managed to cling on to the bend. From up-stream the combination of Hannay's MI and infantry support was unable to develop its own attack because the Boer reinforcements from Bloemfontein had arrived in their rear, and they found themselves fully committed in that area.

Kitchener's brash and personal style of command left him quite devoid of appropriate and adequately planned tactical details, and he appeared to have no notion of shared responsibilities and delegation of command. Instead he orchestrated 'on the hoof', galloping all over the field trying to co-ordinate his attack from every possible direction. In the appalling noise and confusion he rattled off orders piece-meal to whosoever he could lay hands on, whether commanding officers or subalterns, with the result that there was no single-minded purpose to animate any of commanding officers purposefully involved in the offensive. H. Smith-Dorrien, one of the best brigade commanders, later reported, 'I was in a complete fog'. By the time it was half-past ten there was precious little to show for the savage fighting except mounting losses that sickened the older officers. Yet nothing was going to deflect Kitchener from his ultimate and consuming purpose. As the attack on the bend began to wither, he ordered Hannay's MI to disengage itself from the Bloemfontein force, and to move upstream to concentrate everything it had by pushing forward down both banks, and attacking the laager from the north. Hannay's gallant attempt faded about 1,000 yards from the laager, and he reported that further advance was out of the question – his men, like those downstream, were utterly exhausted and unable to go any further.

Kitchener was still not satisfied. He had seen the smoking ruins of the Boer wagons, and the carnage wrought by his guns, and he estimated that the Boer losses equalled his own, except that he had five times more souls to expend than the Boers had. Based on these statistics, therefore, he calculated that in the end he had to succeed. He had no consideration for the loss of lives, and the spilling of blood was not going to deter him. He now decided to leave the south bank, and throw everything into attacking, from both upstream and down, along the entire length of the north bank where the main Boer laager lay. His reply to Hannay's message was – 'the laager must be rushed at all costs. Try to carry the (infantry) support with you, but if they cannot, the MI should do it. Gallop up if necessary and fire into the laager'.Hannay was deeply disturbed – for him these were the words of a mad man, blinded by blood lust. It was three o'clock in the afternoon, and for eight hours, attack upon attack had achieved nothing but five miles of ruin and death to his fellowmen, and to the burghers against whom he was fighting. Yet, resolved upon a soldier's protest, he sent away his staff on various missions of pretext, and then placed himself at the head of a small group of his MI whom he ordered to advance in accordance with Kitchener's instructions. As the group approached the enemy lines, Hannay halted his column and ordered them to hold fast. He then galloped forward, alone, full tilt into the Boer's defences and fell inside the Boer line, his body riddled with bullets. The Boers ceased firing – they retrieved Hannay's body and fired a hero's salvo into the air, while on the other side Hannay's small MI unit doffed their headgear, bowed their heads, and retired to their lines in grief.

The battle raged on – upstream and down the British strove to advance, and it was late in the afternoon when Kitchener launched a frantic last assault from all sides. The men charged with fixed bayonets against the Boers in the bend downstream, as well as along the route of Hannay's last ride. It was at this moment when De Wet suddenly appeared out of nowhere, and without delay, stormed a hill, 'Kitchener's Koppie', a mile or so south of the river, scattering its British occupants far and wide. Kitchener, 'swearing violently', immediately diverted some men and guns to deal with the situation. It was then that Ferreira, having just arrived upstream of the laager, joined hands with the Bloemfontein contingent, and opened up on the batteries pounding the laager, causing the British to divert even more men and guns. Encouraged by these arrivals and given fresh vigour, Cronje's men threw back Kitchener's final assault, and as night came, the exhausted men on both sides laid down their rifles for some rest.

British losses amounted to 1,300 casualties, the cost of Kitchener's daylong efforts to storm the laager. For all this, he was no nearer to success than he had been at dawn, his failure stemming from his neglect to prepare thoroughly, resulting in an attack on the very toughest part of the Boer defences. The situation was exacerbated by Kitchener's failure to communicate battle orders properly, and above all the fact that he had never fought against white men before. He failed to understand and appreciate the Boer's tenacious fighting spirit, which, sustained by the will of Cronje, expressed itself in skill and courage of the very highest order. The resultant controversy that surrounded

Kitchener's performance on the day did not reach public notice because of the strictness of the military censorship, and even a year later, it was generally unknown whether it was Kitchener of Kelly-Kenny who was actually in command on that day.

The Boers' battered laager was not a scene of rejoicing either. The burghers were hardly less exhausted than were the British, and their casualties of 300 on the day were, for them, comparatively heavy. Again, Cronje's commanders urged him to break out, and again he refused. However, he agreed to shorten his line along the river because it had become obvious that the dogged defence of the downstream bend could not hold indefinitely against enveloping attacks. As a result, the positions there were quietly abandoned during the night.

Day 2
Kitchener, now faced with only two miles of front, was eager to resume the onslaught, especially as the entire British field-force was now present. However, the other commanders were emphatically against this course of action, and appealed to Roberts for a final decision. Responding to the seriousness of the situation, Roberts left his sickbed and set off from Jakobsdal to Paardeberg at 10 a.m. On his arrival, there was a message from Cronje requesting a 24-hour armistice to deal with the wounded and the dead. Suspecting a Boer ruse to buy time to enable their reinforcements to arrive, Roberts   rejected the request and called upon Cronje to surrender. Cronje replied – *'Since you are so unmerciful as not to accord the time asked for, nothing remains for me to do. You do as you wish'*. The message was, mistakenly translated from the Dutch original to make Roberts believe that Cronje was surrendering, and when the troops moved forward towards the Boer trenches, they ran into heavy fire and were promptly driven back. Roberts asked Cronje what he meant, to which he replied – *'During my lifetime I will never surrender. If you wish to bombard, fire away.'* It was a defiant, even arrogant, exclamation from a man so doomed in the midst of a charred and reeking encampment, among corpses and carcasses strung along the river, with less than 5,000 men surrounded by six times their number, and exposed to continual   bombardment by scores of guns. Yet even now, Roberts could not be fully certain of success. None of his senior officers, with the exception of Kitchener, were willing to pay a further instalment on the heavy price of another assault.

Day 3
By now, the main concern of all the Free State burghers throughout the entire country was to alleviate Cronje's plight, and from all corners of South Africa, a trek towards Paardeberg was under way. Scores of burghers streamed back from Natal, over Van Reenen's Pass and on to Paardeberg, and in the Cape Midlands, the reduction in Boer numbers even enabled Clements, at Arundel, to head off a lame attack by Schoeman. Back at Paardeberg, Roberts decided not to risk storming the Boer laager, but to reduce it by siege. The day wore on and by the time the guns were in position to launch a telling bombardment, they came under fire from De Wet's commando, dangerously ensconced on Kitchener's Koppie. It became obvious to Roberts, that before he could undertake any further action against the laager, the Boers on Kitchener's Koppie needed to be dealt with and dislodged as urgently as possible.

Day 4

In order to dislodge De Wet from Kitchener's Koppie, Roberts posted a strong infantry force between the hill and the river, and ordered French to lay by with his cavalry on the northern side of the hill. The plan would then be for the infantry to storm the hill and drive the Boers off it and into the arms of French's cavalry. However, De Wet was not one to await encirclement willingly – in a lightning gallop he led his men down an uncovered valley, and got clean away almost unscathed. He raced on to Poplar Grove, between Paardeberg and Bloemfontein, where he linked up with the first of General A. P. Cronje's reinforcements arriving from Natal. Poplar Grove would now become the rallying point for all the Boers who were flocking in to help Cronje at Paardeberg. With Kitchener's Koppie now no longer a threat, Roberts was able to concentrate on his plan to throttle the life out of the laager. He dispersed his troops into two complete rings around it – the further one about a mile-and-a-half from the Boers, and the closer one about three-quarters-of-a-mile. The troops then put on a relentless pressure, and in the west, pushing along the north bank from the ill-starred bend, they succeeded in arriving to within six hundred yards of the Boer trenches.

All this time machine-guns and upwards of fifty pieces of artillery, ranging from batteries of 12pdr guns to four great naval 4.7" howitzers, pounded incessantly on the laager, making all movement within the Boer lines quite impossible, and filling the riverbank with a massive green cloud of lyddite fumes. Yet, in spite of all this heavy bombardment, the burghers were remarkably safe in their entrenchments, and any approaching soldiers were checked short by fierce fusillades of Mauser bullets. It slowly became clear that Cronje's chief danger was not the fire that combed his defences, but the appalling stench of rotting battle carrion, and the risk of disease and starvation from shortage of adequate sustenance.

Day 5

A balloon was floated to a height of 1,000 feet, and an engineer made sketches of the Boer positions, and guided the gunners with their target laying. At Poplar Grove, a few miles east of Paardeberg, reinforcements, pouring in from Natal and the Midlands, boosted the Boer strength to over 4,000 burghers. They decided to hit out on the following day, and to strike hard against the British to the south east of the laager. The intention was to open a clear arc from Kithchener's Koppie to the river, and in so doing, open an escape route for Cronje.

Day 6

Incessant rain pounded down over the Free State veld, bringing all movement to a halt. In the driving rain the attack from Poplar Grove fizzled out into a soaking non-event, and back at the laager, Cronje could do nothing to help because the rain-sodden sky thwarted all attempts at communication by heliograph. With their spirits, and their gear thoroughly dampened, the Boers returned to Poplar Grove, leaving their comrades at Paardeberg more miserable than ever in their flooded redoubts.

Day 7

All during the night and the whole of the seventh day, the rain continued to fall. At Poplar Grove, De Wet decided that the only course now open to him was to distract the British while Cronje tried to fight his way out of the laager. De Wet had somehow to inform Cronje of his plan, and he chose Danie Theron for the difficult task of sneaking through the British lines and into the laager. Theron was a prominent local hero who had formed a voluntary corps of scouts, whose courage and talents regularly assisted in executing clandestine and dangerous missions. Travelling alone in the darkness and the deluge, Theron crawled through the British outposts, swam the river, by now dangerously swollen by the continuous downpour, and reached the laager to hand the message safely to Cronje.

Day 8

Cronje called all his commanders together, and after debating De Wet's proposal, they agreed to attempt the breakout that very night. By now, the raging river waters had risen to over eight feet, and the only way of crossing the swirling torrent was by means of a bridge. It was a demoralising blow for the already over- wrought burghers who were rapidly reaching the limit of their endurance. Imprisoned in their narrow, water logged trenches, unable to still the cries of their wounded comrades – choked to the full by gun-smoke, shell-fumes and the stench of putrefaction and excrement they were only prevented from breaking down completely by the iron will of Cronje. He would not yield, and in spite of the anxiety for their women and children, and for the rapidly dwindling supplies, Cronje kept his men to the task of holding back the relentless pressure of the encircling infantry.

Day 9

Although the building of the bridge had commenced, hardly a word was spoken about the proposed break out, and many burghers openly urged surrender. Cronje remained un-moved but did agree to postpone the break out for two days. In the afternoon, Roberts opened fire with several pompoms, which until now had been a Boer monopoly, and even more serious, a siege train of four howitzers started to drop 120-pound shells with devastating effect. Eventually, one accurately directed salvo destroyed the bridge, and the infantry used the cover of the barrage to press forward to within merely 200 yards of the trenches. It was the last straw. By evening, opinion in the Boers' camp was unanimous – they all agreed that the end had finally come.

The Last Day

February 27th was the anniversary of Majuba, 19 years ago, and Hector MacDonald, wounded on his first day at Paardeberg, had vivid memories of Majuba, where he was also wounded. He sent Roberts a message imploring him to attack the laager, and Roberts agreed that the Royal Canadians undertake to lead the action. In the dark, early in the morning, they advanced to within sixty yards of the trenches, before a withering fusillade cut them flat. They kept up the attack for two hours while the Royal Engineers dug trenches immediately behind them. At daybreak, the Canadians finally took cover in these newly dug trenches.

Danie Theron once again succeeded in slipping quietly through the British lines to tell the burghers at Poplar Grove that the laager's doom was sealed. Between five and six o'clock, here and there the Boers started raising white flags in spite of Cronje's last efforts to stop them. Then at last, and almost as an anti-climax, he bowed his head and sent a message to Roberts that he had surrendered. Roberts immediately ordered the cease-fire, and the battle was ended. Sending one of his generals to escort Cronje, Roberts formed a hollow square of Highlanders opposite his H.Q. and awaited Cronje's arrival. He wore his trim khaki uniform without any badge or embellishment except for the jewelled Kandahar sword by his side. Presently Cronje rode in on a grey, bony horse in his old green overcoat, frieze trousers, rough veldschoen boots and slouch hat. Cronje dismounted and Roberts stepped forward to shake hands. '*I am glad to see you. You have made a gallant defence, sir'* he said. Cronje glowered and said nothing. The two men then had breakfast under a tree and completed the details of the surrender. Later, when Cronje and his wife were finally driven away to captivity in a Cape-cart, the Western Front, except for Mafeking, had utterly collapsed. For the British and the world, it marked the end of the conflict.

Paardeberg – The Aftermath

The end of the battle was curiously muted. On the riverbank, piling their arms in a great stack, the 4,000 Boer prisoners assembled. Their casualty rate was remarkable low thanks to their effective trench system, which had so intrigued the British Staff Officers, that it was the very first object of their scrutiny. Back in Pretoria, Kruger, and the rest of the nation lamented – '*The English have taken our Majuba away from us'*. Wherever they looked they saw their cause suddenly on the descendant.

For the Boers on the central front, the situation was also rapidly disintegrating. – De la Rey and Schoeman had already left for Bloemfontein with most of their men, and even as the events of the last days at Paardeberg were taking place, Clements's men were marching into Colesburg. On his right flank, loyal farmers and empire volunteers, sent up by Roberts under the command of General Brabant, were clearing up the country in a wide arc to the northeast. Farther east, Gatacre was preparing an advance on Stormberg, and after a thirty-six hours fight, dislodged the Boers, and later entered Stormberg unopposed. Thus, without having fired a shot, he finally succeeded in occupying the town that had borne him so many unfortunate memories. Meanwhile, at Paardeberg, those Boers on the run headed for Poplar Grove and Bloemfontein while others simply trekked north, their rear guard fighting tactics only temporarily holding back the British as they lumbered on after the retreating Boers.

In Natal, the events of Paardeberg were matched by an equally dramatic twist in fortune. Precisely as the cease-fire was sounding out over the Modder River, Buller on the Thukela, was preparing his final march on Ladysmith after so many months of defeat and disappointment, for, at last, he had found the key that opened the door to the north and to ultimate victory on the Natal Front.

From Paardeberg to Bloemfontein

Roberts established his Headquarters in Bloemfontein, and settled down to allow his army to recover from the previous months of gruelling warfare. The relaxed and friendly attitude of the townspeople greatly encouraged him, and gave him the equanimity to look at the future with confidence. The astonishing and sudden collapse of the Boer forces and the singing of 'Soldiers of the Queen' by the townsfolk, lulled him into a relaxed optimism which prompted him to make a prediction to Queen Victoria – *'The Orange Free State, south of Bloemfontein, is rapidly settling down. The burghers are laying down their arms and returning to their usual occupations. It seems unlikely that this State will give much more trouble. The Transvaalers (*sic) *will probably hold out, but their numbers will be greatly reduced and it will not be very long before the war will be brought to a satisfactory conclusion. Bu,t now we are obliged to rest here for a short time to let the men and animals recover and to provide the former with new boots and clothes.'*

Yet in spite of all this optimism and enthusiasm, there was an ominous feeling of deep tension between Roberts and his senior officers. Roberts blamed French and Kelly-Kenny for losing one of the great opportunities of the war at Poplar Grove a week earlier. Both French and Kelly-Kenny wholeheartedly agreed, except that they in turn laid the blame four square on Roberts. It was his miscalculations, they claimed, and his reckless re-arrangement of the transport that had crippled the army, especially the cavalry and the artillery, by starving men and horses into a state of total inertia. It was Roberts's blunders, which they all had to endure, they maintained.

Who then, was to blame? The Battle of Poplar Grove on the 7th March shares one feature with many that had disappointed the British in the past – it was easy to say what had gone wrong, but almost impossible to apportion responsibility. Certainly, there had been a chance of making a most sensational bag, one that would have over-shadowed by far the capture of Cronje and his 4,000 burghers. Because, among the 6,000 Boers on the battlefield, that day, was none other than President Paul Kruger himself, who had arrived to give the Almighty a hand to put some fresh heart and spirit into His people. Roberts, however, had only become aware of Kruger's presence on the following day.

The Boers' hastily improved trench defences at Poplar Grove straddled a line of hills on a ten mile wide front on either side of the Modder River, about 30 miles upstream from Kimberley. Roberts's plan of attack was, understandably, the same as the one he had employed at Paardeberg and he ordered French to take his cavalry division, some MI units and the horse artillery on a seventeen-mile detour around the Boer's east flank. He was ordered to make a sweep wide enough to avoid the Boer lines, and then to attack from the rear to cut off their escape route to Bloemfontein. Once the cavalry had passed around the back of the Boer positions, the three infantry divisions, supported by an artillery barrage, would attack from the right. Kelly-Kenny's 6th Division, the Guards Brigade and Tucker's 7th Division assaulting the Boer's main positions on the south bank of the river, and Colvile's 9th Division plus some MI on the north bank.

Roberts's plan was a sound one. The infantry divisions would advance directly onto the Boer positions and flush out the burghers. Meanwhile, the cavalry, safely tucked away behind the hills, would pursue and hunt them down as they fled across the open veld. But, it was never going to be as simple as that. As soon as the Boers spotted the cavalry on their flank in the distance, they leapt onto their ponies and fled pell-mell into the veld behind them. They continued to ride as fast as they could all the way to Bloemfontein and even beyond! Yet even now all was not lost. In fact the cavalry was in a splendid position to launch a chase and hunt down the fleeing enemy. Roberts hastened up to the front to witness 6,000 Boers, led by Kruger himself, fleeing helter-skelter across the open and flat veld, with the cavalry division and forty-two mobile guns thundering after them….

To his dismay, 'thundering' was not what Roberts saw as he gazed in bewilderment through his binoculars. In disgust, he saw that French was not giving chase at all, for instead of hacking and skewering the fleeing forces, the cavalry was advancing at a walk. Indeed, many even fought dismounted. Several thousand cavalrymen were held in check by a handful of riflemen in a lively rear-guard action conducted by De Wet and his men. Roberts blamed French for this fiasco – he was furious at the fact that they could have succeeded in capturing the two State Presidents if only French had obeyed his orders. He also made accusations of 'wretched horsemanship', and accused French that if the cavalry horses had been treated better, they would not have broken down.

French bitterly resented these charges, and instead, blamed Roberts for the poor condition of his men and his horses. The hopelessly inadequate transport arrangements were the cause of the breakdown of the division he said. Douglas Haig, French's Chief-of-Staff, wrote – *'I have never seen horses so beat as ours that day – they have been having only 8lbs. of oats a day and practically starving since February 11th'*. He also severely criticised the formation of *'so many colonial scallywag corps'* which was the reason why there was insufficient fodder to go round for the cavalry horses. According to Haig, the colonial units were *'quite useless – only good for looting and (who) disappear from sight the moment the first shot is fired'*.

Roberts also accused Kelly-Kenny for being far too cautious in his attack on the Boer trenches. In turn, Kelly-Kenny blamed Roberts for the collapse of his men and horses. The 6th Division had been 'starving' ever since De Wet had captured the food convoy at Waterval Drift, and there had only been one water-cart for each battalion – barely enough for half a water bottle for each man. Whoever was to blame, the effects of the Battle of Poplar Grove were disastrous and long lasting for the British. Not only did Roberts fail to capture Kruger, but he also made the crucial deduction from the manner in which the burghers fled, that their morale was broken once and for all, and that surely the war was now nearly over. Although this error of judgement was confirmed in a subsequent action at Driefontein on the 10th March, it proved to be the greatest miscalculation of Roberts's career, and was to cost the British dearly over the months and years to come.

Bloemfontein

Roberts had promised his stay in Bloemfontein would be a brief one, '*to rest for a short time*', and predicted that it would '*not be very long before the end of the war*'. Together both these crucial estimates were to prove disastrously optimistic. The second one in particular betrayed a total lack of understanding on the part of Roberts about the character and the capability of the Afrikaners. Roberts was no outstanding military genius but he was not a fool either – he was a highly successful general, with more than adequate tactical and diplomatic skills resulting from forty years of peace and war in India. But he had no insight into South Africa – he knew nothing of the complexity of colonialism, nothing of the tenacity of Afrikaner nationalism, and nothing at all about the extra-ordinary resilience of the Boers. Significantly, it was Buller, who had served side-by-side with the Boers in the final Zulu war, who accurately predicted the peculiar difficulties of waging a war against the Boer. It would be a 'civilised war' – meaning a war according to the rules of the Geneva Convention – but one fought in an 'uncivilised' country – one with few railways and other man-made assets. It would also be a 'national' war – a trial of strength conducted not in the conventional manner of war between nations or countries, but between an Empire on the one hand, and on the other, a handful of tenacious and highly single-minded individuals, living on farms or in small scattered communities widely spread across an enormous expanse of territory

In this ultra individualistic pioneering society, there was no highly organised machinery of administration, and the central government carried little if any influence or authority. Buller wrote – '*Here time has not yet glorified the seal of Government with a halo of sentiment- to every man his own home is his capital. Hence, there is no commanding centre by the occupation of which the whole country, or even a whole district, can be brought into subjection – no vital spot at which a single blow can be struck that will paralyse every member of the body. There are living organisms which can be divided into a multitude of fragments without destroying the individual life of each fragment.* These were the lessons Buller had learned from history and from his personal insights. He accurately predicted that the set-piece war would change into a fragmentary one, and believed that military strategy based on conventional ideas of the 'single blow' would not bring them any closer to the conquest of the Boers. '*It is useless to capture capital cities unless the territory in between has been subdued. The real task is to beat every man in the field – otherwise to march through the enemy's country is like trying to arrest the flow of a river simply by walking through it. Such a man may indeed stem the force of it on the spot where he stands but let him move where he will and the waters will also close before and behind and around him.*'

Buller had correctly predicted a guerrilla war, and he advised Roberts not to march onto Pretoria before he had thoroughly crushed the Free State armies, otherwise, across the Vaal River, those waters would most certainly close in and around him. Of course Roberts was not going to pay much attention to Buller and his 'good' advice – apart from his personal dislike of the man, he was very sceptical of advice coming from one that had paid so dearly through his own ineptitude and military blunders against these very same Boers over which he was pontificating. In fact, Roberts knew well that it was for those very reasons that he was sent to South Africa, to take away from Buller the supreme command of the British forces in South Africa. Roberts was determined to stay with the conventional idea of defeat and surrender – capture the capital, and you cut off the head of the enemy – then his spirit will also die. In order to smooth his road to Pretoria, he intended to use all the political means possible, the kind so often and so successfully employed in the Indian Frontier wars in the past.

Roberts's first act after entering Bloemfontein was, on the 15th March· to issue a proclamation offering an amnesty for every Free State burgher, except the leaders. All they were required to do was to return to their homes, take the oath of allegiance, and surrender their arms. He then set about, with purpose, to consolidate his position by staying in Bloemfontein until he could build up a larger army, and to prepare it fully for the next 'tiger leap' - the march to Pretoria. His strategy for the moment was defensive – to protect Bloemfontein from Boer raids by De Wet in the north – to re-open the town's water-works some twenty miles to the east, and to re-open the railway line from the south. He ordered Buller to remain on the defensive in Natal, and the only initiative that Roberts himself undertook, was to send out small parties of troops into the country to distribute the proclamation of amnesty, and to collect surrendered arms.

Roberts's refusal to heed Buller's warning in respect of the little influence exercised by the Boer administrative centres on the lives of the individuals was to cost the British dearly in the months to follow. Because, regardless of the fall of Bloemfontein, and later Pretoria, the war continued to be fought bitterly and with great loss and cost for a further two years until the 31st May, 1902. During the time that Roberts's men were making their minor sorties to deliver amnesty proclamations and collect arms, a movement spread across the whole of South Africa, from the Cape Colony in the south, through Natal and the Free State to as far north as Prieska, Mafeking and the Transvaal. The stirring was one of thousands of burghers coming together and preparing to continue the conflict against Roberts and his British Army. All over the country, there were pockets of resistance. Apart from the Boers in Natal, a raiding party of about a thousand burghers under general Steenkamp sparked off a local Afrikaner rebellion in the far northwest Karroo town of Prieska. Then there were some 15,000 burghers scattered around the Free State, as well as five- to six thousand men with De Wet and De la Rey at Kroonstad. In the far north, General Snyman's 1,500 men were still effectively besieging Mafeking, and a large number of Boers under General du Toit were known to be dug-in north of Kimberley. Finally, there were about 4,000 men under General Olivier, who having abandoned Colesburg, were now encamped somewhere in the northeast corner of Free State in the area around Van Reenen's Pass.

General Olivier's commandos would have been a prime target for Roberts, had his intention been to crush the Boer armies in the Free State, because Olivier was effectively trapped a hundred miles behind the main British lines. On the 15th March, Roberts received important intelligence that Olivier, with a column said to consist of 'between six- to seven thousand' Boers, was advancing northwards up the road which passes about forty miles east of Bloemfontein. Yet Roberts did not issue any orders for any of his main army of over 34,000 men to block Olivier, and inexplicably waited until the 20th before ordering French to take a cavalry brigade, a few guns and a handful of MI to proceed to Thaba Nchu, directly astride Olivier's route. To send such a small force so late was little more than a gesture, and Olivier had no problem in side stepping

French, and after an epic march, his ponderous wagon train, 24 miles long, passed safely behind the British lines. Whatever his motives, it was evident that the main reason why Roberts did not make an attempt to crush Olivier when he had such a super chance to do so, was his fallacious belief that the Free State burghers would, if simply left to themselves, accept amnesty, take the oath and then quietly disperse to their homes. It was this pre-conceived belief that the fall of Bloemfontein would knock all the fight out of the Free State commandos that was to be Roberts's most fundamental miscalculation of the overall situation so far.

His second miscalculation was that his own army would be ready to move forward 'in a short time', because by the end of March, after his 'two weeks recuperation' period was over, his forces were still no way nearer to being ready to move than ever. The underlying reason was that Roberts really had very little interest in the dull grind of military administration. The Army Service Corps, Buller's great innovation when at the War Office, did not impress Roberts at all, and he dismissed it as 'one of the aberrations of the Wolseley clique'. It was because of this that he failed to create a competent H.Q. staff to whom he could delegate freely. One of his best friends from India, Major General William Nicholson, Roberts's newly appointed Director of Transport, could not abide Kitchener, who himself was far too self-willed and opinionated to act as anyone's Chief-of-Staff. The result was chaos in the marble hall of the Presidency in Bloemfontein, just as there had been chaos at Modder River.

The problem that had bedevilled everyone from the outset refused to go away. It was that triple-headed monster called 'transport-trains and traction (horses and oxen)', and it was very rapidly growing into nightmare intensity. The Bloemfontein garrison was precariously and dangerously isolated, and tenuously kept alive by the single-track narrow-gauge railway, which ran due south for nigh on a hundred miles before diverging at Springfontein towards the three Cape ports. When Buller had suggested in December, that a special military railway line be laid to extend the Cape railway by a new westerly route directly towards Bloemfontein, Roberts ridiculed the idea. Yet now it was predictably in this very hundred-mile sector that the congestion was most acute. Moreover, Roberts had procrastinated for months before eventually ordering more rolling stock for South Africa and it was only on the 20th March that he cabled England for twenty-five engines and three-hundred wagons as a matter of the highest urgency. It would be three months before they arrived, and in the meantime, every bit of food, ammunition and supplies had to run the gauntlet of those wretched hundred miles of single-track railway. In the end, one of the most serious results of the defects in railway transport was to be a loss of human life that would make Spioenkop look comparatively cheap.

The transport of horses was also in a crisis. They came in their thousands, from India, from Burma and even from Argentina. They all had to come up that same railway stretch, battered and bruised after travelling half way across the world. Roberts' Grand Army swallowed up horses in the same was as a modern army swallows petrol. French's cavalry alone lost 1,500 horses during the relief of Kimberley, and on one single day at Poplar Grove he reported a further 213 casualties. Ever since February there had been a series of plaintive exchanges between Roberts and Pall Mall on the subject of horses, but whatever the outcome, it was clear that he had grossly under-estimated the scale and the complexity of the problem. The crisis was so grotesque that all reason seemed to have disappeared, and to crown in all, in the Cape for example, the vital duties of Director of Remounts, were delegated to an officer who was considered unfit for the job – he was in fact a maniac depressive, who eventually shot himself in a bout of despair.

There was also a third call on transport contributing to the vast drain on resources, namely that required by the Africans. The movement of 11,000 mules led by 2,000 African drivers ate deeply into the already reduced resources available to the regular services. When Roberts's army first arrived in Bloemfontein, they laid the blame for the pitiful state of the under-nourished and exhausted men and beasts on the unavoidable misfortunes of war. In truth, the thoughtless abolition of the traditional 'regimental transport system' was the real cause of the breakdown of men and animals, owing to their being put on half rations following the loss of the unguarded convoy at Waterval Drift.

Another most drastic and painful symptom of the defects in Roberts' military system was the death rate from typhoid. This disease feeds on poor hygiene and overcrowding. In order to prevent it, one needs carefully controlled sanitation, and to treat it one needs careful nursing and a healthy controlled diet. During the siege of Ladysmith, of the 563 deaths in the garrison, 393 were from typhoid, and in Bloemfontein, this grim record of ten deaths per day was soon outstripped. The cause of the outbreak of the typhoid epidemic in Bloemfontein could largely be blamed on the men's dissatisfaction over Roberts's meagre ration of a half-bottle of water per day. They became so over-taken by thirst on the baking South African veld, that they drank water wherever they could find it, including the the Modder River at Paardeberg which had been polluted by Cronje's camp. It was through negligence that the disease spread so rapidly – neglect of elementary sanitary precautions in the military camps as the population soared from 4,000 to 40,000 within a month, and neglect of the patients in the makeshift hospitals, which turned a crisis into a disaster. Hundreds of men lay in the worst stages of the disease in the most appalling conditions, without proper medication or care. There were no nurses, and only three doctors for every 350 patients, and once more, the principal reason for this neglect may be attributed to the failure of the single-track railway line, with its shortage of adequate rolling stock, to provide for the needs of the town, the garrison and the hospitals.

Surprisingly, through all this there appeared an astonishing indifference in Roberts's attitude and action. It was only late April that he eventually got round to sending an S.O.S. to London asking for 300 extra medical orderlies and thirty doctors. It is difficult to understand why he did not act sooner. Perhaps it was his long years of service in India with an army consisting largely of natives that may have dulled his concern and sensibilities to these problems. For example, just a week before his S.O.S. for extra orderlies and doctors, he sent a letter to Queen Victoria stating: *'The health of the men, too, is very good..'* he wrote – *'There are some two thousand in hospital in Bloemfontein but this is only at a rate of 4 per cent – a very small proportion during a campaign. The climate now is perfect and I hope that Lady Roberts and my daughters will be able to come here ere long. They will find it an agreeable change after Cape Town.'*

Around this time, the British High Commissioner in Cape Town, Sir Alfred Milner, paid a visit to Roberts in Bloemfontein to offer him an olive branch of reconciliation. It may appear out of character that Milner, the very man who had precipitated the war at the outset, was now prepared to take a gamble on a shortcut to peace. After all, he had never under-rated the tenacity and resilience of Afrikaner nationalism any more than Buller had, and the political task he had set himself was no less than to 'crush the Afrikaner idea once and for all'. Earlier he had written to Roberts that 'an irreconcilable enemy has tried to extinguish us, and we must destroy him'. It was for this very reason that Milner had suddenly become intensely impatient to get on with the peace. He was very aware of Roberts's shortcomings, and the continuation of the war made him nervous – even afraid. The blunders of Roberts's military administration, the hopeless muddle of the transport system, and the appalling red tape of the military hospital system, were driving Milner near to despair. His life's dream was to forge the weakest link into the strongest in the imperial chain, and here he could not even start with his quest as long as this blundering army remained in occupation. What was more, Milner was more than aware of the one salient fact to which Roberts was so blind, namely that in the midst of all this British dilly-dallying, the Boers were forging a new bond of nationalism in this burning crucible of the war.

There was also a second reason why Milner wanted a quick end to the war, and it was equally fundamental. The secret alliance he had made with Alfred Beit and Julius Wernher depended on the profitability of the Rand mines. Now he had recently received word from Eckstein, the local Wernher-Beit representative and leading mouth-piece for the 'gold bugs', that the Boer authorities in Pretoria had planned a 'scorched earth' policy against the Rand mines by blowing them up with dynamite, and causing damage that would clearly run into millions of pounds. Hence Milner was prepared to lean over backwards to be conciliatory to Roberts until the British Army had finally seized hold of the Rand. Just before his return to Cape Town, Milner, at a civic function in Bloemfontein in honour of Lord Roberts, praised him and his gallant army, and urged that he moved rapidly to an early resumption of his advance on Pretoria and to a final and conclusive victory over the Boer republics. Yet, even as they were hailing the victory and its conquering hero, a great change was happening amongst the Boers in the Free State. One of their most able and audacious leaders, Christiaan de Wet, was actively exploiting Roberts's naïve belief that the will of the Boers had been broken, and that the struggle was nearly over, and was busy re-kindling their determination to fight on. This revival was to grow and grow, and in time to change the entire course of the war to come.

213

12
ROBERTS'S WAR - (b) NEW NEEDS - NEW METHODS

From Bloemfontein to Pretoria
Four days after the fall of Bloemfontein on St. Patrick's Day 1900, the leaders of the Free State and the Transvaal held a krijgsraad (war council) in Kroonstad in the northern Free State, to thrash out the ways and means to continue the conflict and face the threat of Roberts's armies. The Boers examined, and discussed in detail all the aspects of the war to date, on all the fronts. As a result, many sweeping changes were agreed including the banning of accompanying convoys of families and goods, the overall reduction of traction transport to a necessary minimum, the tightening of regulations governing leave of absence from the front, and the setting up of courts for imposing stricter overall military discipline. High on the agenda as well were investigations into the most effective and efficient use of Boer manpower still in the field - about 12,000 near Bloemfontein, and 15,000 scattered about on all the other fronts - and how it could be employed with more telling consequence. One of the up-and-coming stars among the younger of the Boer leaders was Christiaan de Wet, in whose mind the basic principles of a new type of hit-and-run guerrilla warfare were beginning to take shape. In recognition of his successful battle performance and his enthusiastic contribution to the debates, De Wet received promotion to the rank of Commandant-General in charge of all the Free State forces. De Wet's plans were clearly set out and presented to the krijgsraad in direct and simple terms, namely:

- all those burghers whose unreliability constituted a danger to their comrades needed to be weeded out, to leave an elite and dependable striking force.
- mobility needed to be increased by abolishing great wagon trains such as those which proved the undoing of Cronje on the western front.
- defensive tactics needed to be tilted away from conventional methods of blocking and delaying an invasion by fighting on a front. The enormous numerical superiority of the British Army now proved that such a direct strategy was a forlorn hope.
- the Boers needed to develop a 'raiding' strategy behind enemy lines similar to the successful strike against the 180 wagons at Waterval Drift. Apart from the military value of raiding the enemy's lines of communications, it was obvious that the success of Roberts's advance depended principally on the single-track railway to the ports, which needed to be harassed as often and as effectively as possible,
- and most important of all, was the need to revive the burgher's morale – 'give me one day's good work…' De Wet said, 'and I will have the burghers flocking back to join the commandos.'

The krijgsraad accepted De Wet's ideas, but it would be some time before they would be able to put all these ideas into practice. In the meanwhile, the overall fortunes of the Boers were to sink to their nadir. But the credit for avoiding a national collapse that March 1900, must primarily go to De Wet who was now set to give, less than three weeks after the fall of Bloemfontein, a sensational demonstration of what his ideas amounted to, by taking 1,500 men to operate most successfully on the flank of Roberts's great army of 30,000 soldiers. Although both Presidents Kruger and Steyn had agreed to accept De Wet's plans neither fully abandoned the principles of conventional defensive strategy warfare. They had decided to use political methods to stiffen the burghers' shattered morale, and to prevent the Free State men from abandoning their comrades in the Transvaal by accepting Roberts's amnesty offer. Already they had made some important manoeuvres in the propaganda war by addressing, on the 5th of March, a joint appeal to Lord Salisbury, repudiating the accusation that they had gone to war with aggressive intentions. The war, as far as they were concerned, was '*only commenced as a measure of defence and was only continued in order to ensure the indisputable independence of both Republics as Sovereign International States and to protect the Afrikaners from the Natal and Cape who had joined them.*'

This declaration was in truth a challenge to Salisbury to reveal his own intentions, and to expose Britain as an aggressor both in the eyes of the world and in those of the burghers. It was, in fact a ploy to call Salisbury's bluff – he had stated in a speech the previous autumn, '*We want no gold - we want no territory*'. Did that claim still stand today or was Britain truthfully proposing to annexe both Republics? When Salisbury replied, he was quite uncompromising – there was no argument now about the 'oppressed Uitlanders' or the rights of the suzerain power. No, he simply stated that '*Britain was not prepared to acknowledge the independence of either republic*'. Kruger made great play with a copy of a secret Intelligence Department pamphlet entitled, 'Military Notes on the Dutch Republics'. It had been discovered amongst Penn-Symons's baggage at Dundee on the 23rd October 1899, and provided written proof, regardless of all assertions to the contrary, that the British aim, right from the start, was the outright and unequivocal annexation and subjugation of the two republics. In an attempt to discredit the British further, Steyn also arranged for the establishment of a three-man diplomatic mission abroad, and in March 1900, these men, including Jan Smuts' friend and brilliant lawyer, Abraham Fischer, set sail for Europe from Lourenco Marques.

Back on the ground, Steyn, De Wet and De la Rey continued with their 'new style' war. Steyn encouraged the support of foreign helpers, and appointed Col. Comte de Villebois-Marceuil in charge of the Foreign Corps. De Villebois-Marceuil was a colourful Frenchmen, who supported the Boer cause. With the help of his friend judge Herzog, he also pulled together the Free State artillery, left in disarray after Paardeberg, as well as the organisation of the issue of clothing and field transport for the Free State forces. At the end of March, De Wet and De la Rey were ready to move. Information gleaned from spies and informers confirmed reports about the exhausted condition of Roberts's troops and horses, the cause of his long delay in moving out and resuming his advance. The failure to capture Olivier in the east had made Roberts nervous, and it was becoming increasingly obvious that his amnesty programme was not working. He timorously decided to probe the north and establish an advance base at Karee Siding some twenty miles from Bloemfontein. Instead of establishing a base however, he ran into 3,500 Transvalers astride the railway, under the leadership of Koos De la Rey. Threatened with encirclement by a force three times his size, De la Rey skilfully disengaged after some short, sharp action, incurring 40 casualties, as opposed to over 200 British dead and wounded.

Sannaspos

Soon a lively spate of Boer activity broke out all over the Free State. The newly promoted Foreign Corps commander, de Villebois-Marceuil, set off on an enterprise north-east of Bloemfontein, and at the same time, on the evening before the Karee Siding incident, De Wet, with his brother Piet, left for the north-east with 2,000 men, none aware of his purpose nor his destination. De Wet headed south to within a dozen miles of the Modder River north of Bloemfontein. He halted his men near Sannaspos, some twenty miles east of Bloemfontein, the location of the city's water works. He had ascertained that there were only 200 men guarding the pumping station, and he felt confident that with his own force of 2,000 burghers, he should have no difficulty occupying that strategic water-station. The main danger was the close proximity of Roberts's enormous army, so De Wet decided to strike fast and then run fast, relying on speed and secrecy to see him through safely. He anticipated ensnaring some 200 men at Sannaspos, so he was overwhelmed to discover on his arrival, the size of the bounty that had fallen into his trap on the banks of the Modder River.

It was a bigger shock though for Brig. Gen. Robert Broadwood, commander of the 2nd Cavalry Division, when he discovered that soon after dawn on the 31st March, he had walked straight into an ambush. Broadwood, an amiable and able soldier and much admired by his friends, had been appointed by Roberts to take over the 2nd Cavalry Division from Maj. Gen. Babington. Broadwood had what his friends admired most in a cavalry leader – "a hint of impatience and plenty of dash." It was these very traits of 'dash' and 'impatience', which led him into the trap at Sannaspos, because his self-assurance resulted in his neglect to scout and assess the terrain ahead of his column. Broadwood was returning to Bloemfontein after a 'bill posting' expedition in the Thaba Nchu area. After Roberts's failure to block Olivier in the east, sheaves of proclamations were given to the cavalry for distribution amongst the Boers, inviting them to surrender their arms and go back to their farms, in return for amnesty. When this task was completed, Broadwood wired Roberts on the 30th March that he was returning to Bloemfontein via Sannaspos. He had a relatively small force of 1,700 men plus two cavalry regiments, U and Q batteries of the Horse Artillery, and Lt. Col. Edwin Alderson's brigade of 830 MI. He also had a few of Rimington's 'Tigers' and a convoy of 92 wagons belonging to civilians who had been seeking protection with the British.

The pumping station at Sannaspos comprised a collection of outbuildings astride the western bank of the Modder. There was a ford, where the main Bloemfontein-Thaba Nchu wagon road crossed the river, and two-and-a-half miles to the west there was another drift where this same road crossed the Koornspruit, a tributary of the Modder River. The road thus formed the south side of a small triangle of veld, whose east and west sides were the Modder and the Koorn respectively. For twenty miles beyond the Koorn, and right up to the outskirts of Bloemfontein, the veld was practically featureless apart from a small boulder strewn hill called Boesman's Kop, on the south side of the road, about five miles beyond the Koornspruit.

It was midnight before the first of Broadwood's straggling column splashed across the Modder to arrive at the pumping station. This was the advance convoy of 92 wagons and their African drivers, the civilian refugees, and an escort of MI. Broadwood and the rest of the men did not turn up until 3.30 a.m., about a half hour before dawn. Everyone was exhausted after a long slog along the muddy road from Thaba Nchu, and a running fight with Olivier's commandos the day before, and on arrival, the men simply threw themselves down beside the wagons and were soon fast asleep. Neither Broadwood nor any of his officers issued any specific orders to mount a guard over the bivouac because they assumed that any danger could only come from Olivier who was too far away to present any serious threat. Broadwood was ignorant of De Wet's force close to the station, especially after assurances from Major Amphlett, the commander of the barracks stationed at the water works, that the entire area all around was quite clear of hostile threat. Amphlett's based his reports on intelligence received from his routine patrols, which regularly rode out westwards as far as Boesman's Kop.

As soon as De Wet became aware of Broadwood's presence at Sannaspos, he split his force in two, sending his younger brother, Piet de Wet, with a group of 1,600 burghers to the east, with orders to sweep around the north bank of the Modder River, and approach Sannaspos along the Thaba Nchu road. Christiaan de Wet, himself, swung west, skirting Sannaspos, and concealed his group of 400 men, some below the fifteen-foot banks of the Koornspruit, and some in a few near-by farm buildings. At dawn, Broadwood despatched a patrol to scout the countryside behind him in search for any signs of Olivier's forces in the area to the north and east beyond the Modder. A short while later an alarm was sounded when the scouts came racing back to camp, followed by rifle-fire and shelling from Piet de Wet's force, hidden in some koppies to the east of the Modder. In the ensuing panic, Broadwood lost his head, and not thinking matters out clearly, committed a fatal error in ordering the mass withdrawal of his entire force to Boesman's Kop, without first sending scouts ahead to scour the terrain he intended to cross. Soon, a convoy of wagons rumbled off in haste along the road towards Koornspruit, where Christiaan de Wet lay in wait with his burghers at the ready. Accompanying the wagons were some infantry and two batteries of the Royal Horse Artillery, U-Battery commanded by Major Taylor, and Q-Battery under Major Edward Phipps-Hornby.

When the leading wagons reached the spruit De Wet allowed them to cross over unharmed, and then in order not to divulge his presence to the troops following in the rear, he silently dispersed the wagons to the left and right of the road. When the gunners spotted the wagons piling up at the spruit, they concluded that it had to be one of those usual river-fording tangles, and U Battery went forward to sort out the mess. Without creating any alarm, De Wet noiselessly captured the leading echelons of U-Battery, and ordered them to hull down and not to make any noise. After a short while, some gunners managed to break away and raise the alarm, shouting as loudly as they could- '*We're all prisoners! – The Boers are here – They are in amongst the convoy and amongst the guns!'* Phipps-Hornby and his Q-Battery were by now only 300 yards from the ford, and could see a cluster of Boers standing on top of the riverbank. Phipps-Hornby thought that they were un-armed and did not believe the shouted warnings, when suddenly some rifle-fire made him realise that there was an ambush ahead, and that he would have to move his men and his guns away as fast as possible. He wheeled the guns around, and as they moved off, a wave of bullets splashed the ground around them, upsetting one of the guns, which had to be left behind. Somehow, Phipps-Hornby managed to get the remaining five guns into a firing line on a ridge 1,150 yards back from the ford, and hastily opened fire against the black dots on the riverbank. However, under intense fire from the Boers, Q-Battery was soon silenced, and out of the original fifty officers and men, only Phipps-Hornby, one sergeant, one bombardier and eight gunners were left in action when Broadwood eventually ordered the guns to retire. About seventy yards behind the guns was a stone parapet behind which some infantry were sheltering. Phipps-Hornby goaded them into helping him to move the guns, and soon, with the added aid from some volunteers from the Essex Regiment, succeeded in man handling the five guns and limbers and bringing them to safety. Despite the losses for the British, this action was considered to be a glorious one during which four men won the Victoria Cross, and when the remnants of the original force returned to base, the watching troops stood up in the face of a fierce fusillade, and cheered them in.

In the meantime, Piet de Wet was increasing his pressure on Sannaspos from the east, and Broadwood, sandwiched between the two Boer forces, was very aware that his position was rapidly becoming a critical one. He hurriedly despatched an officer of the 10th Hussars to Bloemfontein to inform Roberts of the situation, and to ask for urgent relief. Broadwood waited in vain for a quick response from Roberts, and finally, in despair, decided to evacuate Sannaspos. He was at his tether's end – only a handful of his gunners had survived, and the Boers on the Modder were coming closer and closer. In addition, his ammunition was running low and his men were exhausted. The only solution would be to break out, and by eluding Christiaan de Wet at Koornspruit, possibly reach Boesman's Kop and safety. In a heroic action, volunteers, under cover of fire, rode out from the shelter of the pump station buildings to drag back the exposed guns and limbers of Q-Battery. Then, covered by successive companies of infantry, Broadwood set off. He eventually succeeded in escaping southwards across the spruit, and out into the open veld to Boesman's Kop. His losses totalled nearly 600 men, 117 wagons, seven of his twelve guns, and worst of all, the vital water-works at Sannaspos.

The loss of Bloemfontein's water supply had serious consequencies, for it not only resulted in the necessity of bringing up water supplies by train, thus greatly adding to the strain on the railways, but it also caused an immediate deterioration in the enteric epidemic, which carried off 2,000 people before the end of April. Although the water station was a mere twenty miles from his HQ, Roberts had appeared to sit in a torpid stupor for two entire days, during which time alert after alert poured in from Sannaspos. First, there had been a signal from his Staff Officer, Col. Sir Henry Rawlinson, who had heard the distant rumble of gunfire and had ridden with speed to warn Roberts of the danger. Then there was Broadwood's first SOS, relayed by the post at Boesman's Kop, and finally, the message carried by the officer of the 10th Hussars. Yet, in spite of all these warnings and supplications, Roberts did nothing to help the situation. Instead of investing Boesman's Kop immediately and taking personal control of affairs, Roberts, beset with an anxiety bordering on panic, and fearing that Bloemfontein was in dire danger, sent his best mobile force in that direction to hunt for Boers.

The cavalry floundered about in the vast open plains for two days without finding any trace of De Wet or any of his commandos. In the end, Roberts ordered Gen. Colvile to take his infantry division of 10,000 men, together with the remains of French's depleted cavalry division, and move up to Boesman's Kop to cover Broadwood's retreat from Sannaspos. By the time Colvile's lumbering convoy eventually reached its destination, De Wet, and his entire force, had flown the coup and were well away from the area. With him went the seven guns, five of U- and two of Q- Batteries, plus 117 of Broadwood's wagons and 528 prisoners captured at Koornspruit.

Roberts's inertia confounded and distressed his officers. Ever since Poplar Grove their biggest problem had been finding any Boers to fight, and now, right before them, was De Wet's advance force of less than 500 men, isolated between Broadwood at Sannaspos and Bloemfontein, where Roberts sat with and army of 30,000 men, ready to squash De Wet in his own trap. All that was required was for Roberts to rush a flying column to Boesman's Kop, convert it into a vital communications point, and then to move forward with vast numbers of infantry and overwhelm the Boers. Instead, he allowed valuable time and resources to be wasted on pointless searches for an enemy that was nowhere near there. After Sannaspos, blame and recriminations were tossed about indiscriminately, and in the end, Broadwood was privately censured but officially exonerated. However, it was from the British point of view, a sad reflection that the entire fiasco could have been avoided if Roberts himself had acted with more authority and military acumen.

De Wet continued with his raiding expeditions in the south. With an extremely mobile force of 800 burghers, he confounded the British with lightning strikes, popping up here one day and then fifty miles away on another. On the 3rd of April, he attacked the British garrison of 600 men of the Royal Irish Rifles at Reddersburg, and after twenty-four hours of fierce combat the garrison surrendered, losing forty-five officers and men killed or wounded, and 546 taken prisoner. De Wet's run of success was temporarily stemmed near the town of Wepener, where he laid siege to 1,900 men of the Brabant's Horse Regiment. The Brabant's Horse dug in well and waited for relief from Roberts. After six days, De Wet lifted the siege as Roberts's rescue column approached, and made his way back to his base in the north. But in spite of De Wet's successes with this new type of warfare, both Presidents Steyn and Kruger remained sceptical, still clinging to the notion of blocking Roberts's army of 50,000 men with more conventional tactics. They argued, maybe rightly so, that De Wet's raids, brilliant as they were, did not prevent the British advance northwards, but merely delayed it. Everywhere they looked they saw the net closing in on them – in the east, along the railway from Natal – in the centre, along the railway from Bloemfontein, and in the west, along the railway from Kimberley.

Road to Pretoria - The Plan.
By the beginning of May 1900, Roberts was ready to take on the Transvaal. From Kimberley in the west to Ladysmith in the east, over a frontage of 350 miles, 100,000 Empire troops, Regulars, Colonials, Volunteers, Militia and Yeomanry, massed to sweep aside some 30,000 Boers, about half of whom were positioned, or on their way to oppose Roberts's main advance. Roberts aimed to close in on Johannesburg and

Pretoria from four sides as quickly and as effectively as possible in order to put a speedy end to the war in South Africa. To do so he needed to plan meticulously because he was fully aware of the fact, that although he enjoyed an overwhelming advantage in numbers, in artillery and in equipment, he would be operating in hostile country, and absolutely dependant on a single supply line, which would become increasingly vulnerable the further he advance into enemy country. His numerical advantage would also suffer because of the need to drop off guards and garrisons all along the line in order to protect and secure his rear. This aspect of the campaign was of vital importance, because Roberts knew that the Boers would be operating amongst their own people, who could freely provide them with supplies, reinforcements, and shelter.

The main assault would come from Bloemfontein. Roberts had mustered some 70,000 men and 178 guns north of the Orange River. Kelly-Kenny's 6th division would remain behind to garrison Bloemfontein, while, to protect the capital from the south, Gatacre's successor, General H. Chermside would stand by with his 3rd division. The main advance up the line would be made by French's cavalry division, with Tucker's 7th on the left, and Pole-Carew's new 11th consisting of the 1st Guards brigade and the 18th brigade, astride the railway. Hutton's 1st brigade would precede the 7th and 11th brigades.

At Kimberley, on the western front, Methuen's 1st division, consisting of the 19th and 20th brigades, was joined by a newly constituted 10th division under Hunter, formerly White's Chief of Staff. The 10th was made up of Hart's and Barton's brigades sent over from Natal. In Natal, Buller had three mounted brigades, Clery's 2nd division consisting of the 2nd and 4th brigades, Lyttleton's 4th division, chiefly composed of the Ladysmith garrison, now formed into 7th and 8th brigades, and the 5th, commanded by Hildyard in place of Warren, who had been sent off to deal with the rebellion in the northwest Cape. Roberts ordered Buller to deploy a token force to contain those Boers in the Biggarsberge range in northern Natal, and to take his main force over Van Reenen's Pass into the Free State, and from there to link up with Roberts's advance up the central railway. Buller ignored this request, claiming that it was strategically more important to clear Northern Natal and secure the Durban-Johannesburg railway line on which he depended for supplies. For reasons of diplomacy, Roberts was reluctant to overrule the former Commander-in-Chief, and grudgingly ceded Buller the benefit of the doubt.

Finally, in order to close the trap completely, Colonel Mahon was despatched from Kimberley to Mafeking in the far north. Mahon was in command of the Natal ILH, the Kimberley MI. and 100 of Barton's Fusiliers. His mission was to relieve Mafeking in the far north and then to link up with Colonel Plumer's column of Rhodesians, Queenslanders and Canadians, who were moving down from Rhodesia. Also from Rhodesia another force consisting of Yeomanry, Australians, and New Zealanders under Gen. Carrington, was ordered to stand to on the banks of the Limpopo River in order to invade the Transvaal from the north, should the need arise. In the event, this invasion never happened, and later Carrington's force transferred to the Western Transvaal.

The Road to Pretoria - The Advance

On the 3rd May, the great advance began. Pretoria was 300 miles north of Bloemfontein, with Kroonstad about half way in between, and Johannesburg some forty miles this side of Pretoria. Across the line of advance flowed the rivers Vet, Zand, Vaalsch, Rhenoster and Vaal, where the Boers hoped to make a stand against the British. But, always outnumbered, and with Roberts's mounted troops riding wide to find the open flank, the best the Boers could do, was to delay the advance as long as possible. In that way they could fall back in order to avoid being out-flanked and surrounded, and as they retreated, blow up bridges and railway track in their wake. On the British side, such fighting as there was fell mainly on the cavalry and MI units of French, Hunter and Hamilton. Generally, for the infantry there was little to do but to plod on for mile after endless mile.

Roberts entered Kroonstad on the 12th, where he halted for ten days to repair the damaged railway, bring up supplies, evacuate his sick, and rest the troops and horses. Meanwhile Buller reached Dundee after outflanking the Boers on the Biggarsberg, and forcing them to retire. In the west, Hunter entered the Transvaal, and Methuen was approaching Hoopstadt, midway between Hunter and Roberts. On the same day, by a skilful choice of route and hard marching, Mahon's 900 men linked up with Plumer's 700 from Rhodesia, after having travelled 226 miles in twelve days, and fighting one engagement. Previously, in early April, Plumer's Rhodesians had already tried to reach Mafeking but had been driven back with heavy losses when only five miles from the town. This time, however, when Plumer and Mahon ran into De la Rey and his 2,000 men, a fight ensued, and after five hours, the Boers gave way, and that evening the ILH rode triumphantly into Mafeking. After seven months, Baden-Powell's little garrison was at last relieved. The news of the relief created a storm of emotion in Britain and the Empire, far greater than that provoked by any other incident of the war. The frenetic scenes of rejoicing in London which lasted for over forty-eight hours, placed a new verb, 'to maffick', in the English language. Yet all this euphoric, almost hysterical, response was totally out of proportion to the military significance of the event. Nevertheless, the doubtless 'pluck and wits' of Baden-Powell and his Colonials served as a morale booster for the Empire, and this well merited relief came at a time when victory was at last in sight, the Imperial spirit erupted in unbridled jubilation

When the advance from Kroonstad was resumed on the 22nd May, Roberts must indeed have felt that victory was well within his grasp – in the west, organised resistance had seemingly ended before Hunter's and Methuen's advance, and Methuen was ordered to garrison Kroonstad. In Natal Buller had occupied Newcastle after Botha had removed more than 3,000 burghers over to the central front. During the halt at Kroonstad, Hamilton's column swung east through Lindley and Heilbron, and set off after Steyn, De Wet and the Free Staters. He then cut back into the railway north of the Rhenoster River, his march forcing the Boers to quit their positions on the Rhenoster, and so clearing the way for Roberts' advance. However, although it divided the Free State forces from those of the Transvaal, it failed to prevent them dispersing to the east to face Colvile, Rundle and Brabant, who by now were sweeping up from the south east. Roberts brushed aside advice from some of his colleagues, including Buller, that failing to round up the Free State Boers before proceeding any further would prolong the war. Instead, he adhered to his original plan to cross the Vaal, secure the goldfields, then capture Pretoria and annexe the Transvaal as a British Colony. Acting instinctively on his previous experiences in India and Afghanistan, Roberts was confident that a powerful advance by strong columns through hostile territory, and the subsequent capture of salient strongholds, would suffice to cow the natives into submission. Surely, he argued, a triumphant entry into Pretoria, from whence all the Boer intransigence had sprung, would have the same effect, and with a minimum of bloodletting on either side.

After crossing the Vaal on May 24[th,] Roberts was confronted by Botha and De la Rey holding a range of hills to the west and south of Johannesburg. He decided to advance with the infantry against the junction of the Cape and Natal railways, east of the city, while Hamilton was sent over to the left to join French, and envelope the enemy from the west. Handing over his two mounted brigades for French to press on around the Boer rear, Hamilton launched the 19th and 21st brigades against the Boer right flank at Doornkop, a place of historic significance for both sides for it was here that Jameson had surrendered back in 1896. The attack, led by the CIV on the left and the 1[st.] Gordons on the right, illustrated the different combat methods of the Volunteers and the Regulars. The CIV advanced slowly and drove the Boers off the top of the koppie with rifle and shell-fire, and by so doing they succeeded in avoiding heavy casualties. The Gordons, on the other hand, followed their usual tactics of getting in close with the bayonet, and closed ranks. At 800 yards, they launched their assault under impossible conditions. Later, Private Walker of the 1st Gordons commented, *"If you consider the weight of our kits (anything between 50 and 70 lbs) it is a physical impossibility to charge 800 yards in anything like a short time, up a hill"*. The Gordons were spent by the time they reached the top, and were in utter confusion after discovering that they had taken a false crest. Furthermore, they were now themselves under heavy fire from the Boers. Nevertheless, after half-an-hour, the Gordons charged again, and this time the Boers fled. Hamilton was as thrilled by the ultimate, although costly success of his old Regiment's 1st Battalion as he had been by its 2nd Battalion at Elandslaagte, yet had he waited for French's turning movement to take full effect, the heavy loss of life could probably have been well avoided.

On the following day, the 30th, the British encircled Johannesburg and Roberts demanded its surrender. Dr. Krause, the Boer commandant, agreed on condition that, in order to avoid street fighting and possible damage to the mines, a day was to elapse before the British entered. Roberts's concurrence assured that the goldfields would remain intact, but it also permitted the escape of the Transvaal commandos northwards. Had he not held off, Roberts, may well have succeeded in forcing the Boers into unconditional surrender, for they were all in disarray and in low spirits, and many burghers had already left for their homes. Even their most redoubtable leaders like Botha and De la Rey were deeply pessimistic and despondent. On the 30th Kruger and his government left Pretoria for Middelburg, on the Delagoa Bay railway line. Before his departure, he had ordered the dismantling of the Pretoria forts and he asked Botha to delay the British forces for as long as possible, but told him not to sacrifice his force which by now had dwindled effectively to a mere 2,000 burghers.

On the 31st May, Roberts entered Johannesburg, and on the 3rd June, he resumed his advance on Pretoria. He ordered French to swing north around Pretoria to the west, thereby leaving the Boers' line of retreat open to the east. By now the Transvaal leaders were seriously thinking of surrender, and on the evening of the 4th June, Botha proposed peace talks. Roberts replied that he could only accept unconditional surrender, to which Botha disdainfully responded by setting off to the east, leaving Pretoria undefended. The next day Roberts entered the Transvaal capital. After freeing all the British prisoners of war, he raised the Union Jack and claimed victory. His accomplishments were quite remarkable – on short rations and in trying weather, his weary troops had covered 300 miles from Bloemfontein - nearly 400 in the case of the mounted troops - in thirty-four days, including halts totalling sixteen days. Of the 38,000 who left Bloemfontein, only 26,000 entered Pretoria. The 14th Brigade remained to protect Johannesburg, while others were dropped off as guards. About 3,000 were battle casualties, some had been lost through disease and non-battle wastage, and a high proportion consisted of dismounted cavalrymen or MI left behind because their horses had died or were completely worn out.

On the 6th June 1900, Roberts and the leaders in London justifiably believed that, at last, the war in South Africa had come to a glorious and victorious end. However, their disillusionment would prove to be profound; the Boers, despondent and disorganised as they were, would soon launch into a new type of confrontation that would confound and distress the British. Their resilience and determination would drag the conflict on for a further two years, at the cost of many thousands of lives, both military and civilian, and to an inconclusive end at Vereeniging on the 31st May 1902.

The despairing thoughts of defeat and surrender that had haunted the Boer leaders during those first days of June 1900 were brief and quickly dispelled. Botha and the other Transvaal generals were stunned by a furious telegram from President Steyn, chiding them for their weakness, and assuring them that his Free State commandos would never surrender and, as if to prove the point, his words were speedily matched by the actions of his generals. On the 31st May 1900, the very day that Roberts entered Johannesburg to prepare the way for an end to the war, Piet de Wet captured the prestigious 13th Battalion of the Imperial Yeomanry at Lindley, a small and remote Boer town about thirty miles east of Kroonstad. This seemingly insignificant encounter together with its ensuing incidents had a profound effect on the subsequent course and nature of the war which, in spite of Roberts's optimism, would continue for a further two long and bitter years. The action at Lindley was swift and clinical and the outcome disastrous for the British forces in the eastern region of the Orange Free State. The 13th Battalion Imperial Yeomanry was a unit of high rank and prestige made up of a number of gentleman soldiers from the upper echelons of contemporary Irish and English landed hierarchy and included three Earls, a Viscount and a number of Lords and Squires. The encounter occurred around some koppies on the outskirts of Lindley where the Yeomen were ambushed by De Wet's men. Rather than retreat the Battalion, led by Lt. Col. Basil Spragge decided to fight it out until help arrived. In spite of Spragge's urgent appeals immediate help was not forthcoming and the battle ended with some eighty Yeomen dead and over four-hundred marched away in captivity to the Eastern Transvaal. And this was not all! – at Senekal about fifty miles south of Lindley Lt. Gen.

Sir Leslie Rundle, officer in command of all the British forces in the eastern Free State, on receipt of Spragge's pleas for help, for some obscure reason decided to move his Brigade eastward to bolster the British garrison at Bethlehem A Boer commando in the vicinity succeeded in intercepting Rundle's message to Gen. Brabant stationed at Ficksburg, near the Basutoland border, and ambushed the British column on its way to Bethlehem and severely mauling it and leaving it, in the end, with over 180 men dead or wounded. On top of all this on the 4th June Piet de Wet's older brother Christiaan seized a supply column and 160 Highlanders close to Heilbron and two days later pounced on a battalion of Derbyshire Militia guarding a bridge over the Rhenoster River, succeeded in blowing up the bridge, destroying the railway line and capturing some 500 prisoners and a large quantity of ammunition and supplies.

The Battle of Diamond Hill
In the Transvaal, the Boer leaders, chastened by Steyn's rebuke and encouraged by the success of the de Wets in the Free State, decided to fight on. Botha immediately set off to protect the vital Delagoa Bay railway line from Pretoria to the port of Lourenco Marques in Portuguese East Africa, and to secure the safety of the Transvaal government-in-flight, as well as their gold and ammunition reserves. By the 8th June he had succeeded in gathering around him a force of some 6,000 men and twenty-three guns to hold a 23-mile north-south line of high ground astride the railway. The line centred on Diamond Hill, a prominent outcrop about sixteen miles east of Pretoria and Roberts, alarmed at this Boer threat so close to Pretoria resolved to remove it forthwith. He mustered what was left of French's cavalry division, which was by now so depleted by losses that the regiments were down to squadron strength, and the RHA batteries reduced to 4 guns each. He also committed Pole-Carew's 11th division, and Hamilton's original column less Smith-Dorrien's 19th brigade, which had been sent south with Kitchener. The 19th was substituted by Maj. Gen. Gordon's 3rd. cavalry brigade making a total of 14,000 men, of whom a third were mounted, plus six heavy- and sixty-four field guns. This entire force outnumbered the Boers by two to one. In his anxiety to remove the Boer threat on his doorstep, Roberts, bereft of all but the most conventional of battle strategies, ordered a spurious show of force by Pole-Carew's infantry against the centre of the Boers' position, whilst sending French and Hamilton to turn the Boers' right and left flanks respectively. However, Botha, a shrewd battle tactician, was by now quite used to Roberts's unimaginative tactics, and anticipated the plan. He quietly strengthened and stretched out his wings at the expense of his centre, and when the British attack came on the 11th June, French's two cavalry brigades, supported by Pilcher's and Anderson's MI unexpectedly found themselves pinned down by Botha's well deployed burghers, resulting in a conventional out-flanking manoeuvre which soon was reduced to a dismounted rifle-fire shoot-out. On the far right Broadwood's cavalry brigade became heavily engaged on three sides and, in order to help them Hamilton ordered Bruce Hamilton's 21st Brigade to attack the Boers on the Diamond Hill plateau itself, but by nightfall, the infantry had managed only to take a ridge in front of the plateau.

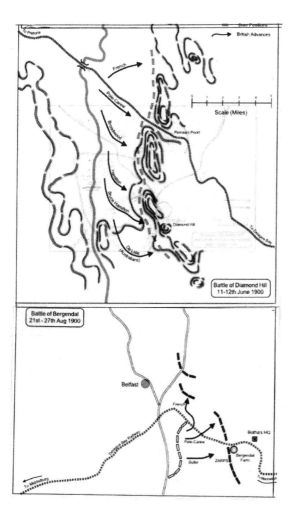

225

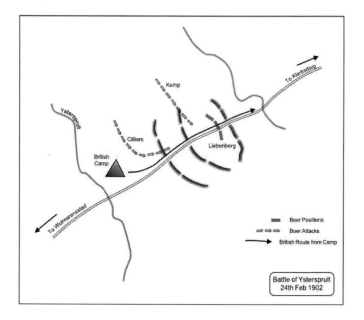

Boer Positions

Boer Attacks

British Route from Camp

Battle of Ysterspruit
24th Feb 1902

The following day Bruce Hamilton again attacked, supported this time by the Guards brigade and De Lisle's MI on his right. The CIV, 1ˢᵗ Derbyshire, 1ˢᵗ Royal Sussex and the Guards fought their way up Diamond Hill, but soon came under intense fire from hitherto unseen positions further back, and also from their flanks. Despite two batteries being sent up to help them, they were unable to advance any further. Meanwhile on the far left, French's position had grown so precarious that De la Rey informed Botha that, given reinforcements, he could throw French back and fall on Roberts's centre. Botha was in the act of sending up the requested reinforcements when a message regarding a development near Diamond Hill made him recall the men immediately. What in fact had happened was that while Bruce Hamilton's brigade had been trying to subdue the Boer fire, De Lisle had spotted that the key to Diamond hill was a koppie at its southeast end. His 6ᵗʰ Regular MI seized a footing at its base and he sent the New South Wales Mounted Rifles, dismounted and with bayonets fixed, swarming up the hill in open order. The Boers, unaware of the exact strength of the onslaught - there were, in fact, only 350 men - fell back rapidly and the Australians succeeded in securing a vital lodgement on the flank of Diamond Hill just as darkness fell.

During the night, Botha withdrew all his men eastwards and by the time his flight was discovered the next morning, it was too late for the British to mount an effective pursuit. De Lisle's men however were tenacious and followed up doggedly and by the following afternoon they caught up with a Boer rear-guard at Bronkhorstspruit. A short action ensued but De Lisle's West Australians were forced to withdraw for want of support. Curiously, the last shots of this penultimate set-piece battle of the war had occurred at the same place as the first shots of the 1881 war. Neither side could claim Diamond Hill as a victory, although they both did.

Roberts now began to realise that the Boers had still to be defeated and that the war was far from being over. He realised that before he could undertake any further decisive action against Botha he urgently needed to deal with the serious threat from De Wet and his commandos in the Free State. Since his arrival in the north-west of the country with Smith-Dorrien's 19ᵗʰ brigade, Kitchener had succeeded in restoring the railway line there, and in fortifying the various British garrisons scattered throughout the region, especially those vulnerable ones barracked at Senekal, Ficksburg and Lindley. Beyond that arc and as far as the Durban-Johannesburg railway line, the Free State commandos roamed at will, mounting telling operations from towns such as Frankfort, Bethlehem and Harrismith on the Natal border. Fortunately, for the British, although the Boers had succeeded in piercing the arc of garrisons in the central railway area, they had been unable to break out southwards through the line between Senekal and Ficksburg, which was firmly held by Rundle's 8ᵗʰ division.

Roberts and Kitchener devised an elaborate plan to corner Steyn, De Wet and the Free State commandos, and to demobilise them for once and for all. It was an optimistic scheme, which included fortifying all the existing garrisons, and despatching three full-strength columns to drive the Boers eastward and hard against the Drakensberg, the precipitous mountain chain forming the full-length boundary between the Free State and Basutoland and Natal. The plan was for Buller to continue his advance up the Natal railway towards Standerton and Heidelberg, and to prevent the commandos from breaking out to the northeast to join the Transvaal burghers. Rundle would press on from the southeast and Clements with his 12th Brigade would link up with Paget's 20th Brigade at Lindley and then proceed to capture Bethlehem with Hunter and MacDonald. On 9th July Hunter and MacDonald reached Bethlehem which had been captured two days earlier by Clements and Paget. Hunter assumed command of all the columns, and prepared to set off in pursuit of the enemy. The Free Staters, 7,500 strong, with Steyn, the De Wets and all their other senior commanders, fell back to the Brandwater Basin, a natural fortress formed by a 75 mile long semi-circle of tangled and jagged mountains enclosing a tract of land along the Caledon River on the Basutoland border. The Basin could only be entered through four passes- Commando Nek to the southwest, Slabbert's and Retief's Neks in the centre, and Naauwpoort Nek to the northeast. No sooner had the Boers reached the Basin, when dissension began to surface amongst the leaders. De Wet immediately realised that what they had thought to be an impregnable sanctuary was in fact a deadly trap, if and when the British eventually seized the passes. After acrimonious wrangling the Boers split into four groups, the first leaving the Basin on the 15th July.

Hunter tarried for six days at Bethlehem to bring up supplies from his distant bases, and to ascertain some detailed information about Brandwater Basin, an area quite inadequately mapped out. As a result of this delay the British troops eventually arrived at the Brandwater Basin Passes on the very same night that Steyn and De Wet, with 2600 men and 400 wagons were sneaking out of Slabbert's Nek. The Boers slipped silently past the British bivouacs and headed back towards Lindley. The next day, when Broadwood realised what had happened, he sent the cavalry and Ridley's MI off in pursuit, but De Wet held them off while his wagons disappeared to the north. Those Boers who remained in the Brandwater Basin now could not agree on a leader, so they abandoned their plans to break out, and barred the passes. With the benefit of some masterly reconnaissance on the part of the Lovat Scouts, MacDonald's Highlanders forced their way through Slabbert's Nek, and by the 26th all four passes were successfully secured by the British. The Boers eventually selected the elderly Marthinus Prinsloo as leader, but by then it was too late to break out, and on the 29th Prinsloo surrendered with 4,500 men and several thousands of sheep, cattle, and horses. Only 1,500 Boers succeeded in escaping over an un-graded track to the east.

It was a considerable achievement by Hunter's troops, and the biggest haul of prisoners since Paardeberg. It was also a bitter blow for the British however that the most determined Boer fighters had got away, including of course, those two most redoubtable of resistance warriors, Steyn and Christiaan De Wet. For a full month after their escape, thousands of British troops were to be employed in trying to catch them as they ran, fought and feinted, first north, then west, then north again, and clean across the Free State and into the Transvaal. Although encouraged by Hunter's success in the Free State, Roberts continued to be plagued with problems throughout July and the first half of August. Even though the hunt for De Wet was now out of his hands and under the control of Kitchener, he still needed to regroup rapidly to overcome Botha's forces in the Eastern Transvaal, capture his stores and supplies, and most important of all, Kruger who was now installed further east at Machadorp on the Delagoa Bay railway. At the same time, it was also imperative to deprive the Boers of this vital rail link with

Komatipoort on the Portuguese East African border. Another thorn in Roberts's side at this time was Buller's stubborn refusal to co-operate. Roberts had asked him to strike out directly to Komatipoort in the northeast to cut off the Boers from the rear, but instead of doing this, he stuck doggedly to the Natal-Johannesburg railway. In spite of these problems, Roberts decided, around the 15th of July, to start his general advance on Middelburg and the Eastern Transvaal. As a preliminary step, he sent Hutton's MI to clear the right flank. Hutton soon ran into very stiff resistance, but instead of receiving help from Roberts, he got orders to stand off, because in the mean time, some fierce fighting had unexpectedly erupted in the hitherto pacified region west of Pretoria.

It was De la Rey who in greatest secrecy, had moved off with Smuts and some 7,000 Western Transvaal burghers, nineteen guns and a variety of Pom-Poms and Maxims, in a wide arc around the north of Pretoria, and established himself in the Magaliesberg range. The Magaliesberg is a prominent chain of hills stretching west from Pretoria for a distance of sixty miles. The only British troops in the entire area were a few garrisons made up mostly from Baden-Powell's Mafeking Column, encamped at Rustenburg, half of Barton's Fusilier Brigade at Klerksdorp, and a few small and scattered posts dotted about here and there. On the 12th July, De la Rey struck simultaneously at three points, capturing three companies of Lincolns and some Scots Greys. As a result, in order to shore up the Pretoria defences, Roberts recalled French from the Eastern Transvaal, and summonsed Methuen from the Free State to join him at Pretoria. Roberts also hurriedly created a new Division out of freshly arrived reinforcements from Hamilton, now fully recovered from his injuries. But, although De la Rey continued his frequent attacks wherever and whenever possible, there were occasions when he ran into some forceful resistance from the British. One such incident occurred at Elandsrivier, where Col. Hore with 500 Australians and Rhodesians from the Mafeking Protectorate Regiment, successfully held off a fierce Boer onslaught for eleven days until they were relieved.

Botha, picking up the cue from De la Rey, struck out eastwards to create a diversion, and sent General Viljoen with 2,000 burghers to take on Hutton's 2nd Royal Irish Fusiliers and the New Zealand Mounted Rifles. The British came under heavy pressure from Viljoen's commandos but successfully managed to hold out until relieved by a counter-attack from the Canadian Mounted Rifles who succeeded in restoring the situation. Roberts was relieved when he heard that De Wet was moving west after his escape from the Brandwater Basin, because he had feared that he would join Botha in the east. As a result he now felt confident enough to resume his advance along the Delagoa Bay railway with French and Hutton. Botha continued to fall back in the face of the British advance, and on the 27th July, Roberts captured Middelburg. There he halted a while until Buller, who had arrived at Heidelberg, confirmed that he was now in a position to link up with Roberts's army in the eastern Transvaal. However, there was still the pressing problem of De Wet. By early August, having crossed from the central railway, he eluded all pursuit and successfully reached the Vaal aiming first to assist Steyn in joining Kruger, and then to continue his effective guerrilla campaign. Kitchener had 11,000 men in five columns advancing from the south to prevent him from doubling back into the Free State and to drive him north against three successive lines, Methuen on the Vaal, Smith-Dorrien on the Klerksdorp-Johannesburg railway, and Ian Hamilton on the Magaliesburg hills, a grand total of 18,000 men.

Nevertheless, in spite of the dogged endurance and tenacity of his pursuers, De Wet managed to keep ahead of them, twisting and turning in his route, always finding an unguarded gap or one blocked too late, keeping himself supplied by friendly farms and maintaining the strictest discipline over his burghers. He continued to take advantage of his pursuers' poor intelligence and tardy communications, in addition to the superior scouting of his own men. De Wet made particularly good use of his co-operation with a corps of foreigners led by the same Danie Theron who had distinguished himself at Paardeberg by carrying messages between De Wet and Cronje through the British lines. On the 14th August De Wet reached the Magaliesberg and slipped through Olifants Nek just a few hours before Hamilton arrived to block it. Methuen, who had been hard on De Wet's heels, believing Hamilton to be safely in position to block De Wet at Olifant's Nek, swung to the left to prevent any escape westwards. This unfortunate manoeuvre enabled De Wet to get clear and break out and into the region dominated by De la Rey. After safely despatching Steyn with an escort to Kruger, De Wet broke up his force into smaller groups and returned, by devious routes to the Vaal from where he once again began raiding the railway.

Bergendal- The Last Set-Piece action of the War
With De Wet back on the Vaal and closely pursued by Kitchener, Roberts could now turn his undivided attention to Botha and Kruger in the east because now, for the first time in the three months since the grand offensive had begun, Buller was at last co-operating with the main army around Middelburg. Leaving one cavalry brigade and two divisions behind to hold the railway between Heidelberg and Natal, he set off with Lyttleton's 4th division and Dundonald's and Brocklehurst's mounted brigades and by the 15th August, he eventually made contact with French's cavalry some thirty miles south east of Middelburg. Between Middelburg and a point eighty miles short of the Portuguese border, the Delagoa Bay railway ran through the northern Drakensberg escarpment, a tangled mass of mountains, about fifty miles wide, which run from the far north of the Transvaal to the Swaziland border. It was on these heights that Botha had deployed his 6,000 men to protect Kruger who was sitting in his railway carriage on the line near Machadadorp.

French was confident that he could successfully run the Boer flank and wind them up from the rear. He urged Roberts to let him take both his own and Buller's cavalry and make a wide sweep southwards via Barberton and cut the Boers' line of retreat. The idea was so bold that it may very well have come off but the ever-cautious Roberts thought it would be too risky a venture, and vetoed the request. In addition Buller was creating difficulties by refusing to hand over any of his mounted troops and what could have been a bold and turning movement offering high dividends and quick success, degenerated into a ponderous advance on the Boer centre around Belfast, with French, Buller and Pole-Carew all bunched up around the railway.

230

On the 25th August Roberts launched his attack of Botha. He despatched French to the north of the railway with orders to break through the Boer right and then swing south to cut the line at Machadadorp. Pole-Carew's infantry was ordered to protect French's right by engaging the Boer right-centre and Buller got orders to move directly eastwards on the south side of the railway line and join up with French at Machadadorp.

French made good progress on the 26^{th,} and the next day, Pole-Carew, who had marched to meet him with the Guards, joined him, while the 18th brigade stayed behind to confront the enemy's right centre. Meanwhile, Buller advanced with the 4th Division supported by a mounted brigade on either flank but he was soon halted by five commandos with two heavy guns holding a line of hills running south east for nearly six miles from the railway. A cavalry patrol then reported to Buller that on the right of his position was a small koppie alongside the railway, just in front of Bergendal Farm. Buller, when he heard this, decided to turn south and break through via the koppie rather than continuing due east into the face of the Boer forces. What Buller did not know, however, was that the koppie was being used as a Boer outpost and was actually occupied by a small force of fifty-seven Johannesburg police (the ZARPS) backed by two small groups of foreign volunteers behind them.

At 11 a.m. on the 27^{th,} began what was to be the last set-piece attack of the war. For three hours Buller's thirty-eight guns laid down a preliminary bombardment on and around Bergendal. Such was the weight of gunfire that no reinforcements could reach the ZARPS, nor could they retire even if they had wished to do so. Grimly they lay low in their trenches and waited for the infantry attack realising that the noise of the bombardment was worse than the actual damage it was causing. As soon as the leading infantry appeared the ZARPS opened a heavy fire with their rifles a Maxim and a Pom-Pom, despite the gunfire that continued to cover the infantry advance. The left battalion, 2nd Rifle Brigade, advanced across the open in short punches, but soon began to sustain severe casualties from the ZARPS, as well as from the hitherto unseen foreign detachment in the rear. The infantry kept going though, alternatively running forward and firing while the reserve companies successfully extended the line towards the 1st Inniskillings. With considerable bravery the ZARPS continued firing to the very end and although some fled as the bayonets closed in over forty were killed, wounded or captured, including their commandant, Philip Oosthuizen. The Rifle Brigade lost fifteen killed and sixty-eight wounded, including their Colonel, and the Inniskillings suffered seventeen casualties.

So ended the Battle of Bergendal It was to be the last pitched battle of the war and the well-led and spirited attack against a courageously defended small post surprisingly caused the collapse of the entire Boer position south and north of the railway. Most of the commandos got away and as they fled eastwards, Roberts's columns tramped after them. In the end, as the burghers disappeared into the mountains and valleys of the Eastern Transvaal, it was clear to both sides that the end to conventional fighting was nigh.

The End of the Beginning

On the 11th September, President Kruger crossed the border at Komati Poort, and headed for Lourenco Marques in Portuguese East Africa. A month later, he set sail for Europe, never to return to his beloved Transvaal. President Steyn returned to the Free State, and Botha, together with his more active leaders, divided up 4,000 burghers still with them into small groups, and made off to the north to continue the struggle against the British in the Transvaal. The remainder of the commandos still in the Eastern Transvaal, about 3,000 in all, together with the bulk of the foreign volunteers fighting with the Boers, formed a rear-guard to defend Komatipoort. As the British approached however, the majority of the Boers crossed the border into Portuguese East African territory, where they sought political refuge. On the 24th September, Pole-Carew entered Komatipoort with the leading British contingents, and found it practically deserted.

It was now just a week short of a year since the war had begun and to all intents and purposes there no longer appeared to be either a Boer army or a Boer state. The burghers had been driven out of Cape Colony and Natal, they had seen their republics annexed, their towns occupied and their leaders in flight, and now they found themselves cut off from the entire world. Yet the fighting spirit of those burghers still under arms remained as strong as ever, and their determination undimmed. They still had the whole of South Africa, from the Limpopo to the Cape, a vast and open space, in which they could ride and strike whenever and wherever they willed.

Following Kruger's flight to Holland and the occupation of Komatipoort, Roberts officially declared the war to be 'practically over'. He informed the British Government that many of the troops, including General Buller, could now return home, since their services were no longer required. He assured the authorities in London that there now only remained the need for 'policing activities' – the 'mopping up' of a few dissident commandos, who would rapidly be brought to heel. Roberts also believed that the Boers' morale was so low that the majority would accept the terms of his latest proclamation inviting them to surrender their arms and return peacefully to their families and their farms. In return, Roberts offered full amnesty, and promised that those who surrendered voluntarily would not be sent outside South Africa, a fate that was feared most of all by the Boers. However, together with this blandishment, was coupled a severe warning that any stock and supplies found on farms belonging to burghers who continued to remain on commando, or who broke their oath of neutrality, would be seized and destroyed.

Yet, in spite of the despondency and despair amongst the Boers and their families in South Africa, there was a growing antipathy throughout the world against what was considered to be Britain and her Empire's unjustified involvement against the Boer Republics. Coupled with this was a strong feeling of sympathy for the Boers, fighting to preserve the legitimate sovereignty of their people and their country. For some Boers, in their deepest despair, there was a faint hope for help from somewhere in the outside world, and incredibly, even from Britain itself! This optimism was based on a waxing tide of sympathy for the burghers in Britain, which, in September 1900, motivated the Opposition in parliament to force the promulgation of a Queen's Proclamation, dissolving parliament, and calling for a general election as soon as possible.

Early in October, the electorate went to the polls to cast its vote in the 'Khaki Election', one of the maddest and most venomous ever fought in Britain. This 'muddy election' was particularly acrimonious, and dirty tactics from all sides were rife. The result was predictable, and the government, with its active anti-Boer campaign, carried the day with a bigger majority than before, winning 134 seats more than the anti-war Liberals and Irish Nationals combined. In actual votes, however, the majority was much smaller, with 2.4 million votes for the government against 2 million for the Liberals, without counting the Irish votes. So if '*every vote for the Liberals is a vote for the Boers*', as pre-election campaign propaganda had asserted, almost as many voters were for the Boers as were against. Ensuing Cabinet changes were inevitable, and heads did roll, although not as many as were expected from the astonishing results. Chamberlain stayed on as Colonial Secretary, Landsdown moved over to the Foreign Office, and his War Office post went to St. John Brodrick. Roberts became Commander-in-Chief at the War Office in succession to Wolseley, now put out to pasture. The command of the army in South Africa fell upon Kitchener, who should have taken up his command in October, but delayed due to the illness of Roberts's eldest daughter.

Roberts began making arrangements for the official handing over of command to Kitchener. He assured Kitchener, as well as the War Office, that there would be no difficulty in mopping up those Boers still at large, since his recently installed policy of farm burning would deprive any would-be guerrillas of food and shelter. Moreover, with the railways and centres of population properly garrisoned, and the countryside adequately scoured by flying columns, Kitchener needed only to conduct a simple policing operation. Roberts's confidence and optimism spread throughout Whitehall, and early in October, the Natal Army ceased to exist as a separate force. Buller sailed back to England to receive a hero's welcome from the crowds, but no honours from the Government. Roberts confidently hoped to follow not too far behind Buller now that the Transvaal was annexed as a Crown Colony and the war 'practically over'

"Bravo Bobs – The Bravest of the Brave" – A Profile of Lord Roberts
At the end of November 1900, Roberts finally laid down his command, and after a tumultuous reception at Cape Town, he set off for Britain. Immediately after he landed, the Queen summonsed him to Osborne, where she bestowed him with an earldom, and made him a Knight of the Garter, an honour not granted to any victorious general since Wellington. On platform 9 at Paddington Station, a stand for 300 distinguished people was erected, and he was met by the Prince of Wales and driven to Buckingham Palace for lunch. The route from Paddington to Buckingham Palace was lined with 14,000 troops, and thousands of wildly cheering spectators thronged six-deep. Parliament voted him £100,000 while the nation and the people generously poured their acclamations upon him, idolising him, lauding him, naming their children, their streets, and even their pets after him! In the face of all this hysteria, it was as if everyone had read the banner headlines, whilst no one had bothered to read the small print underneath. In truth there is no doubt whatsoever that no general was ever in British history, so over-rated, or any country so beguiled.

In the cold light of dawn, a factual analysis of Roberts's achievements reveals a very different picture to the one given to the people and to posterity. His avowed intention, when he embarked for South Africa in December 1899, was to *'end the war in a satisfactory manner'*. His final achievements were exactly the opposite. Instead of ending the war, he protracted it in a most unsatisfactory way, and if he was not entirely responsible for the disaster, at best he sadly failed to prevent the start of an entirely new war, which brought devastation and misery on an unparalleled scale. With it came the wastage of thousands of lives, the loss of millions of pounds and an incalculable impetus to lasting Afrikaner nationalism and antagonism.

Since the legend of Roberts's greatness was seldom questioned, it may be worth looking a little closer at his true management of the war. Only once did he succeed in actually defeating the enemy, and that was at Paardeberg, where in fact, it was Kitchener's bullishness, French's panache, Cronje's pig-headedness, and a river in flood, which eventually brought the Boers to bay. Roberts's reluctance to engage with the enemy, and his preference for protracted siege methods instead of Kitchener's pitched battle policy, provided the Boers in the Cape Midlands with sufficient time to escape, it promoted the spread of enteric, and it caused the inordinate delay at Bloemfontein. It was, in fact, this very delay, which allowed and enabled De Wet to discover new methods of resistance, which, in the end caused the conflict to continue for two further years. For the remainder of the time, Roberts seemed content simply to push the Boers back like water before the bows of a ship, under the happy delusion that he was defeating them. At Poplar Grove, before Bloemfontein, it was his flaccid commands, as much as French's huff that enabled the enemy to avoid a catastrophic defeat. Later, when Hamilton's enterprise at Johannesburg placed the city at his mercy, Roberts deliberately gave the enemy time to escape. At Diamond Hill, which was the only time he was in direct command over the whole battlefield against a reasonably strong Boer force, he allowed the enemy to get away because of his unimaginative battle tactics, confusing orders, and poor reconnaissance.

All these gaffes were hidden from view by his apparent 'triumphant advance', but the very 'advance' was a sham, because Roberts truly believed that as soon as the Boers had lost their main railways and towns they would be incapable of further resistance, and fold like a pack of cards. He would not, nor could not accept that neither railways nor towns meant little, if anything, to a people who were mostly farmers accustomed to travelling in ox-wagons, and living on farms remotely distant from neighbours and from towns. Above all, Roberts erroneously assumed that the capture of Pretoria would bring about the end of the war, and when this failed to come about, his whole strategy collapsed. His one single imaginative strategic move was the projected flank-march right at the very start of his campaign, yet even this was thwarted, when he succumbed to the universal pressure to rescue Rhodes, who was at that time trapped in Kimberly. Yet, even without that, the outcome of campaign was dubious because of the fact that the one only sound railway bridge across the Orange River in British hands, constituted an obvious and juicy target for the many Boer commandos operating in the area at that time. In fact, Buller warned Roberts of the vulnerability of this single crossing, and recommended the construction of an alternate railway route, but Roberts, to his dear cost, simply ignored the advice.

It is tempting to deduce that Roberts's brilliant career in Afghanistan may have been one of the main causes for his failure in South Africa. In that country, troublesome tribesmen were successfully subdued simply by sending columns out to defeat them, and then to impose a fine, burn down their huts and force them to mend their ways. In South Africa, he thought that he could deal with the problem by implementing exactly the same punitive methods, but when the Boers refused to respond accordingly, he found himself at a complete loss. The ensuing retributive devastation of farms and incarceration of women and children from June onwards, branded him the author of a 'scorched earth' policy, which would turn out to be perfectly disastrous from every point of view. In Afghanistan, Roberts's management skills, coupled with his brilliantly successful tactical methods, fanned his mania to be in charge of everything and every detail, and his insistence on running the entire show himself. However, in South Africa things were very different. In truth, he found himself completely overwhelmed by the sheer magnitude of controlling an army ten times bigger than he had ever handled before, across a huge expanse of territory, against a force far superior to any he had ever fought, and in the midst of acute political complexities. In the final analysis, it remained a ridiculous notion that one could annexe countries simply by declaring them 'defeated', and then treating their uncooperative inhabitants as rebels. The solemn running-up of a silken Union Jack woven by Roberts's wife, or even his well reported dramatic or romantic touches like 'you have made a gallant offence, sir' to Cronje after Paardeberg, may raise a whimsical smile, but cannot justify the many lives that were lost through his inability to assert authority over his generals. He lacked the moral courage to sack Buller after Spioenkop, but allowed him instead to continue to blunder along, sacrificing needless lives and materials on the hills of the Thukela.

That Roberts possessed great kindliness and consideration cannot be denied, but his kindliness and personal charm, his elevated moral character, his soldier's courage and chivalry were splendid qualities, which however did not amount to much when assessing his qualifications for making a good general and leader. He was admired for his solicitude for his men, but his bad organisational skills often failed to secure adequate supplies for them, as did his slack regard for hygiene cause them great discomfort and huge losses from epidemics and diseases. His disinclination to risk incurring casualties is a conspicuous example of what can be considered virtues in Roberts the man, but grave weaknesses in Roberts the general. Yet, so it was that when Roberts set sail for Britain, no one seemed to notice that a full year of continuous fighting across thousands of miles had left the greater and better part of the Boer forces intact and still very active. For Roberts the war might have been over, as indeed it seemed to be for many South Africans, for Britain, the Empire and even for the world at large, but the only people who did not think it was over, in fact who *knew* it was not over, were the Boers themselves.

This, in essence, was the core of Roberts's failure- he had no idea of what he was fighting. At first, he thought he was fighting an army, and then he thought he was fighting some rebels, but in fact, his opponents were neither: they were a *nation* in whom the past few months had refined a consciousness of national identity, which until now had lacked coherence or passion.

Resurgence – Cypherfontein and Beyond
While Roberts was preparing his departure from South Africa and the handing over of the 'policing operations' to Kitchener, the South African spring was breathing new life into the veld, and into the commandos scattered all over it. In the southwest region of the Transvaal, De la Rey's burghers quietly slipped back to their commandos, and further south, on either side of the Vaal River, De Wet was back in action in his favourite hunting ground, attacking isolated convoys, and sabotaging the railway line.

At the centre of this activity was a farm called Cypherfontein, situated deep into the Zwartruggens hills about seventy-five miles west of Pretoria. It was here in late October, that a meeting took place between the leaders of both governments, General Louis Botha and President Steyn. De la Rey and Smuts acted as hosts, and the only important absentee was De Wet, who was due to arrive in a few days time. The Boer leaders met to beat out a new policy of warfare and their task was a heavy one. Roberts's policy of large-scale farm burning had utterly changed the state of the war, and the urgent need now was to hammer out a joint offensive strategy to counter it. The discussions at Cypherfontein were serious, urgent, and above all constructive. Botha, Steyn, and especially De la Rey, urged seriously, that in order to continue the conflict effectively, it would be far better for the commandos to operate in their own home areas under their own regional commanders. It was also recognised that there was a need for the men to rest for a while before regrouping for action, but that at the same time, no chances should be lost for striking at opportunity targets wherever they appeared, as indeed, De Wet was doing at that very moment in the Free State. Finally, it was also resolved to carry the fight into the Cape Colony and Natal, where the Cape Afrikaner element were to be encouraged to mount a major insurrection in support of the Boer cause in the Transvaal and the Free State.

Following the Cypherfontein meeting, Botha returned to organise the Transvaal commandos, allocating the west to De la Rey and Smuts, the northeast to Ben Viljoen, and the far north to Beyers, while retaining the southeast for himself, in addition to exercising overall command of all the Boer forces in the Transvaal. Steyn went south to brief De Wet, who since his escape from Methuen in August had been galvanising the Free State burghers into action, and attacking the railway anywhere and everywhere, with impunity. Yet, although he could account for some substantial measures of success, De Wet did not always have it his own way. For example, he had been anxious to be part of the decision-making elite at Cypherfontein, and after spurring his lieutenants into action all over the Free State he crossed the Vaal with a small force, and headed for Cypherfontein. However, he soon ran into a British column of Barton's Fusiliers at Frederikstad on the Klerksdorp railway line, but fared badly, and after five days of desultory fighting culminating in an aborted night charge, he drew off with heavy losses. He then just managed to avoid a British column made up of mounted detachments hastily thrown together by Roberts, whose mobility and speed was a refreshing exception from the usual lumbering 'progress' of the regular 'flying columns'. The commander was also an exception for he exercised a determination, which seriously threatened to corner the fantastic and mystical De Wet. His name was General Charles Knox, who had been with French when overtaking and halting Cronje at Paardeberg. Knox tenaciously hung on De Wet's tail, and two days later caught up with him at a ford across the Vaal River near Parys. Then when an Australian troop succeeded in cuttting through De Wet's rearguard the burghers were all but surrounded and in great confusion.when, mercifully for them, they managed to escape in a violent thunderstorm, and De Wet was able to despatch the bulk of his force in a southwest direction while he himself slipped back into the Transvaal to rendezvous with Steyn, who was by now on his way back from Cypherfontein.

Steyn briefed De Wet on the decisions made at the krijgsraad, and in particular, the renewed proposals to invade the Cape. The moment was opportune because the Afrikaner Bond in the Cape Colony was vigorously opposed to Roberts's annexations and scorched-earth policies. An invasion of the Cape could therefore provoke the wholesale rebellion for which the Boers had so ardently prayed. Besides, Steyn informed De Wet, it would certainly invigorate an awakening in the Transvaal, harness the scattered energies of some of the Free State commandos, and generally distract the British. Together, the two Free State leaders travelled south, and overtook De Wet's convoy, which by now had reached the vicinity of the ruined village of Bothaville, northwest of Kroonstad. Knox continued to stick close to De Wet in hot pursuit, and at dawn on the 6th November, his small advance guard found a Boer picket asleep, and immediately attacked the nearby laagers. Taken utterly by surprise, the Boers rushed for their horses in blind panic. De Wet and Steyn succeeded in rallying most of them, and leading them away at a gallop. The burghers took cover in some nearby farm buildings and an orchard, and fought bravely to save not only themselves but also De Wet's wagons and his eight guns. When they were finally in the clear, they realised that they had left behind 130 men in the panic following Knox's initial attack.

Knox, sensing success, rushed forward an advance guard, which with great resolve, eventually succeeded in engaging the Boers. In the bitter four-hour struggle that ensued De Wet launched a serious counter-attack, and badly mauled the advance guard, threatening them with extinction. However, Knox's main column arrived just in the nick of time, and threw the burghers back. Once again, De Wet managed to escape, this time by the skin of his teeth, but his commando surrendered together with all its wagons, guns, spare horses, and a large quantity of harnesses and saddles, ammunition and clothing. Although it was a notable feat for Knox, it amounted to little so long as De Wet and Steyn remained at large. Within a fortnight, they burst into the news again. After sending their men to recuperate from their setback at Bothaville, De Wet and Steyn crossed eastward of the railway line, gathered equipment and a fresh force of 1,500 men, and set off for the south, with the intention of putting their Cape invasion plan into action. They moved fast, completely outrunning the pursuing British columns, painfully creaking on behind them. The secret of their mobility was their lightly loaded wagons, spare horses, accurate scouting, and an almost total absence of artillery. It was a lesson that the British, to their cost, were yet to learn.

The Boers' route lay through the hills around Thaba 'Nchu. By now, the measures Roberts had taken during his march to Pretoria in order to contain the Boers in the north-east Free State, had been consolidated by a line of fortified posts reaching from Bloemfontein to the Basutoland border via Thaba 'Nchu. These posts, each garrisoned by about fifty men, were spaced less than two miles apart and to all intents and purposes appeared to be impregnable. De Wet, however, by deploying small detachments to keep two adjoining posts occupied at the same time, succeeded in bringing his convoy safely through the cordon, and advanced on the village of Dewetsdorp, named after his father. The British had occupied Dewetsdorp with a small garrison of 500 men, mostly Gloucesters and Highland Light Infantry. At first light on the 21st November De Wet attacked from three directions. He approached the town with caution, only deploying over exposed and open ground in the dark of the night. During the day, his men engaged the enemy by exploiting their superb field-craft and marksmanship to inflict maximum damage on their target. By 4 p.m. on the third day, the British were crowded together into one sector of their trenches with no water and scarcely any ammunition. An infantry subaltern hoisted a white flag over one of the gun-pits, and the garrison finally surrendered. Although there were no less than five major British forces within a 25-mile radius of Dewetsdorp, their reaction was so lethargic that no relief was able to reach the stricken garrison until the day after its capitulation. By that time, De Wet had already moved off and was well on his way south with his haul. Once again, an urgent call went out for General Knox, who soon arrived with remarkable speed. He rapidly picked up his quarry's scent, and surprised Steyn and De Wet one morning as they breakfasted on a farm nearby. The Boer leaders, however, managed to escape, without being detected, to Bethulie, near the Orange River. At Bethulie, the Free State leaders concluded their final arrangements for the invasion of the Cape. Fresh commandos continued to arrive, bringing their total strength up to 3,000 men. Finally, in the last days of November, Judge Herzog arrived with his own substantial force, and it was agreed that both he and De Wet launch their invasions simultaneously, Herzog from the west and De Wet from the east of Bethulie respectively.

When Kitchener assumed the command of the British Army in South Africa in December 1900, he found an enemy that, in terms of fighting men, tactics and leadership, had reached a level that was higher than ever before. Not only had the Boers forced the British army everywhere onto the defensive, they were actually poised to invade the Cape from two directions. It was an illusion to believe that their republics had disappeared, because even if their commandos were scattered, and even if they did lack a seat of government, they were still intact. Even if they had lost their railways and their principal towns and all the other appurtenances of statehood, they nevertheless were still in touch with each other, acting upon a common plan, led by acknowledged leaders, and maintaining their own civil power through President Steyn in the Free State and President Schalk Burger in the Transvaal. In his book entitled 'Good-Bye Dolly Gray', Rayne Kruger penned this final epitaph on the tombstone of Roberts's accomplishments - '*An army scattered but coherent*', he wrote, '*a Government peripatetic but functioning, (and) a people united behind both. What Roberts had won was a shadow. He left Kitchener to grapple with the reality.*'

13
KITCHENER'S WAR – (a) GUERRILLA WARFARE

Kitchener Takes Over – December 1900

When Kitchener assumed overall command of the British army in South Africa, he was confronted with a mountain of serious problems, and found himself facing a more complex task than any British general before him. At first, it looked simple enough – he had 210,000 troops to deal with a mere 60,000 Boers, of which only a quarter were actually on the field at any given moment. At that time about 5,000 Boers had been killed or interned in Portuguese territory, and about 15,000 were being detained as prisoners-of-war. However, out of his 210,000 men, Kitchener found that half were occupied in guarding communication lines, thousands more were on garrison duties, and innumerable others were scattered about the countryside, burning farms and guarding concentration camps and other civil installations, vital bridges and so on. Finally, in response to Roberts's assurance that 'the war was all but over', a steady stream of battle-scarred regulars, yeomanry and colonials was returning home to Britain and the Colonies.

In South Africa, the emergence of mobile MI and various other mounted irregulars was revolutionising the development of warfare, and ringing the death-knell of the cavalry, whose demoded thundering charges across the open veld, with lances aloft, stood increasingly limited chance against well-directed and well-conducted modern rifle fire. In the same way, pitched battle methods of the earlier part of the war, like Magersfontein and Colenso, had become a tactic of the past, as the British generals were at last realising to their cost. The Boers had made it obvious that the age-old and well rehearsed 'parade-ground' attacks, such as controlled volley fire by massed infantry advancing in close-order, simply provided 'sitting-duck' rifle fodder for a well hidden and expert marksman armed with a modern weapon. But in spite of all this, Kitchener's supplications to keep up a flow of fresh Yeomanry and other MI reinforcements were being rejected by the War Office, and to cap it all, the Remount Department had recalled its buying agents from abroad, thereby creating as great a shortage of horses as that of men to sit on them. This new war had caught Britain as unprepared as the old, and although defeat was now an exceedingly remote possibility, so victory, too, was scarcely any closer than it had been during Black Week in December 1899.

Kitchener's first priority was to sort out the immediate problem of appropriate manpower, and he appealed to Britain and the Empire for at least 30,000 mounted and mobile troops. On the 11th December, Brodrick, the new Secretary for War, asked parliament for more money, and as a result more MI was put under training, and the Yeomanry organisation was resuscitated. Soon, recruits were lining up at fifty-one depots all over the country in reply to the call, and at the same time Baden-Powell was raising the South African Constabulary and once again, the colonies came forward, Australia being the foremost. Nevertheless, all these developments would necessarily take months to find expression in the field, so Kitchener had to seek means of making better use of material nearer hand. He immediately set about clearing the army of 'scroungers, loafers and hangers-on' – officers and other military personnel who had established themselves in cosy non-combatant niches such as office workers, mess orderlies, gardeners, cooks and the like. He called for infantrymen to train for the MI and withdrew many of the garrisons that Roberts, in rash and over-confident mood, had created across the countryside, and were providing sitting targets for the Boer commandos. He encouraged new recruitment in South Africa besides the re-enlistment of disbanded volunteer corps, and to meet the threat of invasion in the Cape he sponsored the creation of local town guards and other civil forces.

In the end however, it was obvious that in spite of all Kitchener's frenetic efforts, he would never raise his army to the same level as that which Roberts had disposed of after his optimistic 'victory' claim. Even when the Remount Department hastily started buying again, following Kitchener's requisition for 8,000 horses and 2,000 mules a month – a demand later to be increased – it was doubtful that the shortage would ever be made up. In addition, the fresh recruits now arriving from Britain, the Colonies, and South Africa were not up to the standard of the old seasoned troops sent home with Roberts. They were inexperienced and half-trained men, attracted mainly by the high rate of pay, who when pitched into action, found them unsuited and unfit for the arduous and dangerous tasks expected from them. The seriousness of the military situation had its corollary in the political position, both at home and in South Africa. Chamberlain was accused of having defrauded the public by pretending that the war was at an end, when it was in fact very far from it. The popular press was publishing snide and deliberately hurtful allegations against Chamberlain, claiming that his family's arms manufacturing company was profiteering from the war. In a desperate bid to play down the impact of these allegations, Chamberlain surprised his anti-war critics by declaring that '.*when peace is made, the Boers will be given self-government after an interval to ensure equality in law and in liberty.*'

Back in South Africa Chamberlain's rash face-saving statements were tantamount to the height of provocation for Lord Milner, the newly appointed British High Commissioner whose authority now covered the whole of Southern Africa. His long-standing vision of a single British colonial dependency in all of South Africa was manifested in his own statement that he had 'saved British interests in South Africa' and that, for him, the Boers, whom he disliked intensely, had no individual nor separate role to play in his 'new South Africa'. The Boers from their side detested Milner with equal vehemence. They paid no heed to his so-called 'administrative brilliance' and loathed his condescending arrogance which would signify for all time to come, the Afrikaner's unfortunate impression of the haughty English character. Kitchener at least was a soldier and one innocent of any part in bringing about the war whereas they saw Milner, now flung into their teeth as so-called Governor, as a man who had never hazarded his own life in any war and particularly not this one that was principally of his own making. Milner's policy and attitude not only antagonised the Boers but Kitchener as well. The immensity of the task left undone by Roberts convinced Kitchener that continuing confrontation and total subjugation were never going to resolve the conflict between the Boers and the British. Milner made it clear that he disagreed with Kitchener's ideas that the two sides get together and that genuine efforts made to settle for something less than unconditional surrender.

240

This fundamental difference in outlook between Kitchener and Milner severely shattered any hopes for reconciliation between the British and the Boers. But Kitchener continued to nurture his quest for reconciliation particularly that since the beginning of 1900 there were spurious signs from captured Boers that many among them were beginning to realise the futility of continuing the war and were yearning for its end. Kitchener was quick to interpret these signals as an indication that the Transvaal leaders were beginning to doubt any hope of success and were ready for negotiation. There was good reason for their pessimism because it had become quite clear by now that no substantial assistance was to be coming forth from their fellow Cape- and Natal Afrikaners, nor from Holland, France and Germany, their hereditary and traditional allies in Europe. Soon a number of burghers opted to lay down their arms and for some, even to co-operate actively with the Kitchener. They justified their actions on the basis of a profound fear that any continuation of armed conflict could only end in the ruination of their land, the death of their nation and untold miseries for their families and their kinsfolk.

Soon some leading Afrikaners in Pretoria created a Central Peace Committee and invited Kitchener to speak at their inaugural meeting. Kitchener agreed and did his best to soften the demand for unconditional surrender by a genuinely sympathetic approach, promising to give the fighting Boers every chance to surrender in order to end the war, and usher in an era of just and progressive government. He then issued a proclamation to the Boers still in the field, promising those burghers who surrendered voluntarily, that they could live with their families in government camps, until the end of the war permitted a safe return to their homes. He also promised proper protection for their property and stock, and that anything which had been requisitioned for official use, to be fairly paid for at current market prices. The details of the proclamation together with Kitchener's speech were immediately distributed far-and-wide and to speed things up the news was also disseminated in person by leading members of the Peace Committee who were sent into the Boer laagers in the field with details of the proposals.

In the Free State, Piet de Wet and Commandant S. G. Vilonel set up a movement of informers and guides called the" Orange River Colony Volunteers" Initially its members were not involved in active armed combat against the Boers but operated mainly as guides and intelligence service on behalf of the British army but towards the end of the war, however some did actually participate in a more direct and active fashion. In a letter to President Steyn on 11 January 1902, Commandant Vilonel wrote that the Boer 'bitter enders' were, in fact guilty of waging a 'civil war between the burghers'.

Predictably, their reception was harsh. Their comrades treated them as traitors and cowards condemned them 'in absentia' by court-martial to fines, imprisonment or even death. Sadly Kitchener, encouraged by the activities of the Peace Committee accepted further advice from them and by so doing he was to make one of the most calamitous decisions of the war. Acting on their advice he decided to turn an unofficial refugee policy into an officially declared civilian internment strategy in an attempt to hasten a rapid end to the war. The infamous 'scorched earth' policy, sporadically initiated by Roberts some six months earlier, had caused profound misgivings on humanitarian grounds, and even on question of the military value of such actions. So far, the devastation had been slight, but one of its incidental results had been that women and children in devastated farms faced starvation or molestation by marauding natives. Thus, together with ordinary refugees, swept along by the tides of war, for humanitarian reasons they had been confined by the British columns to informal extensions of their own military camps. Kitchener now decided to make this action official, and openly declared his new policy of rounding up women and children, and confining them to concentration camps, as a calculated and deliberate method of warfare. He clarified his reasons in a memorandum addressed, on December 21st, to his leading officers. – *'This course has been pointed out by surrendered Burghers who are anxious to finish the war, as the most effective method of limiting the endurance of the Guerrillas , as the men and women left on the farms, if disloyal, willingly supply the Burghers, and if loyal dare not refuse to do so.'*

So, now began the declared policy of systematically devastating the farms, and interning all women and children whose men-folk were on commando. Elementary considerations such as the suitability of camps set up solely for military use, or for the availability of doctors or sanitary staff, were simply overlooked. Apart from these mundane aspects, it was committing the army to a task far bigger and costlier than anyone remotely foresaw, and distracting them from their main task of defeating the Boers; for the burghers themselves, although they were now relieved from the burden of caring for their families, it also helped to fan their hatred and temper which would lead to the creation of most tragic and unforgivable consequences. Kitchener himself did not believe this policy to be unreasonable but his decision provided endless material for those intent on depicting him as some kind of monster This was unjust, because not only did he serve under Roberts with soldierly fidelity, but he had also shown an understanding regard for his enemies, and this had made him far more respected than Milner, and more admired than Roberts. The steely judgement of Jan Smuts was that Kitchener was basically a 'kindly man'. The fact remains however, that a combination of factors misled Kitchener into making a decision to which, under different auspices, he might have given deeper thought. It was, after all, a policy originated by his predecessor, and carrying the assurance of some of the burghers themselves that it would hasten the end of the war.

The War Continues – The Second 'De Wet Hunt'
At this time, the most menacing aspect for the British was De Wet's presence near Bethulie, close to the Orange River. Kitchener realised that the Boer menace could easily be turned into an advantage if it could be used to force De Wet into a corner. He called in his columns from far-and-wide to converge on the area in support of Knox. He then deployed some troops along the south bank of the Orange River and strengthened the guard on the railway between the Orange and Bloemfontein. He also strengthened the posts around Thaba 'Nchu, and positioned his troops in a huge semi-circular cordon into which he very much hoped that Knox would drive de Wet.

On the 2nd December, in pelting rain, De Wet and Herzog parted company in order to carry out their invasion to the southeast and the west respectively. De Wet disclosed his whereabouts by making an unsuccessful attack on one of the pursuing detachments, and then for 27 hours, he rode non-stop eastwards while his pursuers thought he was going north,. The rain-swollen Caledon River, flowing down from the Brandwater Basin to the Orange, lay across his path, but he managed to get over with great difficulty. He then rode on to find the ford through which he intended to cross the Orange itself, and when he finally arrived, he discovered that the waters had risen to an impassably high level and, to crown it all, the Coldstream Guards were lying in wait for him on the other side. De Wet was left with no other choice than to turn back north with his horses and his wagons. He left behind his two most daring commandants with a small force to carry out the invasion of the Cape whenever the opportunity offered. One was Scheepers, the other, also a Cape rebel, was Kritzinger, an equally bold and stalwart man. De Wet himself made away, the cordon closing in around him, but, although delayed by a handful of brave Highland Light Infantry at the Caledon, he managed to escape safely, only to find, when he tried to break through westwards, that the railway was bristling with troops. Then, twisting and turning, doubling back on his tracks, feinting first in this direction then that, he made his way northwards. Kitchener continued to pursue De Wet relentlessly, confident that he would eventually find himself trapped in the cordon of reinforcements posted around Thaba 'Nchu.

On their way northwards, the British found hundreds of exhausted and abandoned horses providing some indication that the hunt was telling as savagely on De Wet as it was on themselves. Relentlessly Knox shepherded De Wet towards Thaba 'Nchu, and as dawn broke on the 14th December, he saw, coming through a passage called Springhaans Nek, between the low hills in front of him, the glad sight of De Wet's great convoy. The British watched the Boer convoy heading straight for the line of fortified posts, and then let loose a sudden storm of artillery fire that caused the burghers to fall back in confusion. From the top of Thaba 'Nchu, a heliograph flashed the news back to Knox's columns far behind; at last the prospect of success seemed certain, and the columns spurred on their weary horses, and even as they did so, a Boer advance guard was already engaging part of the British line. General Piet Cronje now seized the chance offered by this distraction by placing himself at the head of the Boer convoy, De Wet bringing up the rear. He found a small gap in the British line where a minor post chanced to be unoccupied and he thrust forward his hundreds of men, animals and wagons in a tumultuous gallop, and while shells and bullets ripped through them from either side, he miraculously succeeded in getting clean away. Arriving at the scene, Knox's men were at their last gasp and quite incapable of further pursuit, and as they watched the clouds of dust settle over the horizon they knew, with despair, that the second hunt for De Wet had failed.

Although De Wet blamed himself for not carrying out his invasion plan, his action by drawing all the British attention upon himself did enable his lieutenants to cross the Orange. Kritzinger, by cutting up a troop of Brabant's Horse trying to stop him, entered the Cape on the 16th December with 700 burghers and rebels. On that same day, Herzog with a thousand men further to the west did likewise. These forces struck rapidly into the colony, and soon vital railway junctions, such as De Aar and Naauwpoort were once more in the news as the call to rebellion again rang through the Cape Midlands. Hastily, troops were diverted to halt the invasion and to guard the railways. Town militias assembled, martial law was imposed in 14 districts, and Kitchener himself came hurrying down to organise defence and offence. The Boers' kinsmen in the Cape were less ready than before to consider active revolt, but almost every farm served as a refuge and a source of supply. Meanwhile, the commandos steadily advanced – Herzog southwest beyond De Aar, and Kritzinger southwards beyond Naauwpoort.

Guerrilla Warfare in the Western Transvaal

Kitchener's first month of command in South Africa was not a happy one. Not only did he have his hands full with all the harassing events in the Orange Free State and the northern Cape, but he was blasted with a continuous stream of alarming signals emanating from the western Transvaal, where the Boers were inflicting serious damage on British garrisons and convoys in that region. These signals from the western Transvaal bothered Kitchener because until now no major threats had been expected from that area. After Roberts's occupation of Pretoria, the western Transvaal had been relatively quiet, because the bulk of the more active burghers had left to fight with Botha's commandos on the eastern Transvaal and northern Natal fronts. Moreover, a large number, not wishing to leave their families and farms alone, had stayed behind, surrendered their arms, and signed the oath of neutrality. The overall effect of these events had left the western Transvaal relatively peaceful, and ostensibly in full command of the British. Now the news was out that De la Rey was back, and with him his 'young lions' – a new generation of young, daring and innovative fighters, unfettered by convention and hungry for independent command. Leaders such as Kemp, Beyers, Lemmer, Celliers, Van Zijl and Smuts, relishing combat in the style of their mentor, De la Rey, scanned the western Transvaal plains, and wrought havoc amongst their British counterparts.

Broadly speaking, the western Transvaal is a vast region lying to the west of the Pretoria-Johannesburg-Vereeniging railway line, reaching for more than 150 miles to the Mafeking-Kimberley railway. The southern perimeter is bounded by the Vaal River from Vereeniging to beyond Christiana, and the northern boundary is dominated by a group of three parallel ridges of the Magaliesberg, reaching due west from Pretoria to Rustenburg and beyond. The greater part of the area between the Magaliesberg and the Vaal is a fertile plateau of drab, flat landscape, with rolling grassland, dotted here and there by small clusters of hills. In a line stretching some thirty miles due east and west of Johannesburg rises the gold-rich Witwatersrand ridge, breaking the flatness of the mid-eastern end of the western Transvaal.

The principal British garrison in the western Transvaal was at Rustenburg, an important settlement about halfway along the strategic wagon road between Pretoria and Mafeking, 180 miles to the west. The Magaliesberg dominated this vital link with the west, as well as other access roads from Pretoria to half-a-dozen lesser British garrison towns to the west and southwest of Pretoria. Farther south, the hills of the Gatsrand straddle road and railway links between Pretoria via Krugersdorp, to Potchefstroom, Klerksdorp and on to Kimberley. South of the Gatsrand, in the Vredefort area, the Vaal River meanders through undulating countryside bordered by low hills in the vicinity of Potchefstroom and Hartebeestfontein, near Klerksdorp.

Immediately after the meeting with Botha at Balmoral, in the Eastern Transvaal, De la Rey sent two of his crack lieutenants, Generals H. R. Lemmer and Sarel Oosthuizen, into the western Transvaal on a covert mission to resuscitate the moribund western commandos, and to stir the burghers there back into action. Both men were apt choices for this crucial and difficult assignment, Lemmer having fought with De la Rey at Kraaipan and Colesburg, and Oosthuizen in the Thukela battles, and around Johanneburg. In response to favourable reports from Lemmer and Oosthuizen, De la Rey moved into the western Transvaal with the rest of his force, and positioned the commandos in various critical locations specifically allotted to his new 'vecht-generaals' - combat generals, with himself in overall command. General Kemp was set up to the east and south of the Magaliesberg, in the Krugersdorp, Rustenburg, Swartruggens and Ventersdorp regions, while Celliers and Lemmer operated in the Lichtenburg, Marico and West-Swartruggens areas. To the south of them, Du Toit commanded the area around Wolmaransstad, Bloemhof and Christiana, and Klerksdorp and Potchefstroom were under the command of Liebenberg. Still further east, in the Gatsrand area, Smuts, who also acted as De la Rey's legal counsellor, took command, and finally, Van Zijl commanded the Griqualand-West rebels in the extreme far west.

The entire terrain offered good cover and opportunity for the stalking commandos to disrupt military traffic and harass enemy columns and patrols at every conceivable moment, and it was in this way that the very first significant encounter occurred, on the 10th July, 1900 immediately after De la Rey's arrival in the area from the eastern Transvaal. He gathered his commandos on the northern side of the Magaliesberg, near the entrance to Silikaatsnek, one of the many passes through the range. On his arrival, he learnt that the south entrance to the pass was guarded by a squadron of the Scots Greys under the command of Lt. Col. W. P. Alexander. A second squadron of Greys was guarding another pass further down called Olifantsnek Pass, whilst a third squadron was posted some three miles away at the Crocodile River Bridge where Alexander had his headquarters. It so happened that on the very day of De la Rey's arrival, the Scots Greys were in the process of being relieved by five under-strength companies of the Lincolns under the command of Col. H. R. Roberts, and both units were resting overnight in the pass.

Silikaatsnek Pass consists of a natural break in the Magaliesberg, at the centre of which is a boulder-strewn koppie. On either side of the pass are high flat shoulders, forming part of the range of hills. The British defenders were bivouacked about a third of the way up these shoulders with those troops who were due to move out the following day, placed under the koppie. The guns were set up in the dip between the two shoulders, and had a restricted field of fire. Early in the morning of the 11th July De la Rey sent two climbing parties, each about 200 strong, to overlook both shoulders along high ground on either side of the summits, directly above the troops encamped on the ledges below. The eastern party reached its destination at about 5.30 a.m., and around the same time, De la Rey himself launched a frontal attack on the koppie. However, the western climbing party was late to arrive and this gave colonel Roberts a chance to send more troops up the western shoulder to face the Boer attackers. As a result, the Boers were unable to take the guns immediately, but later, after the arrival of the delayed climbers, they succeeded in capturing the guns and driving the British off the western shoulder, and finally in surrounding the koppie. At the end of the day, the British, after a gallant defence, and sustaining 72 serious casualties, found their situation quite hopeless and finally surrendered with 189 men. The Boer casualties were also relatively heavy, and included two of De la Rey's adjutants lost during the capture of the guns. On that same day, in another sector south of the Magaliesberg, Sarel Oosthuizen, one of De la Rey's best lieutenants, was mortally wounded on his own farm at Dwarsvlei, during an action against a column of 800 British troops under the command of General Smith-Dorrien.

The incident at Silikaatsnek heralded the outbreak of a new type of guerrilla warfare in the western Transvaal, which continued over the course of the next year-and-a-half. The many hit-and-run encounters that ensued, would in the long-run serve to inflict maximum inconvenience on the British, and help in addition to maintain a high morale among the Boers, fuelled especially by the topping up their supply of arms, ammunition and equipment at the expense of the captured British stores. In a bid to strengthen the western Magaliesberg region, Baden-Powell had been elevated to the rank of Major General with particular responsibility for the Rustenburg area. To maintain the security of the road communications between Rustenburg and Mafeking, Baden-Powell appointed Lt. Col. C.O. Hore, who had been with him throughout the siege of Mafeking, to command a small post at the Elands River, just south of the road from Rustenburg to Zeerust. The post consisted of a force of about 300 Australians and 200 Rhodesians. Its only guns were a muzzle-loading 7-pdr and two maxims. Col. Hore established his main camp and H.Q. on a farm named Brakfontein, and was well positioned on a small boulder-strewn koppie about half-a-mile west of Elands River, and surrounded by open country. Most of the men occupied the koppie itself, but some detachments held two small hills on the bank of the river.

On the 3rd August, a convoy of eighty wagons had arrived from Zeerust, and was awaiting an escort to take it on to Rustenburg. That night De la Rey surrounded the post with a force of 800 burghers, which he subsequently increased to at least 2,000 men. At dawn on the 4th, he launched an intense artillery bombardment on the British positions, and destroyed around 1,000 of Hore's transport animals. In spite of this barrage, and the failure of a rescue attempt from Zeerust by General Carrington, Hore held out gallantly for four days. On the 7th August, De la Rey made an offer to Hore to surrender which he refused. Hore then continued to hold out until De la Rey eventually withdrew his fire when Col. Walter Kitchener arrived on the 16th August.

During the remainder of August De la Rey quietly set about establishing strategic Boer forces in every part of the western Transvaal, the most important of them being the Lichtenburg and Marico commandos under Gen. Lemmer, the Bloemhof commando under Commandant Tollie De Beer, Wolmaransstad under commandant Potgieter and Potchefstroom under Gen. Liebenberg. Command of the Rustenburg and Krugersdorp commandos he kept for himself. At the end of November 1900, the nearest British forces to De la Rey's own commandos were those garrisoned under Brigadier-Generals R.G. Broadwood at Olifantsnek and G.G. Cunningham in Krugersdorp. On the 2nd December 1900, a fully laden convoy of 260 wagons left Pretoria for Rustenburg, and after crossing the Magaliesberg at Breedtsnek, about fifteen miles from Olifantsnek, it approached a spot called Buffelspoort where De la Rey and Smuts lay in wait with about 800 men. The convoy, which extended for about eight miles, was divided into two equal sections each escorted by a force of about 250 men. De la Rey attacked the leading half of the convoy around 5 a.m. Its escort, commanded by Maj. J.G. Wolridge-Gorton, seized two koppies, one on either side of the road. The higher southern koppie, was the more lightly defended, and fell to the Boers around 1 p.m. Despite some vigorous resistance by Wolridge-Gorton on the northern koppie, by nightfall De la Rey had successfully captured 126 wagons. He then hastily beat a retreat to the south of the Magaliesberg by way of Breedtsnek, before any British relieving forces could arrive.

After the Buffelspoort incident, De la Rey was joined by three of the most able of his younger commanders, General Christiaan Friedrich Beyers, thirty-one years old, and Commandants Greyling and Kemp. Beyers had been in charge of operations in the northern Transvaal, but since things were very quiet in that area, he moved south to assist De la Rey in the southwest. On his way Beyers's force was reinforced by Kemp and his Krugersdorp commando, which included the Pretoria District commando led by commandant Badenhorst and 200 Scouts under commandant Lodi Krause, a young lawyer who like Smuts, had been at both Stellenbosch and Cambridge universities. On arrival in the Magaliesberg area, Beyers discovered that Broadwood's cavalry brigade was actively operating in that region. In an attempt to by-pass the British, Beyers mounted a feint attack on Rustenburg thereby luring Broadwood into a post-haste chase in that direction, while he quietly swung south and crossed over the Magaliesberg during the night of the 11th December by way of the old wagon track through Breedtsnek. He then joined up with De la Rey the following day.

When he met De la Rey, Beyers was pleased to learn that the Boers were lying in wait for General R .A. P. Clements, encamped at Nooitgedacht, about five miles away to the east. Nooitgedacht lay under a steep southern face of the Magaliesberg, which, at that point, rises to about 1,000 ft above the valley floor. Clements commanded a force of 1,500 men with nine guns and a pom-pom. Behind him, in a wooded gorge, was a stream which provided water for his men and his animals. A further advantage was a track leading through the gorge up to the crest of the mountain from which he could communicate by heliograph with Broadwood. On the downside however, the site was dominated by great and ominous crags on either side of the gorge – a fact that made Smuts comment on Clements' choice of bivouac *'I do not think it was possible to have selected a more fatal spot in the entire Magaliesberg for a camp.'* It was agreed that Beyers would attack Clements from the Magaliesberg side, both along the top and from along southern slope from the west, whilst De la Rey would attack along the valley from the west directly against the camp itself. Some burghers positioned themselves in the southwest area in order to cut of Clement's possible retreat.

In the early hours of the 13th December, Beyers led a small force up the mountain, leaving Badenhorst to attack along the southern slope. He also posted a further contingent at Breedtsnek to watch out for Broadwood. Beyers himself, with Van Staden's Waterberg commando and Krause's Scouts, moved to deal with the British pickets on the western crest above the camp, while Kemp and Ernst Marais took their commandos along the longer route to the eastern crest. However, before any of them were ready to launch an assault from the top, Badenhorst attacked prematurely from the west at about 3.40 a.m. and was repelled by Clements's MI with heavy loss. Beyers' men opened up their attack on the western crest at about 4.25, followed later by Kemp and Marais on the eastern crest. Soon the out-numbered British defenders were overwhelmed, and as their reinforcements attempted to come up along the track through the gorge, they were decimated by fierce Boer fire. By 7 a.m., the mountain was in Boer hands, with Clements's heliograph captured. A Boer heliographer, in reply to Broadwood's request to send assistance, signalled to assure him that the situation was under control and that no help was required. Realising the precariousness of his situation, Clements left his guns behind and withdrew his troops to Vaal Kop, also known as Yeomanry Hill, two miles to the east. Here he ran into the advance groups of De la Rey's men, and finally realising that all was lost, he moved on to Rietfontein, 23 miles away in the direction of Pretoria. He only managed to escape because the burghers, instead of giving chase and annihilating the retreating British, busied themselves with looting the abandoned British camp instead. At the end of the day the total number of British losses amounted to 628 including 74 dead, 186 wounded and 368 prisoners lost or missing. The Boer losses were about 100, mostly from Badenhorst's commando.

At the end of 1900, De la Rey sent Smuts with a thousand men to the Gatsrand- the fifty five mile ridge lying between Potchefstroom and Johannesburg, where he hoped he could unite dissident elements in the Potchefstroom commando. On the 31st January, 1901 after an engagement lasting forty-four hours, Smuts captured the British post at Modderfontein. By the 1st March, he was back gain operating with De la Rey whom he assisted in an attack on Lichtenburg, De la Rey's home town. General J. G. Celliers was also present at the Lichtenburg raid, giving the Boers' a combined force of 1,200 burghers and one gun. The defending British force commanded by Lt. Col. C, G. E. Mooney, totalled 620 men. De la Rey surrounded the town during the night of the 2nd March, and the next day he succeeded in penetrating the outer defences. In spite of this initial success, he was unable to capture the town, and was forced to fall back after twenty-four hours, during which time Celliers fell badly wounded, and his men were slso obliged to withdraw from the attack. During the retreat, many of the retiring Boers lost their way in the marshy fields around the town and had to lie in hiding in the muddy earth among the reeds during the entire sweltering 5th of March until they were able to make good their escape during that night. De la Rey left behind fourteen dead and forty wounded, together with some prisoners. The British casualties were very much the same, fourteen killed and twenty-four wounded.

Beyers and Kemp left the western Transvaal at the beginning of 1901 and operated briefly together to the east of Johannesburg. In early February, Beyers took the Waterberg and Zoutpansberg commando back to the northern Transvaal, while Kemp rejoined De la Rey in the west, taking the Krugersdorp commando back to its own district. At the age of twenty-eight, he was made a general, and in that capacity served in the western Transvaal for the remainder of the war. Given the task of rounding up inactive Boers south of the Magaliesberg he had by the end of May 1901, a force of 3,000 men with him at Tafelkop, a small plateau on the southern side of the Witwatersrand, about thirty-five miles south-west of Rustenburg.

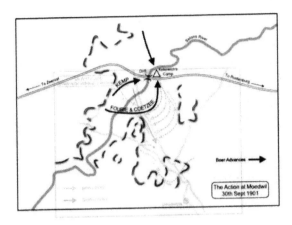

The Action at Moedwil
30th Sept 1901

Boer Advances ➜

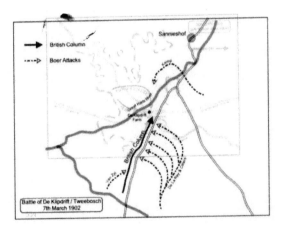

➜ British Column

----➤ Boer Attacks

Sannieshof

Battle of De Klipdrift / Tweebosch
7th March 1902

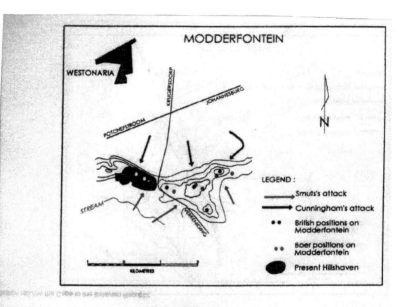

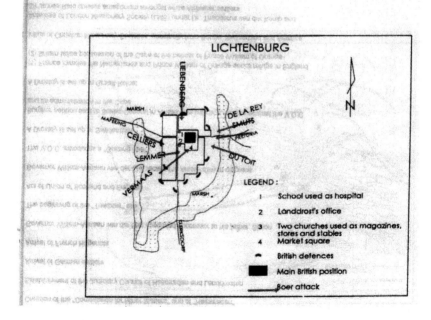

The incidence of regular short, sharp, in and out attacks on British convoys continued throughout the ensuing months. On the 29th May 1901 Beyers attacked a small British force under Brig. Gen. H. G. Dixon at Vlakfontein, about seventeen miles east of Tafelkop. Under cover of smoke from a veld-fire, the mounted Boers charged down on part of the force commanded by Major H. Chance and captured its guns. In a vigorous counter-attack, Dixon recaptured both guns and the ground that Chance had been defending. Another noteworthy encounter occurred on the 30ᵗʰ September 1901. On this occasion, Kemp assisted De la Rey in an attack on a force of 800 men under Col. R.H. Kekewich, commanding officer in Kimberley during the siege, at Moedwil, seven miles east of Magato Nek on the east bank of the Selons River. De la Rey had been stalking the British column for a week, and had assembled a force of 1,000 men by the time he camped at Moedwil. Attacking from the river before daylight, De la Rey's men fired on the camp, causing the horses to stampede. Kekewich was twice wounded in the engagement, but Major R.A. Browne, his second-in-command, dispersed the Boers on the riverbank with a determined bayonet charge. In addition to De la Rey's own attack, the planned supporting assaults from other sectors also miscarried, and the Boers were obliged to withdraw. Kekewich's losses amounted to about 200 men, and the Boer's losses were not stated, but were probably in the region of 50 killed or wounded.

This pattern of initial success followed by failure repeated itself when De la Rey, with Kemp and Steenkamp, attacked a column led by Lt. Col. S.B. von Donop at Kleinfontein, twenty miles east of Zeerust on the 4ᵗʰ October. The 1,000-strong column with seven guns and a hundred mule-wagons was travelling along a road fringed with bush, and dominated by thickly timbered heights, when De la Rey's 500 men charged down on it. They cut through the wagon train in three places, inflicting heavy casualties on the mule teams, the gun detachments and the rear-guard. Von Donop, however, counter-attacked and was able to save his guns and most of the convoy, leaving the Boers with only twelve wagons as the prize for this action.

By the end of November 1901, De la Rey was finding it harder and harder to maintain an active fighting force in the western Transvaal, due to an increasing shortage of man-power, horses and ammunition, and from now, apart from a few minor incidents, he laid low. But, it was not only in the western Transvaal that the guerrilla war was being conducted, with devastating results for both the Boers and the British. On a number of other fronts in the Free State, the Cape Colony and particularly in the eastern Transvaal, almost daily occurrences and encounters between the British and Boer forces occurred. In the eastern Transvaal a number of minor actions, during the early part of 1901, served pertinent notice on Kitchener that the war in the east was far from over. For example,this was overtly demonstrated on the 9ᵗʰ December 1900 by General Viljoen's attack on a British post at Helvetia, south of Lydenburg, resulting in the capture of 250 men and a 4.7inch gun. Ten days later Botha and Viljoen together launched similar and successful attacks on British forces in Belfast, Machadadorp, and other stations on the Delagoa Bay railway.

At this time, Botha nurtured a hope to invade Natal, but his plans were thwarted by Kitchener's first 'grand drive', launched on the 27th January 1901 Botha responded, in the small hours of the 6th February by carrying out a daring attack with 2,000 burghers on Smith-Dorrien's camp near Lake Chrissie, north of Ermelo, penetrating the outer defences by sending back stampeding British horses. Although this attack was eventually repelled, Botha and most of his men escaped, as did the other commandos left behind by to cover the eastward flight of civilians.

Regardless of all the action and counter-action in the eastern Transvaal during this period, it was becoming very clear to Kitchener that there could be no positive outcome to the situation solely with the use of arms, and that some other methods were needed to resolve the problem. He sent word to Botha, through his wife, Annie, requesting a meeting to discuss terms for peace, but only on the clear understanding that the question of independence of the two Boer republics was not on the agenda. Botha, also at the end of his wits, not surprisingly accepted the invitation with alacrity, and a conference was organised to take place at Middelburg on the 28th February 1901. The meeting, attended by Botha, Kitchener and Milner, ended unsatisfactorily and in disagreement, caused mainly by Milner's intransigent determination to negate any tentative attempts at a settlement that did not include the absolute capitulation of all the Boer forces in South Africa. Kitchener, on the other hand for purely military reasons, earnestly strived to reach a more equitable settlement, but his efforts sadly came to nought, once again mainly as a result of Milner's opposition, and London's failure to grasp even then, the gravity of the British military situation in South Africa.

Initially, Kitchener had presented Botha with a 10-point plan namely:
- amnesty for all bona-fide acts of war
- return of prisoners of war
- the two 'new colonies' to be governed, at first as 'Crown Colonies' but 'as soon as circumstances permitted' to be granted self-government
- the use of both Dutch and English languages in schools and law-courts
- Dutch Reformed Church properties to be respected
- payment of all legal debts of the State
- compensation to farmers for loss of horses
- no war indemnity for farmers
- licences for certain burghers to keep their rifles, and finally,
- no franchise to 'Kaffirs' in the Transvaal and the Orange Free State before a representative Government was accorded to the those two 'colonies'.

In the event the British Government, supported by recommendations from Milner, rebuffed the first and the last points, which as it turned out, were in fact the very ones that the Boers had originally rejected outright. When Botha rejoined his government-in-hiding between Piet Retief and Ermelo he was informed that in his absence, Viljoen had accomplished very little, while the British had done a great number of successful things. In fact, a column led by Colonel Benson had succeeded in conducting a number of brilliant night raids south of Carolina, and was becoming a regular scourge to the Boers, who could only mange to avoid disaster by never laagering two nights in succession at the same place, and by saddling-up and beating a retreat before 3 a.m. each day. Botha earnestly set about re-establishing the Boer initiative in the eastern Transvaal, making Kitchener as determined as ever to capture him and put him out of the way. He sent for Rimington and other reinforcements from the Free State, to assist Benson in tracking down Botha and harassing him on every possible occasion. Soon Benson's persistence started showing good effect, and one dawn, following the capture of a dispatch disclosing Botha's whereabouts, the British so nearly cornered him that he barely managed to escape with his son and a handful of followers, forcing him in the panic, to leave behind his hat and a bag-full of correspondence.

In spite of Benson's success against Botha in the eastern Transvaal, Kitchener remained beset by immense problems all around him. In the political arena, Milner and the Colonial Office in London refused to face the gravity of the overall military situation in South Africa, regardless of Kitchener's pleas. In the western Transvaal, De la Rey continued to create havoc wherever and whenever he struck, whilst deep in the Cape Province, roving commandos operated actively against the British in different locations over a vast area of several thousands of square miles. At the same time, in the Free State, De Wet continued to maraud the British convoys and garrisons to such an extent that Kitchener was forced to recall Rimington and his reinforcements from the eastern Transvaal to assist in his new 'grand hunt' for De Wet.

This left Benson on his own once again, this time to face a Botha determined to put the British forces in their place as soon as possible, and with Benson equally set to rid the area of Botha and his commandos, it was inevitable that a major showdown would shortly ensue. Benson set about refitting his force on the Natal railway, and when he was ready, he started ranging abroad again. In due course he set off for Bethal with some 800 horsemen, while leaving about 600 infantrymen to guard his convoy of 350 vehicles. When he arrived near Bethal, his supplies were beginning to run out, and he was obliged to halt a while in order to replenish his stocks. He decided to encamp in the open grassland of the Transvaal highveld, close to Botha's erstwhile headquarters at Balmoral, situated on the Pretoria-Delagao Bay railway line. While the column was moving into position, a party of Boers, closely stalking behind, started harrying it. The order to out-span was given with urgency, and soon, while the column was still strung out along the road, the rear-guard became aware that, in the surrounding mist, the size of the enemy's force had increased vastly, and was looming dangerously close-by.

The fact was that Botha had just arrived on the scene with formidable reinforcements. Such was his speed, secrecy and timing that the British scouts and patrols had failed to spot and report him. It was only when Col. Benson himself joined the rearguard an hour or two later that they became fully aware of the extent of their danger, He immediately ordered the rearguard to retreat to some rising ground half-way back on the road to the camp. The rise was named 'Gun Hill' because two guns had been placed there previously to cover the convoy, and with groups of men scattered around on either flank it formed part of a wide but discontinuous defence arc between the main camp and the Boers.

In the face of the Boer onslaught, Benson and his men fell back. The Boers then galloped out of the mist and charged from several directions into The Buffs, Scottish Rifles and the MI as they converged on the dead ground below Gun Hill. Throwing themselves off their ponies, the burghers then rushed forward on foot, firing into a mass of Benson's soldiers as they fled across the bare veld. Minutes later, entire British gun crews were wiped out, and as officer after officer fell about him Benson, himself wounded in the knee, crawled among the ant-hills, encouraging his men. Conducting himself with great bravery, he was wounded twice again, the last wound proving to be the fatal one. The Boers eventually stormed forward, four or five deep, and overran the British position, leaving behind them, either dead or wounded, 161 of the 178 men who fought with Benson.

At nightfall the Boers removed the guns and allowed the British to take away their wounded. Benson, after being carried back to camp, refused help from the doctors because he believed that their services were more urgently required elsewhere. Then, after conferring his command on Woolls-Sampson and giving him instructions for the defence of the camp, the gallant Benson laid back and died. The British column, having suffered a crippling defeat and 358 casualties, including the death of their commanding officer, was paralysed and entirely at the mercy of its enemy. However, even when it was in his power to wipe out the entire British force, Botha, himself having lost over 100 of his own men, sickened by the sight of such carnage, decided to content himself with his victory, and held his men back from any further needless slaughter. The battle that took place on that day would take its name from a nearby farm called Bakenlaagte, and would go down as one of the worst defeats suffered by the British army throughout its entire campaign in the eastern Transvaal.

The succession of British disasters which marked the closing months of 1901 were such that any detached observer could well have wondered what exactly all that wasteful expenditure of thousands of casualties and millions of pounds had achieved. The guerrilla war, during the very last month of the year alone, exacted as many casualties as those in the combined battles of Black Week the previous December. Even then, the futility of it all did not end there, because, even as the British were taking stock of the overall situation at the end of 1901, the Cape was once again under invasion and threat of rebellion. Moreover, the Transvaal and Free State were more under the control of the Boers than the British, and the Boers were no further from being 'crushed' or 'defeated' as the British were of winning the war, as had been claimed by Roberts on the eve of his departure a year earlier.

What had been increasingly obvious had by now become a stark fact – neither the Boers nor the British were going to 'win this war', nor was either prepared to 'lose' it. A situation of stalemate had been reached, and like two bare-fisted pugilists, the antagonists were slugging it out, blow by blow, until both would eventually drop, side by side, totally spent and near ruination. Even the Boers themselves had begun to realise that they would never win the war, yet they continued to be just as determined not to give in. In the same way, it was now dawning on the British that they were never going to 'defeat' the Boers in this bitter and costly struggle, in which logistically, they were destined to succeed. Yet, even as both parties determined to continue the conflict until the 'bitter-end', it was dawning on the principal characters in this 'no win - no lose' drama that the only means to end it all would be by way of the conference table. Botha, De la Rey, Smuts on the one hand, Kitchener, even Milner and a few in Westminster on the other, each now saw in his own way, the imperative to seek a negotiated end to this pointless devastation.

Into The Third Year and The Struggle Continues..

As the third year of the war began, the picture was as depressing as ever. Huge areas of the country lay silent and bare, and every fold in the vast veld was a snare for the British and safe cover for the Boers. Even in the protected zone of Johannesburg-Pretoria, the British constantly needed to be on the alert against sudden attacks by the nearby commandos. While their two Boer Republican Governments roamed the country in constant but unchecked flight, their three foremost generals, Botha, De la Rey and De Wet, remained as unscathed as did their subordinate commanders from Herzog in the southwest to Viljoen in the northeast. At the same time, Smuts and other Boer generals kept the Cape smouldering under the constant threat of a general uprising. It was a worrying time for Kitchener. He was concerned over the fact that his costly 'spring drives' had produced little effect on the strength and activities of the Boer commandos. He was also aware pf the fact in the course of numerous engagements and minor skirmishes with the Boer guerrillas since Bergendal, the British losses had amounted to over 1,500 men against the Boers' 450.

In Britain too, a deep gloom prevailed in the Colonial and War Offices. On the one hand, there was anger and concern over accusations that the Boers were committing terrible atrocities, such as the use of illegal 'dum-dum', or 'scored' ammunition, and the killing of troops after they had raised the white flag of surrender. On the other hand, there was genuine horror over the tragedy of the concentration camps, compounded by heartfelt resentment in some quarters that the British taxpayer was providing the means to support the enemy's women and children in the camps. There was also protest against the many Boers who had surrendered and then betrayed their oaths of neutrality. Indeed many believed that the British taxpayer was in fact, having to bear the cost of the entire war on behalf of both sides in the conflict. Dissatisfaction with the War Office, rising steadily since the aftermath of Black Week, now reached a crescendo. The Times, normally a supporter of the government, led a revolt indicting the War Office for 'inefficiency'. In addition, public dismay gained no comfort from the knowledge that Kitchener was complaining that many of the mounted reinforcements sent out from England could neither ride nor shoot, and that their officers were under-equipped with military prowess, but overloaded with personal perks such as 'kitchen ranges, pianos and even harmoniums'.

There were complaints and accusations against Kithchener as well. He was accused of being exhausted, and needing to be replaced. He was also criticised for his complaints against the War Office's policies in respect of the reorganisation of the transport and intelligence services, and particularly against his defeatist attitude that 'some sort of peace' be made with the Boers. In one respect, Kitchener's critics were right. He did believe that now a negotiated peace was the only way to end the war satisfactorily for both the British and the Boers. Chamberlain, however, had other ideas. He wanted a substantial extension of the protected zones around Johannesburg and Pretoria for purposes of building and providing facilities for larger numbers of prospective British and Commonwealth immigrants. In addition, he wanted more than anything for the Boer leaders to be hunted down and destroyed. He believed that the forces under Rimington and other officers currently engaged in this task were not sufficient, and wanted the whole army to concentrate on this task to the exclusion of all else. He urged the use of selected columns of one to two thousand men each, supported by paid Native scouts, whose role was to gather information and act as spies. Above all, every effort had to be made to concentrate on Botha, Steyn, and the other senior Boer generals, until they were all captured and the war ended. Kitchener resented Chamberlain's discontentment and interference, and he offered to resign and requested a transfer to India. His request was refused, and it was with that rebuff that he entered into what would become the very last round of the conflict.

Blockhouses, Drives and Concentration Camps.
Goaded by Chamberlain's caustic comments and Milner's criticism, Kitchener was now fired into devising a radical strategy to round up the Boer Commandos, drive them into a vast snare, and when once securely enclosed, to eliminate them as a fighting force. He would cordon off enormous sections of the open plains of the Free State and Transvaal highveld with hundreds of round iron cylinders fitted with A-shaped roof shelters. Each would be within sight of another and manned by seven soldiers. They would be linked with a fence of barbed wire strands, from which hung trip-alarms and pebble-filled tin cans. The plan would then be to drive the Boers into these blockhouse lines, round them up and destroy them. In a short time, 10,000 of these iron cylinders or blockhouses, were erected and strung together in a close pattern across 5,000 miles of South African veld. The inhabitants of each blockhouse kept tight vigilance during the sweltering heat of the day and the bitter cold of the night, making it seemingly impossible for the Boer commandos to escape from its net. In the beginning, the project took off to a slow start but soon a massive blockhouse-network was completed. The two main north-south blockhouse lines lay along the western and the central railways, and further lines were built to cover the areas in between the two railway lines. In agreement with Chamberlain's wishes, Kitchener extended the protection zone around the Johannesburg-Pretoria area from 60 to 120 miles, and following the reinforcement of the protection zone around Johannesburg, the mines were once again able to operate normally, and as a result, they were able to increase their output of gold dramatically. Milner, the British High Commissioner used a portion of the increased revenue from the gold mines to finance the extension of Kitchener' blockhouse patterns across the entire country, even as far as the eastern Free State, the eastern Transvaal, the western Cape and northern Natal.

The Boers who found themselves outside the protected zones remained undaunted, and continued to harass the British with un-relaxed vigour. On the British side, a steady stream of reinforcements was by now arriving in South Africa from Britain, Australia, New Zealand, Canada, and the rest of the Empire in general, thus adding a further 20,000 men to Kitchener's existing compliment of 240,000 men. Ian Hamilton returned to South Africa as Chief-of-Staff to lighten Kitchener's burden of responsibility. Kitchener also had an extra-ordinary and totally unexpected offer of support from the

Boers themselves. After the disastrous failure of the Burghers' Peace Committee's efforts to incite their fellow burghers to lay down their arms and surrender, some of the more influential survivors now proposed to raise a force among their already captured or surrendered countrymen, to fight on the British side. In their sincere belief that their country was conquered, and that the prolongation of war would be a futile tragedy for their nation, they raised a voluntary corps to support the British in their fight against their own people. In the Transvaal, the voluntary corps was named the National Scouts, and in the Free State, it was known as the Orange River Colony Volunteers (ORC Volunteers). Amongst some of the more prominent members of the corps were General A.P. Cronje, captured at Reitz the very night of President Steyn's narrow escape, and General Piet de Wet, Christiaan de Wet's brother. At first, the volunteers received remuneration out of the spoils of captured loot, and gifts from the British administration. Later they received regular payments in addition to awards for social services. Other inducements included privileged treatment of recruits' families in concentration camps, a particularly powerful incentive for the strong family-bound Boer

Conditions in the civilian concentration camps were appalling. In January 1901, Emily Hobhouse, an influential philanthropist, armed with letters of introduction from several leading Liberal members of parliament in England, arrived in South Africa to undertake an inspection tour of the civilian concentration camps. After a thorough investigation, she returned to England with several damning reports of Boer women and children suffering misery and neglect from epidemics and starvation in the camps. She had set out to conduct a dedicated mission to 'waken the conscience of England', and her active agitation had a profound effect throughout the land. As a result of Emily Hobhouse's campaigning, the government appointed the Fawcett Commission, a Committee of Ladies to undertake an official four-month tour of inspection of all the civilian concentration camps in South Africa, and to provide parliament with an official report of their findings. When the Committee of Ladies returned to London four months later, they confirmed all of Emily Hobhouse's findings, and submitted a list of recommendations for urgent action to rectify the situation. As a first priority, the Committee urged the immediate despatch of trained nurses and medical orderlies, together with medical supplies, food and blankets.

Kitchener's priorities at this time lay elsewhere. He needed to exert all his energies and expertise against Botha, De la Rey and De Wet. The protected zone around Johannesburg had cut De la Rey off from the others, and Kitchener grasped the opportunity to leave the western Transvaal alone for the time being, and to concentrate on Botha and De Wet, in the eastern Transvaal and the northern Free State respectively. He determined to employ simultaneously, the two distinct techniques so far utilised, namely the multi-column drive and the single column drive, the former against De Wet and the latter against Botha. By early November, Kitchener had a striking force of 30,000 men ready, well mounted, well equipped, and eager to go forward. He split them into two halves, one for each theatre, and set them loose on the Boers.

Continuing Action in the Eastern Transvaal

In the eastern Transvaal, the Constabulary line, which marked the eastern limit of the protected zone, was pushed still further east. By the 16th November, Kitchener had succeeded in extending it several miles beyond Balmoral on the Delagoa Bay railway, and also across country to near Standerton on the Natal railway. With the blockhouses along the railways themselves, and from Volksrust to Piet Retief in the far southeast, a vast barrier was thus created throughout the whole highveld west of Swaziland. On the 3rd December, the British overran the key centre of Ermelo, enabling Kitchener to construct a further line of blockhouses from Ermelo to Standerton. He then extended this new line northward towards Carolina and beyond to link up with Delagoa Bay Railway and in so doing it cut the highveld into two.

To the Boers, the ominous intent of these moves was clear enough even without the reports of innumerable columns preparing to scour the spaces so confined. With a small escort, Botha hurried the Republican Government northeast to Carolina. The northern-most of the advancing columns were close, and before him stood the blockhouses along the railway. He skilfully feinted and cut the wire entanglements at an unexpected point, and on the 3rd December, the entire party successfully dashed through under fierce crossfire. The Government group then made for the mountains east of Lydenburg while Botha hastened back to the vicinity of Ermelo. For the next two months, the Boers and the British played a frantic game of hide-and-seek, mainly between the meridian of Ermelo and the Swazi border. Compared with their situation during the first great drive under French nearly a year before, the Boers had the advantage of being uncluttered with refugees but many had no horses, and the land was impoverished. Besides, the British troops were now more seasoned, and were able to draw on an endless stream of fresh men and horses. The blockhouses provided a secondary, but equally important function of protecting supply lines, so that the columns themselves were now no longer impeded with cumbersome wagon trains.

Colonel Benson, who had been killed at nearby Bakenlaagte nearly a year ago, had perfected a tactic of energetic night marches, and this tradition was now being perpetuated by his one-time Intelligence Officer, Col. Woolls-Sampson, attached to the General leading the main raiding column in that area. Sampson's headman was a surrendered Boer, who controlled a number of skilful Boer guides, and also a Native spy in every kraal. Soon a successful tactic was perfected whereby several trained Native scouts would ride out each evening to visit the kraals. In the morning, they would report to Sampson, and a target for attack would be selected. Columns would then set out at night, guns situated in the centre in order to muffle the noise of their wheels, and ride up to forty miles in the dark to arrive at their target destination at dawn to thrust home their attack. Throughout December and January, fourteen such raids were undertaken, resulting in Boer losses of over 700 burghers as well as costly supplies and war materials. By contrast, British daytime operations were less successful, as the Boers had perfected new ambush tactics. Small detachments of burghers would be sent out to decoy the British, who would then be set upon by commandos waiting in concealment. In this way, a MI unit lost 135 men south of Ermelo, and further to the south-west, a party of New Zealanders was overwhelmed a fortnight later. On the 4th January, a British unit charged on fifty Boers on a hill east of Ermelo, but it was overwhelmed by a counter-attack that exacted over 130 British casualties in a bitter twenty-minute fight.

By mid February, the campaign had reached a stalemate, as neither night raids nor daylight sweeps could winkle out the Boer commandos. However, by now, the British had succeeded in splitting Botha's force into widely scattered bands, and he began to realise that the game was up for the time being at least. He could find no satisfactory answers to requests from the burghers to give good reason for continuing the war, and and after the completion of the blockhouse grid, communications became so precarious that it was almost impossible to muster any sizable force to face the British columns. As a result, Botha decided to quit the highveld. He gathered some 500 men and rode into Swaziland and then southwards, and by outflanking the Volksrust-Piet Retief line of blockhouses, he finally reached the mountainous area around Vryheid.

With Botha's departure, the eastern Transvaal largely disappeared from the scene, but the fortunes of the two groups which had broken away during the early days of the summer campaign needs mentioning. They were Piet Viljoen's commandos who returned to the Bethal area, and the Government group that had retired to the north of the Delagoa Bay railway. Piet Viljoen managed to break through the line of Constabulary posts and successfully penetrate the protected zone. In scattered bands, his men roamed as far as the outskirts of Pretoria. Kitchener sent a column in pursuit, but a squadron of the Scots Greys was badly cut-up by Viljoen at Heidelberg on the 18th of February. Meanwhile, the vitality of the once so energetic General Ben Viljoen now seemed drained by war weariness. He withdrew his HQ, together with a thousand men, into tranquil retirement in the beautiful mountain hamlet of Pilgrim's Rest, northeast of Lydenburg. He was now so remote from any action and so ineffective, that Kitchener decided to leave him alone and to focus his attention on Botha and De Wet. Ben Viljoen did try to lure the Government group into joining him at Pilgrim's Rest but they declined which perhaps was just as well, because on his way back to his HQ he was surprised and taken captive near Lydenburg. At an earlier time, the loss of Ben Viljoen would have been a severe blow to the Boers, but his effectiveness had by now waned to little if any consequence.

The Invasion of Natal – September 1901
In the beginning of September 1901 Botha and his commandos set off south. Slipping out of their hunting grounds on the remote eastern border of the Transvaal and skirting the mountains on the Swaziland border, they prepared themselves for a raid on Natal. The commandos rode light and fast, with pack mules and horses instead of the cumbersome wagons that had been the bane of earlier campaigns. Botha intentionally left behind all his field guns to facilitate his movements, and his men carried only their Mausers and some Lee-Metfords, which had been taken from captured British soldiers. Botha's intention in invading Natal was to divert British pressure by siphoning off vital reserves from the Cape, Free State and western Transvaal, where the Boer guerrilla activities were causing Kitchener some concern. It was also a deliberate political message that the war was by no means over, and that the Boers were a long way off from throwing in the sponge. His advance took him past Piet Retief, and on across the bleak open veld of the south east Transvaal, still relatively untouched by the war. His

pace was too hot for the British columns to intercept him, but at the same time, it proved too hot for his own horses. In good weather, they might have stood it, but the horses were weak after the icy cold winter and heavy spring rains, which had turned the roads into fast flowing rivers, and the rivers into torrents and vast floods, leaving the horses expended, shivering and starving. By the 14th September, when Botha arrived at a farm near Frischgewaagd, east of Utrecht, the transport problem had become critical. Four hundred horses of the Bethal and Middelburg commandos were so exhausted that he was obliged to halt at the farm for several days for them to recover. The Buffalo, or Mzinyathi, River, which marked the boundary between the Transvaal and Natal, was in heavy spate and a tactical decision now became imperative – to attempt to ford the river or to splash on through the thick mud towards Zululand. Botha's objective was the British garrison at Dundee, ten miles away on the Natal side of the river, where he intended to get fresh food and horses, and then to cut the railway at Glencoe on the main line between Durban and Pretoria. He planned a dawn attack on the same lines as the assault on Penn-Symons's position two years earlier. However, his horses were too weak to undertake a night march, so Botha changed his mind and forged on towards Zululand, hoping to dodge the British patrols and cross the river further south.

As soon as he received the news of Botha's incursion into Natal, Kitchener ordered Major Hubert Gough to take his 24th MI unit and to entrain immediately and head north to intercept the Boers. When Gough arrived at De Jager's Drift, a small camp guarding the main crossing point on the Buffalo River, astride the old Natal-Transvaal frontiers, he received news from the Natal Intelligence Department that Botha with 700 men was in the vicinity, and threatening an attack. On the 17th September, Gough observed through his binoculars a body of two- or three hundred Boers riding northwards from a stony ridge astride the main road leading to Vryheid. The Boers off-saddled at a farm close to Blood River Poort, the mouth of a gorge a few miles from the confluence of the Blood - and Buffalo rivers. Gough sent a message to Lt. Col. H.K. Stewart, who was holding a body of 450 men in reserve a few miles back, to shake the enemy with a good gallop up to the laager, and 'give Brother Boer a good dusting'.

Unfortunately for Gough, Botha had other ideas. He knew that if he delayed, thousands more British troops would be brought in, and he would be vastly out-numbered. But at that moment he knew that his own burghers were the larger force, and he didn't hesitate to make good this unexpected opportunity. Three hundred of his burghers off-saddled at the farm, while his main force, 700 men under his own command, galloped round the right flank of the British who were now holding the ridge. In twenty minutes, the Boers cut through them like a warm knife through butter, and from the centre of the bare plain Gough watched aghast, as Botha's men, hundreds of them, swarmed all over the ridge. Gough rode across to his two field guns where the gunners were trying desperately to fire case shot but, in the confusion, could not find a proper target. At that same moment, some Boers galloped up, pointed their rifles at the gunners and shouted 'hands up'. Gough put his hand down to his holster but it was empty, his batman had forgotten to put in his revolver that morning! He threw himself off his horse and tried to use it as a shield but by then Botha's men had completely overran the site. By the next day, the news of Gough's disaster was out. Capt. Mildmay and ten men killed, five officers and nineteen men wounded, including three officers mortally wounded. Six other officers and 235 men were captured. It was the most humiliating reverse since Clements's smash-up at Nooitgedacht in the western Transvaal, nine months earlier. Botha was elated. He had succeeded in capturing 189 Lee-Metford rifles, 30,000 rounds of ammunition, 200 horses and two field guns as well as all the prisoners and their gear. However, what he really needed was fresh horses, food and fodder and a smooth path into Natal. He found the British horses useless, the field guns too cumbersome for raiding forages and the prisoners a burden. In the end, he simply stripped them of their gear and sent them back to their lines.

To break into Natal, Botha had to ford the Buffalo somewhere, and launch his men down the same road over the Biggarsberg towards Ladysmith that he had taken two years before. Now however, he decided that his force was too weak to cross the Buffalo. 300 of his sick ponies had to be returned to Vryheid, and the remainder continued southeast inside the old Transvaal frontier, tentatively feeling their way into Natal. The rain continued – the men were cold, wet, and hungry and the horses tired. Botha decided to raid two camps in the area for provisions. Fort Itala and Fort Prospect lay enticingly ahead just astride the Zulu frontier. It was at this point, on the 26th September 1901 that Botha succumbed to a fit of over-confidence quite as serious as Gough's earlier on. Botha had received information from some of the local burghers that the two British laagers would be 'easy meat' because they were not entrenched. In fact not only did they have excellent trenches but good men manning them to boot. To cap it all the Boers threw themselves with uncharacteristic recklessness at the trenches at Fort Itala, and in the event lost at least 58 men killed or wounded. The attack on Fort Prospect was equally brave and equally disastrous, and Botha's demoralised men hastily scampered back into the Transvaal at the same time as 15,000 British troops lumbered up after them.

The fiasco of the Natal 'invasion' confirmed what Botha, at heart, had soberly come to recognise since the peace talks at Middelburg, that there were now no other options left but to fight to the bitter end, or to accept Kitchener's peace proposals. The other Boer leaders too were beginning to realise the grim reality of Kitchener's successes since he had taken over the command of the British army in South Africa. In the twelve months following his assumption of command, he had succeeded in hammering and grinding down the Boer forces to about 25,000 men, roughly half the number than when Roberts left, and if that process were to continue, the end, when it came, would indeed be a bitter one.

Kitchener's 'Big Drive' Strategy
Although Kitchener was obviously concerned about Botha's foray into Natal, his mind however, was fully concentrated on what had become by far the biggest thorn in the British flesh – De Wet! Kitchener was determined to flush him out and destroy him, and in so doing, neutralise the entire Boer activity in the Free State. For this single purpose, he allocated 15,000 men, divided them into fourteen columns, and posted them around an area extending some 75 miles south of the Vaal, and 100 miles east of the central railway. He then ordered them to converge on a central point south of Frankfort, shepherding the Boers together into a giant and inescapable trap. Elaborate feints, complete secrecy and meticulously timed marches were the features of an operation that

went like clockwork for five days and on the sixth day, it culminated in the troops' arrival at their destination and the hopeful entrapment of De Wet. They scoured the area from horizon to horizon, but to their amazement, there was not a single Boer in the entire vicinity. In fact, every single British move had been watched by hundreds of unseen eyes and reported by heliograph from hill to hill, so enabling the Boers to slip through the gaps between the columns during the darkness of the night. President Steyn and De Wet were even able to meet unhindered at a council-of-war between Lindley and Reitz, where they laid their own plans for a counter-offensive.

The thwarted British columns returning from their abortive drive actually passed by very close to where De Wet and his men were encamped. They had no awareness whatsoever of the proximity of the burghers to their own lines, and quietly passed by leaving the Boer commandos unscathed. However, Rimington, recalled to the Free State after his earlier encounter with Botha in the eastern Transvaal, managed to discover De Wet's whereabouts through information supplied by a captured burgher. Later there was some doubt whether the informer was not in fact a 'plant', because Rimington, acting on the information he had received, immediately set off to attack De Wet, only to find him lying in wait at a place called Spijtfontein, from where he was forced to withdraw in haste. Rimington next set off to capture a commando led by one of De Wet's ablest lieutenants, Wessel Wessels, who had been harassing blockhouse building operations east of Frankfort. With Rimington rode another notable raiding-column leader, F.H. Damant, whose name had become a by-word for bravery ever since he had left his business in Kimberley to volunteer for service with the British at the start of the war. Now, like Benson at Bakenlaagte, Damant was to be fully tested. By means of the ruse of allegedly wearing khaki dress, the Boers managed to get in close to Damant's column, and isolated his ninety men and three guns at Tafelkop, on the road to Vrede. The attack was launched against ferocious resistance, and the British were only overwhelmed after the gunners had fallen in heaps, and Damant himself was lying on the ground with four bullets in him.

Meanwhile De Wet himself, with the main Boer force, was sighted somewhere between Lindley and Bethlehem, and Kitchener, with unquenched zeal, launched a third all-out drive on the target area, only to find it once again totally deserted. By now the columns were exhausted, having been on the march for six weeks without a break, and as one of them was returning along the road to Harrismith on the morning of December 18th, De Wet sprang an ambush with 900 men at a place called Tigerkloof Spruit. But De Wet was to be severely discomfited. Expecting a fat convoy for easy picking, he was instead, confronted by a column of Imperial Light Horse and Yeomanry under General Dartnell. Dartnell was a considerable character – a Canadian aged 63, he had served with the 'County Downs' in the Indian Mutiny, been head of the Natal Mounted Police for thirty years, trudged with Yule on the night march from Dundee to Ladysmith, and led one of Kitchener's raiding columns formed the previous autumn. He now gave De Wet a serious drubbing, but during this action suffered sufficient losses himself to prompt him to ask Kitchener for reinforcement. When this request was refused, Dartnell responded by resigning his commission.

A shattering climax to this series of operations against De Wet came on Christmas Day. Quite close to the scene of the unsuccessful Tigerkloof Spruit ambush, a line of blockhouses was being built westward from Harrismith. Among the forces which Rundle, the District Commissioner had to protect these works, was a battalion of the Kent and Middlesex Yeomanry, which had been detailed to man a hill called Groenkop near the main road from Bethlehem. On the morning of the 22nd December, De Wet and two of his officers stealthily approached the hill to reconnoitre, while two of his men, riding close by, seized a Native driving some horses, and shot him. The indignant British soldiers opened fire on the two miscreants, thereby exposing their positions, and revealing to the hidden De Wet just the information that he was seeking. He retired to a nearby hill from where he presently observed the pickets taking up their posts for the night, their bayonets visibly outlined against the evening sky. Now, fully acquainted with the lay-out of the camp, De Wet waited until the garrison had settled down to sleep through Christmas Eve. He then rode with a thousand burghers and under a misty scudding moon, reached a side of the hill considered by the British too steep to warrant special precautions. Silently the Boers ascended and found many of the picket asleep, a breach of duty for which most paid with their lives. Worse was to follow. As the Boers' fire greeted the first hours of Christmas Day, a full third of the garrison fled pell-mell from the camp on the slopes below, while the rest strove to mount some confused resistance. By now their position was hopeless, and as the Boers swept down through the tents, the horse and transport-lines were scattered in the midst of wild shouts of terror, stampeding horse and the terrifying cries of the men. Within one hour 348 Yeomanry were either killed wounded or captured, the entire camp was looted, and everything, from plum puddings to clothes and ammunition, was stolen. Although twenty-five Natives were ruthlessly despatched by the Boers, De Wet insisted on nothing but tender solicitude towards the captured British.

On receiving news of this disaster Rundle immediately wired the force nearest to him for help, but the orderly at the receiving office neglected to take any notice of the message, and this omission enabled De Wet to make good his escape. Subsequent attempts to overtake him failed, and making his way northwards towards Reitz, he dismissed his prisoners, and the year ended with the dispersal of his own men to their various districts.

The 'New Model Drive'
Groenkop was to be De Wet's last campaign in such strength, and it was also be the last time that Kitchener would use the 'big drive' system on the pattern which had become so familiar. The past two months of adversity endured by his troops were final testimonies to its failure. Even with his most disciplined troops, improved intelligence, freedom from the distraction of the scorched earth policy, secrecy, the use of blockhouse lines, and cunning feints, Kitchener really had achieved nothing. The British had failed to succeed because the gaps between the advancing columns had enabled the Boers to slip through at night with secrecy, ease and impunity. Kitchener was by now aware of this, but he also suspected that he was failing to assert sufficient control, surprising how this may have had sounded to his field commanders who had become unaccustomed to raising a finger without his express orders. He decided to revolutionise the drive system by the introduction of 'the new model drive', which was destined to

become the marvel of military drill and staff organisation. Kitchener's new plan was to create a dragnet of men literally taking one another by the hand and forming a line from one side to the other, and marching over a given area to flush out its inhabitants. In this way, yard by yard and mile by mile, he would now hunt out De Wet, Steyn and their fighting men in the northeast Free State. Rigidly controlled plans were prepared; provision was made for individual routes for every single man, and also for times and places to halt for food, water, and provisions. Everything was accounted for, every man, every horse every bullet, every bale of forage or roll of bandage – all would form part of a net so close-meshed, that drawn across each yard of the country between blockhouse line and blockhouse line, no living creature without wings would be able to escape.

Through the remainder of January, whilst these plans were being prepared, fresh troops were arriving by rail, food depots were being prepared, and above all, the blockhouses were hurriedly completed. There were two east-to-west blockhouse lines: a northern line from the branch railhead at Heilbron, via Frankfort to Botha's Pass in the Drakensberg, and a southern line from Kroonstad via Lindley and Bethlehem to Van Reenen's Pass, beyond Harrismith. With all the other passes on the Drakensberg fortified, and the Central railway blockhoused, a rectangle 65 miles by 140 miles was enclosed. By nightfall on the 5th of February, Kitchener had 9,000 men drawn in a continuous cordon fifty-four miles long between the northern and southern blockhouse lines - i.e. from Frankfort to a point west of Bethlehem - one man per every twelve yards. Starting on the morrow it was to move westward at a rate of twenty miles a day with an unbroken screen of scouts preceding the main body, the transport and the guns, until it reached the Central railway blockhouse line in two days and three nights.

Detailed and precise orders typifying the meticulous arrangement for maintaining the tight cordon during movements executed in the dark were drawn up and issued by Rimington, one of the originators of the system. Never before was there such a fantastic exercise as Kitchener's attempt to dress 9,000 men in perfect alignment across 54 miles of country, but he managed it. Yard by yard the cordon advanced, while another 5,000 men stood along the blockhouse lines and railways, which were patrolled by seven armoured trains daily. As the circle around him tightened from the east, De Wet called together all his commandos in the area and rode south. Little more than one-third of the 1,800 men concerned heard the summons, or obeyed it if they did. With those who did rally to his call De Wet, accompanied by a huge herd of cattle, approached the southern line of blockhouses somewhere between Kroonstad and Lindley.

Now that one single factor which Kitchener had striven so hard to obviate, asserted itself – that of human fallibility. It was so fated that the bored occupants of some of the blockhouses on either side of the point where De Wet just happened to reach in the dark midnight hours of the 6th to 7th February, were not vigilant enough. De Wet succeeded in slipping through without a shot being fired or any alert raised to summons assistance from reinforcements waiting nearby. Later De Wet drove his great herd of cattle to stampede, and by brute force smashed down the fencing between a number of blockhouses creating a huge escape gap for the remainder of the commando to gallop through to the south and to safety.

Of the commandos who failed, or refused to follow De Wet, one group escaped through the northern blockhouse line, but the rest were forced to ride up and down in front of the ever-advancing cordon, vainly trying to find a gap as they were being pushed relentlessly against the railway. The last hours of the drive had a tingling excitement, as the commandos were pressed harder and harder against the railway blockhouse line, out-numbered by 50 to 1, frantically striving to find a means of escape before dawn. Some did manage to cut their way to safety, some were shot down like game, but the greater part just fell back, stunned and bewildered, into the interior of the trap to await captivity.

In all, De Wet lost 300 burghers. If it seemed a result quite disproportionate to Kitchener's massive enterprise, it did in one sense put an end to De Wet as a real fighting strength. It also heralded a new and final phase of hostilities that gave the Boers in the Free State no glimmer of hope for any future success in the struggle for their freedom, and for the independence of their republic.

Resting his troops for only three days, Kitchener set them in motion once more to sweep clean all the remainder of the north-eastern Free State, which was omitted in the first new model drive. One cordon of columns started near the central railway on either side of the Vaal, and swept eastward towards the northern blockhouse line and the Natal railway beyond Frankfort. It then pivoted southwards towards the Bethlehem-Van Reenen's Pass blockhouse line, its left skirting the fortified passes on the Drakensberg, its right the Wilge River. To guard the river and to seal the area thus bounded, a second cordon approached from the vicinity of Kroonstad. It was a huge undertaking – too huge in fact, since the first cordon spread across sixty miles of hilly, river-gashed country. This time, however, fate dealt the cards in Kitchener's favour. After the initial new model drive, De Wet had slipped back to join his President near Reitz, and now in order to avoid the cordon from the west, they fled across the Wilge, thereby standing square in the path of the other cordon coming down from the north. There appeared to be no escape route open to them in any direction.

Scattered around the enveloped area were about 3,000 fighting burghers, and besides these, a vast mass of civilian refugees who had attached themselves to de Wet and Steyn as they turned north, straight towards the advancing cordon. De Wet resolved to breach the cordon, and summoned all the commandos in the area, but by sunset on the 3rd of March, when a clash with the cordon had become imminent, only 1,200 men had managed to reach him. Acting on information received from his scouts, De Wet carefully selected his point of attack – Langverwacht - about twenty miles south of Vrede. With a mass of horsemen, terrified women and children, a great ruck of vehicles, and yelling natives driving a herd of cattle spread across six miles of veld, he descended on the bewildered British soldiers. De Wets fierce discipline was tested to the full in his attempts to impose some form of order in this chaotic scene. His selected force of burghers whom he had sent into the attack at about 11 p.m. first had to shake themselves free from the mad swell of refugees swarming about them. The portion of the British cordon immediately in front consisted of New Zealanders and Australians, spread across the side of hill, and it was upon them that the Boer advance force hurled itself. The Boers however, forced a gap in the New Zealand line, wheeled and then ploughed through the ensuing gap. Once they were in the narrow but clear passage, the refugee horde forged forward. Soon, about 600 fighting men and a remnant of the refugees together with thousands of cattle, horses, and wagons, were rounded up by the British. One complete commando that included one of De Wet's sons, managed to fall back southwards, but later it was trapped between the jaws of the cordon and the blockhouse line.

Kitchener was in the area to observe the conclusion of the drive, and a message from him on the anniversary of Majuba, caused wild cheering in the House of Commons. The magical name of De Wet, even if only a son, was acclaimed with particular satisfaction, and the final tally of captives, 800 in all, brought the biggest success in the guerrilla war to date, and evoked long and loud jubilations, coupled with enthusiastic tributes paid to the gallantry of the New Zealanders,

The commandos that had not joined De Wet, eventually broke through westwards across the Wilge River, and headed for safety in the Transvaal. De Wet himself once again succeeded escaping, but this time the prospects of further severe losses from the throttling blockhouse lines, and of a renewal of the new model drive had really hit him hard, and he looked about desperately for some form of relief. Steyn proposed a remedy – if he and De Wet, together with his officials, left the northeast Free State, Kitchener might then turn his attention away from that unhappy quarter in order to pursue some other quarry. He suggested an exit from the Free State via the comparatively quiet region of the north-west. De Wet was the only person who could be relied upon to conduct him to safety, and although De Wet was reluctant to leave his burghers, he nevertheless agreed to accompany Steyn. They set off near Reitz at sunset on the 5th of March, spurred on by the news that Kitchener had begun yet another drive across the northeast after allowing his troops only three days rest.

Steyn and De Wet managed to pierce the northern blockhouse line, the railway-blockhouse line, and finally the Kroonstad-Vaal line near Bothaville. Having ridden 200 miles and dared the bullets and entanglements of three blockhouse lines in ten days, they finally arrived on the banks of the Vaal River. By now, Boer resistance was tottering before Kitchener's hammer blows, and as Botha had quit the highveld of the eastern Transvaal, so now De Wet had to quit the northeast Free State. In true De Wet tradition, he did not linger on the banks of the Vaal, but quickly rode on and led his party into the western Transvaal and to De la Rey.

The Invasion of the Cape
Although the principal engagements of the war were now taking place in the eastern and the western Transvaal, elsewhere the daily toll of death and devastation was steadily increasing as well. In the Free State, for example, a column of 200 British soldiers, while clearing a farm near Sannaspos close to Bloemfontein, was set upon by a Boer commando, and overwhelmed. Then, further south, on the 16th September 1901 the Boer general Kritzinger, while preparing to follow General Jan Smuts into the Cape, charged down on a hundred Lovat's Scouts asleep in their camp, killing or wounding half of them.

Smuts had started preparations for the invasion of the Cape Province some months before. Ever since the Boer generals had met at Cypherfontein in the western Transvaal in December 1900, he believed passionately in the need for a third front. He wanted to carry the war into the heart of the enemy's country - into the Cape, which although politically British, was morally the Afrikaner heartland. Outside the towns, the Afrikaner 'volk' still constituted the overwhelming majority, and Smuts realised the many advantages of a campaign in the Cape. In every village and on every farm, friends would be at hand to render help and support. Above all, their farms would not be burned down, nor their herds destroyed, because the Afrikaner-dominated ministries in the Cape would never allow it to happen. Smuts also believed that previous invasion attempts by De Wet, Herzog and Kritzinger had failed because they were not properly co-ordinated, and lacked a joint strategy between the different commandos taking part in the action.

In June 1901, Smuts put his plan to a Boer war council in Standerton, and received its approval. He joined up with Assistant Commandant-General Kritzinger and together they set about re-organising the surviving bands of dispersed commandos in the eastern Free State. On the night of the 3rd September 1901 Smuts, with 250 burghers, splashed across the Orange River at Kiba Drift. Almost immediately, he ran into some trouble. The Africans at Herschel, a native reserve on the borders of Basutoland, received orders from the British to repel all invaders, and this they did by attacking some of Smuts' foraging parties, killing three men and wounding seven. However, they were no match for the Boer rifles, and were soon despatched with heavy losses.

As Smuts headed southwest towards Stormberg, the weather worsened, and a tempest of wind and icy rain demoralised the men and killed the horses. He also became aware that General French was drawing a cordon around him. For three days, from the 9th to the 13th September the burghers sought to fight their way out, but on the third day the British surrounded them at farm situated on the grassy summit of the Stormberg. The situation looked grim – for forty hours, the Boers had been riding without sleep, and now they found themselves surrounded and all the passes blocked. At least that is how it appeared, but suddenly a hunchback on crutches hobbled out of a farm and offered to show them a way out. He led them by a squelching path that brought them so close to the British camp that they could hear voices and the champing of bits, and from there to the edge of the escarpment. From there, the entire commando of 250 men, and at least 500 horses went glissading down the southern face of the Stormberg, across a railway line and out onto the open veld. It was indeed a miraculous escape.

As they forged ahead through the vast open countryside, with French's troops hot on their heels, it became increasingly clear to the Boers that there never was going to be a 'mass uprising' of fellow Afrikaners in the Cape, and that the most they could hope for was hospitality and help as they went on their way. It had become impossible for them to 'live off the country', for the British had taken all the food, the forage and the horses, leaving the farmers only the barest minimum for basic needs.

On the 17th September, Smuts arrived at a long gorge leading to the Elands River valley. At the spot where the gorge started to widen, the commando met a farmer who warned them of the imminent presence of British soldiers, 200 of them with mountain guns and Maxims, laagered on a pass at the end of the gorge at Elands River Poort. Smuts decided to attack at once. The battle that followed was brief, bloody, and decisive. The Boers' shooting was accurate and their battle skills polished by two years of schooling from the master warrior himself, De la Rey. Their opponents, C-Squadron of the 17th Lancers under the command of Captain Sandeman and Lord Vivian were relative amateurs by comparison, and moreover the weather had suddenly sided with the commando, a heavy fog hiding the passes in the north from British view. When the Boer advance patrols made contact with the troops, the British mistook them for irregulars from Colonel Goringes's column, and were surprised when a short, sharp engagement followed during which thirteen soldiers were killed, including Lieutenant Sheridan, a cousin of Winston Churchill. Meanwhile, the main commando had worked up to the British camp from the rear, many of them wearing captured khaki uniforms, which enabled them to approach to within a few hundred yards and thereby gaining an advantage over the British. When the engagement was over, the British losses were twenty-nine killed, and forty-three wounded, and the Boers, one burgher dead and six wounded. After leaving the prisoners and their African retinue behind to fend for themselves, the commando broke out of the Bamboo Mountains to ride in triumph across the open veld, stores and stock adequately replenished, and full of confidence both in the own actions, and in Smuts, their leader.

French now designated Douglas Haig to hunt out Smuts and his commando, and to deal with them accordingly. He issued specific orders that any Boer caught wearing a khaki uniform was to be arrested and shot immediately. For the following four weeks the guerrilla war in the mountains of the eastern Cape Colony centred on a personal dual between Haig and Smuts – a contest between two well matched, though differently armed opponents, each intensely professional, and both relentless drivers of men. It was at this time that French's Field Intelligence Department reported the discovery of six smaller enemy fragments scattered about in the Cape Colony south of the Orange. The information was remarkably accurate, and gave detailed accounts of the location and strength of each of the groups. Among those identified were Commandants Myburgh with a 100 men, Fouche with 100, Wessels with 200, Malan with fifteen, and Scheepers with 250. Add Smuts and his 250 men, and the total south of the river was correctly estimated to be about a thousand. In response to these reports, French and Haig drew up a three-pronged strategy to counter the threats imposed by these fragmented Boer forces scattered throughout the region. First, the scattered fragments of Boer forces were at all costs, to be forestalled from combining into a single large force. Secondly, they were to be harassed continually in order to hinder them from recruiting additional followers, or from raiding the countryside, and thirdly, it was imperative to pursue them relentlessly, hunt them down, and eventually destroy them. On paper it looked to be an easy enough task to round up and destroy some 2,000 men, but Haig was very aware of the fact that his job would not be an easy one. The Boer commandos in the Cape had many advantages over their adversaries. The Cape was huge – four times the area of the old republics, with desert lairs to the west of the railway lines, mountain lairs in the east midlands, and friendly welcomes all round from up-country farmers.

There were also problems created by the extraordinarily unpleasant spring rains that year, which would play a crucial role in the planning of military tactics. Paradoxically, it was one of these very spring storms that caused a Boer commando to come to grief. On the 5th September, when Smuts had slipped across the Orange River at Kiba Drift, Commandant Lotter with a commando of 130 rebels was run to ground by Colonel Harry Scobell's column in a gorge near the village of Petersburg. At that time, a fierce storm had been raging in the Tandjesberge, a tangle of mountains which separated Cradock from Graaf Reinet. It was the fifth night of Scobell's six-day chase after Lotter, and his column was dead-beat. The British force consisted of 1,100 men of the 9th Lancers, the Cape Mounted Rifles, and the Yeomanry, and out-numbered Lotter's force by nearly ten-to-one. Scobell had expected Lotter to spend the night at a farmhouse in a mountain gorge called Groenkloof, but in fact, almost all the commando had taken shelter from the rain in a kraal a few hundred yards away. Before dawn, Scobell disposed his main party along the ridges commanding the farm, and as the sky brightened, he sprang a surprise attack on the Boer party sheltering in the kraal. When it was all over, the Boers party had been overwhelmed, with thirteen dead, forty-six wounded and sixty-one prisoners, including Lotter who later, together with seven other rebels, was executed in Cape Town. Ten Lancers were killed and some wounded, many from their own fire coming from the surrounding ridges.

In spite of all Haig's efforts to prevent the isolated and scattered bands from linking up, little by little Smuts succeeded in enlarging his body of fighting men. As a result of French's drives in the north, many commandos fled southwards in attempts to escape the net, and one such was an active commando led by commandant Scheepers. In his flight to the south, Scheepers succeeded in marauding British columns in areas as close as 100 miles from Cape Town. For the next ten weeks, this bold young leader operated effectively against the search columns in the area northwest of Cape Town, along the Atlantic Ocean, and eventually his commando succeeded in joining up with Smuts. Soon after Sheepers's arrival, a young corporal who had previously fought under De Wet and Herzog linked up with Smuts, bringing with him a well-equipped body of Cape rebels. His name was Salomon Maritz, and his achievements against the British columns in the Cape hinterland were so significant that Smuts rewarded him by conferring on him the rank of General. Now, it would be the combination of his own and of Maritz's forces that would constitute the backbone of the Boer activity in the western districts.

Over a time, Smuts gradually managed to increase his band of guerrillas to about 3,000 men. In November, a hundred burghers arrived from the Free State, and joined up with Smuts after breaking through the blockhouse line along the Orange River and the De Aar railway. The following month, Kritzinger, with a similar force, left the southeast Free State to join him as well. This time, however, the British were more alert, and the 5th Lancers pursued him across 80 miles in the blazing sun, compelling him to shed 110 exhausted ponies before his commando desperately flung itself across the blockhouse line on the De Aar-Naauwpoort stretch of railway, and managed to get away.

The guerrilla bands continued to operate over a vast area 150 miles north of Cape Town, along a broad belt of country extending from Beaufort West on the western railway, to the Atlantic Ocean at Lambert's Bay In November they engaged a convoy at one point, and a fortnight later, in December, another two. These were petty events, but they did serve to create a climate of restlessness, and if this were allowed to intensify, it threatened a general uprising even at this late hour. Kitchener, for his part, carried on pouring reinforcements into the Cape, and soon there were over 9,000 British troops, divided into sixteen mobile columns. The absence of railways meant a slow crawl with wagon convoys, each column a mini-army, complete with staff, Intelligence, police, signallers, hospitals and guns. In December, the launch of a gigantic operation to build a line of blockhouses from Beaufort West to Lambert's Bay, 300 miles west created a dire shortage of transport and labour, thereby severely testing British efficiency.

Throughout most of the month of January, there was a lull as Smuts built up a granary of supplies in several places. Towards the end of the month, the British started a drive, which served only to scatter the bands of Boer forces in the target area. One such band promptly retaliated by aggravating transport problems with the seizure of a convoy of 150 wagons near Beaufort West on the 4th February. The following day another destroyed a second convoy a few miles away, and mauled its escort. Douglas Haig did have some success against a Boer laager on the 13th December, but on the 29th a police post was snapped up by the Boers. Again, Haig launched a combined movement only to succeed in scattering some of the bands as far as into the Midlands, where some guerrilla forces from the northeast had also made incursions. As a result, these areas were once again, teetering on the edge of rebellion. The British then concentrated on putting steady pressure in a northerly direction to drive Smuts clear of the new blockhouse line. Smuts obliged by withdrawing the greater part of his strength across the wastes of the far north-west, and headed for a thriving and rich copper-mining area in Namaqualand. He succeeded in overwhelming several mining centres, and then laid siege to the most important town of them all, O'Okiep, on the 12th April. The British garrison of 900 troops, assisted by a number of white and half-caste miners, successfully held the Boers off until Smuts eventually left the area.

In the midst of the siege, about a fortnight later, Smuts received an unexpected message. It contained urgent tidings – so urgent that he immediately quit the scene with two of his staff, leaving the town unscathed. O'Okiep was finally relieved on the 3rd of May by a British expedition sent out by sea to Port Nolloth. As Smuts made the long journey back he could reflect that he had brought his forces up to a strength of about 3,000, of whom all but one-seventh were rebels, without ever having been beaten by the British forces totalling more than three times his number. In the end, this was his real accomplishment – the tying-up of troops and resource which could have been used more effectively against De Wet and De la Rey in the north.

14
KITCHENER'S WAR (b) – THE ROAD TO PEACE

At the start of the new year of 1902, the end of the war seemed even further away than at its onset in October 1899. By now, it had become obvious to both Kitchener and the Boer generals that neither side was ever going to win the war, yet both were still equally determined not to lose it. In the blistering January heat on the South African highveld, Kitchener's drives were reeking havoc and panic amongst the burghers, whilst hundreds and hundreds of British lives were being sacrificed to Botha in the eastern Transvaal, to De Wet in the Free State, Smuts in the Cape, and in particular to De la Rey in the western Transvaal. As we enter into these last stages of the war, Kitchener and De la Rey were destined to meet again in the context of the decisive battles, which would finally mark the end. It would be appropriate at this stage, therefore, to take a closer look at this outstanding Boer general.

Every feature of De la Rey was big – ears, nose, eyes, forehead, even his grizzled square beard, and yet the impression he gave was not that of a massive man, but that of a 'gentle giant'. He held high values for simple and humane traits such as fair play, kindness, decency, empathy and respect. Because of the bitter feelings aroused by the guerrilla war, many villages refused the burial of the enemy dead in their cemeteries. Yet even before the British had occupied his home town of Lichtenburg, De la Rey had already marked out a portion of the town cemetery, and left instructions that any British dead was to be buried there with full honour and respect. Today many lie there beneath their rows of little crosses with the sculptured likeness of De la Rey turned towards them. In action, he was as able as his theories were sound. At Magersfontein, he had administered the fateful idea of trench and barbed wire, which would underlie the strategy of World War 1. In the same way, the innovation of mobile forces firing on the move was effectively put into practice during the World War II. A notable place in military history must belong to this remarkable man, who had had no martial education and little of any other kind, and whose wise and chivalrous spirit found no satisfaction whatsoever in the thought of war. It was apt that De la Rey should play a leading part in the closing phases of the Boer War, since it was he that had fought in its very first engagement on the 12th October 1899 which resulted in the capture, at Kraaipan on the western Railway, of a British armoured train heading north for Mafeking. Equally apt, too, is that his final opponent was to be Lord Methuen who was the general in charge of British operations in the northwest Cape at the time of the Kraaipan encounter. Later, De la Rey would have the occasion to treat Methuen with exceptional kindness and respect, when he lay defeated and badly wounded and at De la Rey's mercy after the battle of Tweebosch on 7th March, 1902.

Since the last clash between these two men at Magersfontein on the 11th December 1899, Methuen had been half forgotten by the British military command, except perhaps, momentarily when he was foremost in the first De Wet hunt. Now, exercising area command in the western Transvaal, he was pitted, once again, against De la Rey.

By now, tactical circumstances in South Africa no longer favoured the conventional direct head-on clashes of the first six months of the war, and a new type of 'hide, hit and run' warfare had become the order of the day. With fewer troops to enforce his military administration over a huge expanse of sparsely occupied country, Methuen's task had been toiling and unrewarding, while De la Rey and his lieutenants, fully informed by an effective network of scouts using heliographs, were able to sally out at will to pick off a convoy here, an isolated detachment there. In the western Transvaal, the blockhouse lines were still incomplete, leaving wide areas, which the few British columns in the area could not access without the backing of huge and cumbersome supply columns.

In the annals of Boer recollections of Methuen's gentlemanly attitude to his opponents, one can find a touching account of his first encounter with 'Nonnie' De la Rey, Gen. De la Rey's devoted wife. De la Rey's farm at Elandsfontein, near Lichtenburg lay within the area under Methuens's control, and in December 1900, he personally called on Mrs. De la Rey to inform her, with deep regret that he had been ordered to burn the farm buildings. He offered to leave one building standing for her personal use, as well as an alternative offer of a house in Cape Town, but she refused both offers, because as she told him, she was not prepared to accept British hospitality, and preferred to remain near her husband. For the next eighteen months, Nonnie lived an extraordinary life, moving about in her ox-wagon accompanied by six of her children, three African servants, and a small collection of farm animals and pets. In the course of her adventures, about which she wrote after the war, she succeeded in keeping clear of the British, and maintaining close contact with her husband. In the event Methuen did not burn the farm, but used it instead as a billet for British officers, and as a local HQ. One day some Boer scouts, sent there by De la Rey to report on its condition, shot and killed an officer emerging in his pyjamas early in the morning as well as a second who came out to investigate. Not surprisingly, the house was then burnt down, and when De la Rey learned about his scouts's senseless killing of men in cold blood, he was so incensed that he had them severely flogged.

Since the beginning of November 1901, guerrilla activity in the western Transvaal had calmed down considerably, just at a stage when Kitchener was facing a dilemma. Absorbed by the simultaneous campaigns against Botha in the eastern Transvaal, and De Wet in the Free State, and gnawed at by Smuts in the Cape, he needed the reassurance that the limited forces that Methuen, Kekewich and others had in the western Transvaal would prove sufficient to keep De la Rey quiet. From November 1901 to February 1902, this hope was justified, and except for some minor operations at Wolmaransstad and Lichtenburg, De la Rey lay low because of a dire shortage of horses and ammunition. In February, the tide began to run against Botha and De Wet, and they both appealed to De la Rey to act in order to divert some of the pressure from them.

At the end of February 1902, De la Rey's opportunity came. Earlier, Methuen had been recalled to Vryburg for administrative reasons, and the column he was personally commanding was quartered, contrary to usual practice, at Wolmaransstad, which was not situated on a blockhouse line. The outcome of this was that the convoys now needed to travel long distances across open country for supplies. One such, empty except for three all-important ammunition carts, left its last staging camp before Klerksdorp at

4.30 a.m. on the 25th February, 1902 with an escort of 700 men. Soon the convoy was discovered by one of De la Rey's assistants, Commandant Liebenberg, and De la Rey quietly rounded up a force of about 1,200 burghers to intercept it. De la Rey concealed his force in thick scrub by the roadside, near to a stream called Yzer Spruit (Ysterspruit), and when the British drew abreast through the darkness, the scrub abruptly seemed to burst into flames as De la Rey's lieutenants Liebenberg, Celliers and Kemp, respectively bore down on the van, the centre and the rear of the column. Despite the surprise, the escort rallied quickly, the Royal Artillery in particular repeating the steadiness that they had displayed so consistently throughout the war. Unfortunately the commander of the convoy made the mistake of ordering it to press on, and the terrified natives lashed away wildly at the trek-animals causing a turmoil which ended in some wagons becoming stuck, causing a massive pile-up in the rear. This gave De la Rey the chance to gauge his exact moment to unleash an all-out charge. Riding down on the escort in a tumultuous gallop, and firing from the saddle, the burghers created havoc in the British column. When dawn broke it became clear that the British had suffered an unmitigated disaster, with 178 dead or wounded, another 500 captured, horses and mules in plenty seized along with half a million rounds of ammunition. This was the he largest 'bag' of prisoners that had fallen to either side since Gatacre had lost 200, and accidentally left 600 men behind at Stormberg during 'Black Week', and it raised the often-repeated problem in guerrilla warfare of what was to be done with them. The Boers were well aware that if they had been captured, they would have been sent overseas for incarceration, and this knowledge prompted some violent proposals. But De la Rey was having none of that – indeed he even had some of his men flogged for mistreating the prisoners, and on the following day he released all 500 of them to march to the nearest British post. Then eluding immediate attempts at pursuit he withdrew northwards.

As soon as he received the news of the disaster, Methuen, at Vryburg, determined to avenge it there and then. This was to prove an extraordinarily rash decision, as he was only able to assemble a weak column of 1,300 raw troops or surrendered Boers, Cape half-castes and other colonials who were at best more useful as scouts than as disciplined soldiers. But he did not hesitate. Asking Kekewich to send 1,200 mounted men from Klerksdorp to join him a short distance south of Lichtenburg on the 7th March, he set out from Vryburg, ninety-five miles away, with his scratch column, six guns and a convoy of 80 wagons. He started on the 2nd of March and soon began to fall behind schedule owing to the long searches for water over the particularly dry veld. On the night of the 6th he was still some twenty-five miles south of his rendezvous with Kekewich's mounted column, itself moving up rapidly about thirty-five miles to the southeast. Between the two columns, and unknown to either, De la Rey lay in wait with over a thousand men. At 4.30 the following morning Methuen's column broke camp and set off. The ox-convoy was situated a mile ahead of the mule-convoy, and each were protected by a screen of troops and three guns. After they had plodded along for about an hour, De la Rey made his presence known with a preliminary attack on the rear-guard. Half an hour later, he pushed a second wave of burghers forward on the British flank. Methuen, who was in front with the ox-convoy, decided to close up the two groups, but before the manoeuvre could be completed De la Rey attacked again from the right, his burghers galloping up close before leaping from their ponies and pressing forward in the face of British shells and heavy rifle-fire. De la Rey had chosen his moments with precision, his veterans, firing from the saddle, now flung themselves on the crumbling screen of troops around the mule-convoy, whereupon the mounted troops broke and fled for three miles before they drew rein. By now the mule-convoy was totally enveloped, the regulars fighting to the bitter end, and the artillery commander being the last to survive, and by refusing to surrender, the last to die. De la Rey now turned his attention to the ox-convoy and Methuen. It had stopped in a hollow near a dried stream, and around it, braced by Methuen who refused to take cover, stood a thin line of infantry. The infantry was enfiladed by the river, overlooked by the high ground above it and beset on three sides by superior numbers, and within seconds the men were subjected to severe fire from the Boers. Methuen himself fell, badly wounded in the side and the thigh, and his horse, shot beside him, rolled over and crushed his leg. A doctor, going up to dress his wounds was also shot. The sheer hopelessness of the situation allowed of nothing but surrender.

The British had sustained the worst defeat of the whole of the guerrilla war. Nearly 200 men were dead or wounded, 600 others made captive. While his own men helped themselves to booty, De la Rey sought Methuen out, and found him where he still lay near the guns. Thus, the two men finally met face to face in the most poignant encounter of the entire war. De la Rey leant over and extended his hand saying '*I am sorry to meet you in such circumstances*' - '*Oh, it's the fortunes of war*' Methuen responded – '*How is Mrs. De la Rey?*' to which De la Rey replied ' *She's still moving around safely...*' Methuen assured De la Rey that he had always tried to behave in a gentle and friendly manner with the women and children, whom he had to convey to the camps, and that he had only caused the removal of Mrs. De la Rey on the orders of his superior officers. In reply, De la Rey merely nodded, and Mrs. De la Rey herself then came over to see Methuen in her husband's laager, and later sent him some roast chicken and biscuits. To the dismay of his subordinate officers De la Rey set free his wounded adversary, and allowed him to be conveyed to Klerksdorp in his own wagon, having first sent a message to Methuen's wife informing her of her husband's condition and his own sincere regrets. The 600 other prisoners were then given rations and released. (Years later, a fine hospital was built in De la Rey's hometown, Lichtenburg, and named after him. Lord Methuen, along with Lord Kitchener and many other British Generals were among the first to contribute towards its foundation)

Although Methuen was half-forgotten and neglected by Kitchener, Milner, and even the War Office, he occupied that special place in English minds reserved for men who did not give way to adversity. Of Methuen a contemporary observed, '*He was the senior of the British Generals in the field – senior even to Lord Kitchener. Of all those who went out in higher command, he alone remained to the last, refusing to come home even after having been severely wounded, and when the war was over he strove manfully to retrieve the discredit which he thought the sad reverse of Magersfontein had brought upon his name. Younger men were placed above him – his command was reduced at times to a single weak column; yet he continued to serve his country with unabated consistency and zeal. His chivalrous spirit was proof against all slights and discouragements.*' (H.W. Wilson – 'With the Flag to Pretoria')

274

After the Battle of Klipdrift/Tweebosch, De la Rey left the western Transvaal to meet Steyn and De Wet who had just escaped from The British in the Free State. The news of his spectacular success helped to lift their spirits after the disasters of Kitchener's new model drives from which they had just fled. Steyn then stayed with De la Rey, but De Wet, unwilling to serve under De la Rey's command, immediately set off to return to the Free State.

When Kitchener heard the news of the battle, he collapsed and remained in bed without food for thirty-six hours, only telling his most trusted Aide de Camp that his nerves '*had gone all to pieces*'. When he recovered he 'ate a gargantian meal and recovered his poise.' Clearly by now, Kitchener was alarmed over the Boer successes in the western Transvaal, and hastened to introduce his 'new model drive' strategy into that region. He gathered some 16,000 men at Klerksdorp, divided them into four groups under Maj. Gen. Walter Kitchener, the younger brother of Lord Kitchener, and Colonels Kekewich, Sir Henry Rawlinson, and A.N. Rochfort respectively, and in the manner of his Free State drives, added an extensive system of blockhouse fortification lines. Although the construction of blockhouses had already started in the Transvaal in July 1901, there were none in the southwest sector, although they hemmed in the north, east and west, with the Vaal River providing a barrier to the south. It was in this sector, extending 115 miles from north to south between Lichtenburg and the Vaal and 160 miles from east to west between Klerksdorp and Vryburg, that the bulk of De la Rey's commandos under Kemp, Celliers and Liebenberg were now located.

Kitchener then received intelligence reports which placed large numbers of Boers within thirty miles of the Schoonspruit blockhouse line, which marked the eastern boundary of this large area. He ordered 11,000 mounted troops under the four commanders to take up position forty miles to the west of the Schoonspruit line during the night of 23rd March, and then to return to it during the course of the following day, having deployed into a driving formation. In theory they should have trapped Kemp's and Liebenberg's commandos; they should also have caught De la Rey and Steyn returning from Zendelingsfontein with members of Steyn's Free State Council and a small escort, all of whom were in the designated area. In the end all the Boers succeeded in escaping. De la Rey and Steyn slipped through in the small hours of the 24th March and Kemp at about 6 a.m. while the British were still deploying. Liebenberg did not get out until the afternoon when gaps were beginning to open in the 90-mile driving line, but in the attempt he was forced to abandon his guns and wagons. They then all joined Celliers on the Harts River, bringing the total of their combined forces to 2,500 men.

The results of the first drive proved disappointing, yielding only 165 prisoners, three guns and two pom-poms. As a result, Kitchener conferred with his group commanders in Klerksdorp on the 26th March, and decided that while Rochfort would stay on the Vaal, the other commanders would set out westwards in echelon over a period of three days to create entrenched camps at assigned points. At the same time, they were to try to make contact with the Boer forces. In Walter Kitchener's group, Col. G.A. Cookson set off at 2 a.m. on the 31st of March with 1,800 men and six guns, to reconnoitre the Brakspruit, an almost dry stream which flowed towards the Harts River forty miles

275

away. Around 10 a.m. he picked up the trail of a commando, and set off in pursuit until he was checked at a farm called Boschbult, where he fought a holding action while he set up an entrenched camp on the northern bank of the stream. Just after 1 p.m., before he had fully completed his defences, Kemp and Celliers attacked Kitchener from the north, whilst Liebenberg fell upon him from the south. After charging from the south and then again from the northeast, Liebenberg joined Kemp and Celliers, but left his guns behind to shell Cookson's camp from the southwest. The Boers then drove into the British screens but could make no headway against the camp itself. De la Rey, who had his HQ on a farm called Roodewal (Rooiwal), seven miles to the southwest arrived on the scene late in the afternoon, and realising the hopelessness of the situation, called off the Boer action.

The overall situation in the Western Transvaal was rapidly reaching a stalemate. Throughout the area, indeed throughout the whole of South Africa, it was becoming increasingly obvious that the British were not going to overcome the Boers without exorbitant losses, and that the Boers would never surrender even if they had no possible chance of ever defeating the British army in the field. It was inevitable that a settlement of the conflict was now only possible through negotiation. On all fronts feelers for peace were being put about. In Britain, Lloyd-George was making loud noises on the theme of '*make peace now!*', because, according to him '*justice demanded it – and so did commons sense*'. Otherwise, he argued, it would surely cause an embittered Boer nation to seize its chance as soon as Britain ever became involved in a foreign war. This powerful argument was not lost on a country very aware of its international unpopularity and isolation. On the other hand, there was also no real inclination to throw in the sponge especially now that the Empire was, once again, offering increased contingents to fight beside the British forces in South Africa.

In South Africa, requests for peace talks were emanating from various quarters. On the very day of Methuen's defeat at Klipdrift/Tweebosch, Kitchener sent a messenger to the camp of the Transvaal Government, now concealed somewhere in the bushveld, some forty miles north of Balmoral on the Delagoa Bay railway. Since Kruger's departure from the Transvaal in September 1901, Acting-President Schalk Burger, together with State-Secretary Reitz, Lukas Meyer, and other officials continued the management of the Transvaal government function. Following their flight from the Delagoa Bay railway, near Komati Poort in September, they had fled hither and thither across 25,000 square miles of eastern Transvaal, successfully eluding all British attempts to capture them. At first sight there seemed little about Kitchener's overtures to suggest that their wanderings may soon be over. In fact, it was an odd kind of communication. Kitchener himself said nothing, and the contents of the peace overture were simply copies of correspondence between the governments of Great Britain and Holland. From it the Boers gleaned the following story- *On January 25, 1902, Holland's Prime Minister had made a proposal of mediation to the British Government. He had, in fact, been prompted by a passage in a speech made by Lord Rosebury at Chesterfield to the effect that a first step to peace might be an 'an apparently casual meeting of two travellers in a neutral inn'.* Kruger and the Boer delegates in Europe were in favour of the proposal, but Lord Lansdown turned it down. He did, however, add the comment that the '*The quickest and most satisfactory means of arranging a settlement would be by direct communication between the leaders of the Boer forces in South Africa and the Commander-in-Chief of His Majesty's Forces.'*

The correspondence was all that Kitchener sent, and he made no comment on its contents. However, the Boers immediately read into the transaction what they were intended to read, firstly, that the proclamation of the 7th August 1901, which had outlawed them, was forgotten, and that they and not those Boers who had surrendered, the 'hands-uppers' as the guerrillas so contemptuously named them, were being recognised as the true custodians of their people's political destiny. Secondly, although nothing was said about the Boers losing their independence, there was an unspoken invitation to talk things over with Kitchener. In this way, the two nations contrived to wriggle off the stake on which pride had impaled them, and to take the first steps towards trying to end a struggle, which neither of them was ever going to win, and for which both were becoming utterly sickened. Schalk Burger applied for a safe conduct for the Boer leaders to join their Free State colleagues to discuss the proposals. Kitchener readily agreed, so on the 22nd March 1902 Burger and his party entered the British lines at Balmoral, and were escorted by the British to Kroonstad in the northern Free State. President Steyn, General De Wet and the other senior Free State leaders had already arrived in Kroonstad, so discussions started immediately. Talks centred on matters regarding the venue, the constitution, and the agenda for the proposed peace conference, as well as the problems related to the gathering together of delegates from widely dispersed and hostile areas in the midst of military operations. The immediate need was to bring together leaders from their widely scattered spheres of operation, and consequently the strange phenomena occurred of the British co-operating with the Boers in finding and bringing together under safe conduct various Boer leaders – and all this in the midst of military operations, which at the same time, were continuing with unabated vigour. In fact, far from receding into the background, these operations now assumed an even greater importance in view of their possible effect on the peace negotiations. At Kroonstad, it was agreed that the Boer leaders would meet a Klerksdorp in the western Transvaal on the 9th April to thrash out an agenda, and request safe conduct for about sixty Boer delegates from all corners of South Africa to gather at Klerksdorp and participate in the discussions.

Meanwhile, Kitchener became desperate to end the military campaign in the western Transvaal as quickly as possible. On the 7th of April, he released Ian Hamilton from his duties as Chief-of-Staff, and appointed him overall commander of the British forces in the western Transvaal. On Hamilton's arrival at Kekewich's HQ at Middelbult, twenty miles south of Lichtenburg, he immediately started preparations for a big drive southwards from the Brakspruit, past the Harts River on to the Vaal, and then eastwards to Klerksdorp, a total distance of 140 miles. On the evening of the 10th April, the entire British force was positioned on the south side of the Brakspruit, but Kekewich mistakenly placed his division some ten miles to the east, immediately behind Rawlinson. He then partially corrected the error during the night, moving eastwards towards the Harts River, so that his right now ended up at Roodewal, about three miles from the river.

During De la Rey's absence at the peace talks in Klerksdorp, Kemp had assumed overall command of the Boer forces, comprising his own commandos, now under Potgieter, and those of Celliers and Liebenberg. Although Kemp was a very able lieutenant, as a leader he lacked the skills and intuition of De la Rey and tended to act rashly and hastily. Thus, having received reports of a small British force of some 300 men in the vicinity, he decided to move in on their right flank without seeking verification of the report, nor of checking out the situation before the attack.the intelligence reports turned out to be totally out of date, and as Kemp's force topped the ridge about one-and-a-half miles south-west of the main columns at Roodewal, it came within sight of the whole of von Donop's and Grenfell's columns, some 3,000 men in total, not all of whom were even visible to him. In spite of this, Kemp continued his advance towards the Brakspruit, and about a mile from von Donop's column, he inexplicably detached a group of about 700 men with orders to break into a trot and advance directly into the face of enemy in lines, two, three and four deep. As the group approached the British, it threw its wings forward like the horns of a Zulu impi, and at the same time opened fire. The British closed in to meet the attack and by the time the Boers were within 600 yards range, 1,100 rifles and a maxim were brought to bear down on them. The Boers continued without change of pace, throwing their wings even further forward as if to envelope the British entirely, and it was not until they were within a hundreed yards of the troops that they realised that the defenders were still standing firm against the onslaught. The Boers, out-manned and out-gunned, now abandoned their charge, and retreated hastily. Potgieter was killed in this action, and as they continued to retire, the Imperial Light Horse under Col. C. J. Briggs on Rawlinson's right, galloped up to the scene dispersing Liebenberg's commandos who were trying to support Kemp from the east. In this action at Roodewal, the Boers lost 127 men of whom fifty-one were killed, while the British casualties amounted to eighty-seven killed and wounded. It is certain that, had he been present, De la Rey would not have sanctioned the attack that was based on inadequate reconnaissance, not properly planned, lacking the advantage of cover and surprise and gaining nothing. On the other hand, what it did achieve was the drastic weakening of the Boers' negotiating clout at the current round of peace meetings

At Klerksdorp, the Boer leaders opened their deliberations. Present with De la Rey and the Transvaal Government was Louis Botha whose recent whereabouts had hitherto been unknown to British until he emerged in Klerksdorp. Missing for the Transvaal was Smuts; the message that was to recall him from the siege of far-off O'Okiep, was still on its way, and had not yet reached him. Among the Free State leaders present were Steyn, De Wet, Herzog and Olivier. The meeting opened with a prayer, and Schalk Burger called on Botha, De Wet and De la Rey to describe conditions in their respective parts of the country. After deliberation, they decided to negotiate with the British, but on only terms which they wished to submit to Kitchener in person. Kitchener agreed, and that same night they journeyed to Pretoria where he received the Boer delegation with full honours and with warm hospitality. Repeated success in battle had given the Boers great confidence, and many were itching to continue the struggle. It was a bitter blow, therefore, when the news of Kemp's debacle broke the headlines on the very day of the opening of the conference. On the other hand, for Kitchener and Milner, for Britain and the Empire, a faint ray of hope at last glimmered on the horizon.

PART 3

THE END

15
TO VEREENIGING AND THE BITTER END

On the 12th April 1902, the Boer leaders met Kitchener and Milner in Pretoria to open peace negotiations. The Boers were in a confident mood, unanimously aware that they were not seeking a 'peace at all costs', nor that they and their commandos had been conclusively defeated, in spite of the serious setback inflicted on the impetuous Kemp at Rooiwal the day before. Throughout South Africa the Boer commandos were continuing to harass the British, causing them serious damage and concern. De la Rey still had over 5,000 burghers scattered about the western Transvaal, while right on Kitchener's doorstep, General Piet Viljoen had succeeded in penetrating the Pretoria-Johannesburg protection zone. Even as the peace talks were in progress, Viljoen's commandos were inflicting defeat on some British columns only a few miles from Pretoria. In the far east along the Delagoa Bay railway, over 2,000 burghers scoured the mountains and the bushveld, and in the north, General Beyers was once again vigorously active in the area round the town of Louis Trichardt. In the Free State, over 7,000 fighting burghers continued to harass the British in spite of Kitchener's 'new model drives', and with 3,000 men under his command in the Cape, General Smuts was not only causing General French great anxiety, but effectively tying up thousands of British troops, who could otherwise have been put to more telling use elsewhere. Altogether the total of the Boer fighting strength, at the time of the Pretoria conference, amounted to more than 22,000 burghers with their commandos intact and effective. It was this fighting capacity, coupled with their profound spirit of independence, which gave the Boer generals the confidence to submit their own peace proposals to Kitchener and Milner, without hesitation or any doubts over the terms for which they were prepared to settle.

Just as the Boer leaders were united in their resolve, so the principal British negotiators, Kitchener and Milner, were divided in theirs. Kitchener had a clear understanding of what the British were up against. He had since his arrival in South Africa grown to respect and admire the tenacity of the Boers in the field of battle, as well as their blinding faith in the justice of their cause. In the same way, he had grown to trust some of the principal Boer leaders such as Botha, Smuts and above all, De la Rey. In this way he was convinced that nothing less than an honourably and equitably agreed peace would ever resolve the problems in South Africa, and that any more conflict could only lead to further futile loss of life and dignity, and eventually result in ultimate insolvable resentment and hatred between the Boers and the British.

On the other hand, Milner's avowed and deeply rooted imperial idealism blinded him to the realities of the crisis in South Africa. He chose instead to hold out for the outright defeat of the two Boer republics, and their total subjugation to Britain. In this, he was enthusiastically supported by Chamberlain, the Colonial Secretary in London, who sought nothing less than the annihilation of the Boer leaders and their forces, and their surrender and submission to British dominion. Kitchener was frustrated in his awareness that neither Milner nor Chamberlain shared his own enthusiasm for a rapid and honourable end to hostilities in South Africa. In the face of mounting opposition in

Britain to the continuation of the war, Chamberlain ignored the reality and the gravity of the situation in South Africa, and continued to hold out for outright defeat of the two Boer republics.

From the onset of the Pretoria peace talks Milner remained silent, and Kitchener alone responded attentively to the Boer proposals for the establishment of a self-governing Protectorate under the supervision of General Louis Botha, and the surrender of their independence in respect of foreign affairs only. In addition, the Boers confirmed their willingness to hand over a substantial part of the Rand and Swaziland in return for closer co-operation with the British. Kitchener listened to the Boer demands, and at the end of the first day, he informed them that their proposals would be submitted to London at once, but that they would almost certainly be rejected.

Two days later they met again, and the Boers were informed of Britain's outright dismissal of their proposals. This time Milner also joined in the discussions, and confirmed that his Government would not accept any compromise or amendment to its original conditions, and proposed that the whole matter be ended right there and then. Chamberlain's rebuff, and Milner's unsympathetic attitude made the Boer delegation sullen and morose, and many were for abandoning the conference and returning to the battlefield. They informed the British delegation that they had no constitutional authority to negotiate on the basis of surrendering their independence, and agreed that in the circumstance any further discussions would be futile. Kitchener, desperate for the continuation of the talks in spite of Milner, succeeded in luring the Boers back to the conference table by proposing to cable London with a request that the British Government submits its own list of conditions for peace, and to await further developments. After two consecutive Cabinet meetings, Chamberlain transmitted, through the Secretary for War, a reply to Kitchener's petitions. In his reply, he expressed his Government's surprise at the Boers' attitude, and referred them to the proposals offered at the Middelburg Conference a year ago. He added that, in spite of the unnecessary wastage of British lives since then, they would be prepared to stand by the terms of their original Middelburg offer.

In recognition of Kitchener's sympathetic efforts to keep the peace talks alive in spite of Milner's disdainful opposition, the Boer leaders agreed to negotiate on the basis of the British offer. They also submitted two requests of their own, asking that one of their representatives in Europe be allowed to join the peace talks, and secondly that an armistice be agreed to enable each leader to consult his burghers. The British Government refused the first request, but agreed the second, and Kitchener proposed a 'go slow' to enable the Boer generals and thirty delegates from each of the two former Republics, to hold a convention at Vereeniging on the 15th May 1902. With the remit to decide for peace or for war, the Boer leaders were granted free railway and telegraph facilities to hold meetings, and elect the sixty delegates. In the meantime, the war would go on, but for four days prior to the conference, no commando whose commandant was a delegate, would be attacked by the British forces.

The conference then broke up, and the Boer leaders prepared to set off to consult their commandos. Regrettably, before they left, Milner could not resist the temptation to deliver a petulant lecture to the effect that the way to peace did not lie through procrastination, and that he profoundly suspected the Boers of playing a tricky game. The Boers were incensed, and many, including De Wet, were for calling off the whole matter there and then. However, Kitchener met them in private, and with great tact and grace removed much of the effect of Milner's provocative influence. He specifically consoled them by predicting that within two years, the Liberal Party would be in power in Britain, and would grant self-government to South Africa. It had seemed against all the odds at that time, but in the end, Kitchener's predictions were fairly accurate.

During the month that followed the end of the peace talks the war raged on with uninterrupted vigour in the eastern and western Transvaal, but into it were wedged periods of peace which allowed the Boer leaders, with the hospitality and co-operation of the British, to move around quite freely to consult with their commandos. Talks of peace now ranged far and wide, and in Britain in particular, anticipation mounted with the prospects that all would be satisfactorily settled in time for the coronation of the new King Edward VII. Not everyone shared this enthusiasm, however. Milner, for example, was confident that the Boers were hopelessly defeated, and that it would be a folly to allow them to emerge from any settlement with their moral integrity unimpaired. It was to this end that he emphatically opposed any further forms of concession or compromise.

Kitchener openly disagreed with Milner. More than anyone else, he was painfully aware that the Boers were far from being defeated, and that even now they were able to retreat into the vast depths of the sparsely populated Cape, or to the wild untamed regions of the northern Transvaal, and continue a protracted war from there. For him the only answer was a crisp end now, and not a costly and prolonged petering out of hostilities, only to arrive at a settlement in which no one had any faith or confidence. Kitchener's concerns were echoed throughout the world, particularly in Britain where Lord Rosebury's Liberal opposition party's attitude was openly shared by many Union-Conservatives as well. Rosebury was anxious to avoid a war fought to an end so bitter, that any future co-operation between the two white races of South Africa would be impossible to bring about. He wanted terms that would encourage the Boers to come swiftly into the Empire, and work freely and enthusiastically with their English-speaking fellows for the reconstruction of their country.

Amongst the Boer leaders, there was also division. Schalk Burger and Botha had become painfully aware that surrender was inevitable, and sought a peace that would preserve their national integrity and political future, and protect the Afrikaner race from irretrievable ruin. On the other hand, Steyn and De Wet refused to be moved from their passionate belief in the consummate independence of the Boer republics, and to that end they were prepared to sacrifice everything to attain it. They absolutely refused to accept defeat, and actively sought pledges from the Free State delegates that they would never surrender their independence. It was at this time that Smuts arrived from O'Okiep under the 'safe conduct' agreement, and hastily sought to align himself with Botha and the pro-peace faction.

On the 15th May 1902 the Governments of the Transvaal and the Orange Free State, together with thirty delegates from each of the two Republics, gathered on the Transvaal side of the Vaal River in a settlement appropriately named Vereeniging – a Dutch word meaning 'uniting'. The purpose of the meeting was to deliberate and vote on the British peace proposals discussed in Pretoria a few weeks earlier. The meeting was officially opened with the appointment of General Beyers as Chairman of the conference, followed by an address by Schalk Burger, President of the Transvaal Republic. Sensing the division between the Transvaal and Free State delegates, Burger opened with a cautious reminder that the British Government had made it quite clear that it would not negotiate on any basis other than the surrender of Boer independence. He recommended that the delegates accept the British conditions, and declared that if they did agree to submission, the decision needed to be a unanimous one. Louis Botha was the next member to speak. He immediately stated that it would be impossible for a unanimous conclusion to be achieved as long as the Free State delegates considered themselves bound by their pledges to their commandos not to surrender their independence. A legal ruling was then sought, and Judge Herzog, on behalf of the Free State, and General Smuts for the Transvaal concurred that as a principal of law the delegates were not an instrument of the will of the commandos, but were bound to vote only on the basis of their individual judgement. The Free State delegates grudgingly accepted this ruling, on condition that the effect of their pledges was recorded in the official minutes of the meeting.

A negotiating team of five delegates was then selected, and the conference set under way. The chosen members were Generals Botha, De la Rey, and Smuts for the Transvaal, and General De Wet, and Judge Herzog for the Free State. The delegates were immediately informed that since the negotiating team had not been granted any plenary powers, any terms agreed by it required ratification by all the delegates at Vereeniging, as well as the British Government in London. After that point of law was firmly established and agreed, negotiations began at noon on the 19th May, 1902. The Boers set the negotiations under way with a repetition of their proposals for self-government previously submitted at the Pretoria meeting. At this juncture Milner suddenly interjected with an outright rejection of the Boer proposals, describing them as 'farcical'. Kitchener concurred by explaining that they were impractical and unworkable, in both administrative as well as military terms.

The Boers were openly disenchanted with Milner's attitude, and Kitchener, fearing a premature breakdown in the negotiations, anxiously sought other areas of compromise. Milner however continued to discourage all further attempts to reach an agreement, and after some hours of frustrating wrangling, the Boers suggested that Smuts, Kitchener and Milner retire for personal and informal discussions to disentangle the impasse, and seek out some kind of mutually acceptable solution. This gave Milner, the experienced politician and Statesman, a superb opportunity to steer the talks back to the British proposals tendered at the Middelburg Conference. A few hours later, the three men returned to the conference table with a draft preamble to the proposed surrender terms. In a significant concession to the negotiating status of the Boer leaders, they were recognised as acting as the 'Government of the South African Republic', and the 'Government of the Orange Free State', two governments which had, in fact, been abolished by the British nearly two years earlier. In return, the Boers were requested to agree that the burghers would accept King Edward VII as their 'lawful sovereign'. There then followed a proposal that a sub-committee be appointed to draw up an Agreement to add to the Preamble.

At this point General De Wet reacted with some violence against the terms of the Preamble, disclaiming it as 'dishonourable' to the Boers of the Orange Free State, and rejecting any further conditions which may be added to it. Milner, delighted at the possibility of an imminent breakdown of the talks, quickly retorted by stating that in that case, Britain saw no further point in continuing with the peace talks. Kitchener and Smuts, however, were equally anxious to keep the negotiations alive, and hastily intervened with a proposal to draft an appropriate document for De Wet to examine and comment upon, before irrevocably withdrawing from the discussions. Smuts and Herzog then retired with Milner and his legal advisor, Sir Richard Solomon, the Attorney-General at the Cape, and set about drawing up a draft agreement, which was duly submitted to the full negotiating committee for comment and approval. After the addition of one long Addendum, the final text of the draft agreement was cabled to London.

In essence the text was basically identical to the Middelburg conditions with three significant changes, all of them in favour of the Boers. The first was a concession made in favour of the colonial rebels. Milner agreed to request the Cape Government to grant an amnesty for all the Cape rebels, excepting the leaders, exempting them from imprisonment, and letting them off with permanent disenfranchisement. It is interesting to note that the exemption covered the Cape rebels only – those from Natal were left to take their chances under ordinary law.

The second change dealt with the voting rights of the Natives, and proposed to delay the granting of franchise until after the introduction of the two new Colonies, instead of before as proposed at Middelburg. This subtle alteration of propositions suggested that Milner was in agreement with the probability that the exclusion would be a permanent one, because it was a foregone certainty that the Boers would never give the vote to the Africans. This change of attitude was exceedingly significant, because it was made in direct contradiction to Chamberlain's earlier assertions that Britain would never consent to the purchase of a shameful peace through abandoning the coloured population to their pre-war status.

The third alteration concerned the question of repayment of war losses. At Middelburg, Britain had offered to repay the Boer war debts with a grant of £1,000,000. Clause 11 of the new agreement now increased this amount to £3,000,000, and with the addition of a new clause 12, Britain also offered generous loans to the burghers to assist them in rebuilding their lives after war. Further generous offers of assistance were also promised to the Loyalists in the two old Republics, in recognition of their support during the war.

In Britain, the 'terms of surrender' as Chamberlain preferred to call the proposed peace terms, were received with enthusiasm, and after discussions the Cabinet duly agreed them and cabled South Africa on the 27th May, with instructions that they be formally presented to the Boers for a simple 'yes' or 'no' reply. The final document that was laid before the delegates consisted essentially of ten articles. They were:

1- The Boers to put down their arms and acknowledge the King as their lawful sovereign
2- All prisoners and internees to be returned on making the same acknowledgement
3- Surrendering burghers not to lose personal liberty or property
4- No legal prosecution of burghers except for war crimes
5- Dutch to be taught in schools where parents wished; Dutch would also be admitted in the law courts
6- Rifles to be permitted for lawful protection
7- Military administration to be followed by civil management, and subsequently by self-government as soon as circumstances permitted
8- Question of Native franchise not to be decided before self-government
9- No war tax
10- District Commissioners to be set up to assist resettlement, provide necessities lost in the war, and honour Republican bank- or promissory notes, and for this purpose a free gift of £3,000,000 to be provided by the United Kingdom as well as personal loans on liberal terms.

The immediate reaction amongst the Transvaal delegates was 'yes' and for the Free State delegation a resounding 'no'. In the Transvaal, the commandos were becoming increasingly demoralised and depressed, particularly over the sufferings of their women and children who had been left behind to fend for themselves. Most of the families were in a sad state, with little if any food and shelter, and vulnerable to attacks from the Natives who were beginning to assume an increasingly aggressive attitude against them. From Zoutpansberg, in the far north, for example, messages were coming in that they were getting out of hand, and in the south much the same was reported in Bethal and Carolina as well.

Finally, in May, even while the peace talks were under way, the Boers were stunned by an alarming incident at Holkrantz, near Vryheid, in a part of Zululand that had previously been annexed by the Transvaal. After a series of reciprocal cattle raids between the Zulu Sikobobo tribe and some Boers in the area, Sikobobo, the chief of the tribe, successfully repelled a Boer attack by slaying fifty-three Boers, wounding three, and recapturing 380 head of his own cattle. The burghers still in action were horrified by the news of this slaughter, and were rapidly reaching the limit of their endurance. On the other hand De Wet still advocated for an emphatic 'no' vote, and the majority of his followers from the Free State held for a continuation of the conflict until the bitter end. In response to one protester who went on about fighting to the bitter end, De la Rey lost patience, and thumping the table roared back at him – '*Fight to the bitter end - to the bitter end, you say?- Why man, THIS is the bitter end!*'

In the face of this opposition from the Free State, the Transvaal leaders continued to press the case for peace, passionately at first by Schalk Burger, Botha and De la Rey, and later, towards the end, eloquently by Smuts. Gradually the Free State delegates began to falter, and started to accept the fact that the war was ending in any event, and that it was now necessary to expend all energy in winning the peace. Finally, De Wet himself realised hat the Free State could never continue the struggle without the help of the Transvaal, and sat back in bitter resignation.

On Saturday the 31st May, 1902 the delegates assembled to vote for or against the British peace proposals. The negotiating committee laid a motion on the table setting out the reasons why the Boer delegation should accept the British terms. They included the pitiful state of the Boer women and children, due not only to the effects of the war, but also to the unbearable conditions caused by the Natives, especially the so-called 'Holkrantz murderers'. Reference was also made to Kitchener's proclamation of the 7th August 1901 that threatened the confiscation of farms belonging to those burghers who continued to fight against the British forces, and also finally to the Boers' inability to keep and maintain British prisoners of war. The document concluded by admitting that the Boers no longer had any practical means of continuing the war, and certainly no hope of ever winning it. But even then, the disgruntled De Wet and the other Free State delegates grumbled, and manifested openly their opposition to the peace terms. Botha and De la Rey pleaded earnestly with them to accept the resolutions of the treaty, and in the end the recalcitrant Free State members conceded one by one, and finally the majority of them agreed to accept. All the delegates then voted for acceptance of the terms by an overwhelming majority of fifty-four to six.

The Boer leaders returned to Pretoria that same night, where they were met by Kitchener and Milner. At 11.15 pm on the 31st May 1902 the formal peace treaty was signed by President Burger for the Transvaal, then General de Wet for the Orange Free State, and finally Kitchener and Milner for the British Government. It was all over in five minutes, and the two Boer Republics were finally dead and buried. The Boer leaders, looking sad and dejected, retired to their quarters, while Kitchener, with Ian Hamilton, and other senior members of the military staff celebrated their forthcoming departure from South Africa. Milner looked haggard and despondent, aware that he had lost his design for unfettered British dominion in South Africa. It was an exceedingly bitter pill for him to swallow.

Very shortly after the signing of the peace treaty, the imperial army in South Africa started moving out, and soon all but 20,000 of the 250,000 British were on their way home. The Boer commandos too emerged from their laagers with their heads held high and unabashed, as men who had achieved a great victory. Not as conspicuous or proud were those Boers who had reneged to the British ranks during the course of the war. Branded as 'hands-uppers' and 'joiners' ('hensoppers en yoiners') by their own people, these National Scouts and other collaborators would be condemned for years as traitors and social outcasts, whose skeletons would be well hidden away in shameful family cupboards

So at midnight on the 31st May, 1902 it was all over, but it was not to be the end. With the dawn of the first day of June came a new birth, and for the following hundred years South Africa would evolve into full nationhood, and grow to play a significant role on the universal stage of world affairs.

16
THE AFTERMATH

Shortly before midnight on the 31st May 1902 the Anglo-Boer War ended. The 'expedition' that Chamberlain and Milner had predicted to be 'over by Christmas' had dragged on for nearly three long and bitter years. It was a grievous and wasteful war and had cost the British Government more than £200,000,000. The cost in blood was equally high; there had been over 100,000 casualties of all kinds among the 365,700 imperial and 82,750 colonial troops, who had fought in the war. 22,000 of them found their graves in South Africa – 5,775 killed by enemy action or accident, and shovelled into the veld where they had fallen, and a further 16,170 who died of their wounds, or were killed by disease. In addition to the human loss, over 400,000 horses, mules, and donkeys had been lost. Today their sombre last remains can be found all over South Africa, marked by hundreds of whitened stones and countless lines of little crosses.

On the Boer side, the cost in life and suffering was equally trenchant. There were over 7,000 deaths among the 87,500 Boers, foreign volunteers, and Afrikaners from the Cape and Natal, who had fought in the commandos of the two republics. In addition, as many as 28,000 persons, mainly women and children, died in British civilian concentration camps. Farms and homesteads were destroyed beyond recognition, crops were burned, and several million cattle, horses, and sheep had been looted or killed by the British. After the war, the Boers made more than 63,000 claims for war losses, and the British Government paid out compensation grants of over £3,000,000 as promised at Vereeniging. In addition, £2,000,000 was paid to the Uitlanders and other loyalists who had supported the British cause during the war.

Most distressing of all were the untold casualties and fatalities suffered by the Africans during the war. No official records were ever kept of the losses among the 107,000 blacks in the concentration camps, but it has been estimated that over 12,000 died there. In addition, it is also known that there were many thousands of deaths among the 10,000 Africans under arms, who had served on the side of the British as scouts, guides and blockhouse guards, as well as the 40,000 unarmed natives who had worked as drivers, labourers and herders.

The British 'victory' was a rueful one, which ultimately brought to an end their pre-eminence in South Africa and the beginning of unfettered Afrikaner domination for the ensuing seven decades. It was a calamitous and ruinous conflict, which from the start, produced results that no one could ever have predicted or even dreamed. All the initial reasons and justifications for the war were valid enough to those who were involved at the time, yet no one would ever have imagined that before the twentieth century was over all would be lost. At the same time, it would have been impossible to forecast that that the ultimate wielders of political power in South Africa would be neither the Boers nor the British, but the descendants of those many thousands of indigenous South Africans who were forced to toil, suffer, and even die in a conflict that was not of their making.

The fact was that the war had dragged on for too long, and had become an untenable burden to all those who were involved in it. Even before the last shot was fired many of the surviving protagonists clamoured to get away as far and as fast as possible from the mess that they had engendered. On the British side, Buller was the first senior general to return to England. Many of his fellow-officers in South Africa, including Roberts, were relieved to see him go, for it was Buller's misfortune to be condemned for his failures in Natal, rather than remembered for his success in relieving Ladysmith, or his subsequent victories over Botha's commandos in the eastern Transvaal. On his return to Britain he took up his previous post as Commanding Officer of the 1st Army Corps at Aldershot, and it was not long before his reputation once again came under attack, this time in an anonymous letter published in the 'The Times' condemning Buller's Thukela campaign as a 'display of supreme military incapacity'. Buller foolishly over-reacted by making an ill-judged after-lunch speech, in which he defended his conduct in Natal, and blatantly blamed his subordinates, including Warren, White, Hart, and Long, for the many disasters that had characterised the campaign. Buller was severely censured for this attack on his fellow officers, and the War Office relieved him of his command on the grounds of breaching the prohibition on adverse public comment by serving officers. He spent the remainder of his days quietly on his estate in Devon, and died in 1908. In 1905, his many admirers erected an equestrian statue in Exeter, bearing the legend – 'He Saved Natal'

There is no doubt that Buller was the most contumacious of all the British generals in South Africa, and for this reason his reputation was seriously damaged during the period immediately following the Boer War. Fortunately, later historians were inclined to look more favourably on the career of this remarkable soldier, highlighting the wider aspects of his service as a brave and able military leader prior to the Boer War, and particularly his qualities of personal courage and administrative ability. Above all, he remained universally admired for his never failing concern for the well-being of his men. In his book, 'The Boer War Generals' (Wrens Park Publishing, 2000), the Boer War historian, Peter Trew pays homage to this aspect of Buller's character - '*Perhaps the most endearing evidence in his favour is that although many of his officers were critical of him he never forfeited the respect and affection of the ordinary soldiers who served under him.*

Not long after Buller's departure, Roberts also left South Africa, and as we have seen, returned to Britain in triumph. On the 3rd January 1901 he took up an appointment in London as Commander-in-Chief of the British Army, a position with an imposing sounding title, but in fact without any direct operational function, and with merely a little more responsibility than that of a military advisor to the Government. In 1902, the British Cabinet appointed Lord Elgin to set up a Royal Commission with a remit to investigate the activities and efficiency of the British Army in South Africa. Roberts was requested to give evidence on a number of aspects of the conduct of the war, and on any lessons that could be learnt for the future. One of the leading members of the Royal Commission was Viscount Esher, who since the start of the war had taken a keen interest in all aspects of army activities and reform. In his findings to the Commission Esher expressed concern over the restrictions created by the antiquated methods of military management in the War Office, and in the British army in general. As an ardent advocate for reform, he had become aware that in the new climate of improved military structure and style, the office of Commander-in-Chief was obsolete, and that its function could effectively be incorporated into a newly proposed Military Board that would run very much on the same lines as the Board of the Admiralty ran the navy. In 1904, Esher's proposals were adopted, and Roberts's office of Commander-in-Chief of the British Army was scrapped, and its activities incorporated into a seven man Army Council. Roberts accepted his sacking with equanimity, and after accepting an offer to remain as a consultant on the Defence Committee, he retired from his office of Commander-in-Chief with grace.

With the outbreak of the First World War Roberts found that many of his subordinate officers in South Africa had been elevated to high commands in the army. General French had been promoted to commander of the British Expeditionary Force in France, and Kitchener had become the Secretary of State for War. Roberts appealed to Kitchener for the post of Commander-in-Chief of Home Forces but his request was denied. Instead, he was offered the position of Colonel-in-Chief of Overseas Forces in England, and it was in this capacity that, in November 1914, he travelled to France to inspect the Indian Division. While he was there, he caught a chill, and died two days later at St Omer. His body was returned to England, and was buried with due ceremony in St. Paul's Cathedral.

With his task in South Africa satisfactorily completed, Kitchener returned to England shortly after the Treaty of Vereeniging. On the 17th October, 1902, he set off to take up the post of Commander-in-Chief for India, an appointment that he had coveted for many years. He executed this role with enthusiasm and honour, but by 1907 he had fallen out with the Viceroy, Lord Curzon, after a long-standing dispute over rank and responsibility. Although Kitchener eventually won, he ended up with relinquishing his Indian command in 1909, after being elevated to the rank of Field Marshal. Following a short spell of duty as British Agent and Consul-General in Egypt, Kitchener was created an earl, and in August 1914, he took up the appointment of Secretary of State for War. His most remarkable achievement in this capacity was his vital contribution to Britain's involvement in the First World War through his creation of a new citizen's army. The success of his recruiting campaign was epitomised in the famous poster bearing the slogan- 'Your Country Needs YOU'. By September 1914, over 750,000 men had been recruited, and by the time voluntary enrolment came to an end in March 1916, over two-and-a-half million had enlisted. Kitchener's endeavours in this regard constituted one of the major factors in Britain's eventual victory in 1918. In response to an invitation from the Czar to visit Russia and the Russian Front, Kitchener set sail from the Orkneys to Archangel on the 5th June 1916 aboard the HMS Hampshire. Shortly after steaming out the naval base at Scapa Flow in atrocious weather, the Hampshire struck a mine and went down in 15 minutes. There were only 12 survivors and Kitchener was amongst the remaining compliment of 600 men who went down with the ship.

The battlefields of South Africa proved to be a fecund nursery for the making or marring of reputations and careers of many of the other British military leaders who fought in the Boer War. Amongst the less fortunate cases were the fates which befell such officers as Lt. Gen. Sir Hector MacDonald, Lt. Gen. Sir Henry Colvile, and Maj.

Gen. Sir William Gatacre, the author of the Stormberg disaster. The saddest case of all was that of Gen. Hector MacDonald, admirably nicknamed 'Fighting Mac' by his contemporaries. He was an exceedingly gallant and respected soldier who had risen from the ranks as Colour-Sgt. under Roberts in Afghanistan in 1879. In 1881, he served under Gen. Colley at Majuba, and in 1898 with Kitchener at Omdurman. During the Boer War MacDonald commanded the Highland Brigade, and fought once again with Roberts and Kitchener at the battles of Modder River and Paardeberg in February 1900. After the war, he was posted to Ceylon as Commander-in-Chief of the British Army. Regrettably, MacDonald's magnificent career was blighted when following an unfortunate affair with a Ceylonese boy of noble birth he shot himself in the Hotel Regina in Paris, to spare the army, and his wife any further agony and scandal.

General Colvile, who had been sacked by Roberts after his disastrous performance against De Wet at Lindley in the north eastern Free State during one of the first 'drives' in 1901, was killed in a cycling accident at Bagshot near Sandhurst in Surrey. In a bizarre twist of fate it turned out that the car which ran into him, had been driven by Gen. Lord Henry Rawlinson, who had fought beside Colville during the British 'drives' against De Wet in 1901 and 1902. General Gatacre ('Backacher'), who was also sacked by Roberts in South Africa, returned to Britain after the war, and got a job with a rubber exploitation company. Not long after his commencement of duties, he contracted a fatal strain of 'jungle fever' and died in great pain while on an exploration trip in western Abyssinia.

Col. Robert George Kekewich, the British military commander at Kimberley during the siege at the beginning of the war was another officer who terminated his military career by taking his own life. After the relief of Kimberley on the 15th February, 1900 Kekewich went on to serve with Roberts on the Western Front and later against De la Rey in the western Transvaal. After the war, he continued his military career, until in 1914, ill health drove him to desperation, and he ended his suffering with a bullet to his head. On the other hand Kekewich's fellow siege commander Lt. Col., later General Lord Robert. Baden-Powell went on, after the relief of Mafeking, to earn universal recognition as the founder of the Boy Scout Movement in 1908. He died peacefully in 1941, abounding in international honour and renown.

Paradoxically the two officers whom Roberts spurned both became Field Marshals after their departure from South Africa. Lt. Gen., later Field Marshall Lord Paul Sanford, 3rd Baron Methuen of Corsham, returned to South Africa in 1908 as General-Officer-in-Command, whilst General, later Field Marshall Lord George White VC became Governor of Chelsea Hospital, and after his death, was revered by millions for his endurance and his courage.

The list of other senior officers who fought in the Boer War and then went on to become senior commanders in the First World War is a long one and amongst the more notable were those of Generals French and Haig. General, later Field Marshall Lord John French became commander of the British Expeditionary Force in France in 1914, and was later succeeded by Maj. Gen., later Field Marshall Lord Douglas Haig. Other senior British officers to gain distinction were Col., later Field Marshall Viscount Byng of Vimy, Gen., later Field Marshall Sir William Robertson, CIGS, and Maj., later Field Marshall Lord F. W. Birdwood. General Sir Ian Hamilton also advanced rapidly and in 1915, he was appointed to lead the land command of the British forces in the Dardenelles. Later he was made the scapegoat for the disastrous performance of the British forces at Gallipoli and he returned to Britain with his reputation severely compromised. In contrast, Lt. Col., later Field Marshall Lord E. H. H. Allenby's successful performance in the Middle East earned him many honours as well as the unofficial title of 'Conqueror of Palestine'

With such an imposing list of senior British officers who went on from the Boer War to play leading roles in the First World War in 1914 it is interesting to pause here and examine the influence of their experiences on South Africa in their subsequent tactics in Europe. In analysing the performance of the British Expeditionary Force, particularly during the initial phases of the First World War, it is unbelievable to discover just how little the British Army's experiences in the Boer War, that had ended only twelve years before, had influenced its performance in Belgium and in France. In fact, there was little if any evidence of the tactical experiences gained during the numerous military expeditions undertaken by the British during the entire nineteenth century, from Waterloo to the Middle East, Northern Africa, the Crimea, Southern Africa, India and Afghanistan, to Burma and the Far East, and even New Zealand.

In South Africa, British Generals such as Roberts and in particular Kitchener, had become aware of the disastrous results of troops advancing in mass formations over open terrain against small and well entrenched forces armed with superior weapons and firing skills. Yet even with the echoes of Magersfontein, Colenso, Hart's Hill, Nicholson's Nek, and many other battle disasters still ringing in their ears, French and Haig launched waves of tightly packed infantry forward in the face of devastating German entrenchments at the cost of tens of thousands of casualties per day.

Yet before too harsh a judgment be passed against the British leaders, it would be prudent to consider the conditions under which the British Expeditionary Force entered the conflict in Europe in 1914. In the first instance, it was a massive war fought on a grand scale between the principal continental military powers with huge professional forces consisting of conventionally parade-ground trained professional soldiers hired to fight for their sovereign and their country. On the other hand, the relatively small but highly efficient British army had developed along local methods needed for the acquisition, protection and control of the British colonial possessions in all the far-flung corners of the earth. Although enjoying a practical and varied experience of warfare that was without parallel in Europe, the drawback was that its leaders, however apt in handling small-scale expeditions against relatively primitive tribesmen and un-schooled natives, had seldom, if ever, been prepared to direct huge formations on a grand scale. The result was that when, in 1914, the British did go into action in a 'mass encounter' with other huge continental forces it was the protocol of the traditional Continental battle tactics alone that was valid and recognised among the participants. In fact, colonial and overseas small skirmishing practices had no place in the reality of the 'grande guerre' scenario. Initially Britain's relatively small army was obliged to go along with the dictates of her more massive allies, and enemies. Then gradually as

'Kitchener's Volunteers' were trained in post Boer War methods, they joined the fray with much improved arms and skills, especially in fire-power, trench discipline, defence tactics and mobility, which in the end would prove to be a decisive factor in the successful outcome of the war.

Ironically, in the same way as the British military leaders left South Africa as soon as possible after the Treaty of Vereeniging, so too did the leading Boer generals waste no time in travelling abroad to solicit support and aid for their beleaguered people and country. In their close association with Kitchener during the peace negotiations leading up to Vereeniging, Botha, Smuts, and De la Rey had grown to respect and trust him, and concurred in his conviction that nothing less than an honourably and equitably negotiated peace would ever resolve the problems in South Africa. As early as September 1900 there had been there were encouraging signals of opposition to the war coupled with a liberal measure of sympathy for the Boers even in quarters as elevated as the British Parliament. Prominent Liberal opposition members such as Lord Rosebury, Sir Henry Campbell-Bannerman, and David Lloyd George, spoke openly for an early and fair end to the war, and the conclusion of an honourable and equitable peace in South Africa. Even closer to the British public's heart were the despairing reports from influential philanthropists such a Emily Hobhouse and the Fawcett Commission of Ladies, on the appalling conditions in the concentration camps, and the sorrowful plight of the Boer women and children.

Spurred on by encouraging echoes of sympathy and support, Botha, De Wet, and De la Rey were selected to visit Britain and some other countries in Europe in order to solicit aid, and raise funds to alleviate the hardships of the Boer women and children in the concentration camps. The Boer delegation set sail for England in August 1902. In spite of the enthusiastic welcome accorded to them wherever they travelled, they failed in their basic objective, and only succeeded in raising a meagre £105,000, of which a good portion had already been pledged even before the visit. In addition, Chamberlain, although cordially polite, refused to consider any increase to the sum of £3,000,000 for rehabilitation and relief of the war losses, which had been accorded at the Peace Conference. Botha, however, did succeed in meeting and befriending many prominent persons who had taken an interest in the plight of the Boers, and Sir Henry Campbell-Bannerman, leader of the Liberal opposition party in parliament, expressed particular concern, and paid heed to the Committee's and Botha's pleas for help.In the end the three men returned to South Africa virtually empty-handed, but full of encouragement from the tremendous expressions of sympathy of the many influential people and politicians all over Europe. Because of their dislike for, and mistrust of Milner, all the Boer leaders declined an invitation to serve on his nominated Legislative Council. Instead, they set about devoting their resources to sorting out their own affairs, and trying to get their lives in order, leaving Milner to get on in his own way with the post-war reconstruction of the Transvaal and the Orange Free State on the basis of British imperial lines.

Immediately after the signing of the peace treaty at Vereeniging on the 31st May 1902, Milner set about his task of reconstruction with enthusiasm. Kitchener and his military administration had departed, the Boer leaders were safely out of the way, and he was able to gather around him a brilliant band of fellow Oxford University graduates, his 'Kindergarten', and forge ahead with plans to create a new South Africa cast in the mould of pure British imperialistic concepts. For Milner, South Africa would be fulfilment of his dream for a 'little Britain in the veldt'. Milner's immediate efforts in rebuilding the two republics, and lifting them out of the ruins of wanton destruction that characterised the latter part of the war, were amply rewarded. With the help of Chamberlain, and later Alfred Lyttleton after Chamberlain's resignation as Colonial Secretary in 1903, the British parliament voted an allocation of £35 million for investment in South Africa. Milner's 'Kindergarten' immediately put the funds, as well as their multiple talents, to good use, and soon a process of reconstruction, including a comprehensive network of railways and irrigation canals, was launched across the country. Milner realised however, that regardless of all the social and economic improvements he could bring to South Africa, he would never succeed in 'anglicising' the old Boer republics while there was still a majority of Boer voters on the electoral role. Success, therefore, depended on one crucial factor, the need for a majority of inhabitants that would vote in favour of British dominion, and to accomplish this it was critical to encourage as much immigration from Britain as possible.

It was inevitable that Milner's unfettered ambitions would eventually curb his avidity. In his eagerness to achieve optimum productivity and profitability from the Rand mines, he involved himself in a number of issues that alienated not only the powerful Wernher-Beit mining group, but also the miners themselves. He soon found himself in bad grace with the majority of the English and Afrikaans speaking white miners, with all of the black miners, and even with the bulk of the loyal Uitlanders. It was not long before they deserted Milner's cause and aligned themselves with the emergent pan-Afrikaner party, Het Volk', led by their erstwhile foes Botha and Smuts. This climate of unrest and discord put a brake on Milner's dream of a massive influx of British immigrants, and in the end the project collapsed and the Afrikaners continued to remain in the majority throughout South Africa. The substance of the conflict centred around the loss of productivity in the mines caused by the reluctance of many black labourers to work in appalling underground conditions for a pittance in wages. To resolve the problem Milner sought permission to import labourers from China to work in the mines instead. The British government reluctantly consented to Milner's supplications, on the strict condition that the Chinese workers would be treated fairly, and that they would not be flogged in the way that the African miners were.

Milner went ahead with the project in the face of strong opposition from all quarters in South Africa and abroad, and it was not surprising that there was an up-roar throughout Britain and the Empire when it came to light that in spite of his undertakings, the Chinese labourers were being flogged after all. As a result, a vote of censure was passed on Milner in the House of Commons, and in 1905, he was forced to resign as Governor General in South Africa. The drama did not end there. Following Milner's departure, an outcry of resentment and revulsion over the 'slave labour' issue exploded into a full-blown crusade against the ruling Conservative-Unionist government in Westminster, which forced a general election in 1906. The result was an outstanding victory for Campbell-Bannerman and his Liberal party, the absolute rejection of Conservative-

Unionist attitudes against the Afrikaners, and a final seal on Milner's dream of an anglicised South Africa. One of the first acts of Campbell-Bannerman's administration was the granting of self-government to the Transvaal in 1906 and to the Orange River Colony in 1907. In the ensuing general election in the Transvaal in 1907, Smuts and Botha's 'Het Volk' party swept the board. In the end, Kitchener was right in the predictions to Botha at the Pretoria peace talks in April, even if he was a year or two out in his timing! Although this victory put an end to Milner's dreams of British dominion in South Africa, the final act in the drama only closed in 1926, when on a holiday visit to South Africa, he was stung by a tsetse fly, caught sleeping-sickness and died. It was as if Africa, with a cruel twist of the dagger, had finally taken its revenge on Milner, the 'empire-builder'.

In their dedicated quest to rebuild the nation, Botha and Smuts realised that success depended uniquely on the goodwill and support of Britain, and they made every possible effort to ingratiate themselves with the British government and the British public. Not everyone in South Africa, however, agreed with this submission, and Botha and Smuts had to grapple with other more radical leaders in order to win their support. In the period leading up to the Treaty of Vereeniging in 1910, Smuts needed to urge the antagonists 'not to sacrifice the Afrikaner nation on the altar of independence.'

On the 31st May 1910, exactly eight years to the day after the Peace of Vereeniging in 1902 and the end of the Boer War, the South African colonies were united, and as the Union of South Africa, received full independence within the British Commonwealth. From now on Botha and Smuts committed the newly founded Union of South Africa entirely to the British cause, by playing a full part within the empire, including participation on Britain's side in two major world wars. Now as dedicated imperial Statesmen, Botha and Smuts travelled the world making a valuable contribution to international affairs.

The fate of some of the other Boer War generals was destined to be less fulfilling and successful. General Piet Cronje, for example, came to a sad end after being ostracised and rejected by his own people for his bad taste in re-enacting 'The Last Stand of Paardeberg' in the St. Louis World Fair in 1904. De Wet, sorely frustrated in his vain struggle for independence, retired from public life in 1910. In 1914, he emerged, together with generals Kemp, Beyers, and Maritz to lead an armed rebellion against the government. The insurrection was crushed by Botha and Smuts.De Wet, after having served a prison sentence for his participation in the uprising, died alone and forgotten in 1922. It is not certain whether De la Rey supported the rebellion or not, because before he could commit him-self one way or the other he was accidentally shot dead at a police roadblock south of Johannesburg.

After helping Botha to quell the 1914 rebellion, Smuts went on to lead a successful campaign against the Germans in their South West Africa colony and then to assume overall command of the British forces fighting in German East Africa in 1916. Botha and Smuts, with their South Africa Party, later joined with the Union Party consisting principally of British born voters, to form the United Party with a committed allegiance to Britain, and to the cause of racial harmony amongst the white South Africans. On the other side, some of the irreconcilable apostles of Kruger, Steyn and De Wet formed the Nationalist party that actively sought separation from the British Empire, and the ascendancy of the Afrikaners in South Africa.

In 1924, the Nationalist Party gained power under General Herzog, but its majority was too small and ineffectual to pursue a fully blown separatist policy. With the outbreak of the Second World War in 1939, it pressed for neutrality, but was defeated in parliament, and Smuts became Prime Minister once again, and led South Africa into war on the side of Britain. Finally, in 1948, the Nationalists regained power, and this time they stayed in control, until in 1961, Hendrik Verwoerd created the Republic of South Africa, and took it out of the British Commonwealth and into the abyss of apartheid.

The Act of Union on the 31st May, 1910 brought an end to a century of conflict and strife between the white communities of South Africa. A steady process of acrimonious confrontations ended with the Boer War, for which a monumental price was paid in hardship and loss. Yet the cost of suffering was infinitesimal compared to the sacrifices that the indigenous inhabitants of southern Africa had to endure for 250 years in order to sustain white unity and white supremacy.

From the moment of Jan van Riebeeck's first step on Cape soil in 1652, and for the ensuing 250 years the indigenous owners of the African sub-continent were relentlessly and mercilessly disinherited and deprived of their egalitarian rights to the land that was snatched away from them by the whites. Both the British and the Boers were equally guilty of this heinous process of dehumanisation of the indigenous inhabitants of South Africa. In the case of the Boers, their very survival depended on the absolute subjugation of the threat of black power. On the other hand, the British, regardless of fashionable platitudes about equality, the rights of man, and the 'noble savage', depended on an abundant and subservient source of labour, to be exploited at any cost for the benefits of the home economy and the shareholders. In their anxiety to bring the war to a rapid and equitable end, in 1902 the British authorities were willing to go to any length to appease the Boers even if it had to be at the expense of the black African majority. In this way, the inclusion of the subtle, but fateful, proposition "after" was introduced into Article 8, Clause 16 of the Pretoria peace terms. It meant that the question of Native franchise would not be determined until after the granting of self-government to the South African colonies, which amounted, in fact, to never.

When article 8 was inevitably included into the Act of Union in 1910, it put the seal on the fate of any potential coloured representation in a South African parliament for ever. This treacherous dealing between the whites at the expense of the indigenous population happened repeatedly, until the Nationalists finally completed the job. A pact between Herzog's Nationalist party and the Labour Party in 1922 extended the colour-bar to the trade unions, and to industry, and in 1934 a coalition between Herzog and Smuts ensured the removal of the African voters in the Cape Province from the common roll. Then, the return to power of the Nationalist party in 1948, led to the removal of all the coloured voters in the Cape from the common roll, and finally to Verwoerd and absolute marginalisation by apartheid.

Finally, in 1990, against all the odds, the wheel miraculously turned a full circle. With the Boer War finally and completely won, and the Afrikaners securely entrenched in absolute control, white South Africa now had to face a new adversary whose legacy of bitterness, resentment and ultimate resolve far out-matched its own. So, today it is the black majority that is finally in charge of South Africa's destiny, and the lion that once roared loud and long in the jungle of the African sub-continent, has at last been muted and laid to rest beside those white stones and little crosses that mark the 350 years of white Afrikaner dominion in South Africa.

EPILOGUE

Over the course of the past ten years I have journeyed through three hundred and fifty years of South African history, and over three hundred pages of research and discovery, and now find myself back where I started - on the summit of Spioenkop. The melancholy that filled me then has not disappeared and I am still sad, because those haunting rows of blanched boulders and scattered white crosses are still there just as before, only perhaps a bit more pointless and a bit more forlorn.

As a child of an English father and an Afrikaans mother, both descendants of those very people who fought and perished in the long and acrimonious struggle between the British and Boers, I needed to discover the meaning of it all. Why were those forsaken remains of dead British soldiers and dead Boer farmers lying there? It is not enough for me to know that the soldiers who were on the hill that night were paid to be there, that it was their destiny to be employed and rewarded to fight, and to die for whatever their nation's cause. Or that the bones of the Boers lay there as a sacrifice in the desperate defence of their homeland – that very land which they themselves had wrenched away from the hapless indigenous peoples that inhabited it before them.

The bitter irony of it all is that in the end it turned out to be so meaningless, because today, the land that was so bitterly fought for is as far out of Britain's reach as it ever was. And, the Boers who so desperately strived, even at the cost of their lives, to keep their homeland and their nation intact, are today, subjected to the autonomy of those very people whose rights and dignity they had so systematically and ignominiously defiled over the course of the preceding 350 years.

The road from Jan van Riebeeck to Nelson Mandela is a long and torturous one. It is a road drenched with the sweat, tears and blood of the descendants of those very first burghers who were released from the V.O.C. employment, and who set out on their own into the hostile interior to find a new life, a new home, and a new destiny for themselves. It is also drenched with the blood, sweat, and tears of everyone and everything that stood in their way, or tried to take their liberty and their independence away from them. For three centuries the forbears of the Boers of the Orange Free State and the South African Republic, had actively and avidly spurned administrative control and political fealties in order to fulfil their dream of independent nationhood in their very own fatherland, unfettered of all extraneous ties and loyalties.

It also happened that along this road the Boers encountered the British. Why did this come about? There was no real reason for that, either. It was just destined that Britain's Empire, on its glorious path of universal aggrandisement would eventually find its way to the mineral and material rich territories of Southern Africa and, as in every other corner of the world, nothing and no one would deprive it of possession of those truly sparkling jewels to be added to the imperial crown.

The nightmare of the Anglo-Boer War that was fought during the very last days of the nineteenth century ended all these dreams and heralded the beginning of the end of all British and Boer aspirations, because even before the ensuing century was over both the British Empire and the Afrikaner nation and fatherland would be relegated to the history books.

So then, what was it all about? Was it an imperative of possession, or greed, or intolerance, or chimerical dreams of a far away Utopia? Who knows? Today very few people remember and even fewer care about all those soldiers and all those burghers, all those white women and children and all those thousands of black Africans interred under those countless white stones and little crosses scattered, far and wide throughout the southern tip of the African continent.

CHRONOLOGICAL TABLE OF EVENTS

1652
The Dutch East India Company (V.O.C.) occupies the Cape of Good Hope and Jan van Riebeeck lands at Table Bay to establish a revitualling station for passing ships . – Arival of first trickle of imported slaves – mainly from Malaya.

1656
First "free burghers" released from the Company payroll and settled on 28-acre allotments provided by the Company

1657
First armed clash between white settlers and indigenous Khoi inhabitants

1658
Establishment of first school at the Cape and creation of first "Burgher Council"

1662
Jan van Riebeeck leaves the Cape and is succeeded by Commander Zacharias Wagenaar

1679
Arrival of Governor Simon van der Stel

1682
Creation of the "Commission for Minor Matters" and of "Heemraden"

1686
Creation of the "Judiciary Council of Heemraden" and of "Landdrosten"

1687
Arrival of first German settlers

1688
Arrival of French Huguenots

1699
Governor Willem-Adriaan van der Stel appointed as successor to his father Simon

1703
Start of the "Trekboer" era

1707
The Act of Union of Scotland and England

1708
Governor Willem-Adriaan van der Stel recalled to Amsterdam in disgrace
The V.O.C. introduces a "Grazing Fee"

1743
A Drostdy is created at Swellendam

1779
A Burgher Petition is sent to the States-General in Amsterdam with accusations against the V.O.C. and its Administration in the Cape

1785
A Drostdy is created at Graff-Reinet

1795
France invades the Netherlands and Prince William of Orange seeks refuge in England – Britain takes possession of the Cape at the behest of Prince William of Orange

1796 -1802
Influx of Christian Missionary Societies mainly from Britain, Switzerland and America

1799
The activities of the London Missionary Society (LMS) under Dr. Theodorus van der Kemp and Sir James Reid, creates antagonism amongst the white Afrikaner settlers.

1803
Britain returns the Cape to The Batavian Republic

1806
Britain re-occupies the Cape and the Earl of Caledon is installed as first Governor

1810
Establishment of "Circuit Courts" to investigate the London Mission Society orchestrated Khoi complaints against white employers

1811
1- First Circuit Court session
2- Governor Caledon is replaced by Sir John Cradock

1812
Second (infamous) Circuit Court session dubbed by incensed Boers as "The Black Circuit"

1814
Lord Charles Somerset appointed as new British Governor at the Cape

1815
The "Slachtersnek Rebellion" – 5 Boers hanged for insurrection

1820
4000 British settlers arrive in South Africa and are installed around Port Elizabeth in the Eastern Cape

1822
Somerset issues controversial proclomation defining English as the exclusive language for Cape legislature, judiciary and schools

1824
British traders found a trading base in Zululand at Port Natal (Durban)

1826
Cape Colony boundaries extended northwards as far as the Orange River

1834
Abolition of slavery in the Cape Colony

1834-1836
The "Great Trek" – exodus of over 4000 Boers from the Cape Colony across the Orange and Vaal Rivers and the Drakensberg to create the independent republics of Transoranje, Transvaal and Natalia respectively.

1836
Lord Melbourne, British Prime Minister, promulgates the highly provocative "Cape of Good Hope Punishment Act, 1836", declaring British jurisdiction in all Southern Africa south of the 25th parallel

1838
On the 16th December the Boers defeat the Zulus at the Battle of Blood River

1843
Natal annexed by Britain, forcing resident Boers to flee to the Transvaal and Orange Free State

1845
British troops cross the Orange River and defeat the Boers at the Battle of Zwartkoppies

1846
Major Warden installed at Bloemfontein as "British Agent"

1848

Cape Governor, Sir Harry Smith, annexes the Transoranje Republic after the Battle of Boomplaats and installs a British Authority in the freshly dubbed "Orange River Colony"

1852

At the Sand River Convention the British Government recognises and confirms the independence of the Transvaal Republic

1854

At the Bloemfontein Convention Britain restores and confirms the indedepence of the Orange River Republic

1867

Discovery of diamonds in the area around the confluence of the Vaal and Harts Rivers

1868-1869

Britain annexes Basutoland (Lesotho) as a Crown Colony

1870

"Diamond Rush" to Kimberley (in OFS) which Britain promptly annexes to the Cape Colony

1872

Britain grants internal self-government to the Cape Colony

1877

Britain annexes the Transvaal as a Crown Colony

1879

1- British troops crush the BaPedi tribe in the Eastern Transvaal
2- Following set-backs at Isandhlwana and Rorkes Drift the British defeat the Zulus at Ulundi

1800

Boers destroy British column under Col. Anstruther at Bronkhorstspruit in the Eastern Transvaal

1881

Jan. 28 – Boers defeat British force under Gen. Sir George Pommeroy-Colley at Laings Nek in Northern Natal

Feb. 08 - Boers defeat Colley's forces at Schuinshoogte

Feb. 27 - British routed at the Battle of Majuba – Colley killed in action

Mar.06 – Anglo-Transvaal Peace Treaty signed

May 28 – Pretoria Convention – Transvaal gains limited independence

1884
London Convention – Transvaal obtains greater independence

1886
Official proclomation of the Rand Goldfields – Start of great Stock Exchange boom and influx of thousands of British and foreign immigrants ("Uitlanders")

1887
Britain annexes Zululand

1888
Cecil John Rhodes is granted British Royal Charter to explore Matabeleland and Mashonaland north of the Limpopo River

1889
Establishment of the Wernher-Beit Corporation – the principal Rand gold mining house

1896
Dr. L.S. Jameson's raid into the Transvaal in support of the Uitlanders is defeated and Jameson is imprisoned - Rhodes is forced to resign as Cape Prime Minister.

1897
Sir Alfred Milner is appointed British High Commissioner of the Cape Colony

1898
Kruger is re-elected President of the Transvaal Republic and launches a massive re-armament campaign

1899
May-June – Bloemfontein Conference – negotiations break down and Britain and
       Transvaal prepare for war
Oct 09 - Kruger issues ultimatum to Britain to withdraw her troops from the
       Transvaal borders
       - The ultimatum expires and outbreak of war between the Boer Republics
       and Britain
Oct 12 – Boers enter Natal and cross the Western Transvaal borders into N.W.
       Cape – De la Rey captures British armoured train at Kraaipan in the
       first armed engagement of the war.
Oct 12/16 – Boers lay siege to Kimberley and Mafeking
Oct 29 – Battle of Talana (Dundee) in Northern Natal
Oct 21 – Batlle of Elandslaagte (Natal)
Oct 24 – Battle of Rietfontein (Natal)
Oct 30 – "Mournful Monday" – British heavily defeated at the Battle of Ladysmith
       (also known as "Battle of Farqhuar's Farm" or "Pepworth Hill" or
       "Nicholson's Nek")

Oct 31 - Buller lands at Cape Town

Nov 01 – Boers invade the Cape Colony after seizing Norvalspont on the Orange River

Nov 15 – Armoured train wrecked between Estcourt and Chiveley – Winston Churchill captured by Boer patrol.

Nov 22 – Buller leaves Cape Town for Natal

Nov 23 – Battles of Willow Grange (Natal) and Belmont (N.W Cape)

Nov 25 - Battleof Graspan (N.W.Cape)

Nov 28 – Battle of Modder River (N.W.Cape)

Dec 10 – Gatacre repulsed at Stormberg (Central Cape) – 1st disaster of "Black Week"

Dec 11 – Methuen's Highland Brigade severly mauled by De la Rey and Cronje at the Battle of Magersfontein(N.W.Cape) – 2nd disaster of "Black Week"

Dec 15 – Buller suffers heavy losses at Battle of Colenso (Natal) – 3rd disaster of "Black Week"

Dec 18 – Roberts appointed to replace Buller as C.inC. of British Forces in South Africa. Kitchener appointed Chief of Staff

<u>1900</u>

Jan 06 – Battle of Platrand (Natal) – Boers attack Caesar's Camp and Wagon Hill

Jan 10 – Roberts and Kitchener land at Cape Town

Jan 24 – Battle of Spioenkop (Spion Kop) – (Natal)

Feb 05/07 – Buller's assault and withdrawal from Vaalkrantz (Natal)

Feb 11 – Roberts launches his "great flank march"

Feb 14 – Buller launches his fourth attempt to relieve Ladysmith

Feb 15 – French's cavalry charge at Abon Dam followed by the relief of Kimberley
- De Wet captures huge supply convoy at Waterval Drift (OFS)

Feb 18 – Start of Battle of Paardeberg (OFS)
-Lyttelton captures Monte Christo (Colenso Koppies, Natal)

Feb 27 – (a)Cronje surrenders to Roberts at Paardeberg
(b) Battle of Pieter's Hill (Colenso Koppies – Natal)

Feb 28 – Buller relieves Ladysmith

Mar 07 – Battle of Poplar Grove (OFS)

Mar 10 – Battle of Driefontein (OFS)

Mar 13 – Roberts enters Bloemfontein

Mar 18 – Boer War Council at Kroonstad (OFS)

Mar 31 – De Wet ambushes Broadwood at Sannaspos (OFS) and captures Water Works

Apr 04 – Boers maul Royal Irish Regiment at Reddersburg (OFS)

May 03 – Roberts begins his advance on Pretoria

May 12 – Roberts occupies Kroonstad (OFS)

May 14 – Buller drives Boers off the Biggarsberg range in N. Natal

May 17 – Mahon and Plumer relieve Mafeking

May 29 – Battle of Doornkop, by Johannesburg

May 30 - President Kruger and the Transvaal Government leave Pretoria for Machadadorp (E.Tvl)

May 31 – (a) Roberts occupies Johanneburg
    (b) Piet de Wet captures 13th Battalion Imperial Yeomanry at Lindley
Jun 05 – Roberts occupies Pretoria
Jun 07 – Boer guerillas overwhelm British at Roodewal (Rooiwal) – W.Tvl
Jun 11 – Boers maul British troops at Silikaatsnek Pass (W.Tvl)
Jun 11/12 – Battle of Diamond Hill, near Pretoria
Jul 15 – Steyn and De Wet escape from Brandwater Basin in eastern OFS
Jul 21 – Roberts begins advance along Delagoa Bay Railway towards Komatipoort
Jul 27 – British forces occupy Middelburg (E.Tvl)
Jul 30 – Prinsloo surrenders to Hunter in the Brandwater Basin (OFS)
Aug 04 – Boers lay siege to British post at Brakfontein on the Elands River
Aug 14 – De Wet eludes British pursuers at Olifantsnek Pass (OFS)
Aug 16 – British Post at Elands River relieved by Col. Walter Kitchener
Aug 27 – Battle of Bergendal (E Tvl) – the last set-piece action of the war
Sep 06 – Buller occupies Lydenburg (E Tvl)
Sep 13 – French occupies Baberton (E Tvl)
Sep 24 – Pole-Carew occupies Komatipoort on the Transvaal / Portuguese East
    Africa border
Oct 08 – Milner appointed Administrator of the Transvaal and the Orange Free
    State
Oct 19 – Kruger sets sail for Europe from Lourenco Marques (P.E.A)
Oct 20 – De Wet surrounds Barton at Frederickstad (OFS)
Oct 24 – Buller leaves Cape Town for England
Oct 27 – Steyn, De la Rey, Smuts and other Boer leaders gather at Cypherfontein
    to assess future Boer strategy
Nov 06 – De Wet suffers setback at Bothaville (OFS)
Nov 16 – De Wet springs a trap at Springhaans Nek (OFS) and sets off to attempt
    an invasion of the Cape Colony
Nov 23 – De Wet captures Dewetsdorp (OFS) named after his father
Nov 29 – Kitchener succeeds Roberts as C-in-C of British forces in South Africa
Dec 03 – De la Rey captures British supply column at Buffelspoort (W Tvl)
Dec 13 – De la Rey and Beyers inflict damage on Clements's camp at Nooitgedacht
Dec 16 – Herzog and De Wet cross the Orange River into the Cape Colony
Dec 29 – Ben Viljoen captures a British post at Helvetia in the eastern Transvaal

1901
Jan 07 – Boers active in E.Tvl – Botha and Ben Viljoen harass British forces at
    Belfast and other stations along the Pretoria-Delagoa Bay railway line
Jan 27 – French starts a "drive" in the Eastern Transvaal
Jan 29 – Start of "Third Great De Wet Hunt" in the Orange Free State –
    Knox engages De Wet near Parys (on the Free State side of the Vaal River
Jan 31 – Smuts captures British post at Modderfontein, near Johannesburg
Feb 06 – Botha mauls Smith-Dorrien at Lake Chrissie (E Tvl)
Feb 10 – De Wet enters Cape Colony at Sand Drift on the Orange River
Feb 14 – De Wet and Plumer clash at Philipstown in N.Cape
Feb 27 – De Wet and Herzog abandon sterile effort in the Cape Colony and return
    to the Orange Free State

Mar 03 – De la Rey's abortive attack on his home town of Lichtenburg (W Tvl)
May 08 – Milner returns to England "on leave"
Sep 03 – Smuts invades the Cape Colony at Kiba Drift on the Orange River
Sep 07 – Botha invades Natal - Smuts mauls the 17th Lancers at Elands River
Sep 17 – Botha cuts up Gough's force at Blood River Poort (Natal)
Sep 26 – Botha's attacks on Fort Italia and Fort Prospect in Northern Natal
fail badly and as a result he aborts his Natal invasion campaign and
returns to the Eastern transvaal.
Sep 30 – De la Rey inflicts damage on Kekewich at Moedwil (W Tvl)
Oct 24 – De la Rey attacks Von Donop's column at Kleinfontein (W Tvl)
Oct 30 – Benson killed in action during Botha's attack on a British column at
Bakenlaagte (E Tvl)
Dec 07 – Ian Hamilton appointed Kitchener's Chief of Staff
Dec 16 – Boer General Kritzinger captured by British in the Cape Colony
Dec 25 – De Wet captures Yeomanry camp at Tweefontein (OFS)

1902
Jan 25 – Aged and torpid Boer General Ben Viljoen captured by British near
Lydenburg in the Eastern Transvaal
Britain receives offer from the Netherland's Government to mediate in
possible peace negotiations.
Feb 06 – Start of first "New Model Drive" in north-eastern Free State
Feb 13 – Start of second "New Model Drive"
Feb 23 – Steyn and De Wet flee from British by breaking through a Blockhouse
Cordon at Langverwacht (OFS)
Feb 25 – De la Rey captures Von Donop's column at Yzerspruit (Ysterspruit)
Mar 07 – De la Rey defeats and captures Methuen at Battle of Klipdrift (W Tvl)
Kitchener initiates peace overtures on basis of Netherland Government's
proposals of the 25th January 1902
Mar 24 – Start of first "Great Drive" in the Western Transvaal
Mar 26 – Death of Cecil John Rhodes
Mar 31 – Colonel Cookson's column attacked at Boschbult (W Tvl)
Apr 01 – Boers capture town of Springbok in the far western Cape Colony
Apr 04 – Smuts invests O'Okiep, an important copper mining town in the far
western Cape Colony
Apr 07 – Sir Ian Hamilton appointed C-in-C of all British troops in the W.Tvl
Apr 09 – Boer leaders meet at Klerksdorp to discuss Kitchener's peace initiative
Apr 11 – Kemp's disastrous failure against British column near Roodewal
(Rooiwal) a bitter blow for Boer prestige at current phase of peace
negotiations.
Apr 12 – Representatives of Boer Governments meet with Kitchener to discuss
peace proposals
Apr 14 – Further peace talks in Pretoria result in "free passage" for Boer leaders
to consult with their Commandos
Apr 18 – Boer leaders set off to consult with their Commandos in the field
May 15 – Conference of Boer leaders at Vereeniging on the Transvaal side of the
Vaal River to negotiate Boer peace terms

May 31 – Boer leaders agree peace terms at Vereeniging and formal Peace
Treaty signed and sealed in Kitchener's residence in Pretoria that
same night
Oct 17 – Kitchener sails for England to take up appointment of C-in-C for India

1905
Milner relieved of duties as Governor General in South Africa and is recalled
to Britain following the so-called "slave labour" scandal

1906
Transvaal granted 'Responsible Government' status by Britain (6/12/1906)

1907
Orange Free State granted 'Responsible Government status (10/6/1907)

1910
May 31 – Cape Colony, Natal, Transvaal and Orange Free State Colonies are
amalgamated and granted full independence as "The Union of South
Africa". Lord Gladstone appointed as first British Governor-General
and Louis Botha as first Prime Minister

1914
Aug 01 – Britain declares war on Germany and the Union of South Africa assumes
responsibilty for the defence of all British Southern African territories to
free Imperial Garrisons in Southern Africa for service in Europe
Aug 06 – Kitchener is appointed British First Secretary of State for War
Sep 09 – S.A troops enter German South West Africa in action against resident
German forces
Sep 15 – De la Rey accidentally killed at a police road block south of Johannesburg
Dec 20 – Ex Boer War Generals De Wet, Kemp, Beyers and Maritz lead an armed
rebellion against the pro-British South African Government. The
insurrection is swiftly and effectively crushed by Botha and Smuts

1915
Jul 09 - German forces in South West Africa surrender to South Africans at
Tsumeb (SWA)

1916
Feb 19 – Gen. Smuts appointed C-in-C of all British forces in East Afrca and
enters Tanganyika to engage against resident German forces
Jun 05 – Kitchener is drowned when HMS Hampshire, bound for the Baltic Sea
is sunk off Scapa Flow

1919
Aug 28 – Death of Louis Botha – Smuts entrusted with formation of new Cabinet

1924
Jun 17 – South African National Party gains power and Herzog is elected Prime Minister

1926
Milner dies from locally contracted illness while on holiday in South Africa

1939
In September the National Party is defeated in Parliament on the issue of war against Germany and Gen. Smuts becomes new Prime Minister and takes South Africa into the war on the side of Britain and her allies

1949
In May Smuts loses a tightly fought General Election and the National Party regains power in South Africa – Dr. D.F. Malan becomes new Prime Minister

1960
Feb 03 – Harold MacMillan, British Prime Minister on a visit to South Africa makes his historic "Winds of Change" speach to the S.A.Parliament in Cape Town
May 31 – Ruling National Party Prime Minister Hendrik Verwoerd severes all ties with Britain and with the creation of the 'Republic of South Africa' takes South Africa out of the British Commonwealth

1989
Sep 24 – Inauguration of National Party leader F.W.de Klerk as State President

1990
Feb 02 – F.W.de Klerk drops a bombshell in the State Parliament when he inaugurates the democratic transformation of South Africa with the announcement of immediate lifting of all exisiting bans and restrictions on all anti-government and all anti-Apartheid institutions such as the A.N.C., the S.A. Communist Pary, the Umkonto We Sitzwe, the Pan African Congress and all others.
Feb 11 – After 27 years Nelson Mandela, leader of the A.N.C. is released from imprisonment.

1994
Apr 27 – First ever national, free and non-racial General Election held in South Africa
May 31 - Nelson Mandela installed as State President of the Republic of South Africa.

GLOSSARY
WORD	MEANING
Agter-ryer (s)	Rear-rider(s)
Berg/Berge(n)	Mountain / mountain range
BMI	Bethune's Mounted Infantry
Bywoner	Resident white farm worker – squatter
CIV	City Imperial Volunteers
CMR	Cape Mounted Rifles
Dorp	Village – small town
Drift	Ford / drift
Drostdy(e)	Magistracy (cies)
Fontein	Fountain / spring / water source
Heemraad / Heemraden	Administrative Council / Officers
ILH	Imperial Light Horse
ILI	Imperial Light Infantry
Kop / koppie / (kopje)	Small hill / knoll
Korpera(a)l –(e)	Junior Boer Officer(s)
Kraal	Native settlement / livestock enclosure
Krijgsraad	Boer War Council
Laager	Encampment
Landdrost(en)	Magistrate(s)
MI	Mounted Infantry
Nagmaal (Nachtmael)	Holy Communion
NC	Natal Carbineers
Nek	Col / mountain pass
NMP	Natal Mounted Police
NMR	Natal Mounted Rifles
Pan	Pond / pool / dam / stank
Plaas (plaats)	Farm
Poort	Break in a range of hills / gorge/ defile
Predikant	Dutch Reformed Church minister
RA	Royal Artillery
RE	Royal Engineers
Ry-koppies	Ridges of steep-toothed hills
SAC	South African Constabulary
SALH	South African Light Horse
Sangars / schanzas	Defensive breastworks of loose stones
Smous(e)	Itinerant trader(s)
Spruit	Stream / brook
The Great Trek	Mass Boer migration from Cape Colony in ox wagons
TMI	Thorneycroft's Mounted Infantry
Trek	Journey by ox-wagon / to migrate
Trekboer	Itinerant stock farmer
Uitlander	Foreign worker
Vecht-Commandant	Field- (or Fighting-) General
Vee Boere	Stock farmers
Veld (veldt)	Plane / open country / prairie
Veldt Kornet(ten) / Veld Kornet(te)	Boer Police and Judicial Officer(s)
Voortrekker	Boer pioneer
Vrou	Wife / woman
ZARPS	Transvaal Republic Police Force - (Zuid Afrikaansche Rijende Politie)

WHITE STONES and LITTLE CROSSES
REFERENCES, SOURCES, AND ACKNOWLEDGEMENTS

This work is not a scholarly chronicle of the history of South Africa or of the Boer War, but simply a search into the past to find, and if possible to understand the passions and the imperatives which drove the two principal white races in South Africa to a state of mortal enmity and bloody conflict.

I am the South African product of a Boer mother and an English speaking Cape Colonial father – my grandparents fought on opposing sides during the Boer War with all the hatred and venom that they had inherited from over a century of confrontation and conflict. Because of this I have always been driven by an insatiable need to understand where I personally stood in all this. This rapacious quest was constantly fuelled by discussions with anyone and everyone who would be patient enough to put up with me – my parents, grandparents, relatives, friends, teachers, schools, university - books, historical references, libraries, whatever and whenever!.

In this book I have tried to describe my journey through some 350 years of South African history. It is an attempt at a personal narrative of the events which were set in motion with the arrival of the first white settlers at the Cape and which culminated in bitter and bloody conflict between the British and the Boers at very end of the 19th century. The sentiments and the feelings are mine but not being an accredited historian I needed to seek help from the professional scholars and writers for detailed descriptions of battles and personalities. In this regard I am profoundly indebted to all the following authors without whose help I would never have completed my story.

- Thomas Pakenham ("The Boer War" and "The Scramble for Africa")
- Rayne Kruger ("Goodbye Dolly Gray-The Story of the Boer War")
- Michael Barthrop ("The Anglo-Boer Wars – The British and the
      Afrikaners 1818-1902")
- John J. Stephens ("Fuelling The Empire – South Africa's Gold and
      the Road to War")
- Ian Castle ("Majuba 1881 – The Hill of Destiny")
- H.G. Castle ("Spion Kop")
- Oliver Ransford ("The Battle of Spion Kop" and "The Great Trek")
- Peter Trew ("The Boer War Generals")
- Alister Sparks ("The Mind of South Africa")
- Steven Debroey ("Zuid Afrika – Naar de Bronnen van de
      Apartheid")
- Prof. Pert van den Bergh- ("24 Battles – The Battle Fields of the
      North West Proivince")
- Ian Knight ("Colenso 1899 – The Boer War in Natal")
- Professors C.M. van den Heever and P. de V. Pienaar
      ("Kultuurgeskiedenis van die Afrikaner")

311

Finally, on a more personal basis, I wish to express my gratitude and thanks to my many friends who encouraged and helped me in producing this work. In particular I wish to name my friends **Tom Pate** and **Jeremy Cross** who patiently ploughed through my drafts and highlighted the many spelling and grammatical errors that my p.c. keyboard insisting on producing. Jeremy particularly, spent many, many hours restructuring grammatical presentations, correcting errors and offering advice and critiscism of immeasurable value. And then there is **Graeme Black** whose help with the production of drawings and illustrations was also invaluable and, almost as a PS. my very "recently acquired" friend **Douglas Brown** whose account of his personal interest in the 13th Battalion of The Imperial Yeomanry led me to re-write, expand and enliven a large section of my narrative.

Ronnie Hammond
Guthrie, Scotland

Alphabetic List of Works, Authors, Editors and Writers consulted during the compilation of "White Stones and Little Crosses"

-"24 Battles – Battle Fields of the North West Province" (Prof. Gert
    van den Bergh – The North West Tourism Association 1996
    ISBN 0 62019801 X)
-BBC TV presentation – "In the Footsteps of Churchill"
-BBC TV series – "The Boer War" – presented by Kenneth Griffith
-BBC 2 TV series "The First Media War"
-"Colenso 1899 – The Boer War in Natal"
    (Ian Knight Campaign Series No.38 – Reed International Books Ltd-
    Osprey Series- ISBN 1 85532 466 0)
-"Civilization – A New History of the Western World"
    (Roger Osborne – Jonathan Cape 2006 – ISBN 0 224 06241 7
-"Channel 4 TV Series 'The Boer War' presented by Jonathan Lewis
-"Familia Lemmer" (Stephanus R. Lemmer – V&R Drukkery (Edms) Bpk –
    1987 Pretoria – ISBN 0 620 10673 5)
-"Famous Regiments" – Edited by Lt.Gen. Sir Brian Horrocks
-"Fuelling The Empire – South Africa's Gold and the Road to War"
    (John J. Stephens – John Wiley & Sons Ltd. – Chichester
    ISBN 0 470 85067 1
-"Gee Ons 'n Land" – (Prof. H.C.G. Robbertze – V&R Drukkery Pretoria
    1992 – ISBN 1 874861 68 4
-"Geslagregister van die Badenhorst Familie in Suid Afrika"
    HSRC (Pta) Publication No. 35 1991 – ISBN 0 7969 09105
-"Goodbye Dolly Gray – The Story of the Boer War"
    (Rayne Kruger – Cassell & Co. Ltd. LDN 1959)
-"History Of The First World War" – B.H. Liddell Hart
-"Imperial Echoes – Eye Witness Accounts of Victoria's Little Wars" –
    Robert Gidding
-"Kultuurgeskiedenis Van Die Afrikaner"
    (C.M. van den Heever & P. deV. Peinar – Nasionale Pers Bpk.
    Kaapstad 1947)
-"Long Walk to Freedom" – Nelson Mandela –Abacus – Little Brown & Co
    . London
-"Majuba 1881 – The Hill of Destiny" (Ian Castle – Campaign Series No. 45
    – Osprey Publications ISBN 1 85532 503 9)
-"My Early Life" (Winston S. Churchill – Fontana Books 1972 – Collins
    Clear Type Press – Ldn)

-"Payable Gold" – Jas. Gray, F.I.C., S.A. – Central News Agency 1937
-"Pears Encyclopedia (War Economy Issue)- 55th Edition – A&F Pears Ltd-
"Rhodes" (Sarah Gertrude Millin – Chatto & Windus Ldn 1933)
-"Rorke's Drift – Shiyone Self-Guided Trail" KwaZulu Monuments
    Council)
-"Rorke's Drift 1879 – 'Pinned Like Rats in a Hole" (Ian Knight –
    Campaign Series $% -Osprey Publication Series –ISBN 185532 5063
-"Shaka Zulu – The Rise of the Zulu Empire" (E.A. Ritter – Longmans
    Green & Co. LDN-NY-Toronto)
-"Spion Kop" - (H.G. Castle – Great Battles Series –Almark Publishing Co.
    Ltd - !SBN 0 85524 251 5)
-"The Anglo-Boer Wars – The British and the Afrikaners – 1815-1902"
    (Michael Barthorp – Blandford Press Ldn-1987-ISBN 0 7173 1658 4)
"The Battles of Isandlwana & Rorke's Drift"
    (John Laband & Paul Thompson, 1999 - University of Natal Press).
-"The Black Watch – The 42nd Regt.of the Foot" – Philip Howard
-"The Battle of Spion Kop" – (Oliver Ransford – John Murray Ldn. 1969
    7195 1914 4)
-"The Boer War Generals" (Peter Trew – Sutton Publishing Ltd 1999
    ISBN 0 905 778 677
-"The Boer War" (Thomas Pakenham – Wiedenfeld & Nicholson Ltd.1979
    CN 8660)
-"The Cockpit Of Europe – (A Guide to the Battlefields of Belgium and
    France" (Lt.Col. Howard Green,MC FSA – David & Charles
    Holdings Ltd. 1976 – ISBN 0 7153 7006 5)
-"The Great Trek" (Oliver Ransford – Cardinal Edition 1974 Sphere Books
    Ltd. Ldn – ISBN 0 351 17945 6)
-"The Last Trek – A New Beginning" – F.W. de Klerk- Macmillan, London
    ISBN O 331 742642
-"The Mind of South Africa" (Allister Sparks – Ballantine Books NY.
    ISBN 0 345 37119 4)
-"The National Army Museum Book of The Boer War – (Field Marshall
    Lord Carver – Macmillan Publishers Ltd. – ISBN 0 330 36944 X)
-"The Other De Wet" – (S.A. Military History Society
    – http-samilitary.org/vol116mc.html
-"The Scramble for Africa" (Thomas Pakenham – George Wiedenfeld &
    Nicholson 1991 – ISBN 0 349 10449 Z
-"The South and East African Year Book and Guide for 1940 -46th Issue
-"The Story of the Zulus" (L.Y.Gibson – Negro Universities Press NY
    SBN8371 3592 3)
-"The Washing of the Spears" (Donald R. Morris – Jonathan Cape Ltd. 1966
    ISBN 0 7474 01942)
-"Wending en Inkeer – 'n Beskouing oor die Nuwere Afrikaanse
    Letterkunde" – Dr.. F.E.J. Malherbe – Kaapstad Nasuionale Pers
    Beperk - 1948
-"World War I – Catastrophe & Slaughter"(The Sunday Telegraph CD presentation)
-"Wikipedia Free Encylopedia" (Internet)
-"With The Flag to Pretoria – A History of the Boer War of 1899-1900-
    Vol. 1" – (H.W. Wilson – Harmsworth Brothers Ltd. Ldn. 1900)
-"Zuid Afrika – Naar de Bronnen von de Apartheid" (Steven Debroey –
    Uitgewerij de Vroente Kasterlee – D 1982 0052 1)
-"Zulu" (Diamond Films 1964 with Michael Caine – Stanley Baxter & Jack
    Hawkins)
-"Zulu Dawn" (Warner Films 1979 – Peter O Toole – Simon Ward)
-"Zulu War 1879 – Twilight Of A Warrior Nation" (Ian Knight & Ian Castle
    – Campaign Series No. 14 – Osprey Series ISBN 1 85532 165 3)

SOME REMARKS ON SPELLING

1- As far as possible authentic renderings have been chosen for South African place names in accordance with the language in which they are titled – e.g.

Spioenkop (not Spion Kop)
Thukela River (not Tugela)
Sannaspos (not Sannah's Post)

but

Mafeking instead of Mafikeng

2- Rivers are spelled in their titled names followed by the Anglicised/European names in
Brackets – e.g.

Ncomo (Blood River)
Mzinyathi (Buffalo River)

3- Generally contemporary spelling is used for place and feature names – e.g.

Veld (not veldt)
Koppie(s) (not kopje(s))
Kroonstad (not Kroonstadt)

but

Cape Town and not Kaapstad(t)

4- The possessive apostrophe in words ending in **"s"** take an apostrophe plus **s** – e.g.

Roberts's, - Jones's - Harris's - Smuts's

However, words/names ending in **"s"** with an **"iz"** sibilant do not take the apostrophe + s – e.g.

Jesus' - Moses' - Ceilliers'

LIST OF ABBREVIATIONS

aka (a.k.a.)	"also known as..."
Aug.	August
BMI (B.M.I.)	Bethune's Mounted Infantry Regiment
Brig.	Brigadier (or Brigade)
Brig. Gen.	Brigadier-General
Brit.	British
C. Cape	Central Cape
C.I.G.S.	Chief of Imperial Staff
Cape Col.	Cape Colony
Capt.	Captain
C-in-C	Commander-in-Chief
CIV (C.I.V.)	City Imperial Volunteers
CMR (C.M.R.)	Cape Mounted Rifles Regiment
CO	Commanding Officer
Col.	Colonel
Comdt. (or Commdt.)	Commandant
Comdt. (Commdt.)-Gen.	Commandant-General
D.E.I.C.	Dutch East India Company (The)
Dec.	December
Div.	Division
DRC (D.R.C.)	Dutch Reformed Church (The)
e.a. (or "et al")	"et alia" – "and the rest" – or "and the others"
E.Cape	Eastern Cape
E.L.	East London (E. Cape)
E.Tvl.	Eastern Transvaal
et seq.	"et sequens" ("..and those that follow"
F.E.I.C.	French East India Company
Feb.	February
FM.	Field-Marshall
G.O.C.(S.A)	General Officer Commanding (South Africa)
Gen.	General
Gov.	Governor
Gov-Gen	Governor-General
H.M.S.	His (Her) Majesty's Ship
ILH (I.L.H.)	Imperial Light Horse Regiment
Jan.	January
KDG (K.D.G.)	King's Dragoon Guards (The)
KRR (K.R.R.)	King's Royal Rifles Regiment
LMS (L.M.S.)	London Missionary Society (The)
Lt.	Lieutenant
Lt-Col.	Lieutenant-Colonel
Lt-Gen.	Lieutenant-General
Maj.	Major
Maj-Gen	Major-General

315

MI (M.I.)	Mounted Infantry
N. Cape	Northern Cape
N.S.W.	New South Wales
N.Tvl	Northern Transvaal
N.W.	North West – North Western
N.W.Cape	North-West Cape
NMP (N.M.P.)	Natal Mounted Police
Nov.	November
OC	Officer-in-Command
Oct.	October
OFS (O.F.S.)	Orange Free State (The)
ORC (O.R.C.)	Orange River Colony (The)
ORCV (O.R.C.V.)	Orange River Colony Volunteers (The)
P.E.	Port Elizabeth (E.Cape)
P.E.A.	Portuguese East Africa (Mazambique)
Pres.	President
Prev.	Previous(ly)
RA (R.A)	Royal Artillery (The)
RE (R.E.)	Royal Engineers (The)
Regt.	Regiment
Rev.	Reverend
RFA (R.F.A.)	Royal Field Artillery (The)
RHA (R.H.A.)	Royal Horse Artillery (The)
RML Guns	Naval 9-pdr. Guns
S.A.P.	South African Party (The)
S.E.Tvl	South Eastern Transvaal
S.S.	Steam Ship
SA (S.A.)	South Africa
SALH (S.A.L.H) Regt.	South African Light Horse Regiment (The)
SALHA (S.A.L.H.A) Regt	South African Light Horse Artillery Regiment (The)
SALHI (S.A.L.H.I) Regt	South African Light Horse Infantry Regiment (The)
Sept.	September
SLI (S.L.I.)	Somerset Light Infantry Regiment (The)
TMI (T.M.I.)	Thorneycroft's Mounted Infantry Regiment
Tvl	Transvaal (The)
V.O.C.	Vereenigde Oost-Indiesche Compagnie (D.E.I.C.)
W.Tvl	Western Transvaal (The)
ZARPS (Z.A.R.P.S.)	Zuid-Afrikaanische Rijende Politie (S.A. Mounted Police)
-pdr	„-pounder" – Field Gun(s) shell weight calibration
"	Inches (or Seconds per context)
ft	Foot/Feet (Linear)
mm.	Millimetres
2-IC	Second-in-Command

REFERENCE INDEX

319

Burgher(s) – Free Burghers – (15—7 , 19 , 23-4 , 27-8 , 30-1 , 33 , 36-7)
Burgher's Peace Committee, The – (255)
Burgherwacht, De – (The Burgher Watch or Home Guard) – (20)
Butler, Lt.Gen. Sir William – C-in-C (SA) and Acting Governor General (Cape) – (89 , 93 , 98)
Byng, Lt.Col. (later FM) Julien H.G. (CO of the South African Light Horse (SALH) Regiment –
(157 , 289)

C
"C" Squadron – 17th Lancers – (266)
Caesar's Camp (Platrand, Natal) – (122-4)
Caledon (Cape) – (21 , 45)
Caledon River (OFS) – (226 , 241)
Calvinist Republicanism – (13)
Cambridge University (Cambs. England) – (245)
Campbell-Bannerman, Sir Henry – Leader of the British Liberal Party – (121 , 291-3)
Canadian Mounted Rifles Regiment, The – (227)
Cape Afrikaners, The – (92 , 94 , 234, 239)
Cape Agulhas (Cape) – (51)
"Cape Coloureds" / "Half Castes" / "Basters" – (16 , 28 , 34 , 91 , 294)
Cape Court of Justice – (36)
"Cape Dutch, The" – (176 , 185)
"Cape Melting Pot, The" – (27)
Cape Midlands, The – (156 , 164 , 168 , 176 . 178 . 185-7 , 189 , 201-2 , 232 , 241 , 268)
Cape Mounted Rifles (CMR) Regiment – (52 , 102 , 267)
Cape - Natal - Colonial Rebels / "The Cape Rebellion" / Amnesty Concessions for Rebels – (176 ,
185 , 241 , 282 , 286)
Cape of Good Hope Punishment Act 1836 ("Punishment Act 1836") – (46 , 51)
"Cape Rebels (Commandant Maritz's)" – (267)
"Cape Dutch Patois" – (27)
"Cardboard Revolutionaries, The" – (87)
Carleton, Col. (CO of the Gloucester Regiment) – (108-10)
Carlyle, Thomas (1795-1881) - Scottish Scholar and Philosopher – (44)
Carnarvon, Lord – British Colonial Secretary – (56 , 58-9)
Carolina (E.Tvl) – (251 , 256 , 283)
Carolina Commando, The – (139-40 , 144-5 , 148 , 151)
Carrington, Maj.Gen. Sir Frederick – (244)
"Carrington's Australian Unit" – (218)
"Carrington's New Zealand Unit" – (218)
"Carrington's Yeomanry Unit" – (218)
Carter, Thomas – War Correspondent – (78)
Cavalry Division (Lt.Gen. The Earl of Dundonald's) – (117 , 127-32 , 152 , 163)
Cavalry Division (Maj.Gen. (later FM) Lord John French's) – (158 , 168 , 192-5 , 197-8 , 202
205-6 , 208 , 217-20 , 222 , 228 , 265-6)
Celliers, General J.D. – (242-3 , 246 , 271 , 273-4)
Central Peace Committee, The – (239)
Central Supply Park – Regimental – Decentralised Supply Systems – (195 , 209-11 , 253)
Ceres (Cape) – (21 , 45)
Cetshewayo – Zulu Paramount Chief – (57-8)
Chamberlain, Joseph ("Joe") – British Colonial Secretary – (91-5 , 97 , 110 , 121 , 231 , 238 , 253-4
278-9 , 282-3 , 286 , 291-2)
Chance, Major H. – (249)
Chartered Company, The – (88)
Chelmsford, Lt.Gen. Lord Frederick Thesiger – (59 , 111)
Chelsea HospitaL Governor (FM. Lord George White, ret) – (289)
Chermside, General H. – Successor to Command of Gatacre's 3rd Division - (218)
Chermside's (previosly Gatacre's) 3rd Division - (218)

Doornkop (Tvl) – (87 , 167 , 220)
Dordrecht (C.Cape) – 9 185-6)
Dorset Regiment, The – (143)
Downman, Lt.Col. – CO of the Gordon Highlanders Regiment – (183)
Draft Peace Agreement Addendum – (282)
Dragoon Guards, The 7th – (53)
Dragoons, The 1st Royal Regiment – (107)
Drakensberg(e) (Natal) – (46 ,52 , 60 , 65 , 98 , 103 , 114 , 116 , 127 , 147 , 225 , 228, 262-3)
Drakenstein (Cape) – (20)
Driefontein (OFS) – (206)
Drives, Sweeps, Hunts, "De Wet Hunts", "Big Drive Strategy" – (250-1 , 254 , 257 , 259-62
    264 , 269 , 273 , 275 , 278 , 289)
Drostdy(e) - Magistrate, Magistracies – (31)
Du Pre, Alexander, Earl of Caledon - !st British Governor at the Cape – (37 , 40)
Du Toit, General S.P. – Boer General – (208 , 243)
Dublin Fusiliers Regiment, The – (108 , 119 , 160-2)
Dum-Dums, Scored Ammunition – (253)
Dundee (Natal) – (103-8 , 137 , 189 , 213 , 219 , 258 , 260)
Dundonald, Lt.Gen. The Earl of Dundonald -CO of Dundold,s Mounted Cavalry (MI) Dision
    (117 , 119-20 , 127 , 129-32 , 152 , 228)
Dundonald's Mounted Infantry (MI) Division – (127-32 , 157-8 , 163)
Dutch East India Company (D.E.I.C.) – (see under V.O.C.) – (12)
Dutch Language, Patois – (35 , 41 , 43)
Dutch Peace Initiative – (274)
Dutch Reformed Church (D.R.C.) – (28 , 36 , 41)
Dutch Volunteer Corps, The – (103)
Dwarsvlei (W.Tvl) – (244)

E
East Africa (German) – (293)
East Indies and Far East – (12 , 16 , 28 , 32 , 34-5)
East London (E.Cape) – (176)
East Surrey Regiment, The – (158)
Eastern Cape, The – (168 , 186)
Eastern Frontier Boers – Settlers – (27)
Eckstein, F. – Representative of the Wernher-Beit Corporation – (211)
Edgar – "The Edgar Relief Committee" – (90)
Elands River – Elands River Poort (Cape) – (266)
Elandsfontein Farm, by Lichtenburg – Gen. De la Rey's Home – (270)
Elandslaagte (Natal) – (103-7 , 137 , 163 , 220)
Elandsrivier (W.Tvl) – (227 , 244)
Elgin, Lord – Chairman of The Royal Commission on the South African War – (287)
Elsevier, Samuel - Associate of discredited Cape Governer, W.A. van der Stel – (23)
Elves, Lieutenant – British Officer killed in action at Majuba (1881) – (66)
English East India Company – (12)
Erasmus, General "Marula" – (103-5)
Ermelo (E.Tvl) – (250 , 256)
Ermelo Commando, The – (116)
Esher, Viscount – Member of The Royal Commission on the South African War – (287-8)
Essex Regiment, The – (216)
Essex, Major – British Officer at Battle of Majuba (1881) – (66)
Estcourt (Natal) – (110-11 , 116 , 127 , 137 , 168)
Executive Council, The – (167)

German Settlers at the Cape – (21)
German Volunteer Corps, The – (103 , 106, 140)
Germiston Commando, The – (140)
Gilvry, Lieutenant – Naval Gun Battery Commander at Colenso (1899) - (118)
Gladstone, William – British Prime Minister – (60 , 81-2 , 89 , 95)
Glencoe (N.Natal) – (258)
Gloucestershire Regiment, The – (108 , 236)
Gold / Discovery / Production / Rand Gold Mines / Witwatersrand, etc – (56 , 85-6 , 90 , 95 , 220 254)
Golden Age of Dutch Civilisation – (13)
"Goodbye Dolly Gray" – Boer War Book written by Rayne Kruger – (236)
Goodyear, Pvt. – Semaphore Signaller at Spioenkop Battle – (142)
Gordon Highlanders Regiment (previously "The 92nd Highland Regiment") – (74-6 , 106 , 123, 182-3 , 220)
Gordon, General (of Khartoum) / "Gordon Relief Force, The" – (82 , 188)
Gordon's Knoll (Majuba, Natal) – (75 , 77-80 , 82)
Goringe, Col. – British Officer in Action at Elands River Poort (N.Cape) – (266)
Goringe's Column – (266)
Goske, Isdbrandt – Early Dutch Governor at the Cape – (19)
Gough, Maj. Hubert – CO of the The 24th Mounted Infantry Regiment – (258-9)
Graaff-Reinet (Cape) – (21 , 31 , 33 , 41 , 267)
Graham, Col. John – Eastern Cape Commissioner – (42)
Grahamstown (Eastern Cape) – (89)
Graspan (N.Cape) – The Battle – (171-2 , 174 , 189)
Grazing (Fees, Licences, Posts, Stock Posts) – (30-1)
Great Deal, The – (90-1)
Great Trek , The – (24 , 27 , 30-1 , 42 ,44-5 , 51)
Green Hill (Spioenkop, Natal) – (133 , 137 , 139-41 , 143 , 153 , 158)
Greer, Capt. – Artillery Officer at Majuba (1881) - (69)
Grenadier Guards Regiment, The – (169 (
Grenfell, Lt.Col – Officer at Rooiwal (W.Tvl) action in April 1902 - (276)
Greyling, Commandant – (245)
Grimwood, Col. – British Officer at Battle of Ladysmith (Natal) – (108-9)
Griqua(s) – Griqualand West – (52-3 , 55-6 , 166 , 243)
Griqualand West "Rebel Commando, The" – (243)
Grobelaar's Kop (Natal – (119)
Grobler, Jan – Junior Boer General ("Young Turk") - (184)
Groenkloof Gorge (Cape Prov.) – (267)
 Groenkop (OFS) – (261)
"Groote Schuur, De" (Cape Town) – (17)
Guards Brigade, The – (168 , 170 , 173-4 , 181-2 , 205 , 225 , 229)
Gun Hill (E.Tvl) – (251-2)
Gutenberg, Johannes (1400?- 1468) – German Inventor and Printing Press Technologist – (13)

H
H.M.S. Boadecia – (67)
H.M.S. Dido – (67)
Haig, Maj.Gen. (later FM) Lord Douglas – (105 , 185 , 206 , 266-9 , 290)
Hals, Frans – Dutch Golden Age Painter – (14)
Hamilton, Lt. Gen. (later FM) Sir Ian – (77-80 , 106-9 , 122-3 , 227-8 , 232 , 254 , 275 , 284 , 290)
Hamilton, Maj.Gen. Bruce – CO of the 19th and 21st Mounted Infantry (MI) Brigades – (219-20 222 , 225 , 227 ,
"Hands-Uppers" – "Joiners" – (275 , 284)
Hannay, Col. O.C. – CO of the Mounted Infantry Brigade at Paardeberg Battle – (196 , 200)
Hannay's Mounted Infantry (MI) Brigade – (197-9 , 200)
Hapsburg Spain – (13)

Langverwacht (OFS) – (263)
Lanyon, Col.Owen – British Administrator for the Transvaal – (59-61 , 64)
Lee-Metford .303 Bolt Action Rifle – (257 , 259)
Lemmer, General H.R.–Commandant of the Lichtenburg and Marico Commandos – (242-4)
Liberal Doctrines – (37)
Liberal Party / Government, The British- (60 , 231 , 280 , 292)
Lichtenburg (W.Tvl) – (243-4 , 246 , 269-75)
Lichtenburg Commnand, The – (167 , 172-3 , 175)
Liebenberg, General P.J. – Commander of the Potchefstroom Commando – (243,4 , 271 , 273-4)
Liebenberg, General P.J.'s Potchefstroom Commando – (273)
Lisbeeck River (Table Bay) – (14)
Light Horse Regiment (Methuen's) – (166)
Limpopo River (N.Tvl) – (46 , 218 , 230)
Lincoln's Mounted Infantry (MI) , The – (227 , 243)
Lindley (OFS) – (219 , 221 , 225-6 , 260 , 262 , 289)
Little, Maj. – CO of the New South Wales Lancers – (172)
Lloyd-George, David, Chairman of the British Liberal Party – (274 , 291)
London Missionary Society (L.M.S.), The – (39)
Long Hill (Natal) – (108-9)
"Long Tom, The" – Creusot 155mm Gun – (89 , 108-10 , 143 , 197)
Long, Col. – RA Battery Commander at Battle of Colenso (15/12/1899) – (118-20 , 124 , 287)
Lotter, Commandant – Commander of "Cape Rebel Commando" at Kiba Drift – (267)
Louis Trichardt (N.Tvl) – (278)
Lourenco Marques (Portuguese East Africa /Mozambique) – (189 , 213 , 222 , 230)
Lovatt Scouts, The – Unit composed of Scottish Highland Ghillies – (226 , 264)
Loyal North Lancaster Regiment, The – (166 , 169 , 175)
Lunny, Maj. – Officer in !st. King's Dragoon Guards (KDG) at Laing's Nek – (66)
Lydenburg (E.Tvl) – (57 , 61 , 63 , 71 , 256-7)
Lyttelton, Alfred - British Colonial Secretary (1903) – (292)
Lyttelton, Maj.Gen. Neville, CO of the 4th Light Brigade – (117-20 , 124 , 128 , 130 , 143 , 145
    154-5 , 157 , 218 , 228)
Lyttelton's 4th Light Brigade – (127 , 141 , 145 , 253-5 , 158 , 162 , 218 , 228)

M

MacDonald, Lt. (later Maj.Gen.) Sir Hector ("Fighting Mac" – CO of The Highland Brigade –
    (76 , 79-80 , 192 , 203 , 226 , 288-9 ,
MacDonald's Highland Brigade – (226)
MacDonald's Kop (Majuba, Natal) – (75 , 82)
Machadadorp (E.Tvl) – (226 , 228 9 , 249)
Mafeking (N.Cape)–(7 , 87 , 98 , 121 , 164-5 , 167 , 186 , 189 , 196 , 204 , 208 , 218-9 , 242 , 244 , 269)
Mafeking – The Relief of.. (289)
Mafeking Commando, The – (172 , 184)
Mafeking Protectorate Regiment, The – (227)
Magaliesberg(e) – (W.Tvl) – (227-8 , 242-6)
Magato Nek (W.Tvl) – (249)
Magersfontein/Magersfontein Heights (N.Cape) – (7 ,115 , 120 , 122 , 168 , 172 , 178 , 181-6 , 189 ,
    191-4 , 196 , 237 , 269 , 272 , 290)
Magersfontein – The Battle (11/12/1899) – (178 , 181-3)
Mahdi, The / Dervishes, The – (82)
Mahon, Col. CO Kimberley Mounted Infantry (MI) Regiment – (218-9)
Majuba (Amajuba)–"The Hill of Doves"–(N.Natal) – (64-5 , 71 , 73-8 , 80-3 , 88-9 , 96 , 98 , 101
    121 , 121 , 138 , 162 , 203-4 , 294 , 289)
Majuba – The Battle (27/02/1881) – (73-80)
Malan, Commandant Daniel – Boer Commander at Majuba (February 1881) – (76 ,79 , 266)
Malay(a) – (16 ,24 ,28)
Mamusa/ The Battle of Mamusa (1885) – (106 , 124)

329

Manchester Infantry Regiment, The – (106 , 124)
Mandela, Nelson – (296)
Marabastad (N.Tvl) – (62 , 63)
Marais, Commandant Ernst – Boer Commander at Nooitgedeact (W.Tvl) action – (245-6)
Marais, Sarel, - Commander of Germiston Commando at Battle of Spioenkop – (140)
Marico (W.Tvl) – (243-4)
Marico Commando – CO General H.R. Lemmer – (244)
Maritz, General Salomon – "Young Turk" Commander of a Cape Rebels Force – (267 – 293)
Martini-Henry Mark II Rifle – (62 , 100)
Mashonaland – (55)
Massoni, David – Chief of the Korana Tribe (Schweizer-Reneke) – (167)
Matabeleland / Matabele Tribe / Matabele Campaign (1896) – (55 , 166 , 189)
Mauser Rifle(s) – 7mm. 5-round Breach-Clip Magazine – (89 , 100 , 108-9 , 118 , 174, 182-3, 202 ,
    257)
Maxim Machine Gun(s) – (108 , 164-5 , 174 , 227 , 229 , 244 , 266)
Maxim-Nordfelt 1-pdr. Rapid Firing Gun(s–("Pom-Pom(s)" – (89 , 99 , 143 , 155 , 172-4 , 182 , 203
    227 , 229 , 245 , 273)
Maxwell, John – Early English Visitor to Table Bay Refueling Facility – (13)
McGregor, Capt.J.C. – CO of the 3/60th Company at Majuba – (69-70)
Medical Corps, The – (152)
Melbourne, Lord – British Prime Minister – (51-2)
Methuen, General Lord Paul Sanford – 3rd Baron of Corsham – (115 , 124-5 , 166-73 , 175 , 181-7 ,
    189 , 191-2 , 194 , 196 , 218-9 , 227-8 , 234 , 269-72 , 274 , 289)
Methuen's 1st Division – (218)
Meyer,General "Marula" Lukas–Boer Commander - Battle of Talana (Dundee)- (103-4) , 108 , 274
Middelbult (W.Tvl) – (275)
Middelburg (E.Tvl) – (63 , 220 , 227-8 , 250)
Middelburg Commando, The – (116 , 258)
Middelburg Peace Talks / Conference (Feb. 1901) – (259 , 279 , 281-2)
Middlesex Regiment, The – (143 , 145-7)
Migrant Labour (Routes / Movements, etc) – (56-7)
Mildmay, Capt. – Officer in the 24th Mounted Infantry (MI) Regiment – (258)
Military Board, The British, - (288)
"Military Notes of the Dutch Republics" – Author General Ardagh – (95-6 , 213)
Milner, Sir Alfred –British High Commissioner for South Africa – (85 , 88-95 , 97 , 114 , 164-6 , 169
    192 , 211 , 238-9 , 250-1 , 253-4 , 272 , 276 , 278-82 , 284 , 286 , 291-3)
"Milner's Kindergarten" – (292)
Mission(s) – Missionary(ies) – (39)
Modder River (N.Cape) – Battle of Modder River (28/11/1899) – (7 , 168 , 171-5 , 178 , 181-4 , 186,
    189 , 191-4 , 196-9 , 202-5 , 209-10 , 214-6, 289)
Modderfontein (Tvl) – (246)
Moedwil (W.Tvl) – (249)
Moeller, Major – British Cavalry Commander at Talana/Impati Actions) – (105 , 121)
Mohandas Ghandi – (152)
Molteno (Cape Midlands) – (176-7)
Monte Christo Hill (Colenso Koppies, Natal) – (157-9)
Mooi River (Natal) – (168)
Mooi River (Mooirivier) (W.Tvl) – Mooi River Settlement – (46)
Mooney, Lt.Col. C.G.E – British Officer at action at Lichtenburg (W.Tvl) – (246)
Mount Alice (Spearman's Hill, Natal) – (127
Mount Hlobani (Natal) / Engagement in 1878 – (111)
Mounted Infantry (MI) Brigade, The – CO Col. O.C. Hannay – (215)
Mount Prospect (Natal) / Mont Prospect Camp – (65 , 67-71 , 74-7 , 79-81)
Mountain Battery (RA), The / Mountain Guns, The – (134 , 141 , 153 , 266)
Mounted Squadron, The - (66 , 68-70)
"Mournful Monday" – 30/10/1899 (Battle of Ladysmith) – (110)

S

South African Constabulary, The – (237)
South Afircan Light Horse Infantry (SALHI) – The – (102)
Safe Conduct for Peace Talks – (275 , 280)
Salisbury, Lord – Britiish Prime Minister – (94 , 213)
San, The (Bushmen) – (13 , 30, 32 , 34 , 38)
Sand River Convention (1852) , The – (54)
Sandbach, Lt.Col. Arthur ("Sandbags") – British Field Intelligence Officer – (157 , 159 , 162)
Sand (Zand) River (OFS) – (219)
Sannaspos (Sannnah's Post) – (OFS) – (214-7 , 264)
Sappers, The – (Royal Engineers (RE) – (123 , 127, 159)
Scapa Flow (Orkney Islands) – (288)
Scheepers, Commandant, a "Cape Rebel" Commander – (241 , 266-7)
Schoeman,General H.J- Senior Boer Commander at Colesburg (C.Cape) - (186-7 , 197 , 201 , 204)
Schoonspruit (W.Tvl) – (273)
Schreiner, William , Attorney-General of the Cape Province – (92 , 94)
Schuinshoogte / Ingogo (Natal – (65-8 , 70-1 , 73-4)
Scobell, Col. Harry, Britsh Officer at action near Petersburg (N.Cape) – (`267)
Scobell's Column – (267)
"Scorched Earth Policy, The"–Programmed Devastation of Boer Farms and Properties – (234
    237 – 239-40 , 261 , 286)
Scots 6th Fusilier Regiment, The – (158 , 162)
Scots Fusilier Guards, The – (166)
Scots Greys, The – (227 ,243 , 257)
Scots Guards, The – (169 , 173-4)
Scottish Clergymen in the Cape – (41)
Scottish Rifles Regiment, The – (145-7 , 150 , 252)
Scouts, Guides, etc (Boers) – (256)
"Scouts and Scouting" by R.S.S. Baden –Powell (166)
"Scramble for Africa, The" – (85)
Seaforth Highlanders Regiment, The – (181-3 , 199)
Secretary for War and the Colonies, London – (37 , 279 , 288)
Sekhukune War, The (1876(- (167)
Sekhukune, BaPedi Paramount Chief – (56 , 59)
Sekhukuneland (E.Tvl) – (56-7)
Selonsrivier (Selons River) – (W.Tvl) – (249)
Senekal – (OFS) – (221 , 225)
"Sergeant-of-the-Garrison" – Castle Offcial at Cape Revictualling Station – (16)
"Settlers, The 1820" – (42)
Shaka / "Shaka Zulu" – Zulu Paramount Chief – (46 , 50)
Shepstone, Theophilus, Natal Secretary for Native Affairs – (56-9)
Sheridan, Lt. – Cousin of Winston S. Churchill – (266)
Siege of Ladysmith, The – (163 , 210)
Sikobobo / Sikobobo Tribe – (283)
Silikaatsnek (Magaliesberge) – (243-4)
Sims, Col. Commander of the Somerset Light Infantry Regiment – (149)
Slabbert's Pass (Brandwater Basin, OFS) – (226)
Slachtersnek (E.Cape) – (41)
"Slachtersnek Rebellion, The" – (41)
Slave(s) – Slavery – (16 ,19 , 22 , 28-9 , 34-6 , 49)
"Slim Piet" ("Crafty Piet") – Nickname of Comm-Gen. P.J. Joubert – (62)
Slysken, Cape Governor (1795) – (35)
Small Karroo (Cape) – (21)
Smit, Abraham, Boer Commander at Spioenkop – (140)
Smit, Commandant Nicholas ("Nico") – Boer Commander at Majuba – (63 , 67 , 69-71 , 76
    81 , 83)

o   o   o   o   o   o   o

FORCES AND WEAPONS
British Forces:

343

Pole-Carew,s 9ᵗʰ Brigade – (168 , 173-4 , 181-2)
Pole-Carew's 11ᵗʰ Division – (218 , 222 , 229)
"Q" Battery – Royal Horse Artillery (RHA) – (214-7)
Queen's Own Regiment, The – (158)
Remount Division, The British – (237-8)
Rhodeia Regiment, The – (166 , 218 , 244)
Ridley's Mounted Infantry (MI) Regiment – (226)
Rimington Tigers, The – (171 , 214)
Royal Artillery (RA), The – (128 , 138 , 149 , 162 , 181-2 , 206 , 271)
Royal Canadian Regiment, The – (199 , 203 , 218)
Royal Engineers (RE), The – (73 , 127 , 137-8 , 140 , 188 , 203)
Royal Field Artillery (RFA), The – (102)
Royal Garrison Artillery (RA), The – (158)
Royal Horse Artillery (RHA), The – (102 , 215 , 222)
Royal Irish Rifles Regiment, The – (217)
Royal Wiltshire Yeomanry Regiment, The – (166)
Rundle's 8ᵗʰ Division – (222 , 225)
Sappers, The (Royal Engineers) – (123 , 159)
Scobell's (Colonel) Column – (267)
Scots 6ᵗʰ Fusilier Regiment, The – (158 , 162)
Scots Fusiliers Guards, The – (166)
Scots Greys, The – (227 , 243 , 257)
Scots Guards, The – (169 , 173-4)
Scottish Rifle Regiment, The – (145-7 , 252)
Seaforth Highlanders, The – (181-3 , 199)
Smith-Dorrien's 19ᵗʰ Brigade – (222 , 225)
Somerset Light Infantry (SLI) Regiment – (149)
South African Constabulary, The – (237)
South African Light Horse Infantry (SALHI) Regiment – (102 , 119 , 157)
South Lancashire Regiment, The – (162 , 169)
Supply Corps, The British Army – (102)
Task Force, The British Army – (13-8 , 150)
Thorneycroft's Mounted Infantry (MI) Regiment – (102 , 119 , 137-9 , 143 , 151 , 158)
Tucker.s 7ᵗʰ Division – (205 , 218)
"U" Battery, Royal Horse Artillery (RHA) – (214-5 , 217)
Uitlander Volunteers Contingents, The – (102 , 138)
Von Donop's Column – (276)
West Yorkshire Regiment, The – (158 , 162)
Wynne's Lancashire Brigade – (160)
Yeomanry, The – (267)
Yorkshire Regiment, The – (169)

British Weapons
"Joe Chamberlain, The" – 4.7" Naval Gun – (178)
2 ½" Gun(s), RA – (166)
4.7" Naval Gun(s) - (117)
7-pdr Muzzle Loading Gun(s) – (165)
Field Gun(s) RA – (178)
"Lady Ann, The" – 4.7" Naval Gun – (123)
12-pdr Gun(s) RA – (123 , 141 , 174 , 202)
12-pdr Gun(s) for Light Royal Horse Artillery, RA – (101)
12-pdr Naval Gun(s) – (118)
15-pdr Gun(s) with Shrapnel Shells (for The Royal Field Artillery (RA) – (101 , 174)
25-pdr Rocket Tube(s) – (64-5)
4.7" Nal Gun ("The Lady Ann" – (123 , 163 , 178 , 202,3 , 249)
5" Gun(s) of the Royal Garrison Artillery (RA) – (158)

Boer Forces

345

Pretoria Commando, The – (139-40 , 150)
Pretoria District Commando, The – (245)
Rustenburg Commando, The – (244)
Staatsatillerie – The Transvaal Republic Artillery Unit – (103 , 147, 161 , 173-5 , 227)
Standerton Commando, The – (116 , 151)
Swaziland Commando, The – (116)
Transvaal Burghers' Commando, The – (226)
Transvaal Commandos, The – (161 , 167 , 173 , 220 , 234)
Utrecht Commando, The – (140)
"Volunteer Corps of Scouts - Danie Malan's" – (203)
Vryheid Commando, The – (116)
Wakkerstroom Commando, The – (116)
Waterberg Commando, The – (245-6)
Western Transvaal Burghers' Commandos – (227 , 243)
"ZARP"s , The - Zuid-Afrikaansch Rijende Politie ("South African Mounted Police") – (90 , 229)
 Zoutpansberg Commando, The – (116 , 246)

Boer Weapons
120mm Howitzer(s) – (118)
Cruesot 14.75mm Gun(s) – (89)
Cruesot 155mm Gun ("The Long Tom") – (89)
Cruesot Gun(s) – (119)
Krupp 120mm Howitzer(s) – (89 , 118)
Frupp 75mm Gun(s) – (172-3)
"Long Tom" – Cruesot 155mm Gun(s) – (89 , 108-10 , 197)
Martini-Henry Mark-II Rifle(s) – (100)
Mauser Rifle(s)-7mm. 5-Round Breach-Clip Magazine–(100-1 , 189-9, 118, 174, 182- 3, 202, 257
Maxim Machine Gun(s) – (227 , 229)
Maxim-Nordenfeld 1-pdr Rapid Firing Gun(s) ("Pom-Pom(s)") – (See under "Pom-Pom(s)"
"Pom-Pom(s)" – Maxim-Nordenfeld 1-pdr. Rapid Firing Gun(s) – (89 , 155, 172-4 . 182 , 184, 227,
 229 , 273)